PERILOUS GLORY

PERILOUS GLORY

THE RISE OF WESTERN MILITARY POWER

JOHN FRANCE

YALE UNIVERSITY PRESS
NEW HAVEN AND LONDON

For information about this and other Yale University Press publications, please contact:
U.S. Office: sales.press@yale.edu   www.yalebooks.com
Europe Office: sales@yaleup.co.uk   www.yalebooks.co.uk

Set in Adobe Caslon by IDSUK (DataConnection) Ltd
Printed in the United States of America

Library of Congress Cataloging-in-Publication Data

France, John.
  Perilous glory: the rise of western military power/John France.
    p. cm.
  ISBN 978-0-300120745 (cl:alk. paper)
  1. Military history. 2.   Military art and science—History. I. Title.
  D25.F84 2011
  355′.03301821—dc22
                                                                              2011006437
A catalogue record for this book is available from the British Library.

10 9 8 7 6 5 4 3 2 1

CONTENTS

ILLUSTRATIONS AND MAPS

1. A watchtower manned by a warrior in Papua New Guinea, (1961–3). © President and Fellows of Harvard College, Peabody Museum of Archeology and Ethnology. Photograph by Michael Clark Rockefeller.
2. Stele of the Vultures, dedicated by King Eanatum in celebration of his victory over the city of Umma, from Telloh (Ancient Girsu), early dynastic period (*c.*2440 BC). © De Agostini Picture Library/ Getty Images.
3. Tomb of Inty, late Egyptian Old Kingdom (*c.*2300 BC). www. ancienteygptmagazine.com.
4. Egyptian chariot from the tomb of Thutankhamun, Pharaoh of Egypt (1333–1324 BC). © Griffith Institute, University of Oxford.
5. Relief from Sennacherib's Palace, Nineveh (*c.*700 BC). © akg-images/Bible Land Pictures.
6. Terracotta plaque with armed hoplite running (sixth century BC). © De Agostini Picture Library/Getty Images.
7. Terracotta Army of the First Emperor of China (*c.*210 BC). Author's photograph.
8. Chinese bronze dagger-axes dating from the Shang to the Zhou dynasties (thirteenth–third century BC). © Royal Ontario Museum/Corbis.
9. Bronze crossbow lock, Han dynasty (*c.*206 BC–AD 220). Brooklyn Museum, Museum Expedition 1912, Museum Collection Fund.
10. Roman legionary re-enactment costume. Photograph by Roy Edwards.
11. Replica of a Roman ballista, Caerphilly Castle. Author's photograph.
12. Plaque depicting a Tang horseman (ninth century AD). Author's photograph.
13. Detail from the Bayeux Tapestry (late eleventh century). © akg-images/ Erich Lessing.

Maps

PREFACE

I AM DEEPLY INDEBTED TO A LARGE NUMBER OF PEOPLE AND organisations that, at various times, have contributed to this book. The Leverhulme Foundation was kind enough to give me an Emeritus Fellowship which enabled me to travel in China, Iran and Outer Mongolia in 2008–9 to expand my interest in the interactions between the steppe peoples and those of the settled lands which is such an important theme in this volume. On these journeys I met a huge number of people who helped me and responded generously to my questions and this is an opportunity to express my gratitude to them. In writing this book I have inevitably ventured into periods far beyond my own and drawn on the expertise of many people. Professor Jeremy Black of the University of Exeter has been a great source of inspiration. My co-editors of the *Journal of Medieval Military History*, Professor Clifford Rogers of the US Military Academy West Point and Professor Kelly Devries of Loyola College Baltimore, have been immensely helpful. The *Journal* is published by De Re Militari, the Society for Medieval Military History, whose President, Stephen Morillo, and members have been more than generous in discussion, especially in their annual meetings at Kalamazoo. I have had much recourse to their website run by Peter Konieckzny. Membership of the Society for Military History has been invaluable, and I am most grateful to Bruce Vandervort, the editor of their *Journal*. Matthew Bennett of Royal Military Academy Sandhurst and Manuel Rojas of the University of Caceres were always generous with help and advice. I have also been fortunate enough to be a member of the editorial board of Brill's History of Warfare, where the comments of my colleagues, notably Michael Neiberg, on various aspects of modern war, have been very valuable. Many conversations with Professor Bernie Bachrach and his son David have also made their contribution. My first and abiding academic interest in the crusades provided me with a perspective on military affairs, so I must thank the Society for the Study of the Crusades and the Latin East for all their help, and in particular Professor Bernard Hamilton who introduced me to crusading and Professor Jonathan Riley-Smith whose ideas always command attention. I was privileged to act as Director of the James Callaghan Centre for the Study of Conflict at Swansea University, whose members, visitors and speakers provided great stimulus and much information. I am everlastingly grateful to my immediate colleagues in the History Department for their companionship, advice and tolerance. I would especially like to remember Jon Latimer, whose early death robbed the world of a skilled and devoted historian of World War II, and to thank Dr Gerry Oram who has been so helpful on World War I. Members of the Classics Department of Swansea University, notably Professor Alan Lloyd, Dr Tracey Rihll and Dr David Gill were generous with their knowledge of the ancient world, while Dr William Merrin of Media Studies provided vital information on cyberwar. A number of people have read parts of the manuscript, notably Clifford Rogers, Professor Hugh Bowen of Swansea University, and Angela, my wife who has lived with this book for far too long. I am grateful for their help, though I must take responsibility for what is actually published.

All scholars lean heavily on learned institutions, and I owe a great deal to Swansea University and most especially to those who work in its library. The staff of the Institute of Historical Research, the British Library Reading Room and the National Library of Wales all bore with me with patience and courtesy. I enjoyed great intellectual stimulation from my visits to the United States Military Academy at West Point and the United States Naval Academy at Annapolis where Dr Richard Abels was so hospitable and, with his colleagues, so thoughtful. Finally I must mention the staff of Yale University Press, and especially Heather McCallum without whom this book would never have been started, let alone finished, while her colleague, Rachael Lonsdale, has been immensely helpful. The anonymous readers of my manuscript made major contributions, as did my copy editor, Beth Humphries, for which I am truly grateful.

John France
Department of History and Classics
Swansea University
Swansea SA2 8PP

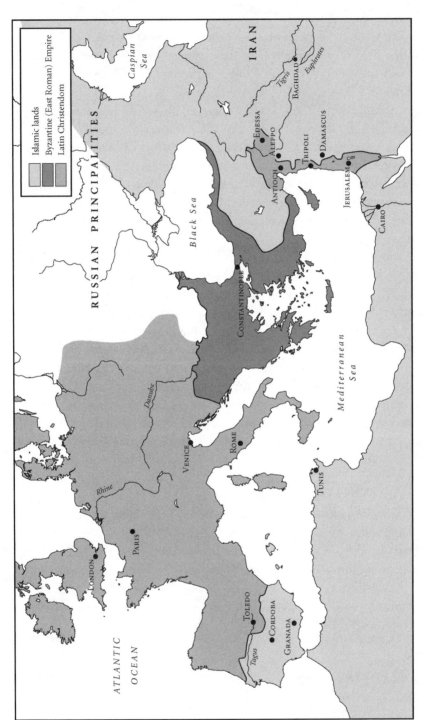

Map 1. The Mediterranean (c.1100 AD). Three civilisations around a sea.

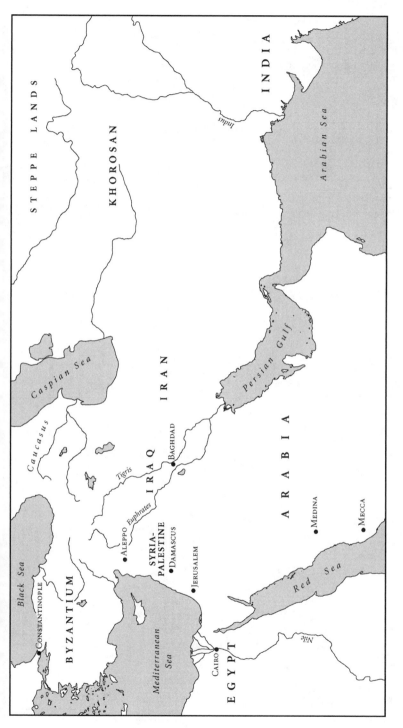

Map 2. The Middle East and west Asia.

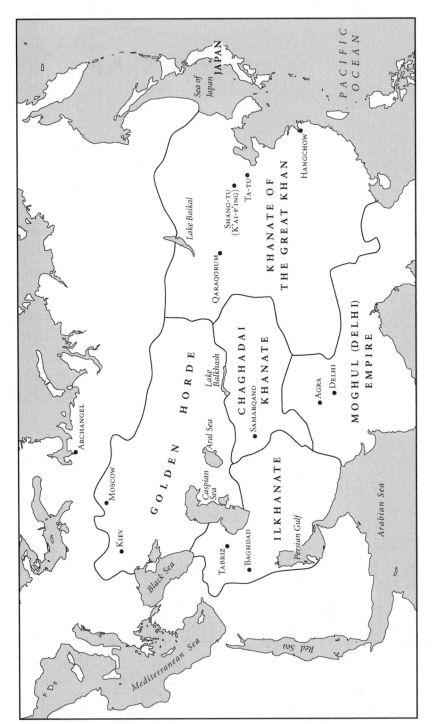

Map 3. China and the Mongol domination under Kubilai Khan (1260–94).

———————◆———————

CHAPTER ONE

THE MANY FACES OF WAR

If a Marine slipped and slid down the back slope of the muddy ridge, he was apt to reach the bottom vomiting. I saw more than one man lose his footing and slip and slide all the way to the bottom only to stand up horror-stricken as he watched in disbelief while fat maggots tumbled out of his muddy dungaree pockets, cartridge belt, leggings lacing and the like. Then he and a buddy would shake or scrape them away with a piece of ammo box or a knife blade.

We didn't talk about such things. They were too horrible and obscene even for hardened veterans. The conditions taxed the toughest I knew almost to the point of screaming. Nor do authors write about such vileness; unless they have seen it with their own eyes, it is too preposterous to think that men could actually live and fight for days on end under such terrible conditions and not be driven insane. But I saw much of it there on Okinawa, and to me war was insanity.[1]

WAR has many faces. This vivid picture of the horrors of the Pacific War in World War II, of men rolling in maggots fattened on the corpses of their comrades and their Japanese enemies, comes from the memoirs of Eugene B. Sledge who served in the rank and file of the US Marine Corps. To us, at the start of the twenty-first century, his recollections are a curious mixture of the strange and the familiar. Since 1945 whole generations of American, British and European people have appeared to enjoy a long peace, and while wars have raged, they have largely been remote from their lives. Sledge describes a virtual moonscape, alien in its unspeakable horror, but some of the fears he expresses are familiar. The squalor repels us, and, for a generation raised in comfort, reinforces his conclusion, that this war (and implicitly all war) is insanity.

Throughout human history there have been numerous such condemnations of war as degrading and horrific. The *Picatrix*, a *grimoire* or magical treatise, was originally written in a Greek pagan world before the birth of Christ, but after the rise of Islam in the seventh century it was translated into Arabic then, in the thirteenth century, rendered into Spanish and Latin. Its message, therefore, circulated in all the cultures of the Mediterranean world:

> Mars . . . is misfortune, damaging, and the author of evil things. And it signified loss, evil works, houses and cities depopulated, drought and preventing rain from falling, fire, burning, disagreements, blood, every impetuosity . . . evil and warped judgements, oppressions, anguish, people's death and damage . . . and every cursed thing which comes about without sense or moderation.[2]

Here then, we might say, is the mad world of war – destructive, squalid, shameful, truly insane. But war cannot just be madness. Rational and thoughtful statesmen commit nations to war, and the organisation it demands is impressive. Nor is it always chaotic. Lt-Colonel John Blackader fought at Malplaquet in 1709, the bloodiest of early eighteenth-century battles, and he has left for us a memory of the ordered lines of fighting men proceeding about their business in that engagement: 'It was the most deliberate, solemn and well-ordered battle that I ever saw.'[3]

War is an organised activity, and generals have always applied their minds to the business of command. About 500 BC the great Chinese military thinker, Sun Tzu, asserted the importance of careful thought in the conduct of war: 'The general who wins a battle makes many calculations in his temple ere the battle is fought. The general who loses a battle makes but few calculations beforehand.'[4] In the early nineteenth century Clausewitz, the great guru of modern western warfare, said much the same:

> The vital contribution of intelligence is clear throughout. No wonder, then, that war, although it may appear to be uncomplicated, cannot be waged with distinction except by men of outstanding intellect.[5]

This is why nations maintain military academies like West Point in the US, Sandhurst in Britain, St Cyr in France and the National Defence University in China, where war is taught as a distinct subject capable of rational analysis and systematisation. An army in action is the product of complex political, social and technological processes which direct and maintain it. Insanity may be a natural reaction to the chaos of the front line – though let us not forget Blackader's words – but it is not an adequate description of one of the most ancient and most universal of human activities which was so important that it stamped itself upon literature almost as soon as writing began.

The earliest epic poem (about 2700 BC) is the story of Gilgamesh, warrior-king of Uruk on the Euphrates in modern Iraq:

> This is Uruk, the city of Gilgamesh,
> The wild ox, son of Lugalbanda, son
> Of the Lady Wildcow Ninsun, Gilgamesh
> Of the vanguard and the rear guard of the army.[6]

The poem recounts the hero's raid to seize timber in the great cedar forest of southern Iran. In preparation, Gilgamesh orders the armourers to forge new weapons for him and his companion, Enkidu. Evidently a vital part of the infrastructure of war, specialised metallurgy, had already evolved.

The very first histories of ancient Greece were about wars. Herodotus (484–430 BC) reports at length the Persian attacks on Greece (499–448 BC), while Thucydides (c.460–c.400 BC) gives a vivid account of the Peloponnesian War (431–404) between Athens and Sparta. It is impossible to read the history of the world without being struck by how universal war is. Describing Europe as a continent torn apart by war is a cliché. The Old Testament, that foundation document of Judaism, Christianity and Islam, records Middle Eastern history as a whole sequence of kingdoms rising and falling in welters of blood. India witnessed a similar series of dramatic changes, which continued when it was conquered by Muslim powers and steppe people. The rise of every dynasty in China was marked by destruction and death on an immense scale. The civilisation of the Moche in northern Peru (AD 100–700) perished in fierce civil strife.

Modern writers have recognised the universal experience of war, but they have tended to emphasise the differences between countries and across times. This is because they are usually specialists, and therefore likely to magnify the importance and distinctiveness of their subjects. A scholar who spends his life studying medieval warfare will not unnaturally see the difference between this and, say, Chinese warfare in the seventeenth century. So it is unsurprising that scholars connect the conduct of war with differences between cultures. And they have been struck too by the supremacy of 'Western Warfare', by which they mean essentially US military power, at the beginning of the twenty-first century. Since the collapse of the Soviet Union in 1989 the US has certainly been the only superpower, which can be defined as

> A country that has the capacity to project dominating power and influence anywhere in the world, and sometimes, in more than one region of the globe at a time, and so may plausibly attain the status of global hegemon. The basic components of superpower stature may be measured along four axes of power: military, economic, political, and cultural.[7]

By this measure the scale of US dominance is astonishing – it spends more on defence than the next fifteen nations in total, the world prices all its key commodities in dollars, its policies can be opposed but never ignored, and American entertainment tastes dominate TV and the Internet. To explain this remarkable situation, many have argued that it arose from the very nature of our culture, that it is peculiar to and rooted in the way Europeans and Americans organise themselves and think, that it is closely connected to our entire experience and our cultural values. One proponent of this cultural view of war argues that there is an intimate relationship between western supremacy and democracy, in that a particular style of war rests on consent and agreement:

> Western armies often fight with and for a sense of legal freedom. They are frequently products of civic militarism or constitutional governments and thus are overseen by those outside religion and the military itself. The rare word 'citizen' exists in the European vocabularies.[8]

To see military power, and actually military supremacy, as rooted in our culture is a comforting idea. But this book adopts a very different perspective. It seeks to examine the history of war as a whole, rather than simply in one period or civilisation. In consequence it presents the history of warfare rather differently and views the present eminence of US power as much more precarious and accidental – hence the 'Perilous Glory' of my title.

Of course cultural experience has some influence upon war, and particularly on why we fight. But this book is primarily about how we fight. It will argue that down to the nineteenth century the major world civilisations, including the western, fought in distinctly similar ways. War may exercise the intellect, as Sun Tzu asserted, but the material conditions of society imposed remarkably similar methods of fighting upon peoples, no matter how diverse their cultures. The city-societies of Europe, the

Middle East, India and China evolved a style of warfare dependent in the main upon mass infantry armies. When these clashed in battle they fought by necessity at close quarters because they lacked dependable missile-weapons, and they organised themselves in tight formations, close-order, as the best way of achieving success.

But because cities were so important in these communities they spent much of their effort in besieging fortified places or undermining them by destroying their economic base in the countryside. This is what is called 'agro-urban warfare'. In pre-industrial societies before the nineteenth century, armies were shaped, to a much greater extent than has generally been recognised, by the geography, topography, climate and agricultural practices of the areas in which they existed. These imposed themselves to such an extent that although there were many great cultures across the world, war was almost everywhere fought in a particular style by armies which were predominantly infantry. This kind of war pre-dated Europe, which was simply an area annexed to Mediterranean civilisation under the Roman Empire. It developed into a distinct civilisation only in the Middle Ages.

On the great Eurasian steppe a quite different style of war emerged, based on fast-moving horsemen. Much of the history of our world has come from the duel and the interchange between these two styles of war. But although this dialogue of death gave rise to changes, they were limited. The most striking fact about warfare is how little it altered over an immensely long period of time. In the nineteenth century Europe and the US radically transformed the basic conditions of human life through the 'Industrial Revolution' and this, in turn, gave birth to the Military Revolution. This is what gives their history a special interest.

In the long epoch down to the nineteenth century war changed, but it did so slowly. And across the world its objectives and value-systems remained remarkably stable. 'Organised theft' is a biting description of war, yet there is much truth in it. Gilgamesh fought for precious wood, while the great Mongol leader, Genghis Khan (c.1162–1227), made a very direct appeal to the greed and lust of his troops:

> The greatest pleasure is to vanquish your enemies, to chase them before you, to rob them of their wealth, to see their near and dear bathed in tears, to ride their horses and sleep on the white bellies of their wives and daughters.[9]

In the 1930s Hermann Goering enlisted the poetry of d'Annunzio to recruit Nazi storm troopers:

Do you wish to fight? To kill?
To see streams of blood?
Great heaps of gold?
Herds of captive women?
Slaves?[10]

War and greed march together across the ages, and even the value-systems of warriors in different cultures resemble one another strongly. There have always been those who rejoiced in war, like the French warrior-poet Bertrand de Born, who died about 1214:

I am overjoyed when I see knights and horses, all in armour, drawn up on the field. I love it when the chargers throw everything and everybody into confusion, and I enjoy seeing strong castles besieged . . . Once he has started fighting, no noble knight thinks of anything but breaking heads and arms – better a dead man than a live one who is useless.[11]

This is no mere anachronistic and antique sentiment. General George S. Patton, perhaps the finest US general of World War II, had a real delight in war, and he tried very hard to inculcate it in his men:

Men, this stuff that some sources sling around about America wanting out of this war, not wanting to fight, is a crock of bullshit. Americans love to fight, traditionally. All real Americans love the sting and clash of battle. You are here today for three reasons. First, because you are here to defend your homes and your loved ones. Second, you are here for your own self respect, because you would not want to be anywhere else. Third, you are here because you are real men and all real men like to fight.[12]

This is the glorious face of war, and glory is indeed part of war's appeal. Arrian, in his *Life*, records that Alexander the Great exhorted his men, Greeks, Macedonians and others, to fight and die for glory:

Gentlemen of Macedon, and you, my friends and allies, this must not be. Stand firm; for well you know that hardship and danger are the price of glory, and that sweet is the savour of a life of courage and of deathless renown beyond the grave.[13]

Glory and self-sacrifice have always formed part of the vocabulary of war. A quotation from the Roman poet Horace: '*Dulce et decorum est pro patria mori'* (It is sweet and honourable to die for one's country) appears on many of the monuments to the dead of World War I. During that conflict the English soldier-poet Wilfred Owen (1893–1918) turned savagely upon this vision of glory and asked scornfully:

> My friend, you would not tell with such high zest
> To children ardent for some desperate glory,
> The old Lie: Dulce et decorum est
> Pro patria mori.[14]

But such bitter cynicism is far from common. Patton may have been exceptional, and it is certainly true that relatively few twentieth-century commanders have spoken as openly as he of death or glory, but soldiers of all ranks know that they depend for life itself on the real virtues of self-sacrifice and courage amongst their comrades. These values are embodied in warrior codes like European chivalry and Japanese bushido, and in the practices of military units. Sledge gives a horrific picture of war, but the Marine Corps motto, *Semper Fidelis*, is never far from his consciousness. This, in fact, is a form of honour, and it was much remarked upon amongst young subalterns of the British army in World War II. A captain of the Lancashire Fusiliers described a new officer joining the battalion in Tunisia:

> He'd be all right. The keen young public-schoolboy type. The kind that hero-worship easily and bust themselves for the honour of the house. You could laugh at them. You could be irritated by them. But they won your bloody wars for you. Because they had been bred and conditioned to bust themselves for the house.[15]

Karna, the great hero of the Indian epic of the Mahabharata, written in the second millennium before Christ, shows the same spirit of self-sacrifice: 'I'll pay Duryodhana with my life for all his kindness and help. I cannot change my loyalty under any circumstance.' In the somewhat later Ramayana, the hero, Rama, kills the demon-king Ravana who had kidnapped his wife. Yet, in a gesture of generosity which warriors of almost all ages and cultures would have approved, he speaks well of his vanquished enemy and urges that his corpse be treated with respect: 'Honour him and cherish his memory so that his spirit may go to heaven, where he has his place. And now I will leave you to attend to his funeral arrangements, befitting his grandeur.'[16]

The values of solidarity, courage and brotherhood are virtually universal because they are the only values which can sustain the individual in the chaos of conflict. Modern armies have inherited them from the distant past and instil them as a means of steeling their soldiers to their dreadful task. Sledge summed up his experience of combat:

> War is brutish, inglorious, and a terrible waste . . . The only redeeming factors were my comrades' incredible bravery and their devotion to each other. Marine Corps training taught us to kill efficiently and to try to survive. But it also taught us loyalty to each other – and love. That esprit de corps sustained it.[17]

A British officer summarised his ideas about why men stand and fight in much the same terms, though with a rather different tone:

> Men are inclined to do what their comrades expect them to do, or, more accurately, because nobody actually wants to fight, they do what they imagine their comrades expect them to do. Whether this be mutual deception or mutual support it does the trick.[18]

The value-systems of warriors are primarily a response to the demands of that most complex and terrifying of all environments, the battlefield, and a huge amount of modern writing about war is writing about battle. Battle has always dominated warfare, because any army going to war must be prepared to face this ultimate test. But this does not mean that battle was always a frequent or even a normal part of war. Our views of how war is fought have been formed by the great Military Revolution of the nineteenth century and the experience of the twentieth whose two great wars were virtually continuous battles. Clausewitz argued that the whole purpose of war is the destruction of the enemy's forces, and, therefore: 'There is no factor in war that rivals the battle in importance.'[19]

But in reality battle was always a chancy business, and even victory in battle might not produce results if the loser retreated into cities and castles to lick his wounds and gather his strength. Because fortifications controlled the land, siege was an immensely important form of warfare. It was also very difficult because of the enormous advantages which fortifications confer on the defender who is fighting behind prepared defences, usually at a height above the attacker, has plenty of shelter, and can draw upon supplies already laid down. The besieger has to improvise his shelter and logistics and must face alerted and well-protected foes. Even in modern conditions an assault on a city is costly in blood and is time-consuming. In 1942–3 the German Sixth Army exhausted itself trying to seize Stalingrad and was in turn besieged and destroyed. In 1968 the North Vietnamese Army (NVA) seized Hué city which the US Marines then had to retake. The NVA suffered over 40,000 killed and inflicted about 10,000 losses on their enemies. It is important to note that in this action about 14,000 civilians were killed; in siege there can be no separation between civilian and soldier.

Partly because of the risks of battle and the sheer difficulty of taking fortifications, armies resorted most commonly to a quite different strategy which the late Roman writer Vegetius recommended:

> It is preferable to subdue an enemy by famine, raids and terror, than in battle where fortune tends to have more influence than bravery.[20]

This is terror and destruction, with a familiar ring for generations who know about the bomber campaigns of World War II and their terrible impact upon civilian populations. We should not let battle dominate our view of war. From the very earliest times, commanders knew that harrying 'civilians' was a highly effective way of subduing an enemy. This was not merely what we describe as 'collateral damage', but deliberately targeting non-combatants. In pre-industrial societies, destroying farms, killing animals and farmers and ruining crops paid huge dividends, for it threatened entire populations with starvation. And looting paid the soldiers and enabled an attacking army to feed itself from pillage.

For millennia, therefore, this kind of war has been essential to commanders because it simultaneously improved an attacker's tactical situation and weakened the defender. Mao Tse-tung, one of the most successful commanders of the twentieth century, simply gave a new twist to the targeting of civilians by suggesting that they should be used to conceal guerrilla forces: 'The popular masses are like water, and the army is like a fish,' he remarked in 1938. Hidden in this way the insurgent could choose when to fight and when to run away: 'The ability to run away is the very characteristic of the guerrilla.'[21] In his view the struggle should not escalate into open battle until the enemy had been so weakened as to make success at the very least highly probable. Of course, the consequence of such tactics, which have become central to all forms of insurgency, are disastrous for the civilian population as events at Hué simply underlined. Beating up peasants, smashing homes, killing women and children, are hardly noble acts, and, unsurprisingly, soldiers have preferred to emphasise other things. Military historians have tended to ignore this inglorious face of war, or at least to treat it as incidental, when in fact it was quite normally of the essence of military operations.

So war is not just battle, but the interplay of this strategy with the two others of destruction and siege. These are not in actual practice separate actions and one can lead into another. An army which is ravaging disperses its forces, exposing itself to defeat by an enemy who keeps his men together; this happened to Saladin at Montgisard in 1177. Battles often arise from sieges. In 1187 Saladin besieged Tiberias and drew the relieving army of the crusader kingdom into a trap at Hattin. If the destruction of the enemy's army is not always the objective, what should it be? And what is the distinction between 'limited' and 'unlimited' war and what conditions apply to them to make them different? Simple statements about war – such as the one with which we began, that it is insanity – will not do. War is a complicated phenomenon with many faces.

It is very hard to make sense of such a complex and widespread phenomenon, especially for generations brought up in the long peace since 1945. In an era of human rights and concern for the individual, it is appalling to confront a human activity whose very essence is the destruction of life:

> We are not interested in generals who win victories without bloodshed. The fact that slaughter is a horrifying spectacle must make us take war more seriously, but not provide an excuse for gradually blunting our swords in the name of humanity. Sooner or later someone will come along with a sharp sword and hack off our arms.[22]

In many ways even more uncomfortable is Vegetius's dictum which suggests that only the armed nation can enjoy peace: 'Therefore, he who desires peace, let him prepare for war.'[23] And the underlying sense of both of these quotations, the inevitability of war or at least the threat of war, is disturbing to generations who regard peace as a norm. Indeed, much thinking about war disturbs. After World War I the British ruling classes were deeply affected by the huge casualties which had been suffered in the trenches, and in particular by the notion of the 'lost gener-ation', the young officers who died in them, depriving future generations of leadership. This dread of losses was a powerful force in 'appeasement' in the 1930s, the desire to placate Hitler and so to prevent war. Once conflict broke out, the political leadership, notably in the person of Churchill, was desperate to avoid casualties, and saw air power as the means to achieve it. Yet the total of aircrew killed, in British Bomber Command alone, was about 55,500, with a further 18,000 prisoners and wounded; around 42,000 British officers perished in World War I.[24] It is an uncomfortable thought that the desire to prevent casualties and the chosen means of doing so produced even greater losses. Calculations of blood of this kind are inherent in the business of war, yet they are also repellent, the more so to people who feel increasingly distant from this kind of conflict. Yet brutal and disturbing as it is, war exercises a terrible fascination, especially for young men; as Dr Johnson remarked: 'Every man thinks meanly of himself for not having been a soldier, or not having been at sea.'[25]

A whole industry has grown up to satisfy our curiosity about war, but it is overwhelmingly focused on the recent western experience. World War II dominates the military history shelves in any bookstore, while TV documentaries make use of the enormous volume of film, some of it in colour, shot in the period 1939–45. As it recedes into the past, World War II is increasingly portrayed as a righteous war. The repetition of this triumph has become something of a comfort blanket, assuring us of our supremacy. 'Our victory' in 1945 is seen as the foundation of the peace which we in Europe and the US (but not everyone) believe we have enjoyed since then. This adds to our sense of military security, which was, in any case, greatly increased by the collapse of the Soviet Union in 1989.

Most of the books and films focus on the experience of individual soldiers. World War II has provided us with an enormous number of personal memoirs, and the best of these, like that of Eugene Sledge, are very vivid and important documents. Works like J. Keegan's *Face of Battle* reject the old style of writing about war in which armies advance and retreat like robots in response to the commands of a general. They prefer to present the experience of the fighting soldier, which gives them considerable popular appeal. But the trouble is that they are essentially descriptive, with a tendency to focus on the minutiae of war – for example, the sound of arrows falling on armour is highly evocative in Keegan's account of Agincourt – and while they go some way to helping us understand what sustains soldiers in the face of suffering, they explain very little else and actually do not tell us a great deal about war. And, necessarily, they tend to focus upon the familiar: we do not have the memoirs of a Mongol horseman or a Chinese soldier of the age of the Terracotta Army. There is a vast literature on the Vietnam War, almost all of it from an American standpoint; it is only very recently that Vietnamese accounts have begun to appear.

Repetition and reiteration of the individual experience of World War II allow us to share vicariously in the agonies of individual soldiers, but this subjective approach enables us to ignore wider and more disturbing questions about why the war happened at all and how it was fought and won. It does not even really explain what makes western men fight because it is too narrow in its focus and invites us merely to cringe at the horrors of war. 'The past is another country; they do things differently there' – the opening of L. P. Hartley's novel is a warning to all historians and the narrow focus on World War II and the recent experience of war is distorting.[26] We see war as the bane of humanity. Things were different in the past. In the drama of the Christian Apocalypse, as the fourth seal was opened: 'Behold a pale horse: and his name that sat on him was Death, and Hell followed with him.' But Death led other horsemen who 'Kill with sword, and with hunger, and with death, and with the beasts of the earth.'[27]

For our ancestors, war was merely one of the scourges of humanity, a killer of men, but a killer amongst others equally deadly: plague and famine. If the harsh conditions of life shaped war, they also shaped attitudes to war. In the summer of 1961 I was cutting grass for the British army in Bury St Edmunds, under the charge of 'Old Bill', a Suffolk man and a veteran of World War I. When I asked him about his experiences, expecting a catalogue of horror, his first reaction was to the effect that 'at least in the army we got three meals a day'. In rural Suffolk before 1914 three meals a day was not taken for granted; it was a world of terrible hardship for working people which bore upon his view of the experience of war. Similarly, my father, who fought in World War II, was born in 1907, one of the six children of a coal miner. But two of his siblings died in childhood – by no means an uncommon experience for his generation, though today we see such mortality as 'Third World'. A child growing up in their generation would have seen animals pouched (cut open) quite routinely, tasted blood sports like dog-fighting and greyhound-racing with live hares, while death and injury in industry were common experiences. Even in the 1940s when I was brought up, such things happened. Children bored a tunnel through a haystack in a Bradford park and some were burned to death when it caught fire. A boy fell from a dangerous pipe-bridge and was dragged dead from the brook by a policeman and a few neighbours. These were not things that made headlines; they were simply part of expectation, of the fabric of existence. Life was rougher in the past, and expected to be so, and the deeper we go into this other country, the more we must beware of taking with us our attitudes, formed by our relatively safe environment and the vicarious experience of war through film and video game.

And our view of the past is too often coloured by another facet of our recent experience. World War II was marked by astonishing technological development, and incredible new devices like the Stealth Bomber have dominated recent conflicts. It is tempting to look at the past in terms of 'weapons systems', but that is a totally false perspective. The trebuchet was a heavy catapult which came into use in the Middle East and Europe at the turn of the twelfth and thirteenth centuries, but it was clumsy, inaccurate and slow. I once fired one and the ball went in the opposite direction to that intended, nearly killing passers-by. There were occasional important technological changes in warfare before the nineteenth century, but in general they were introduced so slowly that nobody got a decisive advantage from them. As late as the 1820s Clausewitz commented on how little new weapons had changed warfare: 'Very few of the new manifestations in war can be ascribed to new inventions or new departures in ideas.'[28] Looking at the past through technological glasses is a distortion, and for the same reason this book does not make much use of military jargon. The sophisticated analytic terms used by armies nowadays are very modern and applying them to distant events is misleading. Ancient generals used subordinates, but the 'General Staff' was an invention of the nineteenth century. Even the distinction between strategy and tactics was not generally recognised before the nineteenth century. Language, therefore, may change the past and make it appear more familiar.

We must not be hypnotised into looking only at our own recent experience. That is rather like looking only in the mirror on the wall – after a while we are bound to think we are the most beautiful of them all. And if there is one obvious fact that the most superficial glance at military history reveals, it is that superiority can evaporate overnight, and that the glory of today produces the dust of empires on the morrow. In matters military, one nation's strength may spring from another's weakness, and, therefore, strength can only be judged in the total context of the competition for power. Moreover, there is a tendency to project the past and the present into the future. Because the US was dominant in 1945 and is strong now, it is easy to assume that this will always be the case: the perspective of history shows that this is not necessarily true. So the present book will look at the military history of the world from the third millennium BC, when we begin to have some substantial records, to the present day.

This book will examine the military development of the powers and nations within the great world cultures: China (understood to include Japan and South East Asia), India, the Asian steppe, the Mediterranean lands and Europe. If the Americas prior to the European incursions in the fifteenth and sixteenth centuries are treated more briefly, it is only because our knowledge of them is limited. The focus is on explaining the present eminence of the 'West', but in the context of world development. War has been a central part of the experience of all civilisations, and many of its manifestations can seem very remote and even incomprehensible, embedded in alien cultures. The Great Wall of China seems, at first thought, the product of far-away and obscure struggles, while it is easy to dismiss the long and bloody history of medieval India as a distant irrelevance. But the Great Wall was the result of a centuries-long conflict between the nomads of Central Asia and the settled peoples on the periphery of the open steppe, the 'Sea of Grass', which, to a remarkable degree, shaped world history. The conquest of what is now Pakistan projected Islam into the Far East and made it into a world rather than a regional religion. Our world, and our means of waging war, has been shaped by the experiences of others, so we need to understand them.

And it is worth emphasising that military history is very important. Military glory is perilous and transient. The way in which military practitioners look at the past influences their present and future thinking and behaviour. Far too many of the current trends of thought on military history simply serve to reinforce and strengthen our trust in the notion of western (and specifically US) military supremacy by asserting that it is culture-specific, that it springs inevitably from the very way in which Americans and Europeans think and perceive the world. This is a comforting but dangerous notion. The history of war is a record of both thought and the application of resources, but it has also been shaped by the most fortuitous events. In the words of Clausewitz:

> War is the realm of chance. No other human activity gives it greater scope: no other has such incessant and varied dealings with this intruder. Chance makes everything more uncertain and interferes with the whole course of events.[29]

And chance governs the rise of leadership, that most important aspect of war. Genius in any field is rare and the emergence of a military leader who possesses it and has command of the material means to achieve success is even rarer. Our modern academies can train soldiers to a level of competence, but they cannot reliably produce an Alexander the Great or a Napoleon.

Military history is particularly significant now because it is almost the only way in which the people of the comfortable and immensely rich countries of the developed world can confront the realities of war. Since the 1960s war has almost become a spectator sport in many countries. This has been encouraged by the rise of relatively small professional armies. While we may have opinions about it, war essentially leaves us untouched. In Great Britain, the Falklands War of 1982 was virtually treated by the media as a sporting event, regardless of the fact that people were dying and being maimed in quite large numbers. France was heavily involved in the events which produced the Rwandan genocide of 1994 which killed at least 500,000 people, but in 2010 the French President airily dismissed such 'mistakes'. The second and third Gulf Wars of 1990–1 and 2003 have been taken rather more seriously, but the use of 'smart' weapons and the showing of TV footage from them has led to comparisons with computer games, and indeed this has become something of a cliché.

Treating war like this is dangerous. Distant wars in distant places have a habit of creeping up on us. In 1851 Bismarck commented that 'the entire Balkans are not worth the bones of one Pomeranian grenadier', but in 1914 Germany, the country which he created, went to war – and lost – over an assassination in the obscure Balkan city of Sarajevo. In the words of Clausewitz, war can 'come along with a sharp sword and hack off our arms',[30] as the whole world saw so vividly in New York on 11 September 2001, in Madrid on 11 March 2004 and London on 7 July 2005.

◆

CHAPTER TWO

MANY WORLDS OF WAR

None of you was there . . . None rose to lend me his hand in my fight . . . None of you came later to tell the story of his heroic deeds in Egypt . . . The foreigners who saw me, praise my name to the end of all lands where I was not known . . . Since ancient times a man was honored for his fighting abilities, but I will not reward any of you, as you have abandoned me when I was alone fighting my enemies.

THE rage of the Pharaoh Rameses II (1304–1237 BC), after his close encounter with death at the battle of Kadesh in 1275/4, is engraved in the stone walls of no fewer than five great temples. The Pharaohs regarded Palestine and Syria as important outposts against attack on their heartland from the east and north. But the Hittite Empire of Anatolia under Muwatalli II (1295–1272), with its access to rich mineral resources, made inroads into Syria. Rameses was determined to drive them back, and in particular to seize the important frontier city of Kadesh in the Orontes valley.

The Egyptians summoned an army perhaps 20,000 strong with some 2,000 war-chariots spread across its four divisions, each named after a god. Rameses commanded the forward division of Amun, followed by his sons in charge of Ra, Ptah and Set. A reconnaissance unit went ahead of the main host to seek out the enemy. As the Egyptians turned up the Orontes valley they encountered spies planted by the Hittites who assured them that the enemy's main force was as far away as Aleppo, leading Rameses to think that he had an opportunity to seize Kadesh; he crossed the Orontes and pressed on hastily with the division of Amun to encamp to the west of the city. When Rameses realised that he had been duped and that Muwatalli had a huge Hittite army at Kadesh, he frantically summoned all his men. As the division of Ra rushed towards him a large force of Hittite chariots burst across the Orontes and destroyed them. They then charged down upon the partially completed camp of the division of Amun. The Pharaoh rallied his chariots:

> His Majesty shone like his father Montu [the god of war] when he took the adornments of war. As he seized his coat of mail he was like Baal in his honour. His Majesty charged into the foe . . . when his Majesty looked behind him he found two thousand five hundred chariots surrounding him.

A desperate struggle followed. But the Hittite horses were presumably tiring, and the lighter and more manoeuvrable Egyptian chariots took their advantage. The Egyptian infantry of the Amun division rallied, and the balance was tipped by the chance reappearance of the Egyptian reconnaissance force which drove back the Hittite charioteers. More Hittite chariots then arrived, but too late to recover the initiative, so the crews abandoned their vehicles and swam back across the river.

Quite why the Egyptian divisions of Ptah and Set failed to help Rameses is not clear, but the Pharaoh's rage at this abandonment is understandable. Nor do we know why the Hittite infantry stood aloof. But the next day the armies in their entirety confronted one another, inconclusively. In his magnificent inscriptions Rameses claimed victory, despite his narrow escape from death. But in essence this was a drawn battle, and Egyptian losses were such that Rameses was forced to withdraw and was never able to reassert his power in Syria. In 1258 BC the warring parties agreed to a peace recorded on a clay tablet, a copy of which is held at the United Nations as the earliest surviving peace agreement. Kadesh presents a sudden and exciting vision of war. Chariots charge and manoeuvre while infantry flee or fight desperately. Blood, mud, dust and confusion – the Pharaoh resplendent in his chariot of gold – the face of battle is suddenly vivid.

The armies which clashed at Kadesh were sophisticated and complex organisms, and very obviously they were the products of well organised states. But long before the state, human communities were fighting one another, sometimes on a substantial scale. For most of their existence humankind depended on a way of life usually called hunter-gathering. Small nomadic groups moved around living upon what they could find, scavenge or kill. This is sometimes thought of as a gentle and environmentally friendly way of life, but in reality it was marked by savage clashes between wandering groups. Hunter-gatherers were tied to a pattern of migration between known food resources which varied with the seasons. If this was interrupted by climatic or other variations, a group had to find a new range, or seize it from others. At Jebel Sahaba in Egypt about a quarter of the bodies dating from the hunter-gatherer period 13,000 years ago show clear signs of violent death. The gentleness of modern hunter-gatherers is the gentleness of the defeated, huddling in hostile environments into which they were driven by us, the successful hunter-gatherers who have long left behind that way of life. After about 12000 BC humans began to grow food plants and to domesticate animals. This gradually enabled them to break their dependence on the vagaries of nature because they could store food to tide them over fluctuations of climate and food supply. The farming life demanded that people live close together in villages where they could help one another to clear land and to keep it cultivated, but this produced no rural idyll.

We have a glimpse of how early farming communities may have waged war. The interior of Papua New Guinea was still a Stone Age society in 1961 when anthropologists made a film, *Dead Birds*, about two villages in strife so continual that the border between their lands was guarded by watchtowers to prevent attacks.[1] The highlight of this remarkable film is a battle. It was a highly ritualised event. Announced beforehand, it took place on a ridge in no-man's-land. The warriors, many of them in finery, bullied and jeered, with individuals rushing forward to throw spears or fire arrows then retreating hastily, never closing to fight hand-to-hand. Once a death was inflicted, both sides withdrew, the killers to rejoice and the others to mourn.

This individualised style of fighting is reminiscent of the battles in Homer's epic, the *Iliad*, where the heroes confront one another while the masses on each side cheer them on. The appearance is of ritualised war with just a handful of casualties. But in New Guinea there was always another and darker side to this warfare – savage raiding. Individual attacks usually killed only a few of the enemy, but their sheer frequency took its toll of men, women and children to the extent that over time whole communities were annihilated and their villages abandoned. This kind of killing produced the high proportion of violent deaths found in ancient cemeteries, and it was interspersed with massacres. At Crow Creek, South Dakota, the entire population of nearly 500, of both sexes and all ages, was slaughtered about AD 1350. All that we know of mankind before the development of the state suggests that, although there were peaceful moments, violence was continual, killing men, women and children generation after generation. It is a myth, albeit an attractive one, that before the state there was no war.

It is therefore no surprise that archaeology reveals that early agricultural settlements were fortified. Banpo village near Xian in China dates from about 4500 BC, long before the rise of any organised state in this part of the world. This was a substantial village covering some 6 hectares but the site is surrounded by a carefully cut ditch some 6 metres deep and 5–6 metres wide. This is far greater than would be needed either to keep domestic animals in or wild ones out. Moreover, it is carefully subdivided by crossing walls to prevent concerted attack. Banpo is evidence of a violent and divided society in which farmers had to be ever ready to defend themselves. Some of the earliest settlements in Britain were the 'Causeway Camps' dating from about 4000 BC, which were surrounded by ditches and banks. Interestingly, in many cases massive concentrations of flint arrowheads have been found around the ramparts and gates: clear evidence of siege warfare.

These settlements of agricultural peoples were much larger and more complex than the transient communities which preceded them. Amongst hunter-gatherers, women had been responsible for gathering and men for hunting. Farming, however, demanded a much higher degree of specialisation. Groups of people had to work together over sustained periods of time following schedules determined by planting and harvesting crops and caring for animals. The villages of Papua New Guinea were guided by their richest members, the 'Big Men', and it was probably people like them who assumed control over the early agricultural settlements, judging quarrels over land and organising people to meet the challenges of sowing and reaping. Measuring time was crucial for the agricultural year, and may have been the preserve of the priesthood. Moreover, farming generated technological innovation: food had to be stored, transported and protected from rival communities by strong buildings and walls. And in many areas the complexities of irrigation and water-sharing could only be regulated by strong authorities. As a consequence, there arose hierarchical societies dominated by 'kings' and their ruling elites who increasingly monopolised power and lived on the labour of farmers. In these new and more complex societies war was the most important task of the rulers. Defending the land was a moral justification for their privileges, and controlling weapons and men of violence was essential to maintaining their dominance over the mass of the population.

In Mesopotamia, complex societies developed most rapidly. The fertile plains produced rich crops, which resulted in increased populations. Over time, the rulers and their retinues separated themselves from the farming communities, whose people actually produced food, by establishing centres of control, in the form of palaces or cities, of which the earliest known to us is Uruk in Mesopotamia (modern Iraq) which dates from 5500 BC. At its height, this was a city of 50,000 centred on its great temples and palaces and ziggurat, defended by a huge mud-brick wall and governed by royal dynasties, one of whose rulers provided the inspiration for the Epic of Gilgamesh which dates from about 2700 BC (see p. 3). Kings usually controlled the cult of the city's gods, so defending the city became a sacred task led by the royal personage who was, in a sense, the mediator between his people and the divine world. These rulers, and the elites around them, lived on the backs of the farmers, and the need to record the wealth they extracted from the mass of the population and the way in which it was spent produced the earliest written records: clay tablets recording taxes and the way in which they were spent. In effect account-books are the earliest known form of writing.

The same pattern of development appeared contemporaneously in the other fertile areas of the Middle East and Asia. In Egypt the Nile watered and enriched the land, providing a great highway along which a common culture developed in relative isolation because of the desert through which it flows. The Old Kingdom (2650–2134 BC), which created the Great Pyramids, united Upper (around modern Luxor) and Lower (the Nile delta) Egypt, and its Pharaohs, like Mesopotamian rulers, claimed to mediate between their subjects and the gods. In north-western India the remarkable Harappan civilisation (3000–1700 BC) built cities with huge populations, such as the 30,000–50,000 of Mohenjo-Daro.

In China the Shang state (1766–1122 BC) developed in the Yellow River valley in the northern part of what is now Henan province. Here on the central plains arose many of the characteristics of Han culture, notably its ideographic style of writing, the fondness for written record together with a tendency to bureaucratic government. The Shang state was built around important cities like Ao, near modern Zhengzhou, and Luoyang. The Shang emperor enjoyed a quasi-priestly authority, but presided over groups of officials, one responsible for royal ritual, another for administration and a third for military matters. These jobs were monopolised by aristocrats who were rewarded with land, while the rest of the population were virtually slaves, tied to the soil. As in the Mesopotamian cities, the royal household controlled virtually all economic activity. The cities of Mesopotamia, Egypt, India and China evolved their own distinctive civilisations, yet shared a common pattern of war.

The large populations of these city-states, supported by agriculture, provided fit young males to fight. Because farming is labour intensive only at certain times of the year, notably the sowing and harvesting seasons, in between large numbers of men are under-employed; and in any case much of the work on the land was undertaken by women. Rulers could employ surplus manpower to build the walls, towers and strong gates with which they defended their centres of power: cities and fortresses. Such strong fortified bases could be attacked only by numerous, well-organised and well-equipped infantry soldiers. At the core of the armies were the kings, supported by their aristocratic followers with armed retinues from amongst whom the commanders were drawn. The elite troops with their splendid armour and weapons were supported by lightly armed conscripts drawn from the ordinary population. Bureaucrats in the cities collected food and oversaw the purchase of weapons and equipment for the army. The city societies were innovative: in India the Harappan civilisation invented the spinning and weaving of cotton and the ox-drawn wagon. Such technological progress fed into military effectiveness.

The discovery of metal, especially bronze, had enormous impact on war, replacing the use of stone for tools and weapons. Copper is widely available and easily worked because of its low melting point, but it is relatively soft. Bronze, an alloy of copper and tin, is harder and capable of taking and sustaining a sharp edge. By about 3000 BC it was known in Harappan India, Mesopotamia and around the Aegean Sea in what is now Greece and Turkey, spreading to China and Egypt before 2000 BC. Shortly thereafter it became common in Western Europe. Because Afghanistan was for a long time the primary source of tin, the invention of bronze was a great incentive to trade. The cities of Mesopotamia lacked metal, so they bought copper from Anatolia and tin from Afghanistan. Securing these and other trade routes was a powerful motive for alliances and war.

The elites who dominated the leading civilisations of the ancient world recognised possibilities for wealth and power which were infinitely greater than could be achieved by a single city and its hinterland. The luxury to which they aspired is very evident in this description of Akkad in Mesopotamia *c.*2000 BC at the height of its power:

Curse on Akkad: the city in its hey-day
So that the warehouses would be provisioned,
That dwellings would be founded in that city,
That its people would eat splendid food,
That its people would drink splendid beverages,
That those bathed [for holidays] would rejoice in the courtyards,
That the people would throng the places of celebration,

That acquaintances would dine together,
That foreigners would cruise about like unusual birds in the sky,
That [even] *Marhasi* would be re-entered on the [tribute] rolls,
That monkeys, mighty elephants, water buffalo, exotic animals,
Would jostle each other in the public squares
Holy *Inanna* did not sleep.[2]

If leaders wanted to increase their power, they had to extend their dominions because they often lacked the natural resources to support this kind
of living. They could not intensify wealth production because agriculture
was the basic resource, and to exploit the peasant too harshly would cause
him to destroy the fertility of the land. Trade and industry, though capable
of more intense wealth production, were limited because tied to agriculture. So empire, dominion over others, was the obvious way to extract
tribute from subjugated peoples and to gain control of mines, forests
and trade networks. Inevitably this incited the envy of rivals, resistance
and war.

The cities of Mesopotamia were very numerous and were built close
together on an open plain with few real dividing features. As a result, although
they developed a common culture, they became locked into complex military
rivalries and diplomatic relationships. Nomadic peoples, generally called
Amorites, swirled across the Mesopotamian plains, threatening the cities. The
Iranian plateau to the east was home to menacing groups, Elamites, Kassites,
Aryans and others from the steppe lands just as anxious to enjoy the luxuries
of dominion as the city people. The whole area could be threatened by attack
from Anatolia and Syria. Egypt feared the kingdom of Kush in Nubia
(modern Sudan) to the south, while the Nile delta was exposed to raiders
from Libya to the west and 'Asiatics' from Canaan (Palestine) and further east.
In China the Shang conducted an aggressive policy aimed at dominating
neighbouring peoples and cities and imposing their increasingly distinctive
culture on them. The Shang state was situated on the central plains, close to
the Northern Zone (roughly between the Great Wall and the country now
called Outer Mongolia) which borders the Eurasian steppe where nomadic
tribes and settled peoples lived cheek-by-jowl.

In this fluid and changing world, city-states competed with one another
and with all other nearby peoples in an almost permanent state of conflict.
In Mesopotamia wealthy cities like Ur, Uruk, Akkad, Babylon, Ashur
(Assyria), Nineveh and Mari were set in the rich plain by the rivers
Euphrates and Tigris. Although they shared a common culture, the ruling
elites were ambitious to increase their wealth and influence, and fearful

that others might do so at their expense. From about 2000 BC, Babylon in the south and Assyria in the north were generally the dominant powers, but they were hostile to one another and the cities in their empires were always restive. Sheer distance and slow communications made it difficult to control them, while violent quarrels within the ruling elites of Babylon and Assyria, especially over who should succeed a dead king, opened the way for rebellion and instability. So although these two precarious empires would dominate Mesopotamia for 1,300 years, they went through many vicissitudes. Similarly, the dynasties of Egypt had trouble holding down the cities by the Nile, and the kingdom was always threatened by division between Upper Egypt and Lower Egypt. The Shang ruthlessly imposed their distinctive culture upon neighbouring lands and their leaders, but they too were plagued by the problems of control at a distance and divisions amongst their chief followers.

Everywhere, cities were the vital instruments by which rulers controlled the countryside, so it is hardly surprising that they were defended by strong walls. In China, the Shang capital of Ao was 3.2 square kilometres, enclosed by a wall 7,000 metres long. This was a massive structure, in places 36 metres wide: some parts still reach a height of 10 metres. The building technique was that of stamped earth: wooden shutters were erected and filled with earth which was then trodden down into a hard mass. It is estimated that these fortifications absorbed the forced labour of 10,000 men over a period of eighteen years. In India the Harappan cities were surrounded by mighty walls of fired brick, but they suffered catastrophic flooding about 2000 BC, which hid much of their achievement. In Mesopotamia and Egypt, mud brick was the universally available material and some city walls were 10 metres thick.

But these ancient peoples did not just rely on mass – they strengthened their fortifications by skilful design. The principle of concentricity, of containing one line of defence within another, was well understood. A contemporary description of Mari records that 'The inner city wall is surrounded by an outer wall, and the palace by an outer wall and a moat.' Great towers projected from walls to provide enfilading fire against attack. Gateways, such as that which survives at Tell-Dan in modern Israel, were provided with flanking towers. The tops of towers and walls were crenellated and pierced with firing loops. Such elaboration was extended to forts covering important points: Samsu-iluna, king of Babylon (1749–1712 BC), 'In the course of two months, on the bank of the Turul river, built Fort Samsu-iluna. He dug its surrounding moat, piled up its earth there, formed its bricks and built its wall. He raised its head like a mountain.'[3] Egypt too established defences in the south against the kingdom of Kush, where Buhen, built about 2000 BC, had a mighty inner circuit towering 11 metres high over a slightly lower outer wall which was defended by a deep ditch with a sloping cleared area or glacis in front. Its great west gate was even taller than the inner wall and was entered by a narrow passageway between two projecting towers of equal height; the use of crenellations and firing loops made this a formidable structure. Machicolations, the system whereby the crenellated top section of a wall was offset to create a gap through which defenders could drop stones on attackers at the foot of the wall, were known. By about 2000 BC, almost all the important design features of fortifications found in the ancient and medieval worlds had appeared in the Middle East. Stone was sometime used to strengthen them in Mesopotamia and Egypt, but its hardness meant that it was very difficult to work, demanded the special skills of the mason and hence was very expensive. Its use, therefore, was generally limited to temples and palaces. Mud brick and earth were used by everyone, so unskilled manpower could be conscripted easily.

But in some parts of the world mud was not available for the construction of defences. In Anatolia, for example, city-states emerged because the area was rich in copper and other minerals. They were never as wealthy as the cities of Mesopotamia in their fertile plain, but the Hittites united them in a formidable empire. They ruled from their capital of Hattusha, which by the thirteenth century BC was protected by building on strong natural features, using roughly worked stones, often of cyclopean proportions. But again mass was not all: Hattusha had towers and recessed gates, and at its heart was a mighty citadel. Further west, at about the same time, the Mycenaean Greeks dominated rocky Greece. The great stone defences of Mycenae and 'mighty walled Tiryns' still amaze, although their cities were much smaller than those to the east.

But their walls, however massive, were not strong enough to save cities from sack. A terrible lamentation commemorates the fall of Ur to the Elamites c.1950 BC:

> Hunger filled the city like water, it would not cease,
> (This) hunger contorts (people's) faces, it twists their muscles.
> Its king breathed heavily in his palace, all alone.
> Its people dropped (their) weapons, (their) weapons hit the ground,
> They struck their necks with their hands and cried.
> They sought council with each other, they searched for clarification:
> Alas, what can we say about it, what more can we add to it?

How long until we are finished off by this calamity?
Ur – inside it there is death, outside it there is death,
Inside it we are being finished off by famine,
Outside it we are being finished off by Elamite weapons,
In Ur, the enemy has oppressed us, oh, we are finished!
They take refuge behind it (the city walls), they were united (in
    their fear).
The palace that was destroyed by (onrushing) waters has been defiled,
    its bolt torn out,
Elam, like a swelling flood, left only the spirits of the dead
In Ur people were smashed as if they were clay pots,
Its refugees were (unable) to flee, they were trapped inside the walls,
Like fish living in a pond they seek shelter.[4]

All over the world the thrust to empire demanded successful siege operations, and this stimulated military organisation. At the core of the city armies were the nobles and their retainers, splendidly armed and armoured. But siege is labour-intensive so that it was necessary to conscript large numbers of peasants to swell the ranks. In addition, mercenaries were often hired for their native skills, perhaps most notably bowmanship. Amorites and other nomads were incorporated into the armies of the Mesopotamian cities, while the Egyptians recruited many Nubians, Libyans and Canaanites. The Shang supplemented their forces with nomadic peoples from the edges of the Eurasian steppe. Only the relatively small cores of these armies were professional and trained: states could not afford to support large standing armies. They had to rely on the native skills within their populations for special abilities, and, if they were not available, to hire people from outside, who for lack of a better word tend to be called mercenaries. Mesopotamian armies were quite commonly of the order of 3,000–5,000 men, though a major effort by one of the greater powers could, perhaps, raise as many as 10,000. Anything larger was probably the result of an alliance of important cities. Egyptian forces were about the same size. In a single year under Amenemhet II (1929–1895 BC) four expeditions returned, from Lebanon, Syria, Sinai and Cyprus. In China the Shang struggled against a myriad enemy states, and armies of about the same magnitude were normal, though by about 500 BC the number of political units had shrunk and those that survived were stronger, fielding much bigger forces.

Agro-urban warfare was based on these large composite armies, supported and supplied by government offices in the cities. The Shang bureaucracy existed for this purpose. Much of the great archive of clay tablets at Mari in Mesopotamia is concerned with the affairs of the army, while troops patrolling the Egyptian frontier with Kush made regular reports on papyrus which were filed in central offices. Agro-urban warfare was, from its origins, bureaucratic. The importance of size and secrecy was well appreciated. Hammurabi of Babylon, about 1792 BC, sent letters to his commanders deliberately exaggerating the size of his forces by a factor of ten: 'When I dispatch 100 troops the one who hears it will quote it as 1000.'[5] This was apparently to confuse enemies if the clay tablets on which the letters were written fell into the wrong hands.

Such armies were primarily designed to attack rival cities, but any such assault demanded substantial manpower, and this created problems of organisation and logistics. The besiegers needed shelter and supplies. One group of Mesopotamians complained they had to 'transport water to the troops day and night from five kilometres away'.[6] Confronted by a strong wall, an army can go over, under or through it: ancient engineers made all these possible. Covering fire was essential for such operations. Our earliest pictures of sieges from Mesopotamia date from before 3000 BC and show soldiers firing bows at the defenders of a city. An Egyptian picture of about 2300 BC shows this too. But archery on its own could not breach walls. The challenge of siege was to bring attacking forces to close-quarter battle with the defenders in the most favourable circumstances. Missile weapons could keep defenders' heads down and kill some of them, but if they were determined they could only be destroyed by close-quarter fighting.

Ladders were the obvious way to climb walls, and by the mid-third millennium we have illustrations of them, sometimes with wheels, being deployed against city walls. But the men on them were very vulnerable, and better means of attack were invented. The siege-tower first appeared in the Middle East about 2500 BC, a tall wooden structure on wheels which could be pushed up against the walls enabling its crew to sweep the walls clear with archery and even to leap on to the city wall. Sometimes the tower incorporated a ram to batter at the lower part of the wall or a gate. Mining or digging through a city wall was a well-known technique long before 2000 BC. The mud brick fortifications of Egypt and Mesopotamia were very vulnerable to this kind of onslaught, and indeed illustrations show men attacking the wall with axes or pointed poles. By 2300 BC wheeled and roofed carts (in medieval Europe called cats or penthouses or tortoises) were used to protect men filling in moats and ditches and to provide fire cover for them. In Mesopotamia earthwork ramps thrown up against the city wall were the most important means of assault, and engineers used mathematics to ensure that the grading of such ramps was sufficiently gentle to allow rams, penthouses, towers and ladders to be brought up for the assault.

Digging and carrying earth to raise ramps, and providing covering fire for the workers were enormously labour intensive, so that siege operations tended to be slow and deliberate, and to focus on one section of the fortifications, even though it was essential first to isolate the city by surrounding it and cutting food supplies and communications with friendly powers. Even if a city was well stocked this was essential because siege is a psychological as well as a physical contest. But the need to concentrate on a narrow section of the defences meant that the defenders could take countermeasures.

We can see the process of siege and counter-attack at work in a series of dispatches to King Zimri-Lim of Mari (c.1765 BC) from his commander, Zimri-Addu, in Hiritum. Mari was an important trading city on the Euphrates in eastern Syria which had allied with Babylon in the face of a threat from the Elamite kingdom of what is now south-west Iran centred on Susa. Hiritum was vital to the Elamite advance, but their determined attack was repelled, and according to Zimri-Addu: 'We set fire to the tower on the lower fringe of the siege ramp, and the enemy are now seeking materials for obtaining another tower.'[7] The siege evidently centred on a siege-ramp, the construction of which was covered by the firepower of a tower. Its destruction in a sally was a major setback for the Elamites, because timber was so scarce in the Mesopotamian plains that such equipment was often prefabricated for carriage to where it was needed. Even worse, the defenders built their own ramp of earth, overtopping that of the attackers. In another dispatch Zimri-Addu reports the success of a sally: 'Our soldiers fought and drove the enemy from his siege-ramp . . . There is no siege-tower left to the enemy. After the enemy withdrew the garrison destroyed the siege-ramp and all the earthworks.'

Sharraya, king of Razama, was a loyal ally of Zimri-Lim of Mari. When his city was attacked by an Elamite alliance, Sharraya conducted an aggressive defence. In an early sortie, 'He went out and felled 500 troops from among the enemy troops. He also killed two leatherworkers and battering-ram makers.' The importance of this kind of aggressiveness and of the vulnerability of specialised equipment and artificers in the complicated business of siege is evident. In a later assault Sharraya did so much damage that the morale of the attackers slumped, and when they heard that Mari was mounting a relief expedition, they fled.[8] Chinese armies of the Shang and Zhou developed much the same equipment, but the massive rammed-earth walls of Chinese cities defied any battering so that tactics were focused on mass escalade, but even here the key was to over-whelm the defenders on one part of the wall. The formidable power of fortifications probably explains why expansionist powers like Egypt, Assyria and Babylon were willing to leave local kings in control of their cities as vassals. This arrangement must have been a useful compromise, achieving subordination and tribute without the tiresome labour and costs of full-scale assault and occupation. But such arrangements, which would remain common until modern times, in part explain the fragility of the ancient empires and the way in which they rose and fell.

Siege invited battle. Only two written accounts of battles in this period, Megiddo (1457 BC) and Kadesh (1274/5 BC), have survived and an illus-tration of a third from the tomb of Inty, a noble judge of Old Kingdom Egypt 2686–2134 BC: all occurred in connection with sieges. The rulers of a target city could choose to try and destroy the attacking army in battle, which was essentially what happened at Kadesh. In the illustration in Inty's tomb the Canaanites, defeated in battle, fell back into their city. Once a siege was set, the defenders could, like Zimri-Addu, sally out to kill their enemies and destroy their equipment. Diplomacy enabled them to call upon allies to attack the besiegers. Battle, the clash of armies in the open field, demanded fighting at close quarters. The key reason for this was the inadequacy of missile-weapons.

Bows, slings and javelins were at all times important, and as they required little expensive metal they were the weapons of the masses. But they had grave limitations, both technical and human. Suitable wood for bows was not available everywhere and without it the weapon was much less effective. Archers and slingers quickly ran out of ammunition. The composite bow, developed about 2000 BC, was made by gluing bone and sinew to a wooden core, producing great strength. It was expensive and complex to make, which limited its use to the elite, and the glue tended to unstick in damp weather. But the gravest problems were human. The javelin requires physique, coordination, skill and a good eye. So does the bow, but states could not afford to train huge numbers of archers – they relied on native skills in their populations, so that accuracy was always unreliable. In the battle scene in Inty's tomb the Egyptian soldiers seem first to have showered their Canaanite enemies with arrows. Significantly, many of the enemy, though stuck with arrows, continue to fight. The Egyptians then advanced in serried ranks and fought with their copper axes at close quarters in a chaotic melee.

But chaos is not the best means of fighting and there is striking evidence that the infantry armies of the Mesopotamian states organised themselves for the close-quarter battle by developing tight formations in close order. The Stele of the Vultures is a stone plaque from Mesopotamia which records an important victory by Eanatum II (about 2440 BC) of Lagash over Umma. It owes its name to its upper part which shows vultures carrying away the heads of dead enemies. But the most interesting part is its portrayal of Eanatum's soldiers who form a tight phalanx, a block of men in close order gathered behind the large shields of the front rank. Bristling through this wall of shields are the spears of their holders and those of the men behind them. The carving implies a formation nine men across in tightly packed files six deep. In another part of the stele, very similar looking infantry follow the king in his great war-chariot, though these bear no shields. Both sets of soldiers wear helmets which may be of leather or copper (examples of the latter have been found in contemporary tombs) and fabric body armour studded with metal plates. It was presumably to counter this armour that bronze socket axes with very narrow blades were developed.

There is plenty of other evidence to suggest that close-order, close-quarter fighting had become the norm before 2000 BC. Almost all illustrations of numbers of soldiers show them grouped together – it is as if the uniform mass is the norm, the mode in which soldiers exist, and this probably reflects a military reality. In New Kingdom Egypt (1570–1070 BC) the infantry were split into divisions of 5,000 common soldiers commanded by 20 officers and 20 scribes, subdivided into companies of 250, each in turn made up of five platoons of 50 men. The rock carvings at the shrine of Yazilikaya near Hattusha, dating from the thirteenth century BC, present us with a picture of Hittite infantry in serried ranks of disciplined soldiers clad in padded armour and helmets, bearing curved swords rather like the *kepesh* of contemporary Egypt. In China under the Zhou dynasty (1045–221 BC) every eight peasant families provided a warrior who was expected to spend one month a year in military training. At the battle of Mu in 1027 BC the commander ordered his men to advance in ranks, and to make sure they kept their order.

In Mesopotamian illustrations and texts, the infantry appear armed with maces (sometimes of stone), bronze axes and, most commonly, bronze-tipped spears and javelins. By the middle of the second millennium the wearing of armour like that of the figures in the Stele of the Vultures was commoner. In Egypt simple armour, such as hair extensions to protect the head against arrow strikes, and leather straps and patches to deflect blows to the chest and abdomen, developed during the Middle Kingdom (2040–1640 BC). The Egyptians had easy access to copper but tin had to be imported from long distances. As a result, copper daggers and axes were used, because bronze armour and swords would have been very expensive. But in New Kingdom Egypt external threats became more severe, and the *kepesh*, a scimitar-like sword, became common while metal armour and helmets were increasingly adopted, as they were throughout the Middle East. Shang China produced huge quantities of bronze, and breastplates made of bronze segments were widely used by its infantry.

Other equipment suggests the anxiety of commanders to keep troops together in close order. Drums and trumpets were used in Egyptian and Mesopotamian armies. Drums have been used in virtually all ages to set the pace for infantry to advance so that they can stay in close order. Trumpets and banners served to signal changes of direction. The men of a unit could rally around their own banner and move in response to the signals of their commanders. All this armament points towards the close-quarter battle as the central event of war, with men rushing against one another in a grim hacking match. The city-based states of the ancient world were highly organised, and this was reflected in their armies which were organised and disciplined to fight in close order: the most efficient way of fighting at close quarters – the essence of agro-urban warfare.

But although all armies were shaped by the pressures of battle and siege, the staple of war was destruction. Whether Henry V of England (AD 1413–22) actually said 'War without fire is as worthless as sausages without mustard' is uncertain, but it represents a great truth. All armies intentionally attacked what we would describe as civilian populations, including the elderly, women and children. This was not 'collateral damage' but absolutely essential and deliberate. Attacking the enemy's population was a good way of breaking his will. After victory over an Arab tribe, Ashurbanipal of Assyria (680–669 BC) proclaimed the triumph of his policy of terror: 'Disaster broke out among them so that they ate the flesh of their children to keep from starving. All the curses which are written in the oath in the naming of my name and those of the gods . . . decreed for them exactly as their terrible destiny.'[9] Such horrors were the price of glory. Egyptian inscriptions boasted of the destruction wrought by their armies: 'This army returned in safety, after it had flattened the sand-dwellers' land. This army returned in safety, after it had sacked its strongholds . . . after it had cut down its figs, its vines, after it had thrown fire in all its mansions.'[10]

The clay-tablet archive of the city of Mari records the surrender of Ishme-Dagan, king of Isin (1953–1935 BC) because his crops had been destroyed and he had 'no grain whatsoever in his lands'.[11] While the well-to-do might be made prisoner and ultimately ransomed, the poor were enslaved and either set to work or tormented for sport. Ravaging and destruction, of course, also served to feed and pay soldiers and so were doubly important. Rules were drawn up for the distribution of plunder, and while they assured the king and senior officers of the lion's share, it was vital to ensure the loyalty of the other ranks by guaranteeing them something. A tablet from Mari in Mesopotamia enjoined a commander: 'Let your troops seize booty and they will bless you. These three towns are not heavily fortified. In a day we shall be able to take them. Quickly come up and let us capture these towns and let your soldiers seize booty.'[12]

From these early times destruction was not an accident of war but a structured part of it, vital to imposing one's will on the enemy and keeping the troops loyal. In every centre of civilisation and style of war it was a staple, an event so ordinary as to be barely worth recording. This is important because military history tends to focus on 'Great Men', strategy, tactics, battle and siege. But the war of destruction was always at the heart of military activity.

And this military activity became ever more elaborate. By 2000 BC infantry were not the only military arm on the battlefields of the Middle East. Animals have been used to carry goods since before recorded history. The disk-wheel, simply a slice across a log, first appeared in Mesopotamia about 3500 BC and this made the ox-drawn wagon possible. Useful as these were for transport, greater speed was needed in war. Donkeys and the untamable wild onagers, with which they could be crossed to produce strong and amenable mules, offered greater speed than the slow ox. The famous Standard of Ur of about 2550 BC, shows mules pulling four-wheeled carts. These were quite small and narrow, and crewed by a driver and a warrior who brandished javelins which were evidently intended to be thrown because each cart has a quiver of them. To the modern eye these carts are clumsy conveyances, and indeed they could not have been very manoeuvrable because they lacked the pivoted front axle, which was not invented until the fifteenth century AD. But they must have had real value as weapons of war because they continued to be used until about 2000 BC.

The two-wheeled wagon, as illustrated in the Stele of the Vultures, which was roughly contemporary with the Standard of Ur, gradually became the standard fighting vehicle of ancient Mesopotamia. None of these could have been very quick, though they may have been capable of 12–15 mph in very short bursts, but by the standards of the age this made them terrifyingly fast and provided armies with a new mobility. Around 2400 BC Enmetena, king of Lagash in eastern Mesopotamia, defeated the hostile kingdom of Umma, capturing some sixty war-carts, which suggests that they were considered useful. In assessing their effectiveness we should also recognise that these were the property of the powerful. On ceremonial occasions kings rode in them and they carried the statues of the gods. Only the richest and, therefore, best equipped and fiercest soldiers would have travelled in them. A well-timed charge of sixty wagons might only have reached 10 mph, but it would have appeared formidable to footsoldiers, especially if it signalled the arrival of the enemy's best forces. The effect of 'cavalry' in all ages has been partly psychological and we should not underestimate these weapons, especially once the warriors in them had learned to use the bow.

But, whether two- or four-wheeled, these war-wagons did not give any one side an advantage. This was because they seem to have evolved slowly from existing farming technologies so that everybody had them at the same time. However, building and maintaining them and breeding the necessary mules would have been expensive, substantially increasing the costs of war. They were for long unknown in Egypt where the Nile offered fast and cheap water transport, and in any case the skein of irrigation canals across the fertile zone would have inhibited the movement of carts. The fast war-chariot, so often shown in films, was clearly a derivative, but the technologies which made it such an effective military device did not come together in the Middle East until after 1700 BC, by which time major political developments had led to a sharply increased militarisation of the powers of the Middle East.

The middle centuries of the second millennium BC saw enormous changes across the whole Mediterranean. In Greece the Mycenaean cities emerged, while in Anatolia the great Hittite Empire centred on Hattusa (modern Bogazköy) became powerful. The Hittites expanded into Syria, threatened Assyria, and achieved a spectacular success by destroying Babylon in 1595 BC. The city recovered under a new Kassite dynasty (1595–1155 BC) from the Zagros mountains in what is now western Iran, whose brutal military regime established an empire in southern Mesopotamia which rivalled that of Assyria to the north. In Egypt a time of troubles (1720–1550 BC) associated with invasions of Hyksos peoples from Asia was ended only by the emergence of the highly militarised society of the New Kingdom whose kings are often portrayed as warriors, splendid in their war-chariots.

But these chariots were very different from the lumbering vehicles which had existed for so long in the Middle East because now they were harnessed to the horse, whose strength and stamina created a new and much more dangerous weapons system, a kind of cavalry. The horse is native to the steppe lands, but not to the Middle East and it was brought there by the 'Aryan' peoples who, over many centuries, had gradually filtered through the Caucasus into eastern Anatolia where they established the powerful Mitanni kingdom; others mounted the Iranian plateau from the southern steppe. On a modern map the Iranian plateau looks like a barrier dividing the nomadic from the settled peoples. But access is relatively easy – even now people on both sides ascend and descend the numerous valleys to retrieve wandering animals. The Caucasus appears very formidable, but its passes offer ready access to the Middle East.

The horse was first domesticated in southern Russia: our earliest evidence of extensive domestication of this animal comes from Dereivka in southern Russia in the fourth millennium BC. Once it could be trained and ridden, the way was open for the development of the pastoral-nomad way of life on the Eurasian steppe, because its superior speed enabled mounted men to control huge herds of horses, cattle and sheep which could live on the grasslands. Some settled peoples, perhaps living in oases and areas of marginal agriculture, chose a nomadic life which offered escape from climate fluctuations and raids. Others may have been driven on to the steppe by enemies or by subtle changes in climate and environment.

However motivated, this change gave them a new focus on mobility and the need to carry goods which had to be made as light as possible. They adapted the wagon, which had obvious uses for their way of life, from the people of the Middle East. But they brought to it the needs of a people for whom wood was rare and lightness an imperative. When steppe peoples adopted the pastoral-nomad way of life, they retained all their old skills, notably in extracting and working metals, producing excellent tools and weapons. Indeed, as time went on the number of weapons increased sharply, suggesting that nomad groups were warring more and more with one another or with others. They were quite prepared to settle if, as in the case of the Mitanni and later the Persians, the opportunity arose. Because they drifted into the Middle East over a long period and mixed with native populations, there was an interchange of ideas between the two groups. As a result of this the heavy Middle Eastern war-cart became the much lighter and more manoeuvrable war-chariot. The horse, with its speed, strength and endurance, was of immense military importance, not least because its appearance stimulated chariot technology.

The Egyptian chariots preserved in the tomb of Tutankhamun (1333–1324 BC) are highly refined, consisting of ultra-light bentwood frames forming a D-shaped platform with low rails at the front and sides.

These must have been formed by soaking and steaming the wood to bend it to shape. The platform was mounted on a new kind of wheel which seems to have been invented by the steppe people: the spoked wheel. This was extremely strong, partly because it was shod with a leather tyre, but very much lighter than the disk-wheel. And for the sake of stability the artisans of the war-chariots attached the wheels at the back of the vehicle, and set them well apart. Improved harnessing and yoke-poles meant that a pair of horses, and sometimes two pairs, were deployed, increasing range and speed. The strong but light war-chariot with its crew of two was very manoeuvrable and its speed could approach 30 mph over short distances. However, even the horse could not sustain high speed for more than a brief period in the heat of the Middle East, so armies trained special infantry forces to keep in touch with their charioteers and to protect them when exhaustion supervened. The fast chariot stimulated the use of the composite bow because this weapon was short enough to be handy in the vehicle, yet by virtue of its strength had superior hitting power. Armies thus developed a weapons system which could strike with fearsome speed.

The Hittite king Hattusilis (1650–1620 BC) took along eighty chariots when he attacked Ursha about 1620 BC. One of his successors, King Mursili II (1330–1295 BC), speaks of his army as 'infantry and chariot fighters'. Hittite chariots were relatively heavy two-wheeled vehicles, crewed by three men – a driver, a warrior with bow and spear and a shield-bearer – but even so they benefited from the speed of the horses which drew them. In Egypt a description of Amenophis II (1427–1397 BC) makes clear the sheer drama of the new weapon:

> Entering his northern garden, he found erected four targets of Asiatic copper. Then his majesty appeared on the chariot like Mont [the war god] in his might. He drew his bow while holding four arrows in his fist. Thus he rode northwards shooting at them, like Mont in his panoply, each arrow coming out of the back of its target while he attacked the next post. It was a deed never yet done . . . Now when he was still a youth he loved his horses and rejoiced in them.[13]

Horses suitable for war had to be bred selectively so stud farms were vital. They needed stables, and much care and food, if they were to be effective. Elaborate harness had to be devised for control. This was very labour-intensive, and sheer expense meant chariots were relatively few in number and always the weapon of kings and their leading men. Charioteers became the elite of the Egyptian army, organised in divisions of fifty.

The chariot was not a super-weapon carrying all before it. In a charge at a formed infantry unit the horses would have been very vulnerable to missile attack, and even if only a few teams were brought down in this way, others would have crashed into them. Sculptures and pictures nearly always show the crew with bows or javelins, suggesting that they manoeuvred their vehicle to fire at infantry or at other chariots. Illustrations of destroyed chariots show horses with arrows or spears in their sides, which suggests the same tactic. Opposite the royal palace at Thebes in Egypt is a long oval area which has been very carefully picked clear of stones, probably so that charioteers could exercise there. The beautifully light and agile Egyptian chariots would, of course, have been damaged by rough ground.

Chariots played little role at Megiddo in 1457 BC, the earliest battle of which we have an account. Thutmose III (1479–1425 BC) of Egypt led an army some 10,000 strong to Canaan to destroy a rebel force gathered at the city of Megiddo which stood across the crucial trade route to Mesopotamia. As they approached, the Egyptians had a choice of three routes. In the interests of surprise Thutmose selected the most difficult of these, a narrow ravine through which his army had to travel in single file. Although Thutmose led the attack in his golden chariot, most of his army fought on foot, and it was their sheer numbers and the element of surprise which led to triumph. But his army fell to plundering the enemy camp and the survivors rallied in the city, which then had to be besieged for some seven months. At Kadesh, as we have seen, chariots played a much greater role. What this suggests is that the chariot offered the capacity to mount a sudden sharp charge which might well shake untried infantry or destroy formations caught on the move in the open. Speed enabled the crew of a chariot to harass infantry formations with their composite bows and javelins with a reasonable expectation of escape. Moreover, they could prevent enemy charioteers doing the same to their own forces. Infantry masses, fighting in disciplined ranks, remained the staple of armies, but the chariot was a weapons system which no army could afford to ignore once it had developed. Chariots made war very expensive, so this strengthened the bigger powers at the expense of the lesser and contributed to the increasing militarisation of the Middle Eastern powers after 1600 BC. Contact with the steppe provided cavalry of a sort, so that agro-urban forces were beginning to take on the shape which would dominate armies down to the nineteenth century: a core of heavy infantry supported by missile throwers and horsemen.

The influence of the steppe people and their horses was not limited to the Middle East, but had a profound influence upon India and China. Although no single people dominated the gigantic expanse of Central

Asia, the exigencies of a harsh environment imposed a common way of life, while people, ideas and devices could pass easily from one group to another. As a result, a common culture based on stock-raising and horses dominated the biggest land mass on earth. The 'Sea of Grass' is confined by the northern forests and tundra, and interrupted by mountainous regions like the Altai. But these are not impenetrable, and the expanses of desert, like the Takla Makan and the Gobi, are not insuperable obstacles to movement because there are numerous oases. The steppe is a poor environment whose most desirable product was the horse. But there are quite numerous areas of arable land and zones with particularly rich grazing.

The life of the steppe people, therefore, was one not of aimless movement, but of purposeful circulation between such important and productive areas. And there was always exchange and interaction with agricultural peoples. They needed to trade and were prepared to settle where there was opportunity. Raiding was a useful way of gaining commodities which they could not afford to buy and of punishing those who raided them. As they probed the periphery of their 'Sea of Grass' they discovered that they could easily reach the Indus valley through Afghanistan. Further east, the steppe merges with cultivated land in the Northern Zone of what is now China.

In India the Harappan civilisation (3000–1700 BC) vanished abruptly and for unknown reasons was replaced by a new people, the Aryans of the steppe. They were clearly pastoralists for whom cattle were a basic form of wealth, and they depended on horses, riding chariots to war. They came as conquerors. Their great god, Indira, is named *Purandara*, the 'breaker of cities' and they conquered the native Dravidic peoples: 'Through fear of thee the dark-coloured inhabitants fled, not waiting for battle, abandoning their possessions, when, O Agni [the fire-god], burning brightly for Puru [an Aryan tribe], and destroying cities, thou didst shine.'[14] But there was no extermination of the native populations. Rather, the highly successful but violent integration of these steppe people resulted in their language, religion and culture being adopted by almost all those who came into contact with them. Like other steppe peoples of this age, they were practised in the making of bronze, and by about 1000 BC they were working in iron. The Aryans may have conquered the Dravidic peoples of India, though they never dominated the Tamil south, but they spent just as much time fighting amongst themselves. However, the India which the Aryans ruled was a relatively empty land. Their clans fought one another and formed alliances with native rulers. Defeated groups moved eastwards into the wild and heavily wooded Ganges valley. They have left us magnificent epic poems, the Mahabharata, perhaps composed as early as 500 BC, and the rather later Ramayana. In both, the heroes fight from chariots with bows and arrows. But in the Mahabharata the two armies are organised in *akshaunis*, large units, thousands strong, each with chariots, war-elephants, horsemen and infantry. The weapons used were little different from those in other cultures where, as we have seen, close-order, close-quarter battle determined the form of armies.

Further east, the steppe people had a profound effect on the warfare of China, most obviously with the chariot. This appeared so very suddenly as a complete weapons system in Shang China that it seems certain that the steppe peoples brought it. The Shang state was aggressively expansionist, imposing its culture and state structure upon the numerous neighbouring states, including the peoples of the steppe fringe to the north. In common with city people all over the world, Shang armies consisted of peasant masses, increasingly well armed with bronze weapons, for whom aristocratic leaders and their professional followers served as nuclei of command. Since most of the competitors of the Shang amongst the Han people of the northern plains were organised around cities, large infantry forces were necessary for the business of siege. Once the chariot became known, it was enthusiastically adopted by the wealthy, though at first it seems to have been used in small numbers as a kind of command vehicle and to emphasise the distinction between aristocratic charioteers and the great mass of armed peasants. In 1122 BC the Western Zhou from the Wei river valley overthrew the Shang at the battle of Muye where the Zhou army was led by 300 chariots. Accounts of the battle suggest that the Zhou used their chariots to outflank the fixed defences of the Shang.

The Early or Western Zhou (1122–771 BC) adopted the culture of the Shang and their state developed along much the same lines as its predecessor. They plunged into relentless war with other semi-Han states, like Qi, as they penetrated the Yangtze and Huai river valleys, absorbing much of the modern provinces of Shaanxi, Shanxi, Henan, Hebei and Shandong upon whose diverse peoples they imposed their culture. The Zhou armies were basically mass-infantry forces commanded from their chariots by aristocrats. Each vehicle carried three men – driver, archer and a man equipped with a close-quarter weapon – and was supported by a group of up to twenty-five foot soldiers. They were organised in squads of five within brigades of twenty-five chariots. This style of warfare would continue into the sixth century BC, with the scale of armies in the bigger states becoming considerable: perhaps up to 4,000 chariots supported by 40,000 infantry. While chariots may at times have been separated and acted as cavalry, this form of organisation suggests that they were primarily leadership vehicles, forming rallying points for mass infantry armies.

Because of the availability of both tin and copper in the north of China, there was plenty of bronze for weapons and, increasingly, armour. The long-handled dagger-axes characteristic of the Shang/Zhou period may well have been developed to enable infantry to fight chariots. Much of the military effort of the Zhou was directed at conquering the peoples in the Northern Zone, the frontier area of mixed agricultural practices inhabited by many non-Han peoples. In 771 an alliance of these peoples defeated the Zhou, whose dynasty then moved east to the city of Luoyang where they continued to rule as the Later or Eastern Zhou (771–221 BC). This event marked the start of the conflict between the Han and their nomadic neighbours, which would last until the Qin (Manchu) dynasty of the seventeenth and eighteenth centuries AD.

The worldwide importance of the horsed chariot and its derivation from the steppe peoples should serve to remind us that for all their literacy and the splendour of their monuments, the city peoples did not enjoy enormous military advantages over others. Eastern Europe was an area rich in metals and produced very fine bronze weapons which were in demand all over the Middle East by the thirteenth century BC. The despised nomadic Amorites seized Assyria about 1830 BC, and in 1595 BC a Kassite dynasty took over Babylon and ruled for nearly 400 years. About 1200 BC the Hittite Empire and the cities of Mycenaean Greece were destroyed in the great Mediterranean-wide movement of the 'Sea-Peoples' which shortly after this permanently weakened Egypt. A great wave of Aramaean peoples swept across Mesopotamia and the Middle East establishing the Neo-Assyrian Empire (934–610 BC) which for a time ruled Egypt before it was destroyed by a resurgent Babylon in the era of the Hanging Gardens of Babylon, a potent symbol of imperial prosperity, marked by the transplantation of the Hebrews to Mesopotamia. But in 539 BC Babylon was in turn destroyed and replaced by the Persians. India was torn apart by the fractious states of the Aryans, while in China the dynasties of Shang and Zhou dissolved into the chaos of the Spring and Autumn Period (722–481 BC).

The great empires of the city-civilisations could usually defeat external enemies because their wealth enabled them to field big and well-organised armies. But this ability rested upon insecure foundations. Maintaining courts, palaces, servants, and above all armies, was enormously expensive. Cyprus exported huge quantities of raw copper. It has been calculated that on this island the labour of 35,700 farming families was needed to support 510 metal-workers.[15] This highlights the huge cost of extracting metal, but it also indicates the strain which the superstructure of these Middle Eastern empires placed upon the subsistence farmers who supported them.

And the superstructures themselves were fairly fragile. The monarchies were subject to frequent succession disputes and other factional quarrels which divided their aristocracies. Subject cities, as we have noted, were often allowed a high degree of autonomy and they were apt to take advantage of such crises at the centre of empire to break away. External enemies were eager to take advantage of any weakness. Conjunctions of such events underlay the rise and fall of empires.

For all the political changes, new regimes did not really alter in any fundamental way the pattern of war which had become established in all the city-civilisations by about 1200 BC. The core of these armies was formed by well-armed and equipped standing forces raised from the city elite and their armed retainers. Beyond that, the needs of siege and battle demanded the conscription of humbler people on specific occasions, augmented by mercenaries. This composite pattern, reflecting the distribution of wealth in the polities, dominated armies for millennia because few societies could afford very large full-time forces, though, as we shall see, there were exceptions. These armies were predominantly infantry forces and they fought in close order which was the best kind of formation for the close-quarter battle. Discipline and morale of course underlay the ability to fight in close order; this must have been strongest amongst the core elements, and much weaker beyond them. But some of the elite fought in chariots which gave the army a degree of mobility and striking power. It only remained for horsed cavalry to emerge to establish the classic form of the 'civilised' army which persisted right down to the nineteenth century.

But there was another pattern of war. Out on the great Eurasian steppe, the Sea of Grass, a different way of life was evolving, based on the herding of domestic animals by men on horseback. It was highly mobile, supporting much smaller numbers than those found on the central plains of China, Mesopotamia or the Nile valley. But in the key military technology of metallurgy the steppe peoples were not inferior, and they enjoyed the enormous advantage of mobility based on their mastery of the horse, to which they would in time add the hitting power of the composite bow. This different way of war was not sealed off from the agro-urban warfare of the cities, as witness the rise of chariots in the Middle East, India and China. The political impact of the steppe peoples was inhibited, though never prohibited, by their dispersed way of life. And their speciality, the development of the horse, provided a new dimension of war for the settled peoples living around them.

CHAPTER THREE

◆

HORSES AND HOPLITES

And yet, I am told, these very Greeks are wont to wage wars against one another in the most foolish way, through sheer perversity and doltishness. For no sooner is war proclaimed than they search out the smoothest and fairest plain that is to be found in all the land, and there they assemble and fight; whence it comes to pass that even the conquerors depart with great loss: I say nothing of the conquered, for they are destroyed altogether.[1]

THE fifth century BC witnessed a fascinating struggle between two radically different ways of war. The Persian Empire, stretching from what is now Pakistan to Egypt and the western coast of Asia Minor, based its power on a great military innovation – cavalry. They were opposed by a much more traditional force, Greek infantry fighting in close order, a phalanx. Greece was a mosaic of small city-states which bickered with one another, usually over petty amounts of land on their frontiers. At the core of their modest armies were citizen-soldiers, called hoplites after their *hoplon*, a round wooden shield reinforced with a central boss and an edge-band of metal, about a metre in diameter and convex in section. It was so heavy that the soldier had to take its weight on his shoulder, rather than simply the arm, through a double strap. His weapon of offence was a spear, about 2.75 metres long, tipped with a metal point and equipped with a butt-spike, though he sometimes carried a sword or dagger. Such equipment was by no means cheap – it cost about 30 drachmas, a third of a year's income for a farmer in Athens. Men of this status were the backbone, though by no means a majority, of the city population and by the sixth century only they were eligible to vote in the city assembly. Only the richest could afford the 100 drachmas to purchase the full hoplite array, which consisted of a splendid bronze helmet enclosing the face and decorated with a feather or horsehair crest, a bronze breastplate protecting the upper body, sculpted to emphasise the muscles of the torso, often with a leather hanging to cover the groin and thighs, and a bronze-covered shield.

According to Herodotus, when war came between Greek cities both sides sought 'the smoothest and fairest plain that is to be found in all the land, and there they assemble and fight'. They lined up in a single massive unit, a phalanx, made up of files usually eight deep. The two sides then closed for battle, being careful to maintain a tight formation even when they began to run for the final collision in the last 100–200 metres. The result was a very intense form of close-order, close-quarter battle in which the front soldiers of the phalanx used their spears to stab under the shield at the enemy's groin or over it at the face. 'Both sides literally collided together, creating the awful thud of forceful impact at the combined rate of ten miles per hour.' Then 'each man pressed with the centre of his shield against the back of the man to his front' in a great scrum, while those in contact with the enemy fought with whatever means came to hand – teeth and bare hands if necessary – in the confusion of the press, seeking out gaps in the enemy line. Whoever fell injured in this convulsion would either be trampled to death or dispatched by the strike of a butt-spike.[2] Unless one side fled before the impact, casualties in a melee of this kind were very high:

> After the fighting had ceased one could see that where they had clashed with each other the earth was stained with blood and the corpses of friends and enemies lay side by side. There were shattered shields, spears broken in pieces and unsheathed daggers, some lying on the ground, some stuck in bodies and others still gripped to strike even in death.[3]

A collision of this intensity in the heat of a Greek summer was necessarily very short, and so exhausting that there could be no long pursuit. Nor was there much room for manoeuvre, because once the troops were packed into this close formation and launched into combat it was virtually impossible to change direction.

The portrayal of Greek warfare as purely an affair of hoplites is, to say the least, a simplification. Hoplites were never the only soldiers in Athens or the other Greek cities. In emergency, cities pressed poor men into service, often equipped as archers and slingers. Mercenaries, such as lightly armed Thracian peltasts, were used as javelin throwers, and Cretan archers were hired. Moreover, battle was rare. When a Greek army attacked a neighbouring state its first target was always the civilian population, whose dwellings and crops were devastated. As always, this served to feed the attackers and to undermine the will of the defenders. Of course it was very difficult for attackers to do permanent damage to olive trees and vines, while much corn was probably taken into the city where the farmer and his family sought refuge along with his livestock. But all primitive agricultural communities lived on the margins of starvation, and any loss, even simply wastage as a result of inevitable haste, could be disastrous; transporting bulky grain from homestead to city would in any case be difficult. If wastage were more than trivial, the consequences would be very serious because most of a family's stocks were for future seed, so immediate loss could have long-term consequences. This is why battles were relatively rare and raids and devastation commonplace. Their effectiveness could be enormously amplified if the attacker established and maintained forts in the territory assaulted. Thus during the Peloponnesian War (432–404 BC) Sparta established a well-defended base at Decelea from which its forces terrorised the Attic plain around Athens. Greeks disliked set-piece sieges because citizen-soldiers had a natural reluctance to risk either the heavy losses entailed in an assault on a prepared and well-defended city or to support the high costs of logistical support for a sustained siege. But they were quite ready to seize a city by surprise and we hear of at least ten cities wiped out in inter-Greek warfare before the Persian wars of the fifth century, far more than the number of known battles in the same period. A city taken by storm was usually destroyed, its adult male population massacred and the remainder enslaved.

Like almost all who wrote about war, Greek writers, Herodotus amongst them, liked to emphasise its noble aspect: the valour of the hoplite, fighting honourably face to face and breast to breast against his enemies. They preferred to forget the sneaking around to surprise and destroy villages and cities, the bullying of peasants and the squalid destruction of their crops. In essence Greek warfare was very like that of the other peoples of the Mediterranean. The armies of the Greek city-states were mixed forces built around a core of its solid citizens, choosing to fight by ravaging, siege or battle as circumstances demanded. The phalanx of close-order infantry was a very ancient and widespread unit of infantry warfare, visible on the Stele of the Vultures dating from the third millennium BC. However, modern writers have regarded the Greek phalanx as something entirely original, and their picture of Greek warfare has carefully forgotten such activities as raiding or pouncing on unprepared small cities, and they have written archers, slingers and light infantry out of the script.

The reason for this one-dimensional picture of Greek warfare lies in a very special perception of general history. In the fifth century BC the Greek states fought off an attempt to conquer them by the Persian Empire. Herodotus presented this as the victory of Greek freedom over Asian despotism and many modern writers have swallowed this in its entirety. They argue that the military institutions of the Greeks sprang from the special democratic character of its city-states where citizen assemblies decided policy. Quarrels between cities were about land on the frontiers between them. Bloody though hoplite confrontations were, it has been suggested that the citizens perceived them as a rapid and efficient way of settling quarrels between states, and certainly better than drawn-out struggles in which severe long-term harm to the countryside and city might get out of hand. Moreover, the brutal violence of this clash of arms with its rigid subordination of the individual to the collective mass was possible because the citizens had agreed to this style of war and thus were bound to it by public commitment. In the words of a proponent of this view:

> The Greeks of the city-states were the first people on earth to contract between themselves, as equals, to fight the enemy shoulder to shoulder, without flinching from wounds, and not to yield the ground on which they fought until either the enemy had broken or they themselves lay dead where they had stood.[4]

Thus there was an inseparable connection between the culture of freedom and the manner of fighting – and it is this connection which forms the basis of the modern notion of a 'Western Way of War'.[5] This, it is suggested, was quite different to the warfare of any other people because democratic decision leads to a ruthless and amoral prosecution of war by the most effective means possible, a direct and brutal confrontation.

I think this is nonsense. Styles of warfare do not arise from democratic (or undemocratic) decisions, but from experience and brute material circumstance. The Greeks were farmers who worked the land on small plains around cities whose walls served as refuges in times of trouble. Because Greece is a poor land, the cities never produced a great aristocracy comparable to that of Egypt, the Mesopotamian cities or the Persian Empire, able to arm themselves and their followers in splendid style. There were richer men, but much of their wealth was devoted to building and maintaining ships which were vital for maritime cities like Athens. In sixth-century BC Athens the law gave equal treatment to 'men who travelled in search of booty or for the purposes of trade'.[6] Even a modest fleet was very expensive, absorbing resources which might otherwise be used for land warfare. Greek cities were certainly not egalitarian societies, but the mediocre aristocrats who led them were not very sharply distinguished from the better-off farmers. As a result, individual leaders had to seek support against their internal enemies in city assemblies, though only the substantial farmers had a real say in forming the policy of the city. The rich might, as individuals, ride to war, but they did not have the means to breed and sustain large numbers of horses. The farmers certainly could not afford such expensive animals on their small-holdings. The mountains, which everywhere hedged about the plains of Greece, were not a good environment for horse-rearing or for cavalry manoeuvre, so there was little real prospect of raising large bodies of cavalry or chariots. It would have been very difficult and expensive to build and permanently man fortifications to block the numerous passes which cut through the mountains between cities.

The people of Athens and the other Greek cities had little choice, therefore, but to become infantrymen, and as such they learned the same lesson as others much earlier: that close-order was the key to success in battle which was necessarily a close-quarter affair. The weaponry and armour useful in such fighting – spear, shield and helmet – was comparatively cheap and clearly more effective than missile weapons, though these too were used. In short, the Greeks reacted in much the same way as other city people by creating infantry armies led by local elites and fighting in close order. As always, the needs of battle shaped armies, even though battle itself was relatively rare and raiding much commoner. As long as Greek warfare was essentially small-scale there was little that was distinctive about it.

However, in the fifth century the Greek cities faced a new enemy, the Persian Empire. In the course of its attacks on Greece it became clear that the hoplite phalanx was a highly effective way of dealing with Persian cavalry. Moreover, Persia intended to destroy the Greek states and undoubtedly the fact that the hoplites were fighting for their cities and farms gave them the courage and the steadiness to stand, strengthened by fighting in the company of families, friends and neighbours. This had little to do with democracy and everything to do with survival. Hoplite warfare reached its highest perfection at Sparta, the most predatory and least democratic of the Greek cities. Its citizens were a military elite, whose youth was in constant training for war, for it was by force that they held down the helots who formed the mass of the population of Sparta. By the late sixth century the Spartan hoplites, distinguished by their scarlet tunics, long hair and fine equipment, were justly regarded as the finest soldiers in Greece. Under the pressure of the Persian wars the Greeks refined the phalanx into a tightly disciplined unit on the Spartan model, though they never completely neglected other arms. The Greek writers who give us our picture of hoplite warfare, Herodotus, Thucydides and Xenophon, are describing the disciplined and developed phalanx as it had come to exist in their day, and projecting it into the past before the Persian wars.

The rise of Persia as a genuine world power was the most important event in the military history of the sixth century. The great civilisations in the Middle East, India and China, had developed separately. But Persian power extended eastwards into India and westwards to Thrace and Macedonia. The Persians were a steppe people of Aryan origin, settled under their Achaemenid kings in the modern Iranian province of Fars, for long overshadowed by powerful neighbours like the Medes of northern Iran and the Elamites.[7] Under Cyrus II the Great (559–530 BC) they conquered both of these and destroyed King Croesus of Lydia whose kingdom dominated Anatolia. Sardis in western Anatolia became a Persian centre ruling the cities of the Ionian Greeks along the Aegean coast. In 539 Cyrus crushed Babylon, and incorporated its empire in Mesopotamia, Syria and Palestine into his own. He then conquered deep into Central Asia, including much of what is now Afghanistan, Turkmenistan, Uzbekistan and Tajikistan. During this campaign Cyrus was killed, and power passed to his son, Cambyses II (530–522 BC), who seized Egypt which had been an ally of both Babylon and Lydia. Under Darius I (522–486 BC) the Persian frontier was advanced into India where Taxila, east of the Indus, formed a very important trading station and centre of Persian influence in South Asia.

The transformation of the modest Achaemenid kingdom of Fars into a world power was first and foremost the result of its having a brilliant leader, Cyrus II, who exploited discontent amongst the Medes to destroy and replace their king, Astyages. The neighbouring Elamite realm was much too divided to interfere and soon also fell victim to his ambition. This gathering of military strength enabled him and his immediate successors to conquer other powers and to draw the aristocracy into their service by offering a share of the fruits of conquest. Once established, the Persians adopted new methods of war which were highly suited to their empire.

After about 800 BC, iron was very widely used for weapons in the Middle East and the Mediterranean, but there is no evidence that Persia enjoyed any advantage in this respect. In fact, the art of iron production was already well known in the Mediterranean and India, although the Chinese only began to use it in quantity in the fourth century BC, probably because they had ample supplies of metals to make bronze and had developed great skills in its production. But the most obvious and most spectacular military development in the period 1000–600 BC was the rise of true cavalry, and it was in this arm that the Persians concentrated their strength.

It is somehow contrary to expectation that the horse was first used to pull the chariot rather than simply ridden. In fact there were good reasons for this. Riding a horse without some form of saddle is uncomfortable, and, if continued for any time, causes sores on both beast and rider. The true saddle, which raises the rider and protects the horse's withers, evolved amongst the nomadic peoples of the Eurasian steppe by the third century BC, but was adopted by settled peoples only in the early centuries AD. Various approximations, usually of leather and padded blanket, had to serve the purpose in the meantime. Harnessing to control the animal had been developed for chariots, but had to be modified. The essence here was to find forms of bit and snaffle which gave the rider control but did not inflict damage upon the beast. Amongst the settled peoples, armour and relatively heavy equipment had become vital in war, especially amongst the leaders of society who were the most likely to ride such an expensive animal as the horse. Therefore, before cavalry proper could appear, something substantially bigger than the steppe pony had to be developed to carry such weight. The chariot is driven by a team which may number up to four, but for the cavalryman the size of the individual horse is everything. Heavy animals could only be produced by selective breeding over substantial periods of time on specialist stud farms. From about 1000 BC, representations of mounted men become more common in the Mesopotamian lands and true cavalrymen appear in the neo-Assyrian period with the magnificent relief carvings of Ashurnasirpal II (883–859 BC). Carvings from Assyria and Babylon probably focus only on the finest beasts, but they indicate that some reached 15–16 hands, much larger than the ponies (up to 12 hands) of the steppe peoples. But the sheer expense of producing and maintaining such animals limited the numbers and a force of 1,000 seems for long to have been unusually large.

At first their use in war was very limited. Horses were high-status transport for the rich. Horsemen were very valuable for reconnaissance, for raiding enemies, and for chasing off wandering peoples like the various

Arab and other nomadic groups who swirled across the Middle East. Deployed for these purposes, cavalry were much more effective than chariots, which could not tackle rough ground. Because saddles were crude and there were no stirrups, the horseman, like the charioteer, was primarily a weapons system for delivering missiles, arrows or javelins, at ranges close enough to be effective while allowing the rider speed enough to escape. Man for man the horse-soldier enjoyed obvious advantages over the foot soldier of height, speed and weight, and horses bred for strength could carry well-armoured riders. But they could not charge into properly formed infantry whose massed weapons would hack them down. However, infantry which lost their close-order could be ridden down and destroyed individually. Movement across irregular terrain, panic induced by the psychological shock of the sudden appearance of cavalry, tiredness, indiscipline, all could cause gaps to appear in the infantry mass, and cavalry had the acceleration to drive into these gaps and open up formations. Infantry caught in the open plain could be isolated and forced into immobility, or harassed into mistakes if they tried to move, particularly by attacks on their rear ranks.

The Persians at the start of Cyrus's career seem to have had no cavalry, but the Medes, whom they incorporated into their kingdom, were famous horse soldiers. The value of their mobility and striking power in the open plains of the Middle East was quickly apparent to the Persians. Their aristocracy were probably already in the habit of riding and hunting and this enabled them to develop quickly into horse-soldiers. As their empire expanded into the southern steppe of Asia and the Indus valley the qualities of cavalry became ever more valuable and the Persian aristocracy soon developed an enormous enthusiasm for fighting on horseback. Herodotus tells us that young Persian nobles were above all instructed in this form of warfare:

> Their sons are carefully instructed from their fifth to their twentieth year, in three things alone, – to ride, to draw the bow, and to speak the truth. Until their fifth year they are not allowed to come into the sight of their father, but pass their lives with the women. This is done that, if the child die young, the father may not be afflicted by its loss.[8]

This does not mean that Persians had no infantry; their 'Immortals', so-called because every casualty was automatically replaced, were an elite corps of 10,000 in close attendance on the monarch, and plenty of other foot soldiers were raised within their empire, especially archers. But the finest troops, the aristocracy and their followers, were concentrated in the cavalry. And the Persians understood the difference between victory, which was a military achievement, and conquest which demanded the creation of a political basis for the new regime. Because of this, although they imposed Persian governors (satraps) on the people they conquered, they were at pains to respect their customs and religion and to allow important native leaders to retain authority. This enabled the Persians to recruit from these conquered peoples to create ever bigger armies, and gave them access to a very wide range of native skills. For example, to attack Egypt Cambyses needed a fleet, and he was able to recruit this from the subjugated Phoenician cities of the Mediterranean coast in what is now Lebanon. Raising troops was made easier because across the Middle East a common system of granting land to soldiers in return for military service already prevailed, while, universally, great men were expected to bring their armed followings to serve the king. This tolerant policy explains the enormous military capacity of the Persian Empire.

When Xerxes (485–465 BC) invaded Greece in 480, his host was said to number 5,283,220, organised in innumerable ethnic contingents. Historians have unanimously condemned this vast figure, and it is now generally believed that Xerxes had about 210,000 soldiers and that the core of the army consisted of Persian, Iranian and Indo-Iranian troops under Persian command. But even if we assume that many of these were servants and support troops rather than fighters, it was a huge army. The Persians organised their forces systematically on a decimal system, with divisions of 10,000 men subdivided into regiments of 1,000, in turn divided into units of 100 and 10. An elaborate logistical service supported the soldiers, and roads were quickly built to link the empire, notably the 'Royal Road' from Sardis in the west to Susa in the Persian heartland, along which dispatch riders maintained communications.

The core of the Persian army was formed by elite units. The Persian aristocracy had enormous wealth, enabling them to afford the finest horses for themselves and their retainers. This meant that the finest soldiers in the Persian Empire were concentrated in the cavalry. The best infantry units, like the famous 'Immortals', came from the Iranian heart-lands, and were of very high quality. These forces were supported by provincial levies of horsemen and infantry drawn from anywhere between what is now Pakistan and western Anatolia. They were of more variable quality, and very large numbers of the foot were only lightly armed troops, many of them archers. This balance of forces would prove crucial in the confrontation with the Greeks.

The remarkable achievement of the Achaemenids becomes more apparent when viewed from a global perspective. In China, the period of the Later or Eastern Zhou (771–221 BC) was one of intense warfare between a series of states which, to a greater or lesser extent, shared a common Han culture. As the power of the Zhou dynasty shrank to a mere localised authority around Luoyang, some fifteen major states emerged, and a myriad lesser ones. The most important were the Qi of modern Shandong and the Jin of modern Shaanxi, while to the south Chu and Wu were the major powers along the Yangtze. In all the states the kings enlisted the support of the gentry, the *shi*, who helped to forge governmental bureaucracies, thereby reducing the authority of the great aristocrats. Confucius (551–479 BC) came from the *shi*, and he created for them an ideology of government emphasising balance and moderation in all things, and in particular the spirit of reciprocity by which one would 'never impose on others what you would not choose for yourself'. This philosophy very quickly became central to Chinese culture. At the same time the Chinese economy flourished. Trade was fostered, partly because the adoption of money, which seems to have appeared simultaneously in all the world civilisations in the sixth century BC, made it easier. The art of metallurgy became highly advanced. These were impressive developments, but the Chinese states were simply not on the scale of the Persian Empire. Perhaps what distinguished them was the relentless insistence that conquered peoples should conform to 'Chinese' cultural norms, in contrast to the Persian practice of tolerance and incorporation of such differences.

Chinese armies about 500 BC, according to Sun Tzu, were enormous infantry forces, as large as 100,000, within which chariots provided officers with mobility and a clearly visible rallying point for their followers. Chinese metal-workers produced splendid bronze weapons. The increasing use of armour and swords are a clear indication that the close-quarter infantry battle was becoming more common. One consequence of this remarkable skill in metallurgy was the invention, probably in the fifth century BC, of the crossbow. The crucial part of this weapon was the bronze trigger-lock which held the bowstring, and some superbly worked examples have survived. This mechanical bow was primarily a weapon of the infantry, and was particularly useful in defending and attacking fortifications. However, it was used in huge numbers and this may, in part, account for another distinctive characteristic of Chinese warfare at this time: the lack of cavalry. Of course, horses were known and ridden, but the sheer firepower of Chinese infantry must have made chariots and mounted men appear redundant. Most decisively, sieges dominated Chinese warfare, encouraging a labour-intensive style of war. Chinese military development was unusual because of the absolute dominance of infantry, in marked contrast to Persian warfare which turned upon cavalry. However, the underlying process of state centralisation, reducing aristocrats to state service, has been noted in the Persian Empire.

Northern India, specifically the Indus and Ganges valleys, also formed a distinct cultural unity which was sharply divided. In the sixth century BC some sixteen states can be traced in this vast area, of which the most important were Magadha and Kosala in the Ganges valley. All, to a degree, shared the Aryan heritage of a caste system which divided society into the priestly learned Brahmans, the warriors or *ksatriya*, the bulk of the population of presumed Aryan origin, the *dvija*, and finally the despised native population or *dasa*. In addition, the Hindu pantheon of gods was clearly ascendant. Increasingly these people inhabited timber cities like Sravasti in Kosala or Rajgir in Magadha enclosed by strong earthwork walls. Despite the political divisions and wars, this was an age of great intellectual and religious vigour, from which Siddhārtha Gautama, the Buddha (between 563 and 483 BC) arose. It was also an age of trading vigour in which Taxila formed a vital connection with Persia through which commodities like horses, gold, textiles and precious stones passed. It was probably because of this exchange that the Aramaic script of the Middle East was adopted in India. The Aryans of India were horse-people, but for their armies they also mobilised huge infantry masses who fought in close order alongside chariots and cavalry. Their armies, therefore, resembled those of the Persians, except that they also used war-elephants which could trample their enemies.

Persia was a global superpower with long frontiers which ebbed and flowed. It suffered from the same weaknesses as all ancient empires. It was difficult to control distant provinces, especially when succession disputes in the ruling house of the Achaemenids were quite frequent, and factional struggles amongst the elite were troublesome. The personality of the ruler was always crucial. It is hardly surprising that control over Taxila was lost in the fifth century, while Achaemenid power in Central Asia came and went. In 499 the Greek cities of Ionia (western Anatolia), amongst which Miletus, Mytilene and Ephesus were the most notable, rebelled and appealed for help from Athens and Sparta, the leading cities of what we would now call the Greek mainland. This revolt was crushed by 494, but Persian pride had been offended by the burning of its regional capital at Sardis, and a forward party of the Persian nobles, amongst them Mardonios, an important member of the imperial family, demanded the conquest of Greece. By 479 this had failed. Astonishingly, the Greeks had fought off an attack by the greatest military power in the world. This was an extraordinary military event which demands explanation.

Once the revolt of the Ionian cities had been put down in 494, the Persians were determined to punish Athens and Sparta for their support of the rebels. This began a series of wars which transformed the cities of Greece and their methods of waging war. In 492 Darius I (522–486 BC) sent a fleet against Greece, but it was destroyed by a sudden storm in the Aegean. In 490 the Persians came again, with every hope of victory. The Ionian Greeks were subdued, and the kingdoms of Balkan Greece, Thessaly and Macedonia had come to terms with Persia, opening the route into Greece from Anatolia. Sparta was a highly authoritarian state whose elite distrusted the relatively popular regime in Athens, while even within that city elitist factions were perfectly prepared to welcome a Persian intervention which would restore them to power. The Persian force gathered in Cilicia and sailed directly to Greece in a fleet of perhaps 400 merchantmen and 200 warships. They captured the city of Eretria on the island of Euboea which was an ally of Athens, and treated its population with great brutality.

Under the guidance of an Athenian called Hippias they then landed in the north of the plain of Marathon where their fleet could be safely beached. Their 1,000 horsemen dominated the open terrain of the plain of Marathon because the Athenians had no cavalry to oppose them. The Persian force was essentially the army of Anatolia, mainly archers and light infantry, reinforced by marines and perhaps some Iranian garrison forces. The quality of their infantry was, therefore, uneven, but so probably was that of the Athenians. Athens mobilised every man possible, including slaves, and this must have produced very variably equipped and trained soldiers. They were supported by 600–1,000 men from the small city of Plataea. It would seem that each side had about 25,000 men. This parity in part explains why nothing happened for four days (7–11 August) after the arrival of the Athenians. Both sides had good reasons for inaction. The Persians would not have wanted to assault the strong Athenian position across the narrow southern end of the plain, and in any case they were anticipating that the pro-Persian party in Athens would open the gates of the city. The Athenians hoped the Spartans would arrive – they had refused to come until the full moon because of a religious festival. The Athenians dared not advance across the open plain where the strong enemy cavalry force would have cut them to pieces. In any case time was on their side because the Persians were very distant from their bases and were bound to run out of supplies.

This stand-off ended on 11 August when the Persians suddenly re-embarked their cavalry and sailed for Athens, presumably hoping to precipitate a coup in the city by their very appearance. It was a bold move, but it meant that the Persian infantry guarding the ships were now outnumbered. Miltiades, the seasoned Athenian commander, saw his opportunity and as soon as the Persian ships had gone he ordered an attack – he and the war party needed a victory if they were to hold the line against their pro-Persian enemies in Athens. According to Herodotus:

> When the Persians saw the Athenians running towards them, they got ready to receive them, but they thought the Athenians must be mad – mad enough to bring about their utter destruction – because they could see how few of them there were, and that their charge was unsupported by either cavalry or archers.[9]

The sudden Athenian advance seems to have surprised the Persian infantry whose best troops were in the centre of their line. What followed was a real soldiers' fight because the Athenians lost all formation as they raced towards the enemy. Herodotus says that the two armies were 8 *stades* (about 1.25 kilometres) apart. No force, let alone the scratch Greek troops, could maintain formation at the run over such a distance. Herodotus says that this running attack was entirely novel in the Greek experience, and it would certainly have been disastrous if the Persian cavalry had been present because they would have outflanked the disordered infantry. But the Persian cavalry had gone and the wild advance had the enormous advantage of momentum once it had passed through the arrows of the Persian archers, because the defenders seem to have built no field fortifications. As the Athenian troops, arriving in small units piecemeal, crashed into the Persians a savage hacking match developed. Herodotus says that 'the fighting at Marathon was long and drawn out'. At first the Persian centre drove back the Athenians, but the lighter forces on their flanks were defeated by the Plataeans on the left and the Athenians on the right, and these forces then turned on the enemy centre and cut it to pieces, killing 6,400 for a loss of only 192. But the Greeks were unable to follow up their victory because they needed to hasten back to Athens to prevent a pro-Persian coup, so the Persians got away in their fleet, losing only seven ships.

It is sometimes thought that Miltiades deliberately weakened his centre to draw the Persian strength into an advance, but it seems very unlikely that any general could have exerted much control in these circumstances or that such a scratch army could have manoeuvred in this way. Miltiades had been chosen as commander of the Athenians because he was familiar with Persian ways, and he deserves great credit for seizing the opportunity presented by the departure of the Persian cavalry. In essence the Athenians won because the Persians divided their own forces and sent away their best troops in the cavalry. Moreover, those left behind were lax in preparing their defence, particularly as they were outnumbered. The Greeks probably fought with great determination and desperation in the face of an enemy whose ruthlessness had been clearly demonstrated by the brutal treatment of Eretria. This was not a victory for the phalanx, because the Athenians must have arrived in loose and extended formations, but the rout of the Persian light infantry by the Athenians whose ranks included the more heavily equipped hoplites was an important indicator for the future.

The death of Darius and the accession of Xerxes caused considerable disruption in the Persian Empire; the new ruler does not seem to have been minded to pursue further hostilities with the Greeks. After all, despite revolts in Babylonia and Egypt at the start of his reign, the western frontier had held. But most empires have a forward party seeking ever more territory and jobs for the boys – and Mardonios, as the king's nephew, seems to have been one of them. Prestige was important; both the burning of Sardis by the Ionian rebels of 494 and the defeat at Marathon demanded revenge. The Phoenician cities of what is now Lebanon were under Persian suzerainty and had expanded their trade enormously, establishing Carthage (in what is now Tunisia) as an important centre, virtually a sub-empire, in the western basin of the Mediterranean. This brought conflict with the cities of Magna Graecia (southern Italy and Sicily), and, indeed, they attacked the greatest of these Greek cities, Syracuse in Sicily, at the same time as Xerxes invaded Greece. The Phoenician expansion held out the prospect of a Mediterranean-wide Persian empire. And conditions in Greece continued to favour a Persian attack. Thessaly, Macedonia and other powers in northern Greece were friendly, while there were parties in both Sparta and Athens who favoured collaboration – indeed there were exiles from both at the Persian court. Preparations for an invasion of Greece began in 484/3 with the cutting of a canal through the Athos Peninsula, and a diplomatic offensive which persuaded many of the Greek cities either to throw in their lot with Persia or to adopt a policy of neutrality. It also increased political tensions within and between its intended targets, Sparta and Athens, who collaborated only fitfully in their Hellenic League.

But at about the same time an enormously rich lode of silver was discovered in the Athenian silver mines at Laurium. The war party in the city, led by Themistocles, successfully urged that this windfall be spent on building a war fleet, with an eye to the developing threat from Persia. A fleet was essential for the Persian thrust into Greece, because an army without sea power could be cut off from its base in Anatolia or by landings in its rear. Ultimately the Persians mustered something like 1,300 vessels, amongst them the very latest thing in sea-power, the trireme. This was 35 metres long and less than 6 metres wide, but its 170 rowers were packed into three tiers with a freeboard of 3 metres. Its light construction and large crew made it fast and highly manoeuvrable, and the bronze-covered ram on the prow was much feared. About thirty sailors and marines made up the crew, but rowers would have been expected to fight as needed. This vessel seems to have originated in the late sixth century BC in the Phoenician cities of the Persian Empire. It was a weapons system which, once introduced, made all existing fighting ships outmoded. Its adoption by city-states like Athens had far-reaching consequences. To build substantial numbers would require huge shipyards and the fortification of Piraeus, the port of Athens. This was hideously expensive. But even more seriously, a fleet of 100 triremes needed over 20,000 men. Ultimately Athens would build 200, manning them with the poor of the city and numerous foreigners. It is hardly surprising, therefore, that there was opposition, but in the end Themistocles and the war party triumphed and a formidable war fleet was created. In agreeing to this the Athenians were recognising that the coming war with Persia would be a fight for the very existence of Athens. This would be a quite different scale of warfare from the inter-city squabbling in which they and all the Greek city-states had indulged for so long.

In May 480, Xerxes and his army constructed two bridges of boats across the Dardanelles and crossed from Anatolia into friendly northern Greece. He set off down the coast towards Athens accompanied by a powerful fleet. This strategy immediately divided the cities allied against him. The Athenians wanted to defeat his army as far north as possible: the Spartans, who had the more formidable army, feared that any expedition would be outflanked and destroyed. They wanted to withdraw into the Peloponnese, and to fortify the narrow isthmus of Corinth, abandoning Athens. But this strategy needed Athenian naval aid, for otherwise the Persian fleet would be able to make landings beyond the Corinthian line. The outcome was a poor compromise: a small allied force was sent to block the road at Thermopylae while the Athenians struck at the enemy fleet in the narrow passages of the sea at Artemisium.

At Thermopylae the mountain was only about 100 metres from the sea so that a small force, some 7,000 in all, under the command of King Leonidas of Sparta, could take up position behind an existing defensive wall to block the advance of the enormous Persian army. In August/September the Persian army arrived and began a frontal assault, which was thrown back with heavy losses. The Greek front was so short that it could be tightly packed, and Leonidas could rotate his units so that each enemy attack always faced fresh men. On the second day of fighting the Persians were again thrown back, but then a traitor revealed to Xerxes that there was a path around the Greek position. Leonidas knew this and had placed a force of 1,000 allies across the narrow path, but they were brushed aside by a strong Persian force; they did, however, warn Leonidas that he was about to be encircled. According to legend he sent all the other forces home and stood with his 300 Spartans to permit their escape. In fact about 1,500 Greeks including the Spartans failed to flee, preventing the Persian cavalry from pursuing and destroying the whole army. Leonidas and his entire force were wiped out. How this came about is uncertain and it is possible that they were simply trapped by the Persians. However this may be, the effect was that many experienced troops got away. A monument to the Spartans, rebuilt in 1955, was erected where they died, inscribed:

Stranger, tell the people of Lacedaemon [Sparta]
That we who lie here obeyed their laws.[10]

A poor memorial, one would think, for the much greater numbers of non-Spartans who died there. But Thermopylae delayed the great army which was already operating late in the season, while bad weather and effective Athenian naval action severely reduced the Persian fleet in the narrows of Artemisium. The people of Athens fled to the island of Salamis, abandoning the city to the Persians, who burned it.

By this time it was early October; the campaigning season was coming to a close which increased the pressure upon the Persians. The main Greek army was dug in behind defences across the very narrow isthmus of Corinth, while the allied fleet stood off in the straits of Salamis. Some in the Persian army urged Xerxes to leave a sufficient force to bottle up the Greek ships by Salamis, while the rest sailed on to outflank the Corinth line, and he actually sent some of his army towards Corinth. This alarmed many in the allied navy who favoured pulling back to prevent it. But Themistocles suggested drawing the enemy into the straits where their superior numbers would count for little. Apparently the Greek ships were heavier and less manoeuvrable than those of the Persians, but experience in the confined waters at Artemisium had shown that if the Persian ships could not manoeuvre they could be defeated. Why the Greek ships were so clumsy is unclear; perhaps it was because each had more fighting men on board or because they had been at sea so long that their sailing qualities were degrading – or both.

To lure the Persians into the straits Themistocles sent messages to Xerxes suggesting that the allied fleet was about to leave the Athenians in the lurch, and urging him to come on to destroy them and receive the submission of the Athenian people. Xerxes probably knew of the tensions in the allied army and was in any case anxious to gain a decisive success before winter, so he sent his navy into the trap. In the narrows between Salamis the superior sailing qualities of the Persian ships counted for little, because they could not manoeuvre to ram their enemies, which was their preferred tactic. Nor, in these confined waters, could they bring their superior numbers to bear. In fact once battle was joined the three lines of the Persian fleet became entangled and the battle resolved itself into hand-to-hand fighting between the crews of individual ships, and in these circumstances the bigger Greek crews probably counted for a great deal. In the words of Herodotus:

> There fell in this combat Ariabignes, one of the chief commanders of the fleet, who was son of Darius and brother of Xerxes; and with him perished a vast number of men of high repute, Persians, Medes, and allies. Of the Greeks there died only a few; for, as they were able to swim, all those that were not slain outright by the enemy escaped from the sinking vessels and swam across to Salamis. But on the side of the barbarians more perished by drowning than in any other way, since they did not know how to swim. The great destruction took place when the ships which had been first engaged began to fly; for they who were stationed in the rear, anxious to display their valour before the eyes of the king, made every effort to force their way to the front, and thus became entangled with such of their own vessels as were retreating.[11]

Salamis was a major victory for the Greeks. Xerxes at this point withdrew with his fleet because a major revolt had broken out in Babylonia, but he left a very large army in Greece under Mardonios.

Mardonios then completed the destruction of the city of Athens. He knew, however, that he could not march south against Corinth leaving the

Athenian fleet in his rear, so he tried to exploit splits amongst the allies. Athenians, whose fleet was the driving force at Salamis, were scandalised by the proposal, supported by the Spartans, to pull back their fleet in defence of the Corinth line. They negotiated with Mardonios and it was only their threat to make peace with Persia that persuaded the allies to move north in the summer of 479. They formed the greatest Greek army ever to assemble: 38,700 hoplites and 70,000 light troops for a total of about 110,000 under the command of the Spartan Pausanias. Mardonios withdrew north-westwards from Athens with his army which had probably been reduced by now to about the same size, even allowing for the inclusion of 20,000 Greek allies. He took up position near Plataea where Thebes, which had submitted to the Persians, could serve as a base.

Mardonios had taken up an east–west position to the north of the river Asopus in a broad plain where his cavalry could be used to best effect. The Greeks approached through the passes of the Cithaeron-Pastra massif, and deployed their forces in line in the northern foothills of this range, some way back from the Asopus and opposite those of the Persians. The Greeks did not dare to cross the river onto the open plain for fear of the Persian cavalry, while the Persians could not easily use their horsemen in the broken country across the river occupied by the Greeks. For much of July there was a stand-off between the two armies.

But Mardonios needed a victory because, although his Greek allies were holding firm for the moment, the Athenian fleet was loose in the Aegean, and might stir up revolt in Anatolia at any time. In August some of his cavalry crossed the river to threaten the supply lines and even the water sources on which the Greeks depended. This forced the Greeks to move towards Plataea on their left. Mardonios then launched his main cavalry force, whose missile tactics caused heavy losses amongst the hoplites: 'Mardonios, delighted by his illusory victory, ordered a cavalry attack. When the cavalry attacked they began to cause casualties amongst the Greeks by their archery and use of javelins since they were horse archers and were difficult to engage.' There followed a series of confused struggles which merged into a single great battle. In one engagement it was the large body of the archers with the Athenians which held the Persians at bay. But the climax of the battle came when the Spartan hoplites held together against the Persian cavalry whose supporting infantry were unable to follow up:

> The Persians planted their shields in a defensive wall and continually
> discharged their arrows ... the Lacedaemonians (Spartans) also advanced

against the Persians who put aside their bows and were ready to meet them. The combat began around the shield wall. When it had been breached a sharp engagement took place around the shrine of Demeter and lasted for some time at close quarters. The enemy would grab hold of the Greek spears and break them. The Persians were not inferior in courage and strength, but they lacked armour, were poorly trained and greatly inferior in skill to their opponents. They broke ranks, and, darting forward in groups of ten, sometimes more, sometimes fewer, they fell upon the Spartan line and were killed . . . The crucial factor in their defeat was that they were unprotected, unarmed men fighting against heavily armoured infantry.[12]

In the confusion Mardonios was killed, and this proved to be the decisive event in the battle. But the Spartans were the most professional army in Greece, and their phalanxes played the major role in holding off the enemy cavalry. Once these were beaten off, the Spartans charged into the Persian infantry. Their bows were short-range weapons and, as at Marathon, this limited the number of arrows that could be fired at an enemy advancing at a run. Once at close quarters the armoured men of the phalanx were at an enormous advantage, and slaughtered their enemies.

It is important to note that it was the Spartans who launched the decisive attacks. Young male Spartans were separated from their families and trained rigorously in athletics, hunting and the use of weapons. They lived in a militarised society which worshipped the cult of collective sacrifice:

> When someone asked Demaratus why the Spartans disgrace those who throw away their shields but not those who abandon their breastplates or helmets, he said they put the latter on for their own sakes, but the shield for the sake of the whole line.[13]

They were heavily equipped with bronze armour, and while this limited their mobility it made them very formidable at close quarters. Above all, they were the best organised troops in Greece with a proper chain of command. Xenophon tells us that the Spartans

> divided the troops into six regiments of cavalry and hoplites. Each of the citizen regiments had a polemarch, four company commanders, eight platoon leaders and sixteen squad leaders . . . Most think the hoplite formation of the Spartans is overly complicated but this is the very opposite of the truth. For in the Spartan arrangements the men in the

front rank are all officers and each file has all that is needed to make it efficient.[14]

Because of their discipline they did not run into battle but advanced steadily to the sound of flutes in order to keep in close order.

The militaristic regime of Sparta was both admired and feared by the other Greek cities, and in the wake of the victory at Plataea it is hardly surprising that the alliance broke up. Some of the Ionian cities rebelled, weakening the Persian position in western Anatolia; Athens created a Delian League to exploit such weakness. Sparta, unwilling to concede the leadership of Athens, pulled out of the war. Athens dominated the whole organisation, collected tributes from the cities of the League, created a great fleet and raised armies which drove the Persians back from the Anatolian coast by 466 BC. They mounted a major expedition to support an Egyptian rebellion, tried to seize Cyprus and organised raids on the Palestinian coast, but none of these expeditions was strong enough to achieve success, and about 449 BC peace was established between Athens and the Persian Empire on the basis of the status quo. By this time there was bitter conflict between Athens and a number of other cities which feared her imperialism. And this is an appropriate word. For the Delian League became an Athenian empire. Athens meddled in the politics of the Delian cities to favour democratic regimes, and planted colonies of Athenians in their lands where they formed military bases. The tributes from the League and the taxes upon foreigners trading with Athens created enormous incomes which could be used to pay rowers for the fleet and to support strong armies. Here was the Athenian culture of leisure and greed at work.

But the Athenian Empire was short-lived, because Sparta helped any city which resisted its dominion. In 431 BC the Great Peloponnesian War between Sparta and Athens broke out. For a long time neither side prevailed, because this was a conflict between a tiger and a shark. The Spartans had the better army, but the Athenians the better fleet and they enjoyed the protection of the famous 'Long Walls' connecting the city and its port of Piraeus, which annulled Spartan military supremacy. The balance was tipped in favour of Sparta by Persian subsidies which enabled it to expand its navy. The war ended in 404 as a defeat for Athens, and Sparta seemed destined to lead the empire of Greece. But Athens soon rallied and offered its support to cities which objected to Spartan domination. In the Corinthian War (395–386) the Persians supported Athens and her allies against the Spartans who had taken over much of western

Anatolia. After 371 Thebes, under a great general, Epaminondas, created a mighty army and in a series of campaigns destroyed Spartan supremacy without, however, being able to dominate the rest of Greece. As a result, there was no Greek empire, and by adroitly playing off the city-states against one another the Persians recovered their dominion in western Anatolia.

The Persian and Peloponnesian wars were a period of sustained conflict, quite unlike anything that the Greek cities had previously experienced, bringing about radical changes in government and warfare. These were really wars of survival, and the power of central governments had to be strengthened if fleets were to be built, fortifications constructed and maintained and armies raised. In purely military terms, the most obvious and distinctive element in the Greek land forces was the phalanx. By the late fifth century the hoplite phalanx had become not merely the core but the dominating force in Greek armies. The individual soldiers wore helmets of leather or bronze and protected their bodies with leather straps or jackets studded with metal plates, together with the great shield. The phalanx was evolving into a very tight close-order formation, unlike the rather looser units which had, for example, fought at Marathon. The problem was that moving and maintaining formation required discipline, a quality notably lacking in Greek citizen armies, with the exception of that of Sparta whose population was dwindling. By the end of the fifth century the phalanx had undergone a decisive change. It was now commonly made up of professional soldiers. The endless wars undermined Greek agriculture, so that men who had once been farmers were now ready to be paid soldiers.

Moreover, armies and tactics became more varied during the long wars. Cavalry and light-armed troops, like the Thracian *peltasts* and Cretan archers, began to be marshalled as separate forces on the wings of the hoplite centre, and their mobility made them very useful. On broken ground the phalanx could not maintain its solidity and thus became very vulnerable. In 426 Demosthenes led an Athenian army against the Aetolians who had only lightly armed troops. He relied on his own archers to repel their attacks:

> But as long as the Athenian archers had arrows and were able to use them, they held out since the Aetolians were light-armed and retreated when they were shot at. But after the commander of the archers was killed, his men dispersed, and the hoplites were worn out through being subjected for a long time to the same fatiguing actions: the Aetolians

pressed them and continued to shower them with javelins. The Athenians were thus routed and fled.

The following year, when the Spartan hoplites attacked his army, Demosthenes sent forward large numbers of light troops armed with javelins, bows and slings, and they harassed the enemy so severely that they could not come to close quarters with the Athenians and so,

> When many of them had now been wounded because they (the Spartans) were continually forced to remain in the same spot, they closed ranks and retreated to their last strong point on the island.[15]

The hoplite phalanx was excellent at close quarters, but once commanders had learned to use light infantry effectively, it had to be used in conjunction with them. This placed a premium on coordination, training and discipline which imposed impossible demands upon citizen-soldiers, reinforcing the trend towards mercenary armies. City-states like Athens and Sparta had evolved the phalanx of spearmen with shields out of necessity, and in the Persian wars it showed great potential against cavalry. But by the end of the fifth century it was clear that only professionals could be trained and disciplined as an element in more complex armies, ushering in a period of tactical experiment. The Athenian general Iphicrates devised a kind of hybrid – lightly armed *peltasts* equipped with very long spears who were crammed very tightly into the phalanx – but this was not sustained. The Thebans at Mantineia in 418 and Leuctra in 371 attempted with some success to overcome the tendency of the phalanx to drift to the right in the attack, as each man sought the protection of the shield of the man on that side, by sending a strong force forward on the left while a weak right was held back. The growing size and diversity of armies placed an enormous burden on the Greek city-states, especially as siege warfare was becoming commoner.

The Greeks were for a long time very bad at sieges and for very good reasons. Citizen-soldiers recoiled from the price in blood involved in storming even modest walls. The alternative, a long siege demanding specialised machinery, was cripplingly expensive. In May of 429 BC the Spartans and their Theban allies besieged the small city of Plataea which had barely 500 defenders. The Spartans showed remarkable ingenuity in that they built a ramp of earth against the city walls and deployed battering rams – the first use of such methods by any Greek city. But they had no archers to cover their attackers and all assaults failed. In the end the Spartans built a wall and ditches around the city – a line of circumvallation – but the siege dragged on until the city's food ran out in the summer of 428 BC.

In the fifth century the Athenians gained a formidable reputation as besiegers, largely because their fleet could move and supply large forces supported by ample numbers of slaves who rapidly dug lines of circumvallation around hostile or rebellious cities. This took time and money; the siege of Potidaea, begun in 432, lasted two years. Athens deployed 3,000 hoplites who were paid 2 drachmas per day plus 1 drachma for a servant. The siege cost 6,000 drachmas (or 1 talent) per day, and, therefore, 2,000 talents in all. The annual revenue of Athens at this time was probably 600 talents, so the siege bit deep into Athenian reserves. Usually, however, the very act of setting the siege and the elaborate preparations for attack strengthened the peace party within a besieged city and a surrender was obtained, either by betrayal or negotiation.

The Athenian siege of Syracuse in Sicily, 414/13 BC, exposed the limitations of this method. Athens had dispatched a huge fleet and army, and although some battering rams were deployed, their generals seem to have been counting on dissent within Syracuse, but the war party in the city conducted a very active defence and checked all efforts to surrender. A Spartan relief force appeared, the Athenians were trapped and they suffered a terrible defeat which, in effect, broke the Athenian Empire.

When, in the fourth century, the Phoenician city of Carthage attacked the Greek cities of Sicily, their methods were quite different. Siege-towers and cats were built to provide covering fire for attacks on the wall, and battering rams were deployed. Above all, they were ready to storm cities, accepting high casualties amongst their soldiers, many of whom were mercenaries. Moreover, terror was exploited as a weapon: cities which failed to surrender were destroyed and their populations butchered as lessons for others. These were the methods of Assyria, Babylon and Persia. The Sicilian Greeks had no choice but to emulate both their elaborate equipment and their brutality.

Greek ingenuity, in fact, added to the horrors of war by inventing the first mechanical bow: the *gastraphetes*, 'belly-bow'. This was originally a composite bow mounted horizontally on a wooden stock within which a slider was drawn back against the bowstring by a ratchet operated by handles. The front of the stock was placed against a wall and the whole was braced by the holder's belly. Once the slider was fully drawn back it was anchored by a trigger whose firing released the arrow. The arrow was much heavier than an ordinary arrow and, because it had a flat trajectory, rather more accurate. This weapon was enlarged and developed to throw heavier darts and rocks, or reduced in size to the classic crossbow. By 340 BC the Greek world had developed torsion-powered catapults. In the two-armed version the large horizontal bow was replaced by two arms each mounted in a coil of sinew, and the string and missile were drawn back by a ratchet. The onager (mule) had a single upright arm whose bottom was buried in a horizontally mounted coil of sinew. The arm was drawn back against the torsion of the coil and suddenly released to kick against a strong horizontal bar, projecting a small stone. All these were essentially anti-personnel weapons, though they could be scaled up to throw stones capable of damaging fortifications.

The military achievements of the Greeks were remarkable, particularly their defiance of the Persian Empire in the fifth century. The phalanx, as the Stele of the Vultures indicates, was an ancient military formation for fighting the close-quarter battle, though of course how tightly it was formed varied from time to time and occasion to occasion. The genius of the Greeks was to realise that the phalanx, which they had adopted out of the same necessity as so many cultures, could be made into a very effective counter to the Persian cavalry, and the sheer desperation of their fight against Persia inspired their soldiers to accept the discipline which would make this effective. At Plataea the defeat of the Persian cavalry exposed the lightly armed Persian infantry to defeat at the hands of the hoplites. Commanders recognised the value of the phalanx, but the spirit of the citizen-soldiers, so vital against Persia, was not something that could always be sustained. In the course of the subsequent intra-Greek wars the vital development was the professionalisation of the phalangists, because the steadier and more disciplined the soldiers of the phalanx, the stronger the formation and the greater the chances of success.

Nothing illustrates better the quality of these professionals than the story of Xenophon and his 10,000. These were Greek mercenaries hired by Cyrus of Persia in his bid for the throne. Xenophon, who later commanded them, makes it clear that Cyrus was seen as providing an economic opportunity for these shrewd Greek entrepreneurs:

The majority of the soldiers had not sailed from Greece to undertake this mercenary service on account of their neediness, but because of the reports of Cyrus' character that they had heard; some brought others with them, while others had spent money of their own on this undertaking and others had abandoned fathers, mothers or children with the intention of earning money for them and returning once more since they had heard that those who served with Cyrus had enjoyed many benefits.[16]

In 401 BC they were victorious at Cunaxa, but Cyrus was killed. This led to negotiations with the victorious party at the Persian court during which their leaders were betrayed and killed by the Persians. The Greek soldiers then formed themselves into a kind of mercenary republic, electing Xenophon as their general, and fought their way up the Euphrates and back to Greece across northern Anatolia.

The Persian wars and then the long quarrels of the Greek city-states created a kind of military laboratory in Greece, stimulating ideas and new developments. The most obvious effect of this was the development of the hoplite phalanx. It became the very embodiment of close-order, a tight mass of men working together, able to resist enemies with their hedgehog of spears and to threaten them by sheer weight and momentum. However, this was only really achieved as the citizen-soldier was superseded by the professional soldier. But the hoplite had never been the only soldier on the battlefield, and commanders began to think seriously about how to combine archers, slingers and javelin throwers to the best effect, creating armies which were much more diverse and more capable of manoeuvre and attack in a wide range of circumstances. This was accompanied by an assimilation of the siege techniques of other peoples, and the invention of new devices like the catapult. What the Greeks did not do was to develop cavalry. That the environment in which they fought – in Greece proper and in Magna Graecia – was not particularly suitable for mounted warfare was a strong reason for this. But, in addition, they may have disdained cavalry because of its limitations: horsemen were missile throwers whose attacks could be held at bay by discipline and close-order, the qualities at the heart of agro-urban warfare as exemplified by the hoplite phalanx.

By contrast, the Persians, who had to fight over vast areas and open plains, continued to focus on cavalry. It is often wondered why the Persians did not train heavy infantry to replace their lightly armed foot. The reasons for this are both general and specific. The Persians had some heavy infantry, the *Karkades*, but they too lacked the means to achieve systematic training and relied on native skills which arose from civilian lifestyles. More specifically, the Greek front was not all that vital to the Persian Empire, and it managed to regain Anatolia by an adroit diplomacy which exploited the quarrels of the Greeks. The priority for the Persian Empire was speed of movement and the ability to fight in other places, especially on the long Asian frontiers where cavalry was the most useful arm. No power can be strong everywhere and in every aspect of war, and the Persian army was no exception to this general rule. And when they wanted heavy infantry, they could always hire them at need from the quarrelsome city-states of Greece whose mercenaries were perfectly willing to serve for money.

In the fifth and fourth centuries BC external attack and internal strife made Greece a forcing house of war. None of the Greek city-states could afford to master all these new techniques, especially as many of them had simultaneously to support fleets. As a result no empire of Greece arose, because neither Athens nor Sparta nor Thebes had the means to consolidate their momentary supremacies. But the military methods which the ingenuity of the Greek city-states had developed could be adopted by others. Moreover, the Greeks lacked cavalry. Thus the classic elements of agro-urban armies down to the nineteenth century – heavy infantry supported by light missile-men – had not yet combined with cavalry. But the horse had enormous potential which was realised under a commander of genius, Alexander the Great.

CHAPTER FOUR

◆

THE GLORY OF EMPIRE, 336 BC–AD 651

Stick together, enrich the soldiers and despise everyone else.[1]

THE rise and fall of mighty empires dominated the great city-civilisations across this period. They all developed professional armies because their military needs exceeded the capacities of conscripts and citizens. The armies of these empires changed somewhat, but remained within the long-established pattern of agro-urban warfare. They were based on mass infantry formations fighting in close order. Cavalry formed a smaller element whose speed was of vital importance. Fortifications forced the adoption of a specialised technology which was remarkably similar everywhere. There were local differences; war-elephants were available in India and Persia, while plentiful supplies of bronze in China led to an intensive use of crossbows. As these empires of the settled city peoples grew, they all, to a greater or lesser degree, came into contact with the radically different warfare of the steppe people which forced unwelcome adjustments upon them.

Those who created empires gained enormously increased resources, but the means to sustain such dominions were finite once the expansive phase was over. Empires ultimately had to be supported from the limited resources of the agricultural societies within them, because while trade and industry were capable of more intense wealth production, they were tied to agriculture whose productivity was circumscribed by the need to preserve fertility. Their ruling elites disagreed about how to direct resources within these constraints, and who should do it. Inevitably, leading soldiers and their armies played a role in these quarrels because imperial regimes were created and sustained by armed might.

Alexander the Great (336–323 BC) stands supreme amongst all the empire builders. King of Macedonia and ruler of Greece in 336 BC at the age of 20, by his death at the age of 32 he had destroyed the Persian Empire of Darius III (336–330 BC) and his imperial rule stretched from the Danube to the Indus. How to explain such breathtaking military success? Persia did not just break down; the nobles remained loyal to Darius. Of the provinces only Egypt, smarting from the defeat of its recent revolt, welcomed the young conqueror. Many more Greek mercenaries fought against Alexander than for him. Persia was destroyed by a better general using new military methods, who inspired his men by example and exploited serious military errors made by Darius and his generals. As ever, the importance of personality should never be minimised, but other factors were at work. The endless wars both between the Greek cities, and against outsiders like the Persians and Phoenicians, had been a forcing house for new military developments which were adapted and systematised by Alexander's father, Philip II of Macedon (359–336 BC).

Philip inherited a peasant militia which he reorganised into six battalions, each of about 1,500 men, recruited on a territorial basis. They were paid for their service and given status as 'Foot Companions'. In effect they had the organisation and discipline of a regular force. He also applied new tactics and equipment. The infantry carried the *sarissa*, a spear 21 feet long with a large leaf-shaped blade and a metal butt-spike, which could be broken into two sections for transport. They fought in a very tightly packed phalanx, literally shoulder to shoulder and at least eight men deep:

> For each soldier in it with his weapons occupies a space of 3 feet when it is compacted and the sarissa is . . . sixteen cubits[2] in length. From this length one must subtract the distance between the hands as they grasp it and the counterweight behind the projecting portion. Thus each sarissa point projects ten cubits in front of the body of each soldier whenever he charges and comes to grips with the enemy. The result of this is that the sarissas of the men in the second, third and fourth rank extend beyond the troops of the front line, and even the sarissas of the fifth line extend two cubits beyond the front . . . Those ranks beyond the fifth cannot use their sarissas to take part in the encounter, but hold their sarissas slating in the air above the shoulders of the men in front and so protect the whole formation by keeping off missiles . . . Also by pressing with the weight of their bodies on those in front during the charge, they create a stronger impetus.[3]

This was a bristling battering ram of enormous power which sometimes adopted a wedge shape, enabling it to exert great pressure on a narrow section of the enemy front. The light leather armour and small shield of the phalangists enabled them to move relatively quickly around the battlefield, and to use both hands to wield the *sarissa*.

But the phalanx was not invulnerable. Mass was its strength, but this in itself made it an easy target for enemy missile throwers. For this reason Philip created units of light infantry, javelin throwers and Cretan archers, to prevent enemy missile-men getting close enough to damage the phalanx – and, of course, they could harass the enemy. But these were of limited use against cavalry who could pounce upon a loose formation on the march, or in battle use their arrows and javelins to inflict heavy losses on the phalanx, and charge into any gaps in the wall of spears. Philip's response was to develop heavy cavalry. The plains and hills of Macedonia made good grazing for horses, and the aristocracy was accustomed to riding and hunting. Once he had tamed their independence, Philip created the 'Companions', an elite aristocratic cavalry. Throughout the ancient world horsemen were primarily missile throwers, but Philip, while retaining this function, insisted that his Macedonian cavalry should fight in close order and destroy their enemies at close quarters. They were heavily armoured, equipped with a version of the *sarissa*, and formed into phalanx-like squadrons of about 200 horsemen, often wedge-shaped to create and enlarge narrow gaps in the enemy line. They could not attack well-formed infantry, but they could crush hostile cavalry and drive them from the field, thereby exposing the footsoldiers to attack.

Philip's army numbered 10,000–12,000 infantry and 3,500 cavalry. He prohibited the enormous trains of servants so characteristic of Greek armies where each man had a slave, and instead compelled the soldiers to carry their own supplies. In this way mobility was not compromised by the needs of logistics. Within the army there were specialised units like engineers who could build bridges and the whole technology of rams, siege-towers and penthouses which, together with catapults, made cities highly vulnerable. Philip built a complex and disciplined war machine such as no Greek city-state had envisaged. To coordinate these separate units he nurtured an inner group of commanders, like Parmenion, who were obedient, but also knew his mind and so could use their initiative. In this way Philip created an army which was highly responsive to his will. Philip's ambition was to conquer Persia and he had already landed troops in Anatolia when he was assassinated in 336 BC, probably by his son and successor, Alexander.

Philip's death inevitably provoked rebellion, and Alexander quickly reasserted Macedonian power in Illyria and the Balkans, and crushed a revolt of the Greek cities, ruthlessly destroying Thebes as an object lesson to all. By the time he crossed into Anatolia in 334 BC Alexander was an experienced soldier who understood how best to use the military machine which his father had built. And he understood, too, the importance of morale and the need to show himself and to lead by example. He had an army of 32,000 infantry and 5,000 cavalry, but he left his Greek troops behind because he was suspicious of their loyalty, especially as he knew that the Persian army of Anatolia included some 20,000 Greek mercenaries. With 12,000 infantry, mostly Macedonian phalangists, and some 5,000 cavalry he advanced to where the river Granicus (Kocabas Çay near modern Biga Çay in Turkey) cut sharply through the open country with banks 5 metres high. On the eastern side, 20,000 Persian cavalry waited, with the Iranian elite in the centre. Behind them on the top of a gentle ridge were 20,000 Greek hoplites. This army seems to have been strung out over 2.5 kilometres to cover all possible lines of approach, and they presumably expected to have time to concentrate their forces when it became clear where Alexander would attack.

Careful reconnaissance, speed, control, aggression and coordination produced victory at the Granicus. Alexander had spied out the enemy positions and he formed his army into attack formation on the march with cavalry on each wing and the phalangists in the middle, eliminating the need for a delay for deployment on arrival which the enemy could have used to counter his movements. He then employed the mobility of his horsemen to great effect. An initial cavalry attack against the enemy centre was sacrificial, and could only have been made by troops with every confidence in their commander, their own officers and the support of the rest of the army. A thrust across the river to the right flank was inspired by Alexander's personal leadership. It dragged the Persian cavalry in that direction and disordered their formations, precipitating a wild struggle: 'Though it was a cavalry battle it resembled an infantry engagement more. Horses and men were entangled with each other in the struggle.'[4]

All this prepared the way for the crushing advance of the phalangists which destroyed the enemy centre weakened by constant reinforcement of the fighting on their left. The failure to move the Greek hoplites against their attack suggests that the enemy commander had lost his grasp. By contrast, the coordination of the Macedonian army was remarkable.

By the autumn of 333 BC Alexander's forces dominated Anatolia and he had advanced into Cilicia with 26,000 infantry and 5,000 cavalry.

When he heard that Darius was in the field with a great army he moved southwards into Syria. But he was then outmanoeuvred, because Darius marched into Cilicia from the north, advanced into his rear, and encamped on the river Pinarus (modern Payas), completely cutting his communications. The Persians, with 12,000 cavalry, 80,000 Persian infantry and 30,000 Greek hoplites, deployed along the western bank of the river on a front of some 4 kilometres between the mountains and the shoreline. Most of their cavalry was on the right by the sea; the mass of their infantry, including the Greeks, were in the centre where the river-bank was at its highest, while other horsemen and the mass of light infantry held the left up into the mountains.

But having seized the initiative, Darius then abandoned it by sitting passively in a defensive posture while Alexander, after retracing his steps along the narrow plain, performed the difficult task of deploying in the plain of Issus in the face of an enemy army. Once again, the coordination of the Macedonian army was remarkable because it moved rapidly into battle formation with the cavalry equally divided between left and right and the phalanxes in the middle. Alexander on foot led the heavy phalangists across the river against the centre of the Persian line. Once they had established themselves he remounted and led the cavalry on his right wing in a wild charge against Darius himself. On the left the Persian cavalry outnumbered the Macedonians, but they were crammed into a narrow front so that their numbers could not be made to count, enabling the veteran Parmenion to fight a careful defensive battle. As Alexander's cavalry drove through the enemy's line, Darius fled and a massacre ensued.

In 331 BC the Macedonian army left Egypt and on 1 October confronted Darius in Alexander's masterpiece battle at Gaugamela. There Darius, with an enormous army, perhaps some 200,000 strong, confronted Alexander with about 47,000. Darius's 40,000 cavalry were drawn up in front of his army. His infantry formed a second line, with the best troops, including the Greek hoplites, close to the king in the centre where he expected the Macedonian infantry phalanx to attack. In front of these he arrayed three groups of about 200 specially prepared chariots with forward projecting spears mounted on the yoke-pole and sharp blades set on the wheel-hubs. To enable them to break up the Macedonian phalanxes they needed smooth ground, so three fairways were prepared. This anchored the Persian army, a curious choice for an army whose great strength lay in cavalry. But clearly, after Granicus and Issus, Darius was mesmerised by the power of the Macedonian phalanx, and counted on sheer numbers to neutralise Alexander's impressive cavalry in the vast open plain.

Alexander advanced with the infantry phalanx in the centre and the cavalry on the wings, positioning himself on the right, but his battle line was about a mile shorter than the Persians'. As the Macedonians approached the enemy, Alexander moved his army to the right. A ferocious cavalry battle developed there as the Persians sought to outflank his approach. As a result of this movement, Alexander's infantry were no longer in the fairways, nullifying the effect of the chariots. However, Alexander's left was very exposed. The Macedonians had provided for this situation by deploying flank guards and organising the infantry so that the phalanx could 'form square' if surrounded. But while Alexander shattered the enemy left causing Darius to flee, Parmenion's men were almost overwhelmed by enemy cavalry, so Alexander had to cut his way through to them in a grim encounter which resulted in many casualties:

> There was no casting of javelins or the counterwheeling that are normal to cavalry battles; rather each trooper tried to cut his way through the men directly opposite him as the only path to safety. In their struggle they killed and were killed without quarter.[5]

Alexander's success owed much to Darius's errors. The Persians did not use their navy strategically to raise revolt in Greece after Alexander plunged into Anatolia. In 332 BC Tyre resisted Alexander's attack for seven months, and Gaza held out from September to November, but Darius made no effort to relieve them and both fell. In battle Darius and his commanders were clearly obsessed with the threat posed by the Macedonian phalanx, and strengthened the centre using their Greek mercenaries. But in each battle their stance was rigidly fixed and they failed to react to Alexander's tactical flexibility. Their army had all the elements possessed by Alexander, except heavy cavalry, but they greatly outnumbered the Macedonian horsemen. However, they were never able to make numbers tell because they lacked real leadership. Alexander's dynamic personality was vital, particularly for his cavalry, and his coordination of forces through trusted companions made his army very flexible. By contrast, Darius and the Persian commanders positioned their armies and then were unable to correct errors in the original deployment or to react to changed circumstances. But perhaps above all, Alexander could count on a superbly trained army of regular troops, with a good balance between all arms, which was capable of responding to his leadership.

When Alexander moved east the flexibility of the Macedonian army was again demonstrated. In Sogdiana, now the site of the cities of Bukhara and Samarkand in modern Uzbekistan, they crushed a guerrilla campaign by the Scythians in 329–327 BC. Alexander then marched into India, defeating Porus, the Rajah of Pauravas on the river Hydaspes (modern Jhelum) despite having to face the novel threat of war-elephants. Alexander wanted to go further, but in June the army mutinied, forcing him into a retreat to Persia where he died on 10 June 323. His empire fell into three major units: Macedonia ruled by the Antigonids, Egypt ruled by the descendants of Alexander's general, Ptolemy, and the rest ruled by the descendants of another, Seleucus.

The successors of Alexander relied heavily on the Macedonian phalanx as the key to military success, though these were augmented by local forces. The Seleucids even used elephants, presumably drawn from their Indian lands, as the writer of the biblical Book of Maccabees shows in his vivid description of Antiochus IV (175–164 BC) attacking Eygpt:

> Antiochus made up his mind to become king of Egypt and so to rule over both kingdoms. He assembled a powerful force of chariots, elephants and cavalry, and a great fleet and invaded Egypt. When battle was joined Ptolemy king of Egypt was seized with panic and took to flight leaving many dead. The fortified towns were captured and the land pillaged.[6]

But the phalanx tended to grow into a massive and rather rigid unit with immense depth, and correspondingly little ability to manoeuvre. External attack and internal rebellion whittled away the Seleucid Empire, especially after a steppe people, the Parthians led by their Arsacid dynasty, took Persia from Antiochus III the Great (223–187 BC). Its troubled remnant was conquered by Rome in 63 BC. In Egypt the dynasty of Ptolemy the Saviour (323–283 BC) would last until the death of Cleopatra VII in 30 BC. Overall, Greek language, civilisation and military methods dominated the Mediterranean lands and reached far into South Asia where, however, another empire was arising.

In 305, Seleucus Nicator (306–281 BC), intent on recovering the full extent of Alexander's empire, invaded India, but came to terms with a great ruler:

> The Indians occupy [in part] some of the countries situated along the Indus, which formerly belonged to the Persians: Alexander deprived the Ariani of them, and established there settlements of his own. But Seleucus Nicator gave them to Sandrocottus in consequence of a marriage contract, and received in return five hundred elephants.[7]

This 'Sandracottus' was Chandragupta (320–297 BC), the founder of the Mauryan Empire which encompassed India from the Bay of Bengal to the Arabian Sea. He was supported by his minister, Kautilya, the author of the *Arthashastra*, an enormous handbook of statecraft, military strategy and economic policy. By the time of his death in 297 BC, Chandragupta had seized almost all of peninsular India, acquiring vast resources:

> But the Prasii surpass in power and glory every other people . . . Their king has in his pay a standing army of 600,000 foot-soldiers, 30,000 cavalry, and 9,000 elephants: whence may be formed some conjecture as to the vastness of his resources.[8]

The rich agriculture and trading wealth of India enabled Chandragupta to sustain a large permanent royal guard and a strong territorial force living on their own landholdings, supplemented at need by a militia, mercenaries and allies. Spearmen in close order formed the core of the army, and they were supported by light troops and cavalry. War-elephants must have been awe-inspiring at first sight, but they were vulnerable to missile fire which panicked them so that they trampled their own men. Logistical support for these troops was provided by an elaborate bureaucracy. The pattern of empire depending on a standing army is very evident here.

Like armies all over the world Mauryan forces often targeted the mass of the population. Ashoka (273–232 BC), in one of his great rock-cut inscriptions, recorded the slaughter in Kalinga of 100,000 people and the deportation of another 150,000, but went on to say: 'On conquering Kalinga the Beloved of the Gods [Ashoka] felt remorse, for, when an independent country is conquered, the slaughter, death and deportation of the people is extremely grievous to the Beloved of the Gods and weighs heavily on his mind . . .'[9] Such of his victims as survived might well have taken a jaundiced view of this remorse, which did not extend to relieving their suffering. Interestingly, these words do not appear on the version of the inscription actually in Kalinga, where they are replaced with clauses urging the conqueror's governors to a policy of merciful assimilation. In India, as elsewhere, civilian suffering was an intended and necessary part of the brutal business of war. By 181 BC internal strife and external attack had destroyed the Mauryan Empire, and it was not until the rise of Chandra-Gupta I (AD *c.*320–35) that a great power once more imposed itself upon India. But the various branches of the Gupta quarrelled, and by 500 AD the dynasty had broken apart. As a result of this vacuum another steppe people found its way into India – the White Huns, who overran Kashmir and the Punjab. They were expelled by an alliance of Hindu powers, but the irruption of steppe people was much more important in China.

There the triumph of Shi Huangdi, the 'First Emperor', ended the long era of the 'Warring States' (475–221 BC). These numerous powers had been anchored by strongly defended cities, and as a consequence war turned on siege. This demanded numerous infantry, for great cities were the nodal points of government, and they were defended by massive rammed-earth walls. Artillery developed to facilitate attacks – it was in China during the time of the 'Warring States' that we first hear of trebuchets. These were lever-action siege engines, capable of throwing heavy missiles; their main purpose, however, was to clear the ramparts because they were ineffective against the massive rammed-earth walls of Chinese cities. In addition, siege-towers and cats were in widespread use, while the techniques of tunnelling and mining were highly developed. Sun Tzu wrote his famous *Art of War* in the fifth century BC, and he regarded 100,000 as quite a normal army size, while by the third century an army of 30,000 was considered small. They were raised by universal conscription of all men aged between 23 and 56 who had to serve as soldiers, or enlist for labour services, for two years, although prosperous people could pay for a substitute. Shi Huangdi conscripted thousands of peasants to undertake such engineering tasks as destroying the defensive walls which the warring states had built against one another, and reinforcing those which faced the steppe.

The size of these armies must be judged in proportion to the enormous population of China and the huge distances. And there are clear signs that, as in the Middle East and India, the real cutting edge of the Chinese armies was formed by elite professionals of war. Shi Huangdi's greatest memorial is the 'Terracotta Army', a huge burial pit containing some 7,000 life-size clay figures of soldiers in full armour guarding his enormous tomb near modern Xian. This force, about the same strength as a Roman legion, appears to be organised in order of march. The archers and crossbowmen flank the unit, but because many are concentrated at the front they were presumably thrown forward to harass the enemy in attacks. The basic unit was the infantry squad of five, three being spearmen and the others archers or crossbowmen. A group of about 100 was commanded from a chariot, and the officers in it are clearly distinguished. These splendid effigies of soldiers wore fine armour and originally carried real weapons of iron and bronze which have now been looted. Crossbows were highly developed and there was even a model with a magazine which fed in a new bolt automatically as the string was pulled back. It is unlikely, however, that all the men in the huge Chinese armies were as well equipped as the Terracotta Army, especially as many of them were simply needed to labour, dig, fetch and carry.

The impression of a professional elite is reinforced by the fact that during the era of the 'Warring States' military professionals had replaced aristocrats as leaders of armies. The *Weiliaozi*, a military treatise of the early third century BC, stressed the directing role of the commander and scorned personal engagement in combat: 'To command the troops and direct their blades, this is the role of the commander. To wield a single sword is not his role.'[10] Adjacent to the main burial pit of the 'Terracotta Army' is a smaller one in which the figures seem to be senior officers conferring like the professional commanders of modern armies.

Moreover, cavalry were becoming very important, and by 300 BC chariots were clearly obsolescent, serving simply as command vehicles for the officers. During the 'Warring States' period the major powers took to employing nomads from the northern plains as mercenary horse soldiers. Interestingly, the cavalrymen in the Terracotta Army appear to have Mongoloid features – suggesting they were specialist horse-soldiers hired from the steppe. The Chinese employed them because they were fine horsemen willing to serve for money. The sophistication of Chinese cavalry developed quickly and by the second century BC some horsemen were wearing armour and using light crossbows cocked by a hook mounted on the warrior's belt.

To sustain these professionals and the huge masses of conscripts in their ambitious campaigns, an elaborate bureaucracy collected taxes ruthlessly. Shi Huangdi disliked the moral code of Confucius (551–479 BC) because it urged governmental moderation and respect for local elites which would have limited his ability to tax. His was a brutal regime and it is hardly surprising that it barely survived Shi Huangdi's death. In the turmoil which followed, a former bureaucrat, Liu Bang, triumphed at the battle of Gaixia in 203 BC and founded the Han Empire (203 BC–AD 220). The battle arose when Xian Yu of the rival Chu kingdom besieged Gaixia. The Chu army was poorly supplied and when Liu Bang mustered a relief force he used it to lure his tired and starving enemies into ambushes which eventually enabled him to kill Xian Yu. Under the Han dynasty Chinese civilisation assumed its classic form, but hardly differed from its predecessor in a military sense.

The Han inherited Shi Huangdi's army and his conflict with the steppe people which would dominate their whole existence. In the year 215 BC,

'The First Emperor then sent Meng T'ien with an army of three hundred thousand to the north to attack the Hu (nomads), and to invade and seize the land south of the Yellow River.'[11] This strike into the Ordos was backed up by Shi Huangdi's incorporation of earlier Chinese fortifications in this area into what later came to be called the Great Wall of China. This was a shattering blow to the Hsiung-nu, the leading tribe of the area. Nomads move on a seasonal pattern following good pasture, and rely heavily on pockets of arable land. The Ordos was part of the Northern Zone where the settled agriculture of the northern plains interpenetrates with steppe, offering opportunities for trade. Its loss weakened the Hsiung-nu in their struggles against the Chinese and their nomadic rivals. They survived because their aristocracy produced a leader of genius in the person of Modun, who was able to reconquer the Ordos in the chaos after Shi Huangdi's death in 210 BC and to dominate the steppe tribes from Manchuria to the Tarim basin.

The Han regarded this empire of the steppe with hostility, but in the great military expedition against Modun in 198 BC their army was totally destroyed. The nomads had strings of horses giving them great mobility, and stirrups enabled them to use the short and powerful composite bow to great effect. These were their long-standing fighting methods, but it was the unity which Modun created that made them so formidable. Steppe people lived in separate tribes spread over huge areas, but Modun brought them into a federation. Though they continued to be outnumbered by the Chinese their intense fighting skill enabled them to overcome the Han, who were driven to a policy of purchasing peace by recognising Modun as an equal ruling over 'All the people who draw the bow', providing him with a Chinese bride, and paying stiff annual tributes of silk, cloth, grain and other foodstuffs.

The conflict with the Hsiung-nu precipitated a debate in Han circles about whether to fight them or to accept coexistence, *ho-ch'in*, in the course of which all the difficulties of fighting steppe people were discussed:

> The configuration of terrain and the fighting ability of the Hsiung-nu differ from those of China. Going up and down mountain slopes, and crossing torrents and streams, the Hsiung-nu horses are better than the Chinese. On dangerous roads and sloping narrow passages they can both ride and shoot arrows; Chinese mounted soldiers cannot match that. They can withstand the wind and rain, hunger and thirst; Chinese soldiers are not as good. These are the qualities of the Hsiung-nu.

Attacking the nomads in the vast wastes of the steppe was futile, as another Chinese adviser suggested:

> If the Han have to strive over many thousands of *li* in order to gain an advantage, men and horses will be exhausted and the Bandits will completely control them. The circumstances will necessarily be perilous. I therefore maintain that this [attacking] would not be better than *ho-ch'in*.

On the other hand it was recognised that Chinese military forces had some advantages:

> However, on level terrain in the plains, using light chariots and swift cavalry, the Hsiung-nu rabble would easily be utterly defeated. Even with strong crossbows that shoot far, and long halberds that hit at a distance, the Hsiung-nu would not be able to ward them off. If the armours are sturdy and the weapons sharp, if the repetition crossbows shoot far and the platoons advance together, the Hsiung-nu will not be able to withstand. If specially trained troops are quick to release [their bows] and the arrows in a single stream hit the target together, then the leather outfit and wooden shields of the Hsiung-nu will not be able to protect them. If they dismount and fight on foot, when swords and halberds clash as [the soldiers] come to close quarters, the Hsiung-nu who lack infantry training, will not be able to cope. These are the advantages of China.[12]

In this debate about dealing with the Hsiung-nu we see the outlines of a classic confrontation between agro-urban and steppe warfare. The skill and mobility of the nomads make it difficult to engage them on favourable terms. Their lack of fixed bases gives them endless space into which to retreat, imposing grave logistical problems upon their attackers. They were not invulnerable, as the Chinese plainly understood, but, as so many peoples would discover, paying tribute was much easier than the alternative.

However, in the end the Han decided to destroy the Hsiung-nu. Tribute was a heavy burden for the Chinese economy and, perhaps worse, for the pride of the Han elite. Moreover, many of the steppe tribes continued to raid China and could not be restrained by the relatively weak Hsiung-nu state, which, nonetheless, protected them from Chinese retribution. This undermined one of the effects which the Chinese hoped for from *ho-ch'in*, that the nomad tribes would be drawn by peaceful contact into the embrace of superior Chinese civilisation. Moreover, the Hsiung-nu frequently gave support to rebels against the Han, so that their destruction became essential to the maintenance of the regime. After the death of Modun in 174 BC, nomad power weakened somewhat. The Emperor Wu-ti (141–87 BC) embarked on war but this necessitated a very expensive reform of the Chinese military. Cavalry were needed against the nomads, and so a network of horse-breeding stations was established. Some Chinese cavalrymen were drawn from the aristocracy and their dependants, but the best came from Central Asian tribes hostile to Hsiung-nu.

Offensive movement, largely the work of the cavalry, pushed forward the frontier against the Hsiung-nu, and fortifications were established in the newly won areas. These were held by the infantry. To consolidate such gains massive transfers of population into the new zones provided an economic base for the garrison and the logistical support for the offensive forces operating out of them. Conscripts were well equipped, particularly with crossbows, and received a year's training before mustering into units. The army was divided into two groups – the active troops, mainly cavalry, who ventured into the field to attack the enemy, and the garrison soldiers who built military roads and guarded the new walls and fortresses. The war launched in 133 BC was very expensive in both men and money. Penetrating the steppe produced logistical problems and appalling setbacks, like the destruction of an army of 30,000 cavalry in 99 BC. But Han pressure and diplomacy broke up the federation established by Modun and thus enabled the Chinese to pick off the separate tribes.

By 119 BC China was no longer paying tribute, had re-established control over the Ordos, and was threatening the Hsiung-nu with annihilation. The battle of Kang-chu in 36 BC indicates the effectiveness of the Han military reforms. Chih-Chih, who claimed to rule the Hsiung-nu, established himself in Sogdiana (modern Uzbekistan). Two Chinese expeditions, each 20,000 strong, moved north and south of the Takla Makan desert and cornered him in a fortified town. The Hsiung-nu cavalry were driven off by crossbow fire while the Han infantry attacked the town. When 10,000 Sogdian allies tried to raise the siege, they were defeated and Chih-Chih was killed. This was little more than a footnote to the long Hsiung-nu wars, but a Chinese intervention so far to the west, in an area once conquered by Alexander the Great, is a strong indication of military efficiency. However, this success was purchased at the expense of terrible strains on the body politic, in particular heavy taxation and the extension and exploitation of government monopolies like salt and iron. The result was serious division in government and shortly before 80 BC the setting up of a conference, the *Discourses on Salt and Iron*, in which reformers called for the end of conquest and a retreat by government from its domination of the economy.

The almost inevitable effect of this continuous warfare was that conscript armies were replaced by long-service forces devoted to their generals. In AD 184 these armies put down a widespread rebellion triggered by court corruption and natural disasters, but the victorious generals were independent-minded warlords at odds with the civilian court, so that by AD 189 the Han dynasty had perished and China was divided between competing kingdoms.

Nomadic peoples played a major role in the struggle which followed. There are no natural barriers between the steppe and the central plains, and Han expansion had brought the steppe tribes into the Chinese orbit. By AD 440 the steppe Toba had created a powerful state in north China and Mongolia, but they were rapidly assimilated into Chinese civilisation as the Wei dynasty. This interplay of the military power of the nomad peoples with the political strength of the educated Chinese elite who controlled the peasant masses was one of the key processes which shaped Chinese history. In the wake of the Han collapse it was largely played out in the northern plains where military development focused on cavalry.

By the fourth century AD the stirrup had become widely known, giving riders a better seat, and they wore more armour. Heavy cavalry began to charge home against enemies. At the battle of Yeh in AD 528 the nomadic Ehrchu launched a mass charge of 7,000 horse which broke through their enemies and slaughtered them. Cavalry could not easily operate in the south where there were great swathes of forest, while its agriculture was dominated by paddy fields and their accompanying water channels which were formidable barriers to horses. The peculiarity of its warfare was the use of fleets on the great rivers, especially the Yangtze. In AD 588 the Sui dynasty, having smashed their northern rivals, created a huge fleet including five-decked ships each capable of carrying 800 troops, to enable their gigantic army, a half-million strong, to cross the Yangtze and conquer the south. The human price of these wars which went on until the late sixth century AD was horrific. The Han census of AD 157 listed 10,677,960 households and 56,486,856 individuals, but under the Jin, who briefly dominated China (AD 265–316) before being confined to the south, this fell to 2,459,840 households and 16,163,863 individuals. War, plague and famine killed many, others fled from the central plains to the emptier south, while many of those who remained ceased to pay taxes by seeking the protection of local aristocrats.

But perhaps the greatest of all standing armies was that of Rome. It emerged in the sixth century BC as a citizen army, the levy (*legio*) 3,000–4,000 strong, bickering with the other small cities in Latium, the area south of the Tiber. The free male population fought in the infantry phalanx while lightly armed poorer men guarded the flanks and the small social elite provided about 600 cavalry. By 396 BC Rome was supreme in Latium, enabling her to raise troops from the defeated cities, and thus to exert influence over the declining Etruscan kingdom to the north. But the decay of Etruscan power opened the way for attack from the north by the Celts of Gaul who were seeking new land. On 18 July 387 BC they destroyed a Roman army on the river Allia:

> The main body of the army, at the first sound of the Gallic war-cry on their flank and in their rear, hardly waited even to see their strange enemy from the ends of the earth; they made no attempt at resistance; they had not even courage to answer his shouted challenge, but fled before they had lost a single man.[13]

The Celts attacked the lighter-armed forces on the flanks of the Roman phalanx which they then surrounded and massacred. They went on to sack Rome. All this prompted the Romans to a major rethink of their military methods, starting with a proper fortification of their city. The Roman legion of 5,000–6,000, was subdivided into maniples, each consisting of two 'centuries' of eighty men. The legion then formed for battle in three lines, in each of which there were ten maniples, aligned so that the maniples in the second line faced the gaps between the units in the front line, and those in the third likewise. In defence and attack this checkerboard pattern enabled the troops to react flexibly to enemy weaknesses. They were equipped for an aggressive style of battle, with javelins to weaken enemy formations, and spears and swords for close-quarter action. Only Roman citizens were permitted to join the heavy infantry of the legions, two of which usually made up an army. In battle their small cavalry units of 300 each, along with the auxiliary forces of allies and tributaries, and occasionally mercenaries, guarded the flanks (*alae*).

Rome suffered many setbacks in her effort to dominate the lands around her. In 321 BC a Roman army was lured into a waterless and barren canyon by the Samnites of southern Italy and forced to surrender. But the drive to empire in the city was strong because this enormously profited its ruling aristocracy and enabled them to buy off social tension by distributing some of the profits of conquest to the poor. Moreover, whatever defeats they suffered, they could tap substantial manpower in Latium and Tuscany which they dominated. In the absence of a strong enemy in Italy the determination of the Roman aristocracy to conquer made Rome a major power in the western basin of the Mediterranean by the mid-third century, when Carthage viewed her as a rival.

Sicily, with its vital position in the western Mediterranean, was the bone of contention between Rome and Carthage in the First Punic War (264–241 BC). In this war with Carthage, sea-power was vital. The Romans had no tradition of naval warfare, but determinedly built a strong fleet. Outmanoeuvred by superior Carthaginian seamanship, they equipped their ships with the *corvus* (literally a raven), a gangway which was suspended from the mast and dropped onto the deck of the enemy ship where it secured itself by an iron spike. This enabled the Romans to fight a land battle at sea. Ultimately they seized Sicily by the treaty which ended the war in 241 BC. This sheer persistence was even more evident in the Second Punic War (218–201 BC), the star of which was the Carthaginian general, Hannibal.

After the defeat in 241 BC Hannibal's father, Hamilcar, and brother-in-law, Hasdrubal, set out to improve the Carthaginian position in Spain where their challenge to Roman intervention eventually precipitated the Second Punic War. Hannibal cultivated the Celts of southern Gaul who resented Roman power in north Italy, traversed their lands with an army of 40,000 including some elephants, crossed the Alps and defeated a much smaller Roman force under Publius Scipio at Ticino in November 218. Scipio's army remained intact and was promptly reinforced by another under Tiberius Sempronius. But the two Roman commanders, each by now having about 20,000 men, failed to cooperate and at Trebia in December 218 Tiberius was drawn into attacking across a river and suffered heavy casualties, mostly amongst his lighter troops because his core legions showed remarkable discipline and got away in good order. On 24 June 217 BC the new Roman commander, Flaminius, failed to make junction with other Roman forces and his army of 30,000 men was ambushed and destroyed in the narrow passage between the mountains and the shore of Lake Trasimene.

The new Roman commander, Fabius Maximus, responded to the Roman losses by avoiding battle, but staying close enough to the enemy army to prevent it achieving anything, though Hannibal moved into Apulia where his army lived on its riches. The Romans then became impatient, and in 216 BC dispatched a huge army of sixteen legions (75,000 men) charged with destroying Hannibal. At Cannae on 2 August Hannibal with 56,000 confronted the Romans. They massed almost all their infantry into a single gigantic phalanx, guarding its flanks with cavalry, but when this great mass charged into the Carthaginian centre and had all but overwhelmed the stubborn Carthaginian foot, the Carthaginian cavalry, having put the Roman horse to flight, surrounded them on both sides in a 'double envelopment' and slaughtered them.

These defeats revealed something of the military weaknesses of Rome. Their cavalry were neither numerous nor very good and Hannibal exploited his strength in this arm, using cavalry to provoke the Romans at Trebia and to destroy them at Cannae. The aggression and rivalries of the Roman elite played into Hannibal's hands, while their impatience with cautious tactical dispositions led to Cannae. But Rome raised new armies and fought on, reverting to the tactics of Fabius Maximus by avoiding open battle with Hannibal and picking off his allies in Spain and Gaul and the few Italian cities which went over to him. By 203 BC Hannibal was isolated, and fled to Africa where he was defeated by an invading Roman army under Scipio Africanus, forcing Carthage to sue for peace. Rome found a pretext to attack Carthage in the Third Punic War (149–146 BC), when, in an act of calculated brutality, the city was destroyed and its 50,000 inhabitants sold into slavery. Sheer determination and a readiness to accept losses underpinned the Roman victory in what turned out to be a war of attrition. Hannibal was a great general who made skilful use of his assets, though his famous elephants did him little good, but his diplomatic skill and military ability were trumped by the doggedness of the Romans.

In 198 BC, angered by his support for Hannibal, the Romans invaded the lands of Philip V of Macedon (221–179 BC), bringing the Roman legion into confrontation with the Macedonian phalanx, then the dominant military formation in the Mediterranean world. At Cynoscephalae the Roman general Flaminius, commanding two legions, advanced northwards up the pass leading to Larissa. His left-hand legion directly confronted Philip's phalanx and was driven back, but his right-hand legion, supported by some elephants, drove into the other half of the Macedonian army which was caught by surprise. Thus the confrontation had resolved itself into two separated battles. A Roman officer in the successful right-hand legion, recognising that the remainder of the army was in danger, detached twenty maniples which charged into the rear of the successful Macedonians cutting them to pieces.

At Pydna in 168 BC the Roman army under Aemilius Paulus again faced the Macedonians, whose initial advance was successful, as Paulus later admitted: 'when he saw the strength of the locked-shield formation and the harshness of the attack, astonishment and terror seized him, because he had never seen a sight more fearful'.[14] But as it advanced, the mass of the phalanx began to break up in the face of uneven resistance and rough ground. The Roman units were able to push into these gaps and were well equipped with swords to fight at very close quarters, where the *sarissa* was quite useless. At both Cynoscephalae and Pydna the legion demonstrated in different ways its flexibility – the quality which the Macedonian phalanx lacked.

By about 100 BC Rome was ruling Italy, parts of southern France and Spain and much of North Africa and Anatolia. The scale and intensity of warfare, often fought in distant places, meant that, as in the Macedonian Empire and China, professional soldiers were needed; the traditional short-service levy simply could not provide the hardened expertise which comes from continuity of service. Under the consul Marius (157–86 BC) the Roman army emerged as a standing regular force built around permanent legions. Tactical deployment was facilitated by the division of the legion into ten cohorts of 480 men each, replacing the old subdivision into maniples of 120. Battle formations continued to favour the triple line, although other dispositions were used according to need and this was easier with only ten sub-commanders to instruct. Equipment changed little. Rectangular plywood shields replaced the traditional oval, while mail gave way to segmented strips of iron bound together with bronze and articulated on a heavy leather base which probably gave better protection from heavy blows. Marius insisted that each man carry his own gear, cooking pots, etc., which is why legionaries were called 'Marius's mules'.

In battle the legions formed the centre of the line, flanked by cavalry and light troops called auxiliaries who included groups like North Africans who were valued for their special skill as slingers. Often they were employed close to their areas of origin, and though sometimes led by their own chiefs, were also officered by Romans because of the risks of defection. Cavalry were formed into *alae*, literally wings, from their usual position in the battle line. They were often recruited from peoples from beyond the borders of the empire. Caesar used German horse-soldiers against the Gauls, and later Sarmatians and Goths were brought in from the steppe lands beyond the Danube. They wielded their traditional weapons, the longsword and the composite bow. Rome had a rigorous system of training for the legions but this focused on discipline, athletics and organisation. It would have been difficult and expensive to teach all the forms of expertise which might be needed in war, so the army was happy to take advantage of the native skills of all kinds of people, even barbarians and especially those from the steppe who provided excellent horse-soldiers.

The rise of the regular legions meant that the army could retain and foster engineering capacity. Soldiers in hostile territory built earthwork camps whose remains stud the landscape of Europe and the Middle East to this day. Many were very elaborate if they were used over time as bases, and some even developed into cities. All over the empire huge engineering projects were undertaken. In 55 BC Julius Caesar wanted to impress the Germans with Roman power, and he chose to do so by constructing a mighty bridge across the Rhine. At Seleucia, the port of Antioch, a tunnel a mile long was driven through living rock to prevent flooding. An inscription records the work of legions IIII Scythica and XVI Flavia Firma. Major fortifications, like Hadrian's Wall and the Porta Negra at Trier, stand as monuments to the skill of the legions, as do the great roads and canals built to carry supplies and men. Engineering was vital in siege warfare at which the Romans excelled.

The culmination of the great Jewish revolt against Roman rule (AD 66–70) was the siege of Jerusalem conducted by Titus, son of the emperor Vespasian (AD 69–79). He fortified the camps around the city and created a great earthwork ramp up which rams were dragged under the protection of siege-towers and heavy catapults whose fire swept the ramparts. The Greeks had invented catapults, but the Romans built and deployed them on a large scale, improving their efficiency in the process. On occasion light catapults known as *ballistae* were used in the field, mounted on carts. Interestingly the Chinese and the Indians, who also created huge professional infantry armies, developed these same skills. Chinese engineers built roads, canals, fortifications and other works on the scale of anything done in the west, while their massive deployment of crossbowmen was an impressive phenomenon. The famous Indian *Arthashastra* urged that infantry should take up close formations, and demanded that they construct camps amazingly like those of which the legions have left such numerous traces.

The long-service paid soldiers who now filled the ranks of the Roman army identified with the unit which formed the framework of their life. The continuous existence of the legions created cohesion and efficiency. The key officers were the centurions whose tombstones proclaim pride in their profession:

To Tiberius Claudius Vitalis, son of Tiberius, of the tribe Galeria, from the rank of Roman *eques* he received the post of centurion in *Legio V Macedonica*, was advanced from *Legio V Macedonica* to *Legio I Italica*, was decorated in the Dacian War with Necklaces, Armbands, Ornaments and a Rampart crown, was advanced from *Legio I Italica* to *Legio I Minervia*, was again decorated in the Dacian War with Necklaces, Armbands, Ornaments and a Rampart crown, was advanced from *Legio I Minervia* to *Legio XX Victrix*, was also advanced within the same legion, was again advanced from *Legio XX Victrix* to *Legio IX Hispana*, was advanced from *Legio IX Hispana* to *Legio VII Claudia*, Loyal and Faithful, was also advanced within the same legion, served in the second cohort as *princeps posterior* for eleven years, lived forty-one years.[15]

Such men formed the backbone of the army, and could be relied upon to marshal their troops and understand the pattern of orders. At a higher level, generals may have lacked formal training, but by working within the military machine they developed tactical skill, and some at least, like the Chinese generals noted in the third-century *Weiliaozi*, cultivated a cerebral professional approach: 'When some said that Scipio Africanus (BC 235–183) had too little aggression, he is reported to have replied, "my mother bore me to be a general, not a fighter." '[16] But in the close-quarter fight inspiration still counted for much. At the siege of Alesia Vercingetorix, the Gallic leader, tried to break through the Roman lines, forcing Caesar to rush to the threatened sector to rally his men: 'Caesar first sent some cohorts to the rescue under young Brutus, then others under the general Gaius Fabius; finally, as the struggle grew fiercer he led up a fresh detachment in person and succeeded in repulsing the attack.'[17]

The Roman legion has gone down in history for its supreme sense of discipline and fighting power. Neither should be exaggerated. After his defeat at Gergovia by the Gauls, Julius Caesar complained bitterly that his troops 'had decided for themselves where to go and what to do; they had not stopped when the recall was sounded nor could they be restrained by the military tribunes and legates'.[18]

In AD 357 the Roman commander Julian (later emperor AD 361–3), with only 13,000 men, was reluctant to engage an invading German army of 35,000 near Strasbourg. However,

The soldiers did not allow him to finish what he was saying, but gnashed their teeth and showed their eagerness for battle by striking their spears and shields together, and besought him that they might be led against an enemy already in sight, trusting in the favour of God in heaven, in their own self-confidence, and in the tried valour of their lucky general.

So battle was joined. But the enthusiasm did not last and when the Roman cavalry guarding his right flank broke under sudden attack by massed German infantry, Julian had to rally them: 'Whither are we fleeing, my most valiant men? Do you not know that flight never leads to safety but shows the folly of a useless effort?'[19] Julian's chronicler likens his hero to Sulla rallying his men in battle in Asia Minor. He could just as easily have cited Vespasian forcing panicked men into a battle line during street fighting in Gamala during the Jewish revolt in Galilee in AD 67 or many another scene of retreat and confusion. Legionaries and auxiliaries, for all the celebrated Roman discipline, were men not machines. And irregular warfare, if it enjoyed widespread support, taxed them severely. The revolt in Judaea of Simon bar-Kokhba in AD 132–5 led to the elimination of *Legio XXII Deiotiana* in a protracted conflict which cost the lives of 580,000 Jews and brought about the destruction of fifty cities and 985 villages.

If the fighting power of the regular Roman army was impressive, the institution had some considerable drawbacks. Soldiers had a sense of loyalty to their units which transcended that to the Roman state. This was accentuated by the fact that legions and auxiliaries were spread out in substantial groups along distant frontiers, often spending long periods in one place. *Legio XX Valeria Victrix*, for instance, was at Chester from AD 88 until the early fourth century. Loyalty, therefore, focused on the generals whose successes earned plunder and generous handouts for the soldiers. And a general who rose to power in the state was in a splendid position to reward his men. Because of this the soldiers became king-makers, backing rival commanders in the civil wars which undermined the Roman Republic and ultimately enabled Augustus (63 BC–AD 14) to create the empire. His reign ushered in a period of relative stability, but the empire had no accepted rule of succession and when this was disputed there was an obvious temptation for military men at the head of the great armies on the frontiers to intervene.

This was not merely a Roman phenomenon. In China the generals on the outer frontiers became independent warlords and were able to over-throw the Han dynasty. In 193 the Emperor Commodus (180–93) was assassinated. The commanders of the armies of Pannonia (the Danube), Syria and Britain then fought for the throne, leading to the triumph of Septimius Severus (193–211) and the Pannonian legions. This set the precedent for a series of generals who aspired to imperial power, producing civil wars which almost destroyed the Empire in the third century. The rise of regular military forces, each with its own ethos and professional way of doing things, was an obvious threat to authority in all states. It was in an attempt to prevent such usurpations that in both China and Rome civil and military power in the provinces were separated. The cycle of military emperors in third-century Rome was only halted in the reign of Diocletian (AD 284–305), who began a new wave of reforms made necessary by changing military conditions.

Once the Roman Empire ceased to expand, it faced the expensive and labour-intensive business of defending long and troubled frontiers. In Britain, Hadrian's Wall had to be garrisoned, while in Europe the Rhine and Danube rivers formed a long northern frontier beyond which numerous tribes tended to coalesce into major units. The Euphrates, where Rome faced Persia, demanded a massive concentration of forces and fortifications. No major enemy threatened the immensely long North African border, but it had to be patrolled against robbers and troublesome tribes. In consequence the army grew. Augustus (27 BC–AD 14) had maintained twenty-five legions, but by AD 193 when Septimius Severus took the throne there were thirty-three in a total force of over 250,000. Thereafter the demands of frontier defence were augmented by the tendency of usurpers to create new legions, so that when Diocletian ruled there were sixty-seven legions in an army of about half a million. During this period the distinction between legions and auxiliaries had broken down as military conditions changed. The legion was originally designed to fight the mass infantry armies of the Mediterranean powers (or other legions in the frequent civil wars). But as expansion ceased, the task of the army changed into fighting often small groups of barbarians along the frontiers. As a result, by the fourth century AD legions seem often to have numbered no more than about 1,000 and to have been little different from other troops. In such warfare speed was very useful. As a result infantry shed their heavy segmented armour in favour of mail, while cavalry numbers increased.

This huge army imposed enormous burdens upon the Roman state. It consumed two-thirds of total imperial revenues. Rations, wages, barracks and fortifications were all costly as were the state factories which produced standardised armour and weapons. The infrastructure of roads was primarily designed to support the military. The large fleet which dominated the Mediterranean was expensive. Once imperial expansion with all its attendant profits had ceased, all this expense had to be supported by taxes, and these largely fell upon the land, which produced twenty times the income from trade and industry.

The army demanded men as well as money, and it proved difficult to fill the ranks. Landowners and local communities were obliged either to pay substantial taxes or to provide recruits for the levy, and service was deeply unpopular. At the start of the fourth century St Pachomius, a young Egyptian, was 'dragged away' into the army and locked up in Thebes where the contrast between official brutality and the care offered by local Christians made him resolve to join their sect. In 313 the emperor Constantine (AD 312–37) believed that sons of veterans, for whom military service was compulsory, were prepared to go to extreme lengths to avoid the draft: 'Of veterans' sons who are fit for military service, some indolently refuse to perform compulsory military duties and others are so cowardly that they wish to evade the necessity of military service by mutilation of their own bodies.'[20] Usually this would involve cutting off the thumb. In a year of emergency, AD 381, the emperor Theodosius (379–95) was prepared to accept such men, but only on the basis of two mutilated in lieu of one whole. The reluctance of Romans to serve is not unnatural. The military life was harsh, while the Empire preferred its peoples to be unarmed and, therefore, docile, and much legislation pointed in that direction.

This was why the army increasingly recruited from 'barbarian' tribes who lived outside the frontiers. When Constantine triumphantly entered Rome as emperor in 312, most of his army was said to be German. Service in the imperial army had obvious attractions for such people: Roman citizenship, regular pay and a career path. Roman commanders were traditionally drawn from the Roman aristocracy and gentry. However, important aristocrats could threaten the throne, and as the army became more professional, specialised commanders were needed at all levels. In effect, the military career became open to the talents by the fourth century, and even barbarians could ascend to the highest ranks. Arbogast was a Frankish general and, under the young Valentinian II (AD 375–92), virtually ruled the Western Roman Empire. Stilicho, the son of a Vandal, married into the family of Theodosius and became guardian of the infant Western Emperor Honorius (AD 384–423).

Barbarians could be recruited as individuals, but sometimes whole units were formed from a particular tribe, and settled within the empire in communities whose inhabitants were obliged to provide hereditary military service. Marcus Aurelius (AD 161–80) planted a community of Sarmatians at Ribchester in Britain. The Teiphali, a Gothic tribe settled on the Loire between Angers and Nantes as cavalrymen, gave their name to the modern town of Tiffauges in the Vendée. Tribal groups like these served under Roman officers and became very well integrated into the Roman world.

But the rise of Sassanid Persia (AD 224–651) vastly added to the military pressure on the Roman state. In 53 BC the Roman leader Marcus Crassus had attacked Persia, which was ruled by a people of steppe origin, the Parthians (247 BC–AD 241), under their Arsacid kings. His army was destroyed by the Parthians near Carrhae (modern Harran in Turkey). The Parthians were originally steppe light cavalry, but once settled in Persia they created from their aristocracy a corps of heavy cavalry, the *cataphracts* whose very horses were armoured. The Romans nicknamed these iron-clad soldiers *clibanarii* (literally boiler-boys) and later imitated them. At Carrhae the Persian cavalry surrounded the Romans who were unable to devise a means of defence against the *cataphract* tactic of charging home, supported by showers of arrows from their light horse. The result was a crushing Roman defeat, though 10,000 survivors subsequently defended Syria very efficiently against Parthian incursions. In itself Carrhae was a single defeat but what is striking is that Rome was never able to conquer Arsacid Persia, despite the fact that it was a relatively weak state.

Under the Sassanid dynasty, however, Persia became far stronger. The extraordinarily able Shapur I (241–72) conquered and plundered Antioch in Syria in 253 and defeated the Roman emperors Gordian III (238–44) and Philip the Arab (244–9). After battle near Edessa in 259 Shapur captured the emperor Valerian (253–60) and celebrated this victory in a rock relief depicting the captive emperor kneeling before him. All descriptions of the Persian army emphasise the role of heavy cavalry, the *clibanarii*, but actually the army was well balanced, as the Roman writer, Ammianus Marcellinus, recorded when the emperor Julian confronted them in AD 363:

> The Persians opposed to us serried bands of mail-clad horsemen in such close order that the gleam of moving bodies covered with closely fitting plates of iron dazzled the eyes of those who looked upon them, while the whole throng of horses was protected by coverings of leather. The cavalry was backed up by companies of infantry, who, protected by oblong, curved shields covered with wickerwork and raw hides, advanced in very close order. Behind these were elephants, looking like walking hills.[21]

The core of this infantry were the archers whose remarkable rate of fire helped to break up enemy formations. In addition, under Shapur I modern siege equipment on the Roman model was developed, enabling the Sassanids to capture and hold fortified cities. In many ways Sassanid Persia resembled Rome, Han China and Mauryan India. A strong bureaucracy based in great cities closely linked to the priesthood of the Zoroastrian religion controlled the government for the 'King of Kings' (*Shahansha*). Adroit administration fostered economic development in the cities which underpinned military power. But the great military advantage the Persians held over Rome was their numerous and efficient cavalry.

The challenge of Sassanid Persia made the Roman army even more costly because it forced the creation of a much bigger cavalry component. Rome, like China, employed barbarian horsemen like the Sarmatians, but even they had to be paid, trained and equipped. All armies relied on 'native skills' so that converting Romans into cavalrymen was a difficult and extravagant process, not least because stud farms and stable complexes had to be built and provision made for the acquisition of enormous quantities of fodder. This was recalibration on an immense scale, but Persian success in the third century made it urgent. A cavalryman costs twice as much as an infantry soldier, but the *cataphracts* with their heavy armour and specially bred large horses must have been even more expensive. By the fourth century about a third of the Roman army was made up of cavalry. Trained heavy infantry remained the backbone of the army, but increasingly cavalry took the offensive while the foot stood on the defensive. To fight off enemy cavalry the Romans increased the proportion of missile weapons in their ranks.

These vast additional military expenses could only be met by immense structural changes within the empire. Under Diocletian a huge central bureaucracy was created to collect and control increased taxation. Government now tried to fix prices and tied peasants to the soil and others to their professions. This takeover of the economy by the state parallels the phenomenon revealed in *Discourses on Salt and Iron* in the Han Empire, which was also stimulated by the needs of war. As in Han China, the size of provinces was reduced, and, to prevent usurpations, civil authority and military authority were very strictly divided within them. The empire in this way was transformed into a centralised military dictatorship. This intensified factional struggles at court because power and responsibility in the provinces were no longer worth fighting for. As in Han China, the person of the emperor was now surrounded by an elaborate court and ritual and housed in mighty palaces. In the fourth century it became usual for there to be two emperors, one for the east at Constantinople (modern Istanbul), which Constantine the Great (AD 312–37) had made his capital, and one for the west (usually Milan), though the unity of the whole was still officially maintained. In the long run, as we shall see, this was to have a malign influence on events.

The Roman military structure was radically altered under Constantine the Great. The army was divided between frontier troops, the *limitanei* who dealt with small border attacks and acted as a tripwire for major threats, which were to be met by the field armies or *comitatenses*. The Han developed a parallel division between active troops and garrison forces. In part this was a solution to the great problem of the third century: usurpations backed by legions long settled in frontier areas. The *comitatenses* were under the eye of the central authorities in cities which were linked to the frontiers by roads and ports, facilitating rapid movement, especially as each major section of the empire came to have its own field army. Overall this subdividing of the army, combined with new fortifications, was an effective form of defence in depth. Its smaller units, of either 500 or 1,000, often of specialists like engineers or crossbowmen (*arcubalistaria*), provided flexible building blocks for the creation of substantial forces. The whole expensive structure could be afforded, though with some difficulty, and, in moments of defeat, it must have seemed burdensome. After the city of Amida was destroyed by the Persians in AD 359, Ursulus, the state treasurer complained bitterly: 'Behold with what courage the cities are defended by our soldiers, for whose abundance of pay the wealth of the empire is already becoming insufficient.'[22]

The Roman army of the fourth century was well organised and structured for the obvious tasks it faced, but ultimately it failed to preserve the state as a whole. This is doubly surprising because the eastern part of the empire ruled from Constantinople, which alone faced a strong rival in the form of Persia, survived, while the western was replaced by a series of really quite minor tribes. What happened to this mighty army? The answer is a conjunction of events, none of which in itself threatened the existence of the state. The barbarians on the frontiers became more formidable at the very moment when military misfortunes and internal strife racked the empire. In dealing with these, judgements were made which ultimately proved catastrophic.

The pattern was established under Constantius II (337–61), the successor of Constantine the Great. Constantius at first ruled the east from Constantinople while his two brothers took Africa and Europe. But tensions and intrigues exploded in the west, his brothers were killed and

Constantius faced a series of rebellions, the most dangerous of which was that of Magnentius who was crushed at the battle of Marsa Major (Osijek in Croatia) on 28 September 351. But there were in all nearly 60,000 Roman casualties.

The consequences of such infighting were very clear: the barbarians of Germany invaded Gaul. Constantius appointed his cousin Julian as Caesar and charged him with clearing them out. At the battle of Strasbourg in AD 357 Julian, with only 13,000 troops, defeated King Chlodomar and 35,000 Alamanni. Such a formidable barbarian federation had arisen partly from contact with and imitation of Roman political institutions and partly from the Roman habit of buying allies and encouraging them to build up strong kingdoms beyond the frontier. A chronicler records that in AD 358 Constantius ended a campaign on the Danube by appointing a king to rule over the Sarmatians: 'a man even then surely suited for the honours of a conspicuous fortune and (as the results showed), loyal'.[23] But not all were as faithful. And even more dangerously, the barbarian army at Strasbourg organised itself and fought well – it is more than likely that many in its ranks had fought for Rome in the past. It was in the end defeated, though not before it had routed Julian's cavalry. Nor was this an isolated event. In AD 355 a strong German army had sacked the great Roman city of Cologne on the Rhine, though barbarians were not usually good at siege warfare. When, in AD 360, Julian as emperor (360–3) tried to destroy Persia, he could raise no more than 60,000 men, because he had to leave substantial forces along the frontiers to prevent incursions. As a result, his army proved inadequate for the chosen task and Julian perished in the attempt along with some of his finest troops.

But the most decisive disaster was the battle of Adrianople in AD 378. In 376 some Gothic chieftains, fearful of the rise of the Huns in Eurasia, asked to be allowed to cross the Danube into Roman territory. This kind of immigration had often been permitted, but the newcomers were always dispersed to settlements across the empire, rendering military service and improving tax yields. This was why the eastern Emperor Valens (364–78) was advised to agree to the request:

> which unexpectedly brought him so many young recruits from the ends of the earth that by the union of his own and foreign forces he would have an invincible army; also that instead of the levy of soldiers which was contributed annually by each province, there would accrue to the treasuries a vast amount of gold.[24]

The problem was that the Goths were very numerous. Once across the Danube, the machinery of government proved inadequate to cope with them, particularly as corrupt local Roman officials tried to exploit the Goths. As a result, they began to ravage the countryside.

However, the Goths lacked siege equipment, and the local general, Sebastianus, was confident that he could harry them into submission. But the random factor of the personality of Valens interacted with the tensions always present at the imperial court. Valens regarded the Goths as an affront to his prestige. He was suspicious of Sebastianus and envious of his cousin Gratian, Emperor in the West (AD 375–83), who had enjoyed victories over the peoples of western Germany. He therefore gathered an army 15,000 strong at Adrianople and summoned help from Gratian. Despite receiving news that Gratian was close by, Valens decided not to wait for him and to give battle. On 9 August 378 he marched his troops for some seven hours up to the Gothic camp. There were negotiations, but officers eager to attract imperial approval appear to have begun fighting and dragged the whole army into an engagement without realising that much of the Gothic army, especially its cavalry, were absent from the camp. As the Romans, in confusion, attacked the camp, these returned, took them in the rear and slaughtered them – the body of Valens was never recovered. The new eastern emperor Theodosius I (AD 379–95) was unable to defeat the Goths and agreed to their settlement in the Balkans as 'allies' (*foederati*) by treaty in AD 382. Nominally this was what they had asked for in 376, but of course they had not dispersed and had conquered much of the Balkans whose revenues were thus lost to the empire. Undoubtedly Theodosius was driven to this treaty by the loss of skilled soldiers at Adrianople and the need to retain considerable forces on the Persian frontier.

Theodosius I was the last ruler of a single united Roman Empire, but he only defeated rivals in the west at the cost of appalling casualties, notably at the battle of the Frigidus, 5–6 September 394 where losses seem to have been comparable to those at Marsa Major. He was succeeded in AD 395 by his very young children: in the east Arcadius (395–408), in the west Honorius (395–423) whose guardian, Stilicho, was the real power. The big problem was that the Goths were established in the Balkans between Italy and Constantinople. Stilicho quickly showed that he was capable of defeating them, but the court of Constantinople did not want to see his power expand into what they saw as their part of the empire, and prevented a decisive victory, perpetuating Gothic power in the Balkans. Although the empire was in theory still a unity, in practice the two courts of Rome and Constantinople were developing different interests. These conflicts drew much of the western Roman army into Italy, weakening the Rhine frontier where, in the bitter winter of AD 406, the river froze, enabling the Burgundians, Alans, Suevi and Vandals to cross into Roman territory and opening the way for others to traverse the Danube and to settle there.

Barbarians had broken into the Western Empire before. But now the emperors could dispatch few troops to the provinces because they were preoccupied by events in Italy and the Balkans. Moreover, the barbarians were better organised and equipped, and correspondingly more difficult to evict. Constant fighting pressed hard upon civilian populations who were targeted by both sides, provoking rebellions by the Bagaudae, the suffering peasants who sometimes allied with the invaders in an attempt to free themselves from exploitation by the Roman state. Pressure on the frontiers demanded increased military expenditure, but the devastation simultaneously reduced the ability of large areas to pay taxes.

Under this kind of pressure the Western Roman Empire began to disintegrate. In AD 410 the emperor Honorius abandoned Britain, 'sending letters to the cities in Britain ordering them to guard themselves'.[25] In the same year the Goths of the Balkans sacked Rome. The gatherings of tribes who had crossed the Rhine in AD 406 began to establish kingdoms which were only nominally subordinate to Rome. The Burgundians set themselves up in south-east Gaul. The Suevi and Vandals settled in Spain in 409, nominally as federates, but in practice as an autonomous kingdom like the Goths in the Balkans. The emperor Honorius persuaded some of the Balkan Goths to settle in Aquitaine (south-west France) to attack the Vandals, supporting them with grain from North Africa until they were established. In response to this pressure, the Vandals under King Gaiseric (428–77) conquered the province of Africa which had long been the breadbasket of the empire, dramatically impoverishing the imperial government. The Visigothic kingdom of Aquitaine then expanded into Spain.

In effect the Western Empire was being reduced to Italy and a few outposts, presiding uneasily over a network of barbarian federates whose forces would sometimes be put at the disposal of Rome, but only when it suited their leaders. In these circumstances the resources to train and equip new levies of soldiers were limited. The bitter civil wars of the late fourth century had eroded the Roman army and the rapid and sudden loss of territory and, therefore, tax resources, meant that it was impossible to train and replace troops in the traditional way. In the early fifth century

Vegetius wrote a tract on the improvement of the Roman military which testifies to the decay of the Roman army. He said little about the cavalry, which he thought satisfactory 'Thanks to the example of the Goths and the Alans and Huns',[26] but argued that infantry discipline had decayed to the point where soldiers threw away their heavy armour. The quick fix was to recruit even more barbarian bands, but their loyalty was provisional, to say the least. Even this was expensive, and unpaid barbarians were likely to defect. At this stage in the early fifth century a new and major threat appeared from the steppe.

Attila was born into the ruling family of the Hun Empire whose sway he extended by AD 434 over the entire western steppe from the Dneiper to the North Sea. His brilliant cavalrymen raided so ferociously that Attila was recognised as an equal by the emperors of east and west from both of whom he extracted huge sums in tribute. Enlisting his services enabled the Roman emperors to cow other barbarians within and without the empire. Because of the weakness of its army, Rome was reduced to playing off its enemies in a precarious balancing act in which Attila sometimes figured as an ally and sometimes as an enemy. In 451 an alliance between Rome and the Goths of Aquitaine and others defeated Attila at Châlons in Gaul, but this was the swansong of the army of the Western Roman Empire which formed only a fraction of the victorious force. Attila threatened Rome in 452, extorting tribute, but his death in 453 destroyed the unity of the Huns. This removed a dangerous threat, but also a useful element of equilibrium in the diplomatic game. Thereafter the few outposts of Roman military power in the west were simply swallowed up by the barbarians.

The western Roman army vanished with a whimper rather than a bang. Its epitaph is recorded in the life of St Severinus (AD c.410–82), a holy man who lived in Roman Noricum (roughly modern Bavaria and Austria) in the fifth century. His friend and biographer Eugippius, who was writing about AD 500, recorded that at Passau there were some Roman troops, but he had to explain to his audience what they were and something about them: 'Throughout the time that the Roman Empire existed, the soldiery of many towns were maintained at public expense for the defence of the frontier. When this practice fell into abeyance, both these troops and the frontier disappeared.' This imperial remnant, probably in the 470s, sent some of their number to Italy for their pay but they 'were killed during the journey by barbarians'.[27]

The Eastern Empire was richer and easier to defend. Syria and Egypt were insulated from major enemies by deserts, except in the north where the cream of the army, supported by a network of fortifications, was concentrated against Persia. Constantinople on its peninsula was guarded by a double wall running some 5.6 kilometres from the Sea of Marmara to the Golden Horn, built in AD 413–14 by Theodosius II (408–50). The inner wall was 5m thick and 12m high with 96 towers rising to 18–20m, while the outer was 20m away, 2m thick and 9m high, topped by 96 towers set between those of the inner wall. The towers projected from the wall at 50m intervals, enabling their garrisons to enfilade any attack with missiles. In front of this mass of masonry was a deep moat which could be flooded in time of attack. Some 65 kilometres westward the Anastasian wall, built in the later fifth century, formed the outer edge of a fortified zone defending the city. None of the barbarian peoples had the sea-power necessary to circumvent the city which, therefore, effectively closed off Asia from Europe. In general the two parts of the empire drifted apart, and in 476 Odovacar, imperial commander in Italy, deposed the last western emperor, Romulus Augustulus, and was recognised by Constantinople as king of Italy.

East Rome preserved the Greek civilisation that had been dominant in the eastern Mediterranean since the time of Alexander. Its buoyant economy underpinned military muscle which, in the sixth century, led to the reconquest, albeit temporary, of Vandal North Africa, parts of Spain and most of Italy. By contrast, living standards in Western Europe sank dramatically and literate culture became confined to the high aristocracy and the clergy. This was the result of the particular way in which the empire collapsed.

The invaders came not to destroy, but to enjoy the wealth of the empire, just like the nomads who fought their way into the Han Empire. But the eastern nomads, like the Toba, became Chinese – why did this not happen in Europe? The answer is probably because a large number of small groups of 'barbarians' flowed into the west while the Roman armies were distracted by internal disputes and major enemies. None of these barbarian groups could dominate the others, so no great empire was able to take over in the same way that the Toba seized much of north China. The Toba needed Chinese administrators to run their vast lands, but the western incomers simply did not have the same need for their rather petty kingdoms. In Noricum St Severin negotiated with whole groups of barbarians and their kings whose memory has all but passed away, and names like Franks and Goths disguise the fact that they were disparate groups of tribes and alliances whose settlement had to be arranged piecemeal.

Some of the relatively small groups of incomers were stiffly resisted, first by the Roman army and then by the native populations, resulting in massive destruction of the wealth of the countryside and the cities, as in the Balkans after 378 and Britain after 410. Many of the early barbarians were replaced by others. In Italy, Odovacar's pre-eminently Hun army was replaced by Ostrogoths in 493 who in turn were overthrown by the prolonged Roman reconquest under Justinian (527–65), whose governors were later driven out by an invasion of Lombards in 568. In southern Gaul the Goths were conquered in about AD 505 by the Franks. In Spain the Visigoths drove out the Vandals. In Britain the competing native princes employed German mercenaries who rebelled and overcame bitter resistance from their former employers, ravaging the province.

The mechanics of conquest, therefore, had a lot to do with the destruction of the Roman west. All the great empires had external enemies and civil wars, but underlying these was a deeper problem. The drive to empire created enormous wealth for those who controlled it, because they took over huge resources. In China each new dynasty formed a new regime which 'liberated' the wealth of those it defeated, creating a buoyant situation. But ultimately the limitations of an agricultural economy imposed themselves, adding bitterness to the various internal divisions. The Western Roman Empire was much poorer than India, China or even its eastern half, so that when the enemy came much of its economy collapsed quickly. With it went much of Roman culture and civilisation which were simply not as deeply rooted as Aryan Hinduism in India or the Han culture of China. Cities, those bastions of Roman civilisation, did not always disappear, but faded to a shadow of their former selves, small communities huddled around Christian cathedrals. Cities of stone were gradually replaced by mud and daub. This was a world on the downgrade, the clear consequence of military failure.

The armies of the great civilisations were the most numerous and formidably organised war machines of their age. But all over the world, and irrespective of differences of culture, they enjoyed only the most limited technological advantages over their enemies, largely in engineering and siege warfare, which were not always decisive areas. The evolution of agro-urban armies into regular standing forces brought enormous benefits in discipline and expertise, but provided no guarantee of victory. They could be committed to impossible tasks, as in the attempted conquest of Persia in AD 363, or the Han attempt to conquer the steppe. Poor command decisions, as at Adrianople in AD 378, led to defeat. Nor did they ensure the existence of the state, as they generated their own loyalties and could plunge it into internal strife or replace it, as did the warlords at the end of the Han in China. These predominantly infantry forces were profoundly influenced by contact with the steppe, out of which arose their substantial cavalry components. But agro-urban armies always found it difficult to defeat the steppe people, especially when, united by a Modun or an Attila, they could muster large forces. It was only the sheer difficulty of achieving extensive rule on the 'Sea of Grass' of the Eurasian land mass which relegated the nomads to a secondary role and prevented a truly decisive intervention in the fragmentation which characterised the Mediterranean, China and India in the fifth and sixth centuries.

But this period of collapse is of special interest because out of it emerged Europe, hitherto merely an annexe of the Mediterranean world. Many of the great Roman landowners survived and came to terms with their new barbarian masters, preserving something of Roman culture. They staffed the Christian Church which looked to the bishop of Rome as its ultimate authority. And the Church brought about a remarkable transformation in the sixth and seventh centuries, converting the barbarians, enlisting their leaders as its protectors and imposing a respect for its literacy. The rulers of this emerging civilisation had to devise a new military organisation because Roman administration had decayed. The demise of the tax-collecting state meant that in Europe there could no longer be the regular armies so characteristic of the great empires. And this new civilisation of the West needed protection because it was surrounded by enemies, amongst which the greatest was the new religion of Islam which burst upon the world in the seventh century.

CHAPTER FIVE

◆

IDEOLOGY AND WARFARE, 500–*c*.1200

O believers, when you encounter
The unbelievers marching to battle, turn not your backs to them
Who so turns his back to them,
Unless withdrawing to fight again
Or removing to join another host,
He is laden with the burden of God's
Anger, and his refuge is Gehenna –
An evil homecoming.[1]

So Muhammad (*c*.570–632), the Prophet of Islam, brought a new spirit into the conduct of war. He welded the many tribes of Mecca and Medina into a single religious community, the *umma*. This was protected and spread by war which, therefore, became a sacred duty: 'Prescribed for you is fighting, though it be hateful to you.'[2] Soldiers had always prayed to their gods, but pagans had so many that holy war on behalf of one against another was almost inconceivable. Islam, however, was a monotheistic religion with a monolithic structure, aiming at universal domination, within which a spirit of holy war, jihad, is prescribed. Moreover, much of the Koran is actually about the wars which Muhammad waged against his enemies in Mecca and Medina. His victory at Badr in 624 was important in imposing unity upon the feuding tribes of Arabia. This was only possible by uniting sacred and secular authority, ensuring, therefore, that violence was a sacred act. By contrast, Christianity always preserved the separation of sacred and secular, and regarded killing as murder. Christians wanted to defend the Roman state, so that when the very existence of Byzantium[3] was threatened by the war with the Persians from 602 to 629, the delivery of Constantinople from their siege of 626 was ascribed to the intervention of the Virgin. The emperor Heraclius (610–41) regarded the campaign against Persia as a holy war. But the Church in the Eastern Roman Empire never elaborated any theological foundation for the idea, and it was not until the eleventh century that its western branch produced a doctrine of holy war.

On Muhammad's death, power in Islam passed to a succession of caliphs, the 'Commanders of the Faithful'. Their military forces fell upon the exhausted empires of Persia and Byzantium. At the battle of Yarmuk in 636 the Muslim army defeated the Byzantines, opening the way for the conquest of Egypt and Syria. Sassanid Persia was defeated at al-Qadisiya in 637, and from there the Arabs pushed into Afghanistan and the steppe lands where Samarkand and Tashkent on the Silk Road became Islamic cities. Muslim armies from Egypt seized Byzantine North Africa, and then exploited a succession dispute in Gothic Spain to conquer almost the whole peninsula in 711; later they even threatened Gaul. This astonishing wave of conquest demands explanation.

The Arabs had no technological advantages over their enemies, and they were not especially well organised, because they fought in tribes under traditional leaders. Nor were they very numerous: at Yarmuk, 20,000 confronted 25,000 Byzantines. Some of their leaders were very able and occasionally rapid movement of their armies may have surprised their enemies. However, the Arab way of war, like that of their enemies, depended on mass infantry armies fighting in close order, supported by cavalry. But the nomadic life of the desert Arabs produced fine warriors who, inspired by religion and led by good generals, made effective soldiers. As the Koran acutely observes:

> Now God has lightened it for you, knowing that there is weakness in you. If there be a hundred of you, patient men, they will overcome two hundred; if there be a thousand of you they will overcome two thousand by the leave of God: God is with the patient.[4]

Never would the truth of Napoleon's maxim that in war 'The moral is to the physical as three to one' be better demonstrated. In a world where close-quarter fighting was decisive, the will to fight could tilt the balance in any combat.

A gigantic new Arab empire arose, built around a religion which united its many peoples in the name of God. Islamic doctrine was inspirational, and the struggle on the frontiers against Byzantium and the shamanist peoples of Central Asia attracted young volunteers, *muttawi'a*, motivated by religious belief. On the other hand, religion added its own disputes. The death of the Prophet raised the profound problem of who was to be authority in the *Umma*, and it was all the graver in that sacred and secular power had to be combined as required by the Prophet. The first caliphs were the companions of Muhammad but a strong tide of opinion favoured the succession of a member of his family, resulting in the choice of his nephew, Ali (656–61). The civil war following his assassination eventually produced the Umayyad dynasty which ruled from Damascus until 750, but the adherents of Ali, the Shi'ites, resented their rule and clung to other supposed descendants and in time elaborated a rather different and more austere form of Islam as opposed to the orthodox Sunni. Conversely another sect, the Kharijis, believed that any one of the faithful could be chosen as caliph, and launched a violent struggle which lasted for 200 years; they still survive as the Ibadi sect. Ideological opposition was obviously very dangerous to ruling groups, who quickly developed a vested interest in damping down and controlling zealots.

Religion made Islam different in many respects from other world powers, but in some respects it was remarkably similar. The predator empires of the ancient world plundered the assets of those around them and cultivated a sense of superiority. The Greeks and Romans disdained all 'barbarians'. Chinese emperors could not stomach the claims of steppe people to equality. Zoroastrian Persia imposed the cult of its supreme god, Ahura Mazda, on defeated enemies. An Arab ambassador told the Shah of Persia: 'Once the Arabs were a wretched race, whom you could tread under foot with impunity. We were reduced to eating dogs and lizards. But now for our glory, God has raised up a prophet among us.'[5] And the Arab elite was as predatory, unscrupulous and materialistic as any other – and as prone to internal faction. The soldiers of the Arab armies fought in expectation of reward. In the early years Islam was embodied in the 300,000 *muqatila*, soldiers settled in and around the major cities of conquered provinces. In Iraq, Basra and Kufa supported significant garrisons, the names of whose soldiers were recorded on registers, the *diwan*, so that each could be assigned a share of the taxes levied on the region. The soldiers regarded this income as their booty, the *fay*, to which they and their descendants were entitled as a return for their exertions. It was obvious that higher authority would regard this claim to hereditary pay with little enthusiasm. But in the early years the Arabs, like other conquerors, liberated vast sums from the defeated, stimulating at least for a while the economy of the lands they ruled.

And as in other powers the issue of authority was ultimately decided by military force. In 661 the Umayad family won because they controlled the army of Syria which crushed all opposition. They established a capital at Damascus and created a great empire with its own coinage, army and a strong navy. Their authority depended on their ability to pay the soldiers, and military expansion was the time-honoured way of achieving this. The obvious enemy were the Byzantines against whom warfare could be justified in religious terms. Thus the instincts of a predator regime and the fervour of a new religion worked together. This prompted the Umayyads to create an Arab fleet which in 671 began an abortive seven-year assault on Constantinople. This was renewed in 717–18, but the Arab land army was attacked by Byzantium's Bulgarian allies, while at sea her fleet deployed Greek fire, a form of liquid fire projected from siphons mounted on the prows of Byzantine ships. The Arabs broke off their attack on Constantinople, never to return.

The Umayyad army evolved into the classic Middle Eastern paid professional force supported by a bureaucracy. Its tactics remained typically agro-urban. Horses were primarily used to transport men to battle, where they then fought on foot. Tactics were fairly simple, as one commander explained to his men: 'The first part of the fighting is the shooting of arrows, then the pointing of spears, then the thrusting of them to left and right and then the drawing of swords. That's all there is to it.'[6] Military development and political faction combined to destroy the Umayyads. The Syrian army was important because its garrisons across the Arab world enforced the authority of the Umayyads. But two much more efficient fighting forces evolved on the exposed frontiers. The Jaziran army faced modern Armenia and Azerbaijan, and the Khorasanian defended Central Asia. Because these armies were fighting against Turkish horsemen on the steppe, they developed good cavalry, including armoured horsemen like the *cataphracts* of Persia and Byzantium. The leaders of these two armies were bitter rivals. When Marwan II (744–50) used the Jaziran army to seize the Caliphate and rewarded its officers, the Syrian army became alienated. The army of Khorasan, fearful of the ascendancy of the Jazirans, backed a new contender to the Caliphate who claimed descent from al-Abbas, uncle of the Prophet. The rival armies clashed at the battle of Zab in 750 where the Khorasanian army was triumphant. The Abbasids ruthlessly eliminated the Umayyads, although one of them, 'Abd ar-Rahman, survived and established a kingdom in Al-Andalus (Spain). The Abbasids moved the capital to Baghdad where their regime, with its largely Iranian army, marked the revival of a Persian Empire in which Arabs played a limited role.

This vast Islamic empire and its great trading activity, reaching to East Africa, India and China, provided a huge tax base, but this was strained by the need to support a regular army of 100,000. Most Abbasid soldiers were Persians whose heavy cavalry were highly effective, but the bulk of the army fought on foot. Military specialists increasingly commanded the army which was equipped for siege with *manjaniq*, traction-trebuchets working on the swing-beam principle. The Arabs acquired knowledge of these weapons from the Chinese with whom they traded along the Silk Road and across the ocean to Guangzhou. The Abbasids maintained 25,000 troops against Byzantium, because the prestige of the dynasty demanded commitment to jihad. Their attacks on Byzantium continued to attract *muttawi'a*, but these expeditions were increasingly futile because Byzantine resistance had hardened and the Caliphate largely stood on the defensive.

The succession dispute of 811–19 which brought the caliph al-Ma'mun (813–33) to power was a decisive event in the history of the Abbasid military. At the battle of Rayy in May 811 Ma'mun won because his cavalry destroyed the enemy infantry. After a bitter siege, 811–13, Baghdad surrendered to him. But because both parties had enlisted sections of the Khorasanian army, this force was totally shattered, and a new one had to be built. The Khorasani remained important, but to them were added Magheriba from the desert fringe of Egypt, Faraghina from the frontier with Central Asia and, most significantly, nomadic Turks from the steppe lands. This was a change of world importance, because the Turks were horse-archers whose effectiveness was the result of technological developments which enormously enhanced the military power of the nomadic peoples.

Horse-archers had been an important element in the armies of Byzantium and Persia down to the sixth century, but thereafter they were little used. This was probably because horsemen who paused or slowed to shoot or throw were vulnerable, while infantry formations had learned how to cope with heavy cavalry. However, stirrups developed on the steppe in the fourth century and the Avars, a people of Turkish origins who settled in what is now Hungary in the mid-sixth century AD, brought them to Europe where they were in general use by the eighth century. At the same time saddles were radically improved, giving riders greater security and comfort. The steppe peoples, whose very lives depended on the horse, mated this technology with the composite bow. The result was that Turks were capable of rapid and accurate fire from the backs of their fast-moving horses, and were even able to shoot backwards. An Arab remarked: 'The Turk can shoot at beasts, birds, hoops, men, sitting quarry, dummies and birds on the wing, and do so at full gallop to fore or to rear, to left or to right, upwards or downwards, loosing ten arrows before the Kharijite [Arab tribesmen] can nock one.'[7] Moreover, warriors kept strings of animals, and this enabled them to move quickly over long distances or to sustain high speeds during periods of combat. Al-Ma'mun recruited Turks, despite the fact that many of them were not Muslims, as the cutting edge of his new armies.

The army of the Abbasids became a Turko-Iranian force, bitterly resented by the native populations. To prevent friction, they were housed at Samarra, about 120 kilometres north of Baghdad. The Samarran army was much smaller than its predecessors, numbering 15,000 Turks and an equal number of others, mostly mounted. They were very efficient, invading Byzantium and sacking the cities of Ankara and Amorion in 838. This expedition had a supply train, equipment for siege warfare and the support of specialist units of sappers and even medical services. Such elaborately equipped forces were not cheap, especially taking into account the need to fortify frontier districts, to maintain a fleet and to support other troops in garrisons.

The Turkish commanders had lavish incomes and they forged connections with factions at court. In a series of civil wars the leading Turks made and unmade caliphs with the intention of improving their power and wealth. But the Islamic Empire had ceased to expand and, like other empires, found supporting its gains difficult, so that paying this standing army was becoming more onerous. The civil wars at the heart of the caliphate paralysed central government, enabling provincial governors to seize power and retain taxes. Abbasid rule shrank to a part of central and southern Iraq, and by the mid-tenth century a military faction, the Buyids, had reduced them to the status of figureheads. In effect the soldiers in this rump of empire had taken over their paymasters under the nominal rule of the caliphs, and the old Arab–Iranian empire collapsed. The substantial army of the caliphs was no more, but in the provinces each ruler retained about him a small *askar* of professional soldiers, often Turks, who could form the nucleus of larger armies when necessary.

Even the spiritual authority of the Abbasids was challenged. Civil wars and reports of luxury and indulgence at the Abbasid court had aroused widespread disgust, which promoted the cause of the Shi'ites. In Tunisia they established a Fatimid caliphate whose rulers claimed descent from Fatima, daughter of the Prophet. In 969 they seized control of Egypt and waged war against the Abbasids, extending their authority over Palestine and Syria. Although this was an ideological struggle, Turkish horse-archers fought on both sides. Their fast-moving style of war suited the open dry countryside of the Middle East. Heavy cavalry backed them up. Infantry remained an element in Islamic armies but it was less and less important. In this way the influence of the steppe modified Islamic military methods. The mass of the rural population had no role in these events, merely paying taxes to whoever was in a position to collect them. But Islamic rulers had to keep an eye on the Arab factions in the cities whose people contributed the educated manpower and imposts which sustained their regimes.

The rise of Islam in the seventh century AD had affected the whole known world. The Umayyad conquest of Sind took the new religion into India. It spread onto the steppe, and in 751 the Arab governor of Tashkent defeated a Tang army at the battle of Atlakh on the Tal river, forcing the retreat of Chinese influence from the borders of Persia. To the west the old unity of the Mediterranean was replaced by three distinct and mutually hostile cultures. Islam was by far the mightiest, posing a grave threat to the other two. East Rome, centred on Constantinople, clung to the remains of its empire in Anatolia, Greece and the Balkans. In the remains of the collapsed Western Roman Empire a mosaic of petty kingdoms formed the new civilisation of Catholic Europe. The decay of the empire of Islam had profound consequences for all these.

The Byzantine Empire had been impoverished by the loss in the seventh century of her richest provinces. Her cities, lacking the tribute of foreign powers, their trade shattered by the disruptions attendant on the Islamic expansion, shrank to mere isolated garrisons, embattled fortresses anchoring her hold on an Anatolian plateau swept by Arab raids. The emperors at Constantinople desperately needed soldiers to fight off Muslim attack. In the centuries before 1000 the empire never had more than 120,000 men under arms, and individual armies as big as 12,000 were unusual. Its stance was defensive. Anatolia was divided into provinces called themes whose governors united civil and military authority. In each theme, military settlements were created, whose men supported themselves by farming but could be mobilised at need. They garrisoned a dense network of fortifications along the roads and in strategic positions, which made life difficult for Muslim raiders trying to find food by ravaging. In addition, the thematic forces could mass to fall upon raiding parties, forcing them to concentrate and thereby minimising their destructive capacity. The *tagmata*, the standing army based at Constantinople, formed the core of any large army raised to fend off major enemy attacks or, more rarely, to sally into enemy territory.

The collapse of the Caliphate coincided with economic recovery in Byzantium which, from the time of Constantine VII Porphyrogenitus

(913–59), sustained a new Byzantine army. At its heart were professional infantry, frequently foreign mercenaries, who were trained and disciplined to fight in close order, often forming square to protect their cavalry. They were accompanied by light troops and substantial bodies of archers some of whom were horsed but dismounted to fight. Light cavalry performed reconnaissance duties, softened up hostile formations and pursued scattered enemies. The cutting edge of the army was the armoured cavalry, the *klibinarioi*, who destroyed their enemies by shock charge. This balanced force was highly effective, and pushed the Byzantine frontier eastwards, capturing Antioch in 969. The obvious value of a strong central army led to neglect of the thematic armies, whose aristocratic leaders became deeply resentful and rebelled against Basil II (976–1025) who survived by enlisting a corps of Russian mercenaries. Basil's main achievement was the conquest of Bulgaria, hence his nickname *Bulgaroctonus* – the Bulgar-Slayer. But his inheritance was an expensive mercenary army. The aristocrats of Asia Minor who led the thematic armies resented a government which neglected their forces in favour of the regulars for whom it taxed the provinces. For the Byzantines, as for their Abbasid enemies, keeping a regular standing army was an enormous burden. By the mid-eleventh century Byzantium was torn by rivalries which threatened to erupt into civil war at times of succession disputes. Even so, with the Abbasid Empire in decay and its Fatimid rival facing grave internal difficulties, there seemed to be no fundamental threat to Byzantium.

But the vacuum of power in Islam was suddenly filled by a new force. About 975 Islamicised Turks created the Ghaznavid Empire in Afghanistan, Persia and India. Another Turkish dynasty, the Seljuqs, perceived the weakness and fragmentation in the old Arab lands and invaded the Middle East. In 1055, in alliance with Turkish factions in the city, they seized Baghdad. They respected the Abbasid Caliphate, but their leader, Tughril, took the title of Sultan and seized secular authority. The Seljuq Empire by 1070 controlled what is now Iraq and Iran and pressed into Syria, bidding to destroy the Fatimids of Egypt in the name of Sunni orthodoxy. Its best soldiers were the Turkish horse-archers backed up by small numbers of very heavily armed cavalry of Iranian origin and clouds of light horsemen recruited from across the Caliphate, sometimes supported by infantry. Some Turkish tribes disliked Seljuq control and raided across the Byzantine frontier. The emperor Romanus IV Diogenes (1067–71) attacked Seljuq Syria in order to force the Sultan to control them. In 1071 Romanus made a major effort, advancing to Erzerum in eastern Anatolia with an army of 40,000. The Sultan gathered a rather smaller force to support the tribes. The two armies clashed at Manzikert on 19 August and the Byzantines were defeated. Romanus got good terms from the Sultan, but his enemies blinded and deposed him, opening the way for ten years of bitter civil wars.

These civil wars enabled the Turkish tribes to penetrate Anatolia. The cities of this area had defied the Arabs for centuries, and as the Turks had no knowledge of siege warfare they should have been able to hold out. But while the Arabs had raided, the nomad Turks saw the Anatolian plateau as a desirable environment for their flocks. They had come to stay, not simply to raid. The various pretenders to the Byzantine throne after 1071 rarely had much connection with the land and enlisted the military aid of the Turks in their struggles, handing over the cities in return. By 1081, when Alexius Comnenus (1081–1118) restored order, Anatolia was controlled by petty Turkish sultanates. Because Anatolia, the traditional recruiting ground of the Byzantine army, had been lost to the Turks, and because they were Muslims, it is hardly surprising that he turned to a source of Christian soldiers to help him reconquer his lost lands.

Europe was an impoverished mosaic of peoples descended from the tribes who had destroyed the Western Roman Empire, but despite their diversity, elements of a common culture had emerged, so that Europe was now something more than a geographic expression. The key factor which bound its peoples together was a form of Christianity whose language was Latin and whose spiritual head was the pope, the bishop of Rome. But in addition, across the whole of Western Europe the countryside was dominated by land-holding magnates amongst whom kings were little more than first among equals who lacked the apparatus of a state. The Roman collapse had disrupted governmental organisation and crippled the economy, so that states shrank and the collection of taxes failed. As a result, the leaders of society drew most of their wealth from the land, and although they competed at royal courts for profitable offices, this patronage was much less important to them than their territorial holdings. Because the state was weak, each great man necessarily kept an armed retinue, so that this was a highly militarised society.

The laws of the kingdoms of the West required that all freemen should come to war on the king's summons, the richest with the full panoply of an armoured cavalryman, helm, mail shirt, round shield, lance and longsword; lesser men with horse, shield and lance; and the humblest as footsoldiers with spears, bows and arrows. However, real military power depended on the well-armed retinues of the king and his great magnates. As time went on, the gap between the mass and this elite became more marked. The Franks were a Germanic people settled along the Rhine who had long provided Rome with soldiers, but by 486 they had established their own kingdom extending from the Rhine to the Loire. Under King Clovis (481–511) they annexed Burgundy and converted to Catholicism. In 507 Clovis defeated the Goths, who dominated southern France and Spain, at the battle of Vouillé near Poitiers. This was largely an infantry battle with the leading men on each side fighting on horseback:

> King Clovis met Alaric II, King of the Goths, on the battlefield of Vouillé, near the tenth milestone outside Poitiers. Some of the soldiers engaged hurled their javelins from a distance, others fought hand to hand. The Goths fled, as they were prone to do, and Clovis was the victor, for God was on his side. . . . Clovis killed Alaric, but as the Goths fled, two of them suddenly rushed up in a scrum, one on this side and one on that, and struck at the Frankish King with their spears. It was his leather corselet which saved him and the sheer speed of his horse, but he was very near to death.[8]

The Goths fled to their Spanish kingdom, while the Franks became the dominant force in Gaul. The descendants of Clovis, the Merovingian kings, dominated northern Europe, extorting tribute from the pagan Saxons and other German tribes to the east. But dynastic infighting led to the rise of a new family, the Carolingians, who threw up a leader of genius, Charles Martel (714–41), who tried to reassert Frankish ascendancy over neighbouring powers. By this time the Arabs were in firm control of Spain after their destruction of the Visigothic regime in 711. In 732 the Umayyad governor, 'Abd ar-Rahman, decided to take advantage of the turbulence amongst the Franks to invade Gaul. He encountered Charles Martel on the road between Poitiers and Tours:

> He confronted the consul of Austrasia by the name of Charles, a man who proved himself to be a warrior from his youth and expert in things military . . . After each side had tormented the other with raids for almost seven days, they finally prepared their battle lines and fought fiercely. The northern peoples remained as immobile as a wall, holding together like a glacier in the cold regions. In the blink of an eye, they annihilated the Arabs with the sword. The people of Austrasia, greater in number of soldiers and formidably armed, killed 'Abd ar-Rahnan when they found him, striking him on the chest.[9]

The Arab army was largely infantry supported by light cavalry, while the Franks relied on foot, close packed 'like a glacier', to repel them. This was a highly significant battle. Charles Martel's power was contested amongst the Franks, and defeat would probably have destroyed his whole position, opening the way for this Arab raid to turn into a campaign of conquest. Disunity had let the Arabs into Spain and could easily have done the same in northern Europe. Indeed, when Charles tried to conquer Provence, some local leaders called in the Arabs who were not expelled until the end of Charles's life. In fact, 732 marks a turning point in the history of Islam, especially taken with the failure of the Umayyad siege of Constantinople only fourteen years before.

The peoples of Europe could not afford regular armies like those sustained by taxation (albeit with great difficulty) in the Caliphate and Byzantium. The European model, by which soldiers took over land in order to support themselves, was a necessary simplicity. European armies lacked the means to support large numbers of horse-soldiers, but their military technology was no worse than that of their neighbours. They were familiar with fortifications and siege equipment. Under Charlemagne (768–814) the Franks conquered all of western Germany and Saxony, asserted their power over Bavaria, destroyed the Avars of what is now Hungary, seized the Lombard kingdom of Italy, advancing their rule down to the Byzantine south, and created a march (border zone) in northern Spain based around Barcelona. In recognition of these conquests, on Christmas Day 800 Charlemagne was crowned Emperor of the West, an elevation bitterly contested by the Byzantines who regarded their own ruler as sole emperor in the Christian world.

This was a remarkable achievement. Charlemagne had a very limited and barely literate governmental structure and no standing army. His armies consisted of the men settled on the royal lands in return for service, and the retinues of his great lords who would support him if he could lead them to loot and glory. Victory was the cement of an empire which was necessarily predatory on its neighbours. He could call upon the mass of free Franks and undoubtedly did on occasion, but the professionals could be mobilised more quickly and were much more effective in offensive operations. But at best the support of the lords was episodic and conditional. In these circumstances Charlemagne exploited victory cautiously. In 774 he defeated and deposed the Lombard king and crowned himself as their king, but guaranteed the laws and privileges of the Lombard aristocracy, who would serve him well. In 788 he deposed Tassilo, duke of Bavaria for treachery, but only after a painstaking show of legality and he was careful to conciliate the Bavarian nobility. His armies were transient affairs and he did not have the means to occupy hostile lands.

This in part explains why Charlemagne's wars against the Saxons dragged on for so long. The Franks had traditionally asserted overlordship of this pagan people, but the Saxons rejected Carolingian authority. They threatened the Christian lands of western Germany which accepted Frankish leadership and even raided the Frankish heartlands. It was therefore a vital matter for the regime to curb them. But the Saxons had no single monarch, capital or focus, and making an agreement with some of their lords simply alienated others. There were no Roman roads east of the Rhine, while weather and distance took a toll of armies and imposed terrible strains on the Carolingian kingdom. Professional Frankish warriors sought loot, but Saxony yielded little of that and plenty of hard knocks. There was a limit to the number of times the host of freemen could be summoned, for they were the backbone of agricultural production. Charlemagne persuaded the Frankish lords to support him, but their support was inevitably spasmodic. Moreover, military enterprises elsewhere detracted from Frankish efforts in the Saxon wars. In 778 the Abbasid Caliph of Baghdad persuaded Charlemagne to join an attack on Umayyad Spain. The Franks gathered much booty, but as their army returned across the Pyrenees its rearguard, under Count Roland, was wiped out by a Basque ambush, encouraging another round of Saxon resistance. Little wonder the Saxon war, begun in 772, stuttered on until 804. Charlemagne was not particular about his methods. In 782, in response to a Saxon revolt and a Frankish defeat in the Süntel mountains, he ordered the massacre of some 4,500 prisoners. But the back of Saxon resistance was broken by a winter campaign in 785. To sustain an army in winter was enormously difficult, but the effort paid off because it caught the Saxons dispersed and vulnerable in their villages. The following summer most of the Saxon leaders capitulated, and some 10,000 men with their wives and children were forcibly exiled and settled in various parts of the Frankish realm. Even so there were serious Saxon revolts down to 804.

Charlemagne was successful because the Franks were united and could raise more soldiers than any other power in Western Europe. But large armies would have perished without good logistics, and it was here that Charlemagne excelled. In 806 the emperor wrote to one of his great lords, Abbot Fulrad of St Quentin ordering him to prepare his troops to join the army:

You are to come with your men to the aforesaid place equipped in such a way that you can go from there with the army to whatever place we shall command – that is with arms, implements and other military material, provisions and clothing. Each horseman is to carry shield and spear, long-sword and short-sword, bow quivers and arrows, and your carts are to contain implements of various kinds – axes and stone-cutting tools, augers, adzes, trenching tools, iron spades and the rest of the implements which an army needs. And provisions in the carts for three months following the assembly, weapons and clothing for half a year. And this we command in absolute terms, that you see to it that whichever part of our realm the direction of your march may cause you to pass through you proceed to the aforesaid place in good order and without unruliness, that is you presume to take nothing other than grass, firewood and water.[10]

'Axes and stone-cutting tools, augers, adzes, trenching tools, iron spades' are not the stuff of heroics but they were vital for the kind of war which the Franks were waging in Saxony in which it was important to build marching camps, and to destroy hostile fortifications. Siege was a much more frequent activity than battle, which was rare. 'Provisions in the carts for three months' were essential because all armies march on their stomachs. This kind of attention to detail meant that large Frankish armies could be maintained and could operate effectively over extended periods of time.

In addition, production of iron was much greater in the Frankish lands than elsewhere in northern Europe, and Charlemagne, aware of this limited technological advantage, forbade merchants to sell arms and armour to possible enemies:

They are not to take arms and coats of mail to sell; and if they are discovered carrying them, all their stock is to be taken away from them, half going to the fisc [royal income], the other half being divided between the aforesaid *missi* [king's agent] and the discoverer [who had shopped the merchant].[11]

And after initial success, conquered peoples could contribute to the Frankish armies – the Lombards provided very substantial forces.

But the long Saxon war gradually took on a very special religious character. Since the time of Clovis the Frankish kings had always emphasised their Catholicism. The long Saxon resistance demanded a massive mobilisation of Frankish resources and prompted a radical development in the conduct of war, somewhat paralleling Islamic jihad. Charlemagne saw

Christianity as a powerful cement of empire; he believed that the Christian king should care for the souls and bodies of his subjects and this influenced the conduct of war. In 772 he destroyed the Irminsul, the sacred oak of the Saxons, which was the focus of their religion. He and his predecessors had long sponsored Christian missionaries east of the Rhine, hoping that conversion would pacify the enemy. But the Saxons were devoted to their pagan beliefs, and in the face of their obduracy the Franks increasingly portrayed the conflict as God's war. Miracles were reported. In the revolt of 774 the Saxons seized Fritzlar:

> But when they set themselves to burn the church dedicated by the blessed martyr Boniface in the place which is now called Fritzlar by its inhabitants and were vainly trying to bring this about, a sudden terror sent by God entered into them and they fled, confused and cowardly in their fear, back to their own homes.[12]

The Saxon rebellion of 782 was provoked by a savage law code, the 'Saxon Capitulary', which imposed Christianity. Forcible conversion became so common that a few senior Frankish churchmen protested against it – in vain. On one occasion it is said that the Franks pushed Saxon prisoners at spear-point through a river while a bishop further upstream blessed this 'water of baptism'. The 'Saxon Capitulary' was ultimately rescinded, but conversion was effectively compulsory.

This gathering sense of holy war was very evident in the last great campaign of Charlemagne's reign. The Avars were a steppe people settled in what is now the Hungarian plain. They were ferocious raiders who skilfully exploited dissent amongst their neighbours. It was probably the deposition in 787 of their ally, Duke Tassilo of Bavaria, which provoked serious Avar attacks on Bavaria and Italy in 788, convincing Charlemagne of the need to destroy them. In a letter to his wife he emphasised spiritual preparation: 'We for our part have observed, with the Lord's aid, three days of litanies . . . We beseeched the mercy of God that he would vouchsafe to grant us peace and safety and victory and a successful expedition.'[13] But mounting a campaign so far from his home territory also required careful preparation. New border fortifications served as bases and Frankish engineers even attempted to build a canal between the Rhine and the Danube to facilitate the flow of supplies from the Frankish heartlands, but this ran into insuperable engineering problems. Prefabricated bridges were constructed to speed movement. But above all the expedition was from the first touted as holy war. By 796 Charlemagne had destroyed the Avars, and gained an enormous booty. Churchmen were impressed by the expansion of Christianity brought about by Charlemagne's armies, and were not unduly fastidious about his methods. But no doctrine of holy war emerged, though from this time the notion that God approved of war against infidels became current amongst the ruling groups in Europe.

Carolingian expansion had ended by about 800. Umayyad Spain and Byzantine South Italy were too strong to conquer. The Slav frontier demanded an active defence, but the trackless wastes of Central Europe were hardly inviting. The Danes constantly launched raids on the Frankish world using their new longships, but the ageing emperor failed to invade their lands. Military effort is always expensive, and as conquest ceased so did the flow of tribute. But troops were still needed to protect the frontiers and the Carolingian government called up the levy of the Franks, causing great discontent. Such defensive war yielded little booty so the lords used their positions in the state to further their private interest. Charlemagne legislated against the evils of this situation:

> Poor men complain . . . that if a man refuses to give his land to a bishop, abbot or count or any of their servants, these seek opportunities whereby they can harm that poor man and make him go on every occasion to fight in the army until he is impoverished and hands over or sells his land, like it or not. They say that others, who have handed their land over, are allowed to stay at home without any trouble.[14]

This was the lethal syndrome which shortly after so crippled the Abbasids and which, indeed, afflicted all the ancient and medieval empires. The competition for shrinking resources embittered succession disputes in the Carolingian family and opened the way for outside attack. Some of southern France fell to Islamic conquerors from Spain who remained until 972. In the ninth century, Byzantine Sicily was seized by Muslims from North Africa who spilled over into Italy and extorted tribute from the papacy. The Slavs, the Vikings of Scandinavia, and the Magyars, another steppe people who settled on the Hungarian plain, were fought off, though at the cost of much destruction. Dynastic failure brought the empire to an end, because after 876 there was a sequence of short-lived rulers and, therefore, a terrible vacuum of power.

In France, Germany and Italy the military aristocracy became the effective rulers, displacing distant and little known kings. Their worst enemies were each other, so that war was fought on a petty scale by lords anxious to protect and expand packets of land spread across vast areas. In these circumstances they relied upon fortified houses – castles that were garrisoned by hired bully-boys always prepared to fight. It was convenient, therefore, to be served by a few well-equipped soldiers who could gather quickly to meet any threat or to make themselves into one. The result was the rise of the knight, who was essentially a heavy cavalryman, and western warfare from this time onwards was uniquely focused on this military arm. Why was this?

In a continent deeply seamed by rivers and mountains, with an agriculture dominated by arable farming, there was no room to raise clouds of light horse and little in which to manoeuvre them. It is no accident that successive waves of nomadic horsemen, Huns, Alans, Avars, Magyars, settled in the last extension of the Eurasian steppe, the Hungarian plain. Further west the land challenged both their logistics and their tactics. This was of the highest importance to the military development of Europe. But if huge numbers were impossible, careful breeding and feeding with grain could produce bigger, stronger animals capable of bearing the weight of defensive armour and offensive weapons. In addition, by the end of the eighth century the peoples of Europe had adopted the stirrups and improved saddles developed by the steppe people, making the rider more secure and, therefore, more capable of fighting at close quarters.

Western society could not afford eastern specialisation, so the knight was an all-purpose warrior capable of fighting on foot or horseback. In the mid-ninth century the Vikings had posed a grave threat to northern France; for example, in 859

> The Danes ravaged the places beyond the Scheldt. Some of the common people living between the Seine and the Loire formed a sworn association amongst themselves and fought bravely against the Danes on the Seine. But because their association had been made without due consideration, they were easily slain by our more powerful people.[15]

The implication is clear – the Vikings were a menace, but for the lords self-directed peasant military power was even more dangerous. The knight was a policeman, charged with defending the social order. Because of this knights aspired to holding land of their masters and emphasised their common lifestyle which centred on war. For war demanded dexterity in arms, and knights had the wealth and leisure to train for it. Hunting was a vital exercise for mounted men, while mock combats, tournaments, became popular. By a combination of superior arms and athletic skill the knight became the soldier *par excellence*. Knights lived around their lords, either retained in the household or on land in return for military service. When large forces were needed, more had to be hired and they were drawn from the sons of poorer landed knights whose families provided them with equipment as their share of the patrimony.

The equipment of a knight was expensive. By the fourteenth century a plough horse cost 30 pence, but a fine warhorse for a great noble might cost as much as £200. Even a simple knight needed a riding horse (to save his warhorse), costing ten times the price of a plough animal, and a pack-horse, while greater men would have many more. The basic protection of the knight was the hauberk, a shirt made of 30,000–40,000 rivet-closed iron rings, each about 1 centimetre across. This was split at the groin and the skirts hung down to the knees. Increasingly they were made with integral hoods (*coifs*), sleeves and mittens, while separate leggings and shoes were available. The hauberk was worn over a padded tunic (*aketon*), and by the thirteenth century elbows and knees often had leather or steel-plate coverings. A pointed or domed iron helmet protected the head, leaving the face exposed, but by the twelfth century some had a great helm which provided all-round protection at the price of limiting vision to eye-slits. All this could be supplemented by plates of boiled leather (*cuir bouilli*). Shields of laminated light wood offered additional protection. The lance was the knight's weapon of first resort – a 2.5-metre spear which could be used to throw or thrust, or couched under the arm so that the weight and momentum of horse and rider could be concentrated into the point directed at the enemy. For close-quarter work the sword was essential. Overall the knight's equipment weighed about 60 pounds, but this provided good protection. A true blow from a lance or hit from an arrow at close range would penetrate the mail shirt, but in the scrimmage of battle glancing blows were more common, and armour and cloth padding deflected these. Knights were individually formidable, but lacking practice in mass formations, were best used in small groups of men who knew one another. Even so, lack of cohesion was a major problem. Medieval Europe could not afford the state-paid soldiers of Byzantium and Islam, and its armies resembled those of earlier civilisations, mass infantry forces built around mounted elites.

Infantry were needed because the broken European countryside gave cover against cavalry, and bad weather sometimes made riding precarious. Because of the network of castles war turned on sieges in which the horseman's role was limited. Infantry were raised from amongst a lord's peasants, poorly trained and equipped because military investment was focused on the elite. They accompanied knightly retinues but when armies gathered they had no training. Thus infantry, whose essential quality is mass, lacked cohesion. Most footsoldiers carried spears, and sometimes had steel caps and padded clothes for protection. Archers were valued, but their quality was variable and they were not always available. Crossbows were very effective, but relatively uncommon because expensive. Mercenaries were the best footmen because they were willing and experienced fighters, but they were costly and so retained only for short periods.

The armies of medieval Europe were smaller than those of Islam and even Byzantium and they lacked their capacity for fast manoeuvre on the battlefield. Even when a really important leader called together a large force, numbers were limited. In 1066 William the Conqueror prepared to invade England. This was a vast effort, yet his army did not number more than about 7,000 fighting men including perhaps 2,000–3,000 cavalry. Throughout the twelfth century an army of 5,000 was remarkable. Western European warfare was based on the sheer fighting power of small forces of armoured knights, usually on horseback and supported by bigger infantry formations. This was a slow-moving style of war, for warhorses had to be conserved and even in battle had limited endurance. Topography, geography and climate made fast movement difficult.

Nevertheless, European armies were very formidable. Speed and tactical acumen were important in battle, but ultimately victory was usually won by hard fighting at close quarters. The sheer force of hard and heavily protected men on big horses was overpowering in these circumstances. But western armies, like most others, tended to avoid battle. It was always a chancy and unpredictable affair, and leaders were, quite reasonably, chary of risking their own lives. To assemble a large army, a king had to persuade nobles to assemble retinues which they might be reluctant to commit to the hazard of battle. The soldiers in these followings were not used to fighting together, let alone as part of a large force, and this simply increased the element of danger. Further, while the results could be spectacular, as they were at Hastings in 1066, more often the loser retreated into fortifications to recover.

In a poorly policed world where the ruling elites were riven by factions, every substantial landowner needed at least one fortress. Castles were centres of power from which lords dominated the countryside, intimidated their peasants and threatened their aristocratic rivals. In the tenth and eleventh centuries they were, for the most part, simple earthwork and timber structures, but by the twelfth century mighty stone structures were being built. The principle of concentricity, of presenting any attacker with successive obstacles, was well understood. A common model was the simple enclosure castle, a 10-metre-high stone wall studded with towers which projected from the walls providing enfilading fire against any attack, surrounded by a ditch 4–6 metres deep. In the middle a massive stone tower, perhaps built on a mound, provided a place of last resort. Castles were great economic and social foci of power, replacing (or at least supplementing) cities, which were few and small in northern Europe.

Castles were always much more than merely blockhouses. They may appear cold and austere to us, but the finest of them had luxurious apartments for their owners, hung with tapestries. And a splendid castle was a status symbol. Hedingham in Essex is a five-storey tower rising in white stone from the flat countryside. It was built by the De Vere family to celebrate their creation as earls of Oxford. In such places the remarkable code we call chivalry was formed as part of the interaction of nobles and knights. This was fundamentally a warrior ethic celebrating the qualities of loyalty and bravery and asserting the right of warriors to dominate society by violence. To it were grafted various ideas about knights as the servants and protectors of the poor which gave a veneer of morality to brute and crude turbulence. Out of this society arose a literature, largely the long poems which we call *chansons* and *romans*, in which war played a central part. These cultural creations portrayed idealised warriors, ever ready to sacrifice themselves in a noble cause, in which heroes perform valiant deeds:

Samson the Duke on the Almanzor runs:
Through gilded shield and painted flowers he thrusts;
Naught for defence avails the hauberk tough,
He splits his heart, his liver and his lung,
And strikes him dead, weep any or weep none,
Cries the Archbishop: 'This feat was knightly done!'[16]

Inspiring though this might be to the aspiring knight, war did not consist of individual jousts and brave deeds such as this. Chivalric literature is about as useful a guide to the nature of western medieval warfare as Superman is to twentieth-century crime fighting.

The sheer numbers of castles and their strength intensified the basic nature of war, which was destruction. They presented a great challenge to any attacker, and while weak or unprepared fortifications could be stormed, anything more formidable demanded a systematic siege which was very difficult for the relatively incoherent forces of the day. The attacking army needed to provide itself with shelter, to organise food supplies and to build equipment that demanded rare and specialised skills which might not be available. As a result, ravaging, which undermined the economic base of the enemy, was the staple of war. A contemporary praised William the Conqueror, king of England (1066–87) because 'He sowed terror in the land by his frequent and lengthy invasions; he devastated vineyards, fields and estates; he seized neighbouring strongpoints and where advisable put garrisons in them; in short he incessantly inflicted innumerable calamities upon the land.'[17] This pattern of war, turning upon fortified strongpoints and reliant upon devastation, was common to armies across the whole world because it was economical and effective. Western warfare was unique only because it was little influenced by the steppe peoples.

Their limitations in the circumstances of Western Europe had been cruelly exposed in 955 at the battle of the Lechfeld. The Magyars were steppe horse-archers who settled in Hungary in the ninth century, and took to raiding their neighbours. They used speed and manoeuvrability to surround their enemies and the firepower of their composite bows to break up their formations in preparation for close-quarter battle. The Germans had defeated them at the Riade in Eastern Germany in 933, by closing quickly in a mass formation, as their king advised:

When you sally out to the field of battle let no one ride faster than another but keep together. The shields of each should guard his neigh-bour so that they can receive the first volley of arrows from the enemy. Then charge very fast before the enemy can fire again for the weight of your armour will prevail.[18]

Despite this defeat, in 954 many Magyar nobles supported rebels against the German monarch Otto I (936–73) in the hope of plunder. In August 955 they besieged Augsburg in the open plain of the Lechfeld, seeking to draw Otto onto a battlefield of their own choosing where their speed would be advantageous. Otto understood the risk and preserved his army by approaching the enemy through broken and wooded country, emerging close enough to the Magyar siege-camp to prevent any manoeuvre by their cavalry. The Magyars then feigned flight to draw the German cavalry out onto the plain, but Otto did not try to follow them, and so the Magyars dispersed for a fast return to their native land. Their routes home lay across a network of rivers, all in spate due to heavy rains. Local forces, alerted by Otto, destroyed the Magyar bands as they tried to cross these, and Otto deliberately hanged all their leaders. Weather, topography and shrewd tactics together foiled the Magyars who were, essentially, fighting outside the natural habitat in which their tactics had evolved. The Germans clearly saw this fight against the pagan Magyars as a holy war and this is demonstrated very clearly in the life of Udalric of Dillingen, bishop of Augsburg (923–73). He actually led his city's resistance, and was later venerated as a saint.

Christians had evidently come to regard war against 'the other', the outsider as defined by religion, as entirely proper, and the Church accepted this. It also tried to mitigate the horrors of war between Christians. The 'Peace Movement' of the eleventh century demanded that soldiers should not harm the persons and property of the Church and the poor, and that war should be avoided on Sundays and other sacred holidays like Easter. By the twelfth century it was common for victors in war to ransom defeated enemies, albeit only the knights and nobles, and the notion of honourable surrender in the face of overwhelming odds was widely accepted. Self-preservation was at work here – the winner might reflect that next time it could be his turn to be defeated. Peasants and non-combatants were no longer enslaved by the victors, and although they were often the victims of war, it was rarely primarily directed against them. This was partly because churchmen argued for such mercy. But the decisive factor was that the western elite drew their wealth primarily from land, whose yield was inseparably connected to labour. Most European war was about possession of land, and nobody wanted to acquire a desert. There is no doubt that the Church was a convergent cultural influence, directing men to moderate the horrors of war. Paradoxically, however, this sacred influence also sanctioned greater violence against non-Christians.

In November 1095, at the Council of Clermont, Pope Urban II (1089–99) preached a great expedition to free Jerusalem, which had been enslaved by God's enemies: 'If a man sets out from pure devotion, not for reputation or monetary gain, to liberate the church of God at Jerusalem, his journey shall be reckoned in place of all penance.'[19] This is salvation through slaughter, holy war in the name of God and at the direction of the papacy. And while Urban insisted on 'pure devotion' he did not forbid monetary gain or reputation. The Byzantine emperor had asked Urban for military assistance shortly before Clermont, because he needed troops to exploit the civil wars in the Seljuq Empire. But Urban had his own agenda. For the first time a counter-jihad was launched, in an explicit attempt to roll back the tide of Islamic conquest. This was a reaction to a very real threat. Islam had conquered Spain and the Turks had recently conquered yet more Christians in Anatolia. Where Islamic armies triumphed, other religions withered away. In an age when religion was the focus of existence, and in a Europe only just uncertainly emerging from the shadow of invasions, it was hardly surprising that a doctrine of holy war should emerge with enormous potential for deployment against all those proclaimed to be enemies of God – not merely Muslims. In the long history of violent confrontation between Islam and the west, crusading was a rare and relatively short period of European aggression. For two centuries crusading launched highly motivated western soldiers into the Middle East (and in fact inspired Christian soldiers, including the conquerors of the Americas, right down to the eighteenth century). The immediate consequence of Urban's appeal was the First Crusade and the seizure of principalities in the Middle East amongst which Jerusalem, captured in 1099, was the greatest.

This was in principle a clash of cultures because religion was the principal defining element in these cultures. For the most part human cultures were little interested in war, which was shaped by the material circumstances in which it was conducted. But the crusades injected a new and dynamic motivation into warfare – the hatred of exclusivist religions for those who differed from them. This ideological commitment added a new fervour and savagery to war, particularly as both sides believed that those who were killed would directly enter paradise. Religious sentiment was the most direct way in which culture invaded war before the nineteenth century. Its influence, however, was intermittent because before modern times the means did not exist to stir up ideological excitement over long periods of time. But there were limits to the intensity and scale of ideological war in the Middle Ages. In his moment of triumph after Hattin in 1187 Saladin massacred the 300 surviving members of the Military Orders, monks sworn to a life of ideological warfare against Islam. After his capture of Acre in 1191 Richard of England (1189–99) massacred its garrison of 4,000 and all their dependants. But these events were the product of particular circumstances. Saladin had achieved an unexpected and total victory in 1187, but he confined massacre to the Orders who were special enemies, and allowed ransom of the secular nobles he captured. Richard in 1191 was anxious to march on to Jerusalem and Saladin was refusing to pay the ransom for the garrison in the hope of delaying him. Crusading warfare was certainly unremitting and much crueller than war in the west, but the conflict fell some way short of the kind of total war which prevailed upon the eastern front in World War II. Truces were common and both sides exchanged prisoners for ransom. Sieges were usually terminated by surrender on terms, though if a city was stormed the defenders were at the attackers' mercy. The fleets of the

Italian city-states were essential to link Jerusalem to the West, but they always continued to trade with Islamic powers, especially Egypt.

Crusading precipitated a fascinating confrontation of military methods between the slow-moving agro-urban war style of Europe and the modified steppe methods of the Turks. The word modified is important, because although the Turks were superb horse-archers, they augmented their armies with other cavalry and some infantry, and learned the arts of fortification and siege. The clash of fighting styles is exemplified by the first great battle between crusaders and Turks at Dorylaeum on 1 July 1097. After capturing Nicaea, the army of the First Crusade broke into two sections, a vanguard and a main force separated by some 5 kilometres. Its total strength at this time was 50,000–60,000, but of these only about 6,000 were knights, about two-thirds of whom were in the main force. The crusaders knew the Turks were about, but on the morning of 1 July 1097 the vanguard were surprised by an attack from 10,000 Turkish horsemen. The speed of these Turks and their technique of surrounding their enemies was a novel and terrifying experience for the westerners. A priest who endured the battle, huddled and fearful amongst the other non-combatants in the crusader camp, later recalled: 'Stunned, and almost dead, and with many wounded, we immediately fled. And it was no wonder, for such warfare was new to us all.'[20]

The knights panicked and fell back on the camp which the infantry were pitching. But this disordered mass of cavalry, foot, half-pitched tents, carts and animals drew the Turks into a close-quarter hacking match which gave the main force time to arrive and drive them off. Luck and numbers brought victory, but the army learned and became more disciplined and more effective as time went on. Crusader infantry went to the fore in battle, and with their spears, bows and crossbows kept Turkish horse-archers out of effective range of the knights' horses until the moment came for the westerners to unleash what their Muslim enemies would later call their 'famous charge', the mass assault of knights in close order with their lances couched which, if it fell upon the main force of their opponents, could shatter them beyond hope.

These tactics served the First Crusade and the western settlers in the Holy Land very well. They demanded great discipline, and the western settlers, aware of being massively outnumbered, always demonstrated that. But the First Crusade had almost been undone at Dorylaeum because it was a collection of armies with no overall commander, and this lack of a command structure dogged all crusades, including the Second (1147–9), which was poorly coordinated. Crusades suffered from all the hazards inherent in any military undertaking, and in addition took place far from home in a strange environment. The Crusade of St Louis (1248–50) captured Damietta, then tried to advance to Cairo through the Nile delta, but was undone by the enemy's closer knowledge of the hydrology of the area and its complex web of channels and canals.

The great military problem for the Turks was that although their light cavalry could sometimes triumph, often by luring Frankish cavalry into a premature charge, victory usually had to be won in close-quarter fighting, the great strength of the western knights. Slowly the Muslim powers built up heavier cavalry forces but even then they were often outmatched. Moreover, the fortified cities like Jerusalem, Antioch, Acre and Tyre anchored the crusader states. Any Turkish attempt to seize one would be frustrated by the crusader field army. And the settlers studded the countryside with castles which, individually, could do no more than serve as refuges and bases for raids on enemy communications, but which collectively made life very difficult for invaders. But perhaps the gravest problems of the Turks were political.

When the First Crusade arrived the Seljuq Turks who dominated Syria were in bitter conflict with the Shi'ites of Egypt. Worse, the Turks were divided amongst themselves, and they continued for long to be racked by feuds. In addition Turks were a hated and alien ruling elite. Many Arab nobles were perfectly prepared to ally with the westerners against them. The Turkish leaders quickly grasped that the best way to consolidate their power was to unite the Sunni in a jihad which was directed at the westerners and at Shi'ites.

Saladin (1138–93) was the leader who brought together the elements necessary to break the Franks. Nur ad-Din Zengi ruled Syria and when Egypt began to dissolve into factional disorder sent an army to seize it before the Latins could. His commander there, Saladin, rebelled, and on Nur ad-Din's death in 1174 seized control of Syria before the Zengid family could act. Saladin is remembered in the West as a humane and even amiable ally, but in reality he was a tough politician. He was a Kurd and as much a stranger in the Arab Middle East as the Turks associated with him. However, he posed very skilfully as the champion of jihad against the Latin settlers, although in reality he spent more of his life fighting fellow Muslims, as illustrated by his ruthless disinheritance of the heirs of Nur ad-Din. But his union of Syria and Egypt squeezed the Latin kingdom of Jerusalem and meant that he could raise about 34,000 mounted men. Moreover, by the time of his ascent to power the Turks had come to recognise the need to develop a heavy cavalry and had managed to a considerable extent to do so. The mounted archers in his army were still vital, but they were better armed than ever before and backed up by more heavily armed lancers.

But by 1187 Saladin was under pressure. He had failed to make much impression on the kingdom of Jerusalem, one of whose leaders, Raynald of Châtillon, the 'Elephant of Christ', had recently sacked Jedda, the port of Mecca, and disrupted Muslim pilgrimage in the Red Sea. In these circumstances Saladin proclaimed jihad and raised an enormous army of 30,000, mostly cavalry. He passed south of the Sea of Galilee and besieged Tiberias. In response, King Guy of Jerusalem (1186–94) gathered a very large army, 20,000 strong with 1,200 knights at its core, and encamped in a strong position at the Springs of Sephoria 26 kilometres to the west. Saladin's strategy was obvious – to draw the Franks into a long march to relieve Tiberias across open country ideal for cavalry action where they would find little water. The Franks were uncertain about their response. Tiberias was a minor town whose destruction would do little harm, and after its fall Saladin's army would simply withdraw. On the other hand, here was an opportunity to crush the enemy, and if it were not taken there was a risk that all Galilee would fall to Saladin.

Despite the obvious risks, Guy decided to seek battle. The course of events illustrates the qualities of two highly motivated and well-organised armies. Guy arranged his cavalry into three squadrons. Each was surrounded by foot-soldiers to keep the Turkish horse-archers at a distance; the Franks clearly anticipated harassing attacks but hoped to force Saladin to deploy for battle, perhaps by marching on his camp. All day Saladin harassed his enemy, keeping his main force close enough to deter the Franks from making substantial attacks on his clouds of light cavalry and far enough away to avoid presenting a target against which they could charge. This army of Jerusalem encamped overnight on inhospitable land, desperately short of water. The Muslims set fires to make their thirst worse, and the next morning, although they surrounded the Franks, held back from attack until the sun was at its highest. The crusader infantry panicked and fled to a nearby hill, the Horns of Hattin, exposing the cavalry. The knights remained solid and made desperate charges as the enemy closed in. However, their horses were tired and the Muslims had created throughout the century a relatively heavily armoured force which managed, in these favourable circumstances, to contain their enemies and slaughter them. With its army destroyed, the kingdom of Jerusalem rapidly fell into Saladin's hands.

The Frankish knights showed great determination and discipline in holding together, and at the last their cavalry remained formidable. The key factor was that Saladin slowed them down badly on 3 July, depriving them of water, and on 4 July exerted such pressure that the morale of their infantry collapsed. The Turks had adapted intelligently to warfare against westerners and skilfully used their mobility in the approach to battle. In 1191, after he had recaptured Acre, Richard I of England led the army of the Third Crusade southwards down the coast of Palestine towards Jaffa. They were in precisely the same formation as the Franks at Hattin, but they could receive supplies and water from a fleet on their right. Saladin was quite unable to stop this battering ram, and his forces were mauled at Arsuf on 7 September. On the other hand the manoeuvrability of the Turks enabled Saladin to escape with his army largely intact.

The crusades accelerated the militarisation of Syria and Egypt, forcing their rulers to exploit tax-collecting machinery rigorously to maintain the soldiers. In 1250 Egypt was under attack by the crusade of St Louis, king of France (1226–70), and it was the Mamluks, the disciplined corps of Turkish soldiers created by Saladin's family, which fought them off. They then extinguished the house of Saladin and created their own Mamluk Sultanate under whom a formidable standing army emerged. The leading Mamluks, each with an armed following, formed a kind of military republic whose intrigues and coups determined the choice of sultan. The regime recruited direct from the steppe and since office was not hereditary, there was a constant change of personnel as new leaders arose from the ranks. The army was primarily a cavalry force, but although they continued to use the composite bow, the state equipped them superbly with fine weapons and armour which made them the equal of western knights and paid them well enough to sustain high levels of recruitment. They were trained on standardised patterns using military manuals, could be augmented by hired soldiers when needed, and were supported by effective logistics and specialist units of engineers whose modern siege equipment was vital to the capture of the Frankish cities and castles. In March 1291 a great Mamluk army, 60,000 strong and equipped with 100 siege engines, captured Acre despite a strong defence. The Mamluks formed a regular standing army about 20,000 strong, sustained by massive taxation of the quiescent Egyptian peasantry. It made them the single greatest land power in the eastern Mediterranean. Theirs was a steppe regime skilfully adapted to Middle Eastern conditions.

How far did the crusades influence western military development? The raising and supplying of large armies for long journeys to the east must have increased expertise and provided westerners with new kinds of experience, but we do not know how or even whether this was transmitted.

The armies of Jerusalem were able to use the mass cavalry charge as a means of destroying their enemies because their forces, constantly at war, were disciplined. Such charges were barely known in the west until the thirteenth century, during which western cavalry improved radically. In 1266 German knights at the battle of Benevento almost destroyed their French enemies by moving forward in close order like a juggernaut. But it is impossible to say how far this was due to the example of the fighting in the east. In any case, by the end of the thirteenth century infantry were increasing in importance. The real lesson of the crusades in field warfare was the need for solid formations and coherence, and western soldiers knew that anyway. The problem was how to achieve it with their part-time armies.

The westerners in the Holy Land certainly developed the art of fortification. The cities of Palestine and Syria with their Roman walls were the anchors of the Islamic regimes of the Middle East. Castles existed but were less significant because this was a more urban society. The settlers naturally built their lordships around castles. Because timber was uncommon in Palestine, castles were constructed of stone, often taken ready cut from the remains of ancient civilisations. But as the threat from Islam grew, the westerners developed the principle of concentricity in new and interesting ways.

Belvoir, high over the Jordan valley, 'set amidst the stars like an eagle's nest and abode of the moon',[21] was built by the Hospitallers in 1168–70. It is a remarkable intellectual concept. An outer wall 130 × 100 metres has square towers set at the corners and in the middle of each side. It is protected by a formidable rock-cut ditch 20 metres wide and 14 metres deep. Inside is another castle with higher walls and strong corner towers covering the spaces between those on the outer circuit. Bows and catapults on this inner wall could thus support the fire of the outer enceinte. All the structures are massive, but what is most striking is that great storage spaces have been incorporated into the walls within which are shooting galleries provided with loopholes and slits so that the garrison could fight from cover. After his capture of the kingdom Saladin besieged Belvoir for two years before it surrendered.

It is difficult to trace crusader influence on western fortifications. The principle of concentricity was well understood in Europe long before the crusade. What is novel about Belvoir, and later castles like Crac des Chevaliers, was the careful design with tiers of shooting galleries buried in the walls and inner defences able to assist the outer ones against assault. Western castles rarely brought all these features together. Mighty

Caerphilly, begun in 1271, is quite different in that it was built around water defences. The castles of North Wales, erected at the end of that century by Edward I (1272–1307), were massive, but they mostly exploit the strengths of their sites. Only Beaumaris (1295–8 and unfinished) really follows the model of Belvoir. Truly concentric castles were very expensive, and it was only the spur of constant warfare which led to their development in the east. It is significant that Belvoir was built by the Order of the Hospital, an immensely wealthy organisation and one dedicated wholly to warfare. But even the greatest castle was vulnerable to determined attack if there was no strong relief army in the offing. Crac des Chevaliers fell in 1271 and Marqab in 1285, each after a siege of one month.

The capture of Crac des Chevaliers, built by the Hospitallers about 1202, illustrates both the strategy of castle-building tactics and the technology and tactics of siege as they were practised all over the world. The castle is built on a mountain spur and the land falls away sharply on all sides except to the south where the fortifications are, therefore, at their most massive. The whole hilltop was carefully sculpted to accommodate the mighty walls. The outer walls are higher on the outside than on the inside: the lower courses set against the rock and soil of the hill have immense resistance to battering, while the inner castle is also set upon the living rock. It commanded an area with a friendly native Christian population whose taxes provided food, but near to the Muslim cities of Homs and Hama which for long paid tribute to avert raids by the garrison. After 1260 Egypt seized Syria and the income from tribute ceased, which is probably why its defences were never modified.

The outer wall is 9 metres high and set with massive round towers at 35-metre intervals and its defences are tiered so that the maximum firepower can be concentrated at any threatened point. Men could obviously fight on top of the walls, though they were very exposed. Below them set within the massive thickness of the masonry are shooting galleries with narrow openings covering all approaches. Just below the fighting top these galleries have box machicolations, which jut beyond the main wall, each providing an arrow slit in the outer face and another in the floor so that there was no dead ground in which attackers could shelter. Below them more shooting galleries have narrow slits through which to fire. The inner castle is set on higher ground with similarly tiered defences of equal strength and complexity, and on the south side two great towers rise from an enormous masonry *talus* or slope, from which supporting fire for the outer wall could be provided. In the highest level of all, most remote from enemy fire, there are wide openings, and these were intended for giant crossbows whose power and height enabled them to outrange almost anything brought against them. At the foot of the *talus* was a large cistern which served to protect the inner castle from efforts to undermine it. How to take such a mighty fortress?

The Mamluk Sultan Baybars (1260–77), knowing that no crusader force could, for the moment, challenge his field army, brought a huge force, equipped with numerous catapults to Crac in 1271. The tactics of siege were everywhere the same: to attack the fortifications on a narrow front (or, more rarely, fronts), deluging them with fire. The defenders might be well protected, but sufficient fire-power could make even shooting galleries untenable. This would open the way for assault by ladder, by siege-tower or by mining, which was used by almost all armies. It could take two forms. A deep mine could be dug, creating a chamber under the foundations of the wall or tower which were supported until they could be burned. At Rochester in 1216 King John ordered twenty flitches of bacon whose fat was needed to set the fire, but specified that they need not be of the best quality. Alternatively, an armoured roof or cat could be pushed up to the wall to unpick its lower courses and foundations. Traditional rams were little used because their crews were vulnerable. All these were methods known to the ancient world and all were open to countermeasures. A deep mine could be countermined – there is such a counter-tunnel, dating from the twelfth century, still in existence at Bungay Castle in Suffolk. 'Cats' were vulnerable to heavy stones dropped upon them, or fire attack. Mobile towers were hard to move and could be battered by the catapults of the defenders, held at bay by heavy beams or set on fire.

The most spectacular form of attack was by catapult. Here technology had advanced markedly since ancient times. The Greeks and Romans had used catapults based on torsion: the arm or arms of the machine were caught in twisted skeins of rope, and drawn back against their pressure. However, torsion machines could throw only relatively small stones. Chinese engineers in the fourth century BC developed the traction-trebuchet. This was a beam pivoted on a solid framework which fired a missile from a sling when the front end was pulled down by a firing team. Such weapons were commonplace all over Europe and the Middle East at the time of the crusades. Most were relatively light machines firing stones of the order of 15 pounds something like 120 metres. City and castle walls were massive at the base, but the crenellations at the tops of walls and towers were single layers of stones which missiles could dislodge and make untenable in preparation for an assault. At the siege of Jerusalem the crusaders threw an enemy spy against the wall using one of these. Much more effective was the counterweight-trebuchet, again a beam pivoted on a wooden frame, but built on an altogether more massive scale. The throwing end of the beam was wound down by a winch or winches against a great counterweight on the front. About 1270 a French engineer drew a blueprint for one of these machines and cautioned:

> If you want to make the strong engine which is called a trebuchet, pay close attention here. Here is the base as it rests on the ground. Here in front are the two windlasses and the double rope with which one draws back the beam as you can see on the other page. There is a great weight to pull back, for the counter-poise is very heavy, being a hopper full of earth which is two *large toises* [roughly 12 feet] long and nine feet across and twelve feet deep. Remember the arc of the *arrow* [the missile, commonly a stone] when discharged and take great care, because it must be placed against the stanchion in front.[22]

This instrument had long been known in China, but first appears in Europe and the Middle East in the late twelfth century. Sizes varied, but the very biggest could throw a stone of more than 100 kg about 150 metres. This could make an impression on even the strongest wall. But these were not super-weapons. Trebuchets are unreliable: I once operated a traction-trebuchet which threw its stone in the direction diametrically opposed to that intended. A little later I witnessed a counterweight model throw its ball vertically, so that it came down just where the operators would stand. In both types the ropes stretch and perish and the moving parts need constant maintenance. The counterweight trebuchet was really very clumsy – in 1287 sixty ox-carts were needed to transport one around Wales. It was difficult to change the range or direction once the machine was set up. And the crew were very exposed to counter-fire. While 150 metres might represent a maximum range, in practice a little over half that was more typical, because it was preferable to hit the higher and thinner parts of a wall. This brought the weapon comfortably within bow-range, and shields had to be raised to mask the crews. In addition, castles mounted machines on their walls, notably giant crossbows and torsion-driven *springalds* which could be brought to bear upon these machines.

At Crac, Baybars focused his attack on the south-west corner of the castle, and his counterweight trebuchets profited from being sited on higher ground. The defenders seem to have had no heavy engines capable of breaking them. The fire of these heavies augmented lighter machines and sleets of arrows which simply saturated the defences. At Marqab modern archaeologists found masses of arrowheads embedded in the interstices of the blocks around arrowslits. Under cover of this kind of fire the Mamluk engineers were able to undermine Cruc's tower and part of the southern wall. Once the enemy gained the outer wall the garrison decided to surrender. Immediately after its capture the Mamluks not only restored the south wall, but they also built a massive square stone tower in the middle capable of supporting a counterweight-trebuchet. They did not want their defences to be outranged. Any fortress would fall to determined attack, but to achieve a result as quickly as this took the discipline to accept heavy casualties, organisation, and fine equipment. By the end of the thirteenth century the Mamluk army was supreme but their sea-power was very limited.

In the age of the crusades Mediterranean naval warfare was still conducted by ships which would have been recognisable to the Athenians and Carthaginians. The light winds of the inland sea in the sailing season meant that oars were useful as ancillary power for all ships and vital for warships. The Byzantine galley or *dromon* was broadly representative of this kind of ship in the Mediterranean. It was about 30 metres long, driven by fifty oars per side arranged in two banks. For longer journeys there was a pair of lateen sails. Its range was limited because it carried a large crew in relation to its size and lacked space for food and water. Even the lighter western galleys of the twelfth century, which had only one bank of oars and carried more provisions, could only stay at sea for five days before they needed water. Ancient galleys had used the ram, but medieval ships were bigger and carried boarding castles at the prow. This was a missile platform – the Genoese were famous crossbowmen – but the main purpose was to board and seize enemy vessels. Merchant ships were much larger, powered by sails and with much smaller crews. Their great freeboard gave them a height advantage over galleys which have to be low so that their oars can bite. But merchant ships were very clumsy, with poor sailing qualities. All vessels proceeded by coast-hopping from port to port, avoiding the open sea. When Byzantium recaptured Cyprus in 965 the army moved overland to ports on the Anatolian coast close to the island, minimising the hazards of movement by sea.

The Byzantine fleet based in the Aegean and Cyprus and Arab fleets based in Egypt, North Africa and Spain were the most important naval forces in the Mediterranean on the eve of the crusades. The Mediterranean was isolated from northern Europe, because although passage from the west through the Gibraltar strait was easy, the current made the reverse extremely difficult. Ships going west needed a network of ports, all of which were controlled by Islamic powers, in which to wait for favourable winds. Venice had a well established trade with Constantinople but took care to exclude competitors from the friendly ports which made this possible. The crusade and the subsequent creation of western states in Palestine was an enormous incentive for cities like Pisa and Genoa, and ultimately Venice, to reach eastwards and tap into the luxury trade between the Middle and Far East. Moreover, because the crusaders had quarrelled with Byzantium their new states were totally dependent on sea-power for communication with the west. Western pilgrims travelled by sea on the biannual fleets which sailed to the Holy Land. Their fares earned vast profits for the Italians which could be used in the east to buy the silks and spices which commanded great prices in Europe.

The wind patterns in the Mediterranean generally favoured navigation along its northern edge, and as the key islands – Crete, Rhodes, Cyprus – fell under western control so western naval supremacy grew. The growth of the European economy, fostered by the Italian cities, encouraged northern traders to enter the Mediterranean, a process greatly helped by the reconquest of Spain from Islam. As a result European shipping technology improved, and by the fourteenth century large round ships, cogs and carracks, derived from northern European models, dominated trade. Alongside the big merchant ships the Italians devised the 'Great Galley', a very large fighting vessel, wind-powered but equipped with oars to provide rapid manoeuvre. The crusades were a major force in the creation of a substantial and deep-seated European technological advantage in naval warfare which sustained the western states in the Holy Land. However, western naval power suffered from the bitter wars between the Italian city-states. The blue-water sailing capacity fostered by the crusades had enormous military potential, but this was for the future.

Much of Islam was uninterested in the crusader settlements and looked to threats and opportunities elsewhere. The Sind had long been Islamic while the Ghaznavids conquered much of the Punjab centred on Lahore. From there they launched profitable and destructive plundering raids across the plains of northern India. India was rich, with fecund agriculture and thriving trade. The spices, so prized in Europe and the Middle East, originated in what is now Indonesia, and they were exported to India in return for cotton goods. Arab traders then rode the monsoon winds across the Indian Ocean to the ports of Egypt and the Persian Gulf. Indian smiths forged crucible steel which found fame in the west as Damascus and Toledo blades. But India was divided. Surveying the history of its empires and kingdoms, principalities and powers, tribes and dynasties is rather like looking at the statue-encrusted façade of an Indian temple: one is impressed by the overall effect, but the details escape the eye. When Islam appeared in India there was no violent reaction such as it provoked in Europe. Its main religion, Hinduism, is an infinite pantheon of gods profoundly influenced by Buddhism. So Islam was simply yet another cult amongst many. Even the terrible destruction wrought by the Ghaznavids was little different from the depredations of Hindu powers. Moreover, in a scene of ever-changing dynasties and powers, there was little devotion to specific political structures.

The Islamic conquerors of India were Central Asian freebooters who might occasionally proclaim their Muslim devotion. The Ghaznavids established their dominion in Afghanistan, seized Iran and mounted destructive raids into India, but they were driven from Iran in 1040 by the Seljuqs and faced great resistance from the Hindu Rajputs. Muhammad of Ghor in Afghanistan drove the Ghaznavids out of India and recognised the possibilities for conquest in the divided state of the Indian powers. Defeated by the Rajput rulers of Delhi at the first battle of Tarain in 1191, he appealed to the religious enthusiasm of his followers, and this enhanced the solidarity of his motley crew of Afghans, Persians, Arabs and Turks. Muhammad allegedly made those who deserted him during the battle wear nosebags and eat grain. More probably, the lure of Indian opulence and the fear of being hanged separately if they did not work together did the trick. His victory on the same battlefield a year later owed much to traditional steppe tactics, for Muhammad seems to have feigned retreat before the enemy army then fallen upon them as they were drawn out of formation. The Delhi Sultanate which he founded dominated the Indus and Ganges plains until the mid-fourteenth century. In the period 1296–1312 sultans led a series of highly profitable raids deep into south India, but threats from Asia prevented any conquest there and the regime itself was destabilised by internal rivalries and replaced by smaller, albeit Muslim powers.

The Muslim domination of northern India was a remarkable phenomenon, but it seems to have owed little to religious enthusiasm. The sharp-edged delineation of religions and powers, so characteristic of the Mediterranean, simply did not exist in India. Muslim rulers imposed the traditional poll tax on non-believers, denounced Hindus as idolators and occasionally, in deference to their more extreme followers, destroyed temples or dismissed non-Muslim advisers. In some areas, like poorly populated East Bengal, huge Muslim settlements created a stable base for an Islamic regime, but the Delhi Sultanate and its successor states, whether Hindu or Muslim, were so mixed in population that accommodation and tolerance were the order of the day. It was less religious enthusiasm than sheer military competence that produced the Muslim ascendancy.

And, as always, access to the ample horse herds of Central Asia sustained dominance in India. The plains of India were excellent theatres for cavalry, but the climate did not lend itself to horse-breeding. The Central Asian connection was therefore vital to sustain cavalry armies. The Hindu powers did not enjoy the same access – often relying on a seaborne trade across the Indian Ocean from Arabia. Soldiers were a special caste in Hindu India, enjoying high status, but war was left to them, and the city people had little interest in bitter resistance. They were used to a situation where dynasties and governments came and went. The mass infantry armies of the Hindu powers were very effective and often fought well, but their cavalry was limited in numbers and lacked the strings of horses of their enemies, and hence manoeuvrability. Elephants provided excellent firing platforms to terrorise cavalry and infantry, but horses could be trained to tolerate them, making their crews easy targets for mounted bowmen. The armies of the Delhi Sultanate drew on many peoples, but their best soldiers were steppe Turks, very like their Mamluk contemporaries in Egypt. Muslim rulers tended to be absorbed into the Indian state system and the raw zeal of religious fanaticism was easily blunted by the luxuries they encountered. But the skill of Muslim nomads from the steppe was a constant, always in high demand from Hindu and Muslim princes alike.

No great religion animated warfare in China, where the exclusivism demanded by Christianity and Islam (and certain Buddhist forms) never took hold. But aristocratic Chinese factions and external invaders from the steppe fought for control over an efficient bureaucracy. Successful dynasties proclaimed an imperial ideology which appealed to the Han precedent of a united people ruled through administrative centralism which was seen as benefiting all people. So refined was the machinery of Chinese government that it conducted censuses as a basis for levying taxes. The bureaucrats were so efficient at this that ambitious Chinese dynasties and their supporters championed the ideology of imperial unity. Even steppe people who seized parts of China were drawn into this system; thus the Toba adopted Chinese ways and even the name of the Wei dynasty.

But this unity was simply the victory of one faction over others. The Sui dynasty (581–619) united China, and extended the Grand Canal, to link the Yangtze to Beijing, bringing grain taxes from the south. But they over-extended themselves in campaigns to conquer the Koguryo Empire of Korea. In 612, despite deploying a great fleet and thirty armies, each of 4,000 cavalry and 8,000 infantry with archers and support troops bringing the total to 20,000, they failed because of the hostile climate, the harsh terrain, the short campaigning season and the numerous Koguryo fortresses. When elements of the army bypassed these strongpoints terrible logistical problems forced them to retreat. Their best soldiers came from military settlements, but they had to be augmented by conscripts of uncertain value. Cavalry were mostly heavily armoured but supported by lighter forces recruited from the Turks of the steppe lands whose internal divisions guaranteed quiet on that long frontier. The Chinese pressed on in 613 and even in 614, but the enormous military pressures provoked rebellions which ended only in 628 with the victory of Li Shimin, founder of the Tang dynasty (618–907) who ruled as Tang Taizong (626–49). Imperial unity proclaimed obedience to an absolute emperor, but the reality was that all government rested to a degree on consent, and the Sui had stretched that to breaking point.

The civil wars which attended the Tang seizure of power had a very grave effect upon China. The 609 Sui census recorded 8,907,546 households and 46,019,956 individuals, but by about 640 the census reported 2,874,249 households and a population of 12 million. Powerful local lords absorbed peasant family lands and withdrew them from the tax lists. It took time for the Tang to re-establish central control. A strong military was essential and regimental headquarters (*fubing*) were established in areas where soldiers were settled on farms. The various *fubing* contributed to a rota of guard duty at the capital, Chang'an, as a means of maintaining contact and loyalty, and when not doing that or fighting, supported themselves by farming. The system provided some 600,000 soldiers who could be drawn upon to form an expeditionary army. Typically such a force had 20,000 men: 14,000 combat troops, including 4,000 cavalry, 2,200 archers, 2,000 crossbowmen with the remainder being spear-armed infantry. The fifty-man platoon was the tactical unit which could be combined with others to constitute bigger forces.

The Tang family had steppe origins, and the need to fight the nomads had enormous influence on their armies. The founder, Li Shimin, was a canny general who won his victories by drawing his rivals into areas where their support was not good and establishing strong positions which they had to assault. Once they were engaged, Li Shimin personally led massed cavalry charges into their ranks. His forces were then ruthless in slaughtering their enemy in the pursuit. He eschewed the very heavily armoured horses and riders which had become usual in Chinese armies and reverted to light horse, often archers, with well-protected riders capable of fast movement. Tang infantry were comparatively heavily armoured and included a very high proportion of archers and crossbowmen to tackle their main enemy, the fast-moving horsemen of the steppe lands. Many of the Tang officers were themselves of Turkish origin and Tang armies frequently included substantial contingents of nomads. In 629 they overwhelmed the eastern Turks at the Iron Mountain (near modern Hohot). In 664 they began a war which imposed Tang supremacy on Korea, albeit at the price of sharing power with the southern kingdom of Silla which, by 675, was in total control of the peninsula. During the Korean imbroglio a Tibetan empire arose in the west, and the eastern Turks also reconstituted their power.

This continuous military pressure, which forced the Tang empire to plant garrisons along its exposed frontiers in the north and west, could not be sustained by the *fubing* system, and the result was the rise of regular armies stationed in the frontier provinces. This regular standing army, some 500,000 strong, including perhaps 80,000 cavalry, was much more expensive. In addition it was quite usual to enlist steppe tribesmen under their own leaders for particular expeditions. It proved convenient to give commanders extensive civil power over their areas, thus breaking the rule of separating civilian and military command which had been adhered to since the Han. These armies were very effective, though not always successful. However, as long as the frontiers held the imperial government was complacent. The Tibetans were pushed back and serious attacks from the steppe prevented by a combination of fortified walls and strong-points held by infantry, and aggressive raids conducted by cavalry. The Tang army was a well-balanced force, in many ways very like the army of the Roman Empire. Its costs were enormous – by 755 about 75 per cent of total imperial income. In that year An Lushan, commander of the north-eastern frontier army, was goaded into rebellion by enemies at court. His revolt triggered others and a long and destructive civil war raged until 763. By its end many provincial governors had become warlords with their own armies and imperial rule unravelled, so by 907 the Tang were confined to part of south China. Once again regular forces showed the tendency to overwhelm their political masters.

Two dynasties emerged from the subsequent bitter wars. In the central plains the Song (960–1127), ruling from Kaifeng, were dominant. The Khitan nomads of Manchuria and north-east China were their rivals, adopting the Chinese name of the Liao dynasty. The Song resented these steppe barbarians, but lacked the strength to evict them. By the Chanyuan

Covenant of 1005 the Song agreed to recognise the Liao regime and to pay tribute, ushering in a century of peace. The rise of another steppe people, the Tanguts on the north-western frontier, was checked when the Song reorganised their army. Much of their army was in garrisons on the long frontiers, with the main field force kept around Kaifeng to crush any sustained invasion. This regular army, on the Tang model, was well equipped and enjoyed real success in the later Tangut wars.

But peace was the order of the day. In 1040 a poet remarked on the unpreparedness of the Song armies in the face of Tangut attack: 'For thirty-three years there has been peace. All the soldiers who have had any experience of war are either dead or decrepit. Those who have been recruited later know nothing of actual warfare.'[23]

For all armies, prolonged peace was a challenge. The Song took to heart the lesson of the Tang collapse and tried to avoid following the same route by subjugating the generals under very tight civilian control. This was a re-affirmation of traditional imperial policy, and had obvious benefits, but the degree to which the military were excluded by the Song from decision-making ultimately proved very dangerous. The long peace brought enormous economic benefits, especially as the canal system connected all the great resources of China. By 1078 the area around Kaifeng was producing 125,000 tons of iron, and bituminous coal was being made into coke for smelting. A vigorous commercial and industrial economy had come into existence and Chinese trade was reaching across the oceans. This stimulated technological innovation which was applied to military purposes. A form of Greek fire was in use by Song navies on the Yangtze and in sieges by the tenth century. In a remarkable military application of this technological advance, gunpowder was developed:

> In the third year of the K'ai Pao period of the reign of Sung T'ai-Tse [969] the general Feng Chi-Sheng, together with some other officers, suggested a new model of fire arrow. The Emperor had it tested, and as the tests proved successful presents of gowns and silk were bestowed upon the inventors.[24]

Such advances were impressive, but provided no decisive aid to victory. And in fact the Song were driven out of north China by a combination of political and military mistakes.

In the early twelfth century the Liao regime came under pressure from a new steppe people, the Jurchen of Manchuria who were unified in 1115 by Wanyan Aguda who declared himself emperor. The Song allied with

Aguda to destroy the Liao. But the Jurchen were far more dangerous than the Liao had ever been. In 1127 a surgical strike by the Jurchen seized the court at Kaifeng and some of the imperial family, but the emperor Gaozong fled to the south. There the climate and geography were very unfavourable to the horse-armies of the Jurchen who also lacked any kind of fleet to cross great rivers like the Yangtze. Refugees from the north were a strong faction at the southern Song court, consistently demanding attacks on the Jurchen. But the Song lacked cavalry, which was vital for any attack on the northern plains. On the other hand they had plenty of footsoldiers and a powerful fleet, so the Jurchen could not move south. The Jurchen distrusted and disarmed the native population and so lacked infantry and the means to cross the great rivers. Moreover, they were distracted by their steppe rivals, the Tanguts, whose Western Xia Empire had formed a modest third party in Chinese politics since 1038. The result was the Treaty of Longxing of 1165 by which the Song paid a modest tribute to the Jurchen and stabilised their frontier on the Huai river. The Jurchen were drawn into the civilisation of China and their rulers took the dynastic title of Jin (1115–1234).

China was unusual in that its ruling elites proved highly resistant to all the exclusivist religions. Even Buddhism, popular under the Tang, never succeeded in dominating the state. This was perhaps because Han culture was far more ancient and elaborate than that of the Mediterranean world and Europe, and had enshrined ancestor worship, often in association with a form of Daoism which is essentially quietist. Hence, although the rise and fall of empires and dynasties in China was bloody and brutal, the driving force of an exclusive religion was lacking. By contrast Christianity dominated, indeed almost monopolised all cultural expression in Europe as Islam did in its sphere. In these civilisations religion was the greatest and virtually only cultural influence upon the direction and sometimes the spirit of war, though this tended to be intermittent and confined to special circumstances which pitted the faithful against outsiders.

On the other hand the Han elite of China had a pride of race and contempt for neighbouring peoples which in some ways paralleled the exclusiveness of the great monotheistic religions. The Chinese did not wage war in a way radically different from the other great civilisations, for they depended on mass infantry armies with smaller cavalry components. But in the great northern plains which are at the heart of Han civilisation the threat of the steppe people meant that the cavalry assumed enormous importance. The nomad challenge was their chief military problem and visibly it was growing as nomadic peoples established their own empires and aspired to rule over China proper. The same challenge was very evident in India, while by the twelfth century the Middle East was ruled by Turks from Eurasia. Europe was largely immune to the challenge of the steppe, and there the importance of cavalry arose from the relative poverty of states which could not afford very large armies. The rising power of the nomads rested on the sheer military skill of their horsemen who adapted very well in the different cultures over which they ruled. This underlines the simple fact that culture had a very limited impact upon war compared with brute circumstances, which had so far limited the impact of the steppe people upon Europe and would continue to do so.

CHAPTER SIX

THE STEPPE SUPREMACY,
*c.*1200–1683

Yuan [Mongols] arose in the northern areas. By nature they are good at riding and archery. Therefore they took possession of the world through this advantage of bows and horse.[1]

WHEN Temujin, better known as Genghis Khan, was born about 1162 on the Onon river in Mongolia, the state of the world witnessed powerfully to the accuracy of the above statement. His own people, the Mongols, were comparatively obscure but other steppe tribes had spread their authority far and wide. The Jurchen (Jin dynasty) ruled northern China. Further west the Tanguts held their Western Xia Empire. The Khitan who had survived the Jurchen onslaught formed the Qara-Khitan (or Western Liao) Empire in modern Kyrgyzstan. The Uighur Turks had splintered into three: in Chinese Gansu, around Turfan and close to Samarkand where as the Kara-Khanids they converted to Islam. The Khwarazmian Shahs dominated south Central Asia between Afghanistan and Anatolia, and parts of Persia. Syria and Egypt lay under Turkish dominion while a Seljuk offshoot held Anatolia. The Delhi Sultanate, of steppe origin, dominated northern India.

Why had these steppe people achieved so much, despite ferocious opposition? Their way of life bred hardy fighters whose riding skills enabled them to shoot the composite bow to great effect. The hunt accustomed them to group discipline and fast manoeuvre. Strings of mounts enabled them to cover vast distances and to sustain speed in battle. This meant that it was difficult to engage them on any except their own terms. Battle was usually decided at close quarters, but their speed and hitting power enabled them to choose the moment and the conditions for this. Their lack of fixed bases gave them endless space into which to retreat and imposed major logistical problems upon their attackers, while their nomadic way of life minimised the type of operating frictions imposed on most armies by the needs of supply.

Their weakness was numbers and dispersion. The steppe is poor, supporting sheep and cattle for subsistence. The only export was horses, which were in high demand amongst the settled peoples. But a single horse needs 120 acres of steppe grazing, so a warrior with a string of five horses consumes the resources of 600 acres, plus whatever he needs to consume himself. This was and is a dangerous environment. The climate is harsh with winter temperatures falling to minus 40. The bland appearance of the steppe is deceptive, for vegetation varies and it is seamed with changes of level and scattered with marsh, a deadly trap for the unwary.

Natural problems were compounded by human threats. The thin population lived in tribal groupings, each of which needed to guard an enormous range against all others. Conflict was inevitable and this meant that life was highly militarised. The terrain provides innumerable opportunities for hidden approach and ambush. Tribes had to be vigilant against attack and intelligently flexible in response. Survival demanded discipline. In the hunt the men of a tribe formed a great crescent and drove miles across the steppe herding game against an obstacle. Those who led these groups needed to be men of proven ability and military cunning. To survive was to be a soldier, to lead required the skills of a general. Steppe rulers shared the tastes of all elites for power and luxury goods like silks and spices from the settled lands. They had to make arrangements with other tribes across whose ranges they needed to drive their horse herds to exchange them for such fine goods. Alternatively, they could subjugate them. Such tribal war created small steppe federations which provoked neighbours to form similar groups in order to resist. Out of the interplay of such ambitions and needs arose real steppe empires. The sheer distances over which authority had to be exercised meant that they were always somewhat federal in nature. The name of the Uighur Turks, who about 745 had established a great empire, means 'united' or 'allied'. They were destroyed by a Turkish people of Siberian origin, the Kirghiz, whose name means 'forty tribes'.

Temujin, born into this predatory aristocracy, understood the needs and the rivalries of the various peoples of the Mongolian steppe and its neighbouring areas. The Naiman of the Altai mountains were a Christian Turkish tribe, bitter enemies of the Kereyids of the Orqon and Tula rivers, while the Merkids lived in the forests south of Lake Baikal. He played them off against one another: in alliance with the Jin he destroyed the

Tatars of Lake Dalai. At an assembly of leaders by the Blue Lake in 1206, he was hailed as Great Khan (Genghis Khan) of all the Mongol peoples. He quickly reduced the Tanguts (Western Xia dynasty) to tributary status and in 1211 attacked the Jin, who became tributaries. Genghis respected the autonomy of steppe tribes, provided they were obedient and contributed to his army. But when the Khwarazmian Shah, Ala ad-Din Muhammad (1200–20) defied him, Genghis descended in person, and in a seven-year campaign, 1218–25, destroyed every city which failed to surrender promptly. Deliberate terror of this kind sent a very clear message to his enemies. Other Mongol armies pushed into Georgia and Armenia and even defeated the Cumans of what is now southern Russia. By the time of his death in 1227 Genghis Khan ruled the greatest empire the world had ever seen.

In 1222 Genghis raided the Indus valley, but the Mongols' conquest there was halted by a ruler of genius, Sultan Balban (1246–87) of Delhi who was himself of Turkish descent. Balban came to terms with Hulagu, the Mongol ruler of Persia in 1260, and defeated Mongol incursions in 1279 and 1285. The Delhi Sultanate enjoyed a vast income from taxes and used it to maintain a substantial standing army. A network of fortifications was built across the Mongol lines of approach. They were manned by native infantry, largely spearmen and archers, (*payaks*) who were experienced in siege operations for which Indian armies had developed sophisticated machinery. Mongol raids became enmeshed in these defences and then fell victim to Balban's strike force of cavalry recruited from the steppe Muslims. In battle war-elephants were highly prized as good platforms for archers and for their morale effect. But Balban himself noted:

If this anxiety . . . as guardian and protector of the Mussulmans were removed, I would not stay one day in my capital but would lead forth my army to capture treasures and valuables, elephants and horses, and would never allow the *Rais* and *Ranas* [Hindu rulers] to repose in quiet at a distance.[2]

The Delhi Sultanate saved India from the Mongols, but the Mongols saved most of the subcontinent from the Delhi Sultanate. The Mongols had their revenge, one of their raids in 1285 killing Balban's son and all hope of a dynasty.

Despite such setbacks, under Genghis Khan's son and successor, Ogodei Khan (1227–41), the tide of Mongol conquest continued. Russia was invaded by the Mongol general Subedei. Its ancient capital of Kiev was destroyed in 1240 and even distant Novgorod in the far north found it wiser to submit. In 1241 Subedei turned westwards. On 9 April 1241 a Mongol force of some 30,000 destroyed a German–Polish army at the battle of Liegnitz, and on 11 April the main force crushed the army of Hungary and briefly occupied much of that country. Despite succession conflicts and regencies at Karakorum, expansion continued, and under Möngke Khan (1251–9) another Mongol thrust was launched under Genghis Khan's grandson, Hulagu, capturing Baghdad with a dreadful slaughter in 1258, then sweeping into Syria where Damascus surrendered in 1259. The attempt to conquer Egypt was defeated by the Mamluks at Ain Jalut in 1260 and the Mongols were driven from Syria. However, they remained strong in Persia where they created the Il-Khanid regime (1256–1353).

The Mongol eruption was not an elemental surge but a carefully planned and organised political movement directed by a predatory elite who made the best use of the fighting qualities of the steppe warriors. They had an ideology of sorts – that the house of Genghis Khan was divinely destined to be universal emperors over all people. Khan Guyug (1246–8) responded to a papal embassy in 1247:

> In the power of God, all lands, from the rising sun to its setting, have been made subject to us . . . You in person, at the head of the kinglets, should in a body, with one accord, come and do obeisance to us. This is what we make known to you. If you act contrary to it, what do we know? God knows.[3]

Genghis Khan established a capital at Karakorum where he issued laws for his tribal federation. He was supported by a literate bureaucracy based on Persian and Chinese models. Restive tribes, like the Merkids, were broken up, but obedient ones were allowed a continued existence. The fluidity and volatility of political forces on the steppe were always threatening to any great regime, hence the severity of his treatment of the Khwarazmians and the Cumans. In this way one conquest generated the need for another.

The Mongols gathered intelligence carefully and were skilled diplomats. They knew the Song dynasty of south China hated the Jin (Jurchen) of north China, and in 1234 it was in alliance with them that the Mongols eliminated the Jin. It was no accident that the invasion of Hungary in 1241 was undertaken at a time when Europe was bitterly divided. In religious matters the Mongols pursued a politic tolerance. Shamanists themselves, they respected the rich mix of faiths which had grown up in

Central Asia – Manichees, Nestorian Christians, Muslims, Buddhists and others. When Hulagu prepared to invade the Muslim Middle East, he approached the crusader states and their European patrons for an alliance.

At the heart of the army was the guard (*keshig*) which protected the Khan and acted as a training unit for young men who would be promoted to command other units. The guard, therefore, was a solvent of tribal distinctions. This welded the army together and created a command structure staffed by men who knew one another's minds and that of their commander. The army was divided into units of 10 (*arban*), 100 (*yaghun*), 1,000 (*minghan*), and 10,000 (*tumen*) which formed a hierarchy in which each commander reported to that above. Mongol horses were hardy and adapted to steppe life by their ability to forage under snow. Their dependence on grazing for subsistence freed the Mongols from the burden of carrying fodder and grain, but meant that their movements over the steppe had to be planned and timed to find grass and to avoid overgrazing. But this limited the size of their armies when they entered different climatic zones. Much of the draconian discipline of the Mongol army was dedicated to enforcing care of horses. As Mongol armies advanced they sent out spies and strong reconnaissance forces, and took with them agents whose main task was organising supplies. They also established lines of communication with gallopers to carry messages.

The Mongols were not, at least at first, very numerous, but their mobility created an illusion of numbers which they were at pains to cultivate. Their advantage in horse-breeding was enormous. When Kubilai Khan (1260–94), attempted to raise horses from within northern China the most strenuous efforts produced only 70,000 animals: a single Mongol *tumen* would have had 50,000 animals. In battle the Mongols always preferred open spaces where their advantage in mobility could be made to tell. The Mongols had quickly appreciated that they could not rely on horse-archers alone, and they developed strong forces of armoured lancers. In battle these better armed troops were masked by clouds of horse-archers. Rapid movement, and especially feigned retreat, was designed to weaken and confuse the enemy, and draw them into an ambush by the main force. After every success they incorporated the troops of the conquered people. And they learned new methods when they made war on settled peoples. In 1211 Genghis Khan's failure to capture Beijing brought home the need to diversify the army if they wanted to attack cities. In 1218 against the Khwarazmians he took a siege-train with catapults and even explosives, manned by Chinese troops as well as 150,000 cavalry. The city of Merv defied the Khan and suffered a terrible fate calculated as a warning to others, when it surrendered: 'The people of Merv were then distributed among the soldiers and levies and, in short, to each man was allotted the execution of three or four hundred persons.'[4]

In 1258 the Mongol general Hulagu took Baghdad with the same kind of well-equipped army, and perpetrated a similar massacre. Mongol adaptability was demonstrated by the conquest of Song China under Kubilai Khan. South China was dominated by rice-paddies which were a barrier to cavalry and the Song had important fleets, notably on the Yangtze. In 1161 the Song navy had inflicted major defeats upon Jin attempts to cross the Yangtze at the battles of Tangdao and Caishi. The Song navy deployed fast paddle-wheel ships powered by men on treadmills, some of which were equipped with trebuchets firing gunpowder bombs. But the Mongols recruited infantry from the Chinese population and created their own fleet on the Yangtze, focusing their campaign on a siege of the twin cities of Xianyang and Fancheng. Their fall in 1273, after a seven-year assault, doomed the Song whose capital, Hangzhou, perhaps then the richest city in the world, surrendered in 1276.

The great collision of the Mongols with western armies was essentially a by-product of their conquest of Russia in 1237–40. Bela IV of Hungary (1235–70) had given shelter to the Cumans who were fleeing before the Mongol onslaught, thus provoking the Mongol commander Subedei to attack. This prospect, widely expected in Central and Eastern Europe by 1240, brought together Bela IV, Wenceslas of Bohemia (1230–53), the rulers of Poland and other minor powers. Such a coalition could have successfully resisted the Mongols. Subedei advanced into Hungary with about 80,000 troops, but he sent 30,000 under Baidar and Kadan into Poland, presumably to divide his enemies. Duke Henry II of Silesia, the most important of the Polish princes, gathered 10,000 men and awaited support from Wenceslas near Liegnitz where Baidar and Kadan challenged him to battle. Henry did not realise that Wenceslas was only a day's march away, and chose to give battle on 9 April 1241, splitting his army into four divisions: the Bavarian gold-miners and other peasants; the forces of Greater Poland; the other Polish princes with the Teutonic knights; his own Silesian troops and mercenaries along with small contingents of Templar and Hospitaller knights. The Mongols masked their main force and their light horse drew the western cavalry into an ambush. Accounts refer to the Mongols using smoke to confuse the westerners: this was almost certainly gunpowder which the Mongols had acquired through contact with the Chinese. Henry was killed, most of his troops were slaughtered and the Mongols sent home nine bags of ears as a token of triumph.

Meanwhile Subedei and Batu invaded Hungary. The response was very sluggish. The Hungarian aristocracy were devoted to their privileges which they suspected King Bela wished to curb. More particularly they were afraid he would use his Cuman allies to crush them. Accordingly they assassinated the Cuman king and many of his followers, weakening their own army. On 15 March the Mongol advance guards reached Pest, where the royal army was gathering, then retreated drawing the Hungarians after them until they reached the banks of the river Sajo at Mohi where, on 10 April, Bela drew up his army in a fortified camp. The Hungarian lords, even at this late stage, were far more afraid of Bela than the Mongols, and because of their quarrels failed to register that the main Mongol force, twice their strength, was on the opposite bank of the Sajo. Indeed, the Hungarians did not even garrison the river bridge some 7 kilometres to the north-west despite its obvious importance. It was only because they were warned by an enemy defector that, on the night of 10 April, a substantial force ambushed the Mongols as they tried to cross. Batu attacked the bridge again, deploying seven engines which threw stones and firebombs, and although the Hungarians resisted fiercely they were eventually forced back to their camp. In the meantime Subedei, though at great cost, forced the passage of the river to the south, and his forces now surrounded the camp, bombarded it with missiles, and on 11 April destroyed the Hungarian army. In many ways this was a quite untypical steppe battle. Victory was achieved by intense fighting on two very narrow fronts, and there was none of the sweeping manoeuvre so characteristic of steppe armies. But this merely illustrates the sheer adaptability of the Mongols, and their ability to exploit the errors of their enemies.

These resounding Mongol victories had limited consequences. Hungary was devastated and raids were made into Austria, but the Mongols then withdrew. There were good reasons for this. Ogodei had died in 1241 and Subedei needed to return to Karakorum to pursue his own claims and ambitions. After heavy casualties at Liegnitz and Mohi the Mongols could not advance into Europe, and Hungary could not long sustain all the Mongol horses. By contrast, there was ample grazing in Russia where the Mongols established a permanent presence. But why did they not come again in strength? They raided Poland throughout the thirteenth century and were certainly not fearful of the military power of a divided Europe whose people were terrorised by this new enemy. But the cramped and seamed countryside of Europe with its mainly arable agriculture was not congenial to steppe horsemen, and the damp climate could dissolve the glue on their composite bows. None of this was, however, insuperable, for the Mongols were highly adaptable and a determined thrust would, as in China, have attracted allies. But Europe was far from the centres of Mongol power, so that sustained conquest would have been difficult. Moreover, Europe was much poorer than China, and hardly, therefore, worth the immense trouble. Decisively, after Ogodei none of the great Khans totally dominated the other Mongol leaders who acknowledged their authority, and they all developed different priorities which, as it happened, did not include the conquest of Europe.

Europe survived essentially by chance, but in India and the Middle East the Mongols suffered clear military defeats at the hands of steppe people already in possession who were very familiar with the tactics of the Mongols and had evolved militarised societies of their own. The Mamluks who ruled Egypt after 1250 were Turkish soldiers recruited from the steppe where the upheavals associated with the Mongol invasions had created a great market of military men. Ruthless exploitation of the peasantry enabled the Mamluks to support a standing army of some 20,000 cavalry who were well armed and highly trained. When Hulagu conquered Damascus in 1259, the Mamluks recognised the gravity of the threat to Egypt. Hulagu returned to Karakorum on the death of the Great Khan Möngke (1251–9), leaving his colleague, Ketbuqa, to hold Syria with limited soldiers of inferior quality, forced to depend on unreliable local allies like al-Ashraf of Homs, to make up his muster of perhaps only 12,000 men. The Mamluks under Sultan Qutuz (1259–60) decided to take advantage of this moment of weakness and gathered an army which was bigger than that of the Mongols.

In August 1260 they concentrated at Acre, the last crusader city in the Holy Land whose rulers observed a benevolent neutrality towards the Egyptians. Ketbuqa, aware of his numerical weakness, took a strong position with ample water in the narrow plain between Mount Gilboa and the Hill of Moreh which was suitable for cavalry. Between two very similar armies on such a confined battlefield there was little room for manoeuvre, and on 3 September 1260 Qutuz, supported by his general Baybars, lined up his squadrons and threw them against the Mongol line whose left was anchored on the spring of Ain Jalut. The decisive factor was that al-Ashraf Musa, ruler of Homs, who was on the left of the line, betrayed his Mongol allies and went over to the Egyptians. Luck also played a part, as Qutuz survived bitter fighting while Ketbuqa was killed. The victory opened the way for a Mamluk reconquest of Syria, but they were not able to make an impact upon the Mongol dominion in Persia which contested control of Syria for the rest of the century and beyond.

The Mongol defeats in India and Syria occurred at a time when the Mongol Empire was breaking up. Kubilai Khan was nominally the Great Khan of all the Mongol peoples, but in fact he was increasingly focusing on his role as Chinese emperor, and his steppe dominion slowly dissolved. By the time of his death the Chagatai Khanate ruled Afghanistan and parts of north-west India together with Central Asia from Turfan to Samarkand. The Khanate of the Golden Horde, extending from Siberia to the Ukraine, embracing the Caucasus and the Aral Sea, extracted homage from the Russian princes as far north as Moscow and Novgorod. The Il-Khanid descendants of Hulagu ruled Persia, much of Anatolia and parts of the Indus valley. None of these had the drive and resources of the united Mongol peoples and all entered into alliances: the Il-Khanids approached western powers in their war against the Mamluks. These were, nevertheless, gigantic empires, and it must not be forgotten that the Delhi Sultanate and Mamluk Egypt were also steppe powers whose armies were constantly renewed by recruitment from the 'Sea of Grass'.

This was a world dominated by the cavalry peoples of Asia. Europe was relatively poor, distant from Mongol power-centres and masked by the Polish kingdom and the Russian principalities which absorbed the energies of the Golden Horde. European soldiers, therefore, mostly fought one another untouched by the dominant military tendencies of the age. But the Mongol Empire imposed peace upon the Silk Road, and trade brought Europe into contact with China. A Venetian colony grew at Yangchow, while Marco Polo became famous as a traveller. Such connections brought to Europe a new technology with very obvious military applications – gunpowder. An English friar, Roger Bacon (1214–94), recorded the recipe for this explosive mixture about 1257. Europeans were soon using primitive cannon; the earliest picture of one is in a manuscript by Walter de Millemete, dating from 1326. This new technology contributed to the momentous changes in European warfare which began in the early fourteenth century.

European warfare before 1300 was really dominated by the knight, whose preferred style of war was mounted. This was fundamentally because European states could not afford to raise, train and sustain infantry forces whose strength lies in mass. Yet war in Europe demanded footsoldiers, and as a result knights often had to dismount to fight, thus stiffening the large numbers of poorly armed footsoldiers. Mercenary foot were often employed, but because of the expense they were dismissed as soon as practicable. Yet there were circumstances in which disciplined foot were raised and trained. The city-states of Italy, especially Milan, defended their independence by insisting that all able-bodied men should serve in their militia – the rich as cavalry and the poor as infantry. These men lived and trained together, fighting with their relatives and neighbours against the enemies of the city. At the battle of Legnano in 1176 the cavalry of the German emperor scattered the horse of the Milanese and their allies, but the Milanese foot held out in their camp until their cavalry could regroup to put the Germans to flight.

The cities of Flanders were equally proud of their independence from their count and his master, the king of France. In 1302 some of the cities revolted against the French king, and the combined rebel army, with the militia of Bruges at its heart, besieged Courtrai. They had 10,000 men including a few sympathetic nobles and about 900 crossbowmen. All the Flemings seem to have had iron caps and most wore some kind of armour. They were armed with pikes or the long heavy club called the *goedendag* (literally Good Day). A French army under Robert of Artois came quickly to the rescue of Courtrai. Artois had about 3,000 cavalry supported by 6,000 lightly armed foot, amongst them 1,000 crossbowmen. The Flemings were trapped between this force and the river Lys, and formed their battle line with the river and the town of Courtrai behind them. However, between them and the French was a network of streams and dykes which they improved and extended by digging pits. Moreover, the weather was poor so the streams were full and the ground which the French had to cross was wet and slippery. Artois reconnoitred the enemy position and secretly bought a map of the obstacles from a defector, and with this he planned his attack.

On 11 July 1302 when battle was joined, the French crossbowmen first went forward and there was an inconclusive exchange of fire with the Flemings. The French cavalry then advanced across the streams to charge into the rebel ranks. But there was insufficient space between the streams and the Flemish ranks for the French knights to develop the momentum of a real charge, so they came to a halt before the pikes of the Flemish foot. A savage scrimmage then developed across the whole line as Flemish foot with swords and *goedendags* sallied out, doing mortal damage to the knights and their horses. The French pulled back to regroup, but the Flemings advanced and the cavalry were tumbled into the streams in a terrible slaughter. This was a spectacular victory, but like Legnano possible only because the cavalry chose to attack infantry in an entrenched position. At Mons-en-Pévèle on 17 August 1304 the Flemings tried to attack the French army, but movement broke up their dense infantry formations and they suffered heavy casualties at the hands of the enemy cavalry. It had always been recognised that steady infantry in a strong position were very hard to defeat. The difficulty was how to replicate the qualities of bravery and coherence which city militias developed as a result of the upbringing of their citizens.

European states could not yet raise sufficient taxes to train and maintain large standing armies like those of the Egyptian Mamluks, the Delhi Sultanate, and the Chinese. But they were becoming richer and an increasing professionalism was starting to emerge. In Italy constant fighting between the petty city-states in the thirteenth century exposed the limitations of citizen militias – principally that merchants and workmen could not afford to be constantly fighting. The militias were at first augmented and later replaced by hiring mercenaries in companies whose commanders kept them in being. There thus arose a corps of regular professional soldiers whose leaders, the *condottieri*, bargained with the cities over terms of employment. The city-states kept small standing forces and hired more for short periods, but demand was so great that mercenary companies stayed together, developing military skills, discipline and cohesion. The rewards of this kind of life could be very great. Muzio Attendolo, nicknamed Sforza (1369–1424),[5] was a mercenary leader whose son, Francesco, became duke of Milan (1450–66), founding a dynasty which would last almost a hundred years.

Of all the mercenary companies the most successful was the Grand Catalan Company. This was originally recruited from Spain and consisted of 1,500 knights and 4,000 *Almogavars* – tough infantry from the frontier with Islam. The Company was a highly disciplined and ruthless force. During fighting in Italy 300 French knights charged a force of *Almogavars*, who 'hurled darts so that it was the devil's work they did, for at the first charge more than 100 knights and horses of the French fell dead to the ground. Then they broke their lances short and disemboweled horses.'[6] After Italy, the Company served Byzantium in 1303, and was so successful against the Turks of Anatolia that the Byzantines, fearful of its power, assassinated its commander. After devastating much of the Byzantine Empire in revenge, in 1310 the Catalans joined the French duke of Athens, Walter V of Brienne. Once again they were too successful for the comfort of their employer, and Walter recruited 700 knights and numerous foot and confronted them on 15 March 1311 at Halmyros. The Catalans raised field fortifications in a secure position and flooded the plain in front of them, miring the Athenian cavalry charge. They and their following infantry were slaughtered and the Company then took over rule of Athens until 1388. Their strength lay in their discipline and organisation. Leadership emerged from the most important knights, and they were respected and obeyed by all others because the members of the Company appreciated that if they did not stick together and obey they would be destroyed. Logistics and pay were in the hands of a single person, the Procurator General. They were able to absorb Greeks and even Turks into their ranks without losing cohesion or fighting ability.

In northern Europe it was in England that the most important changes appeared. After a sustained peace in the thirteenth century, the English crown under Edward I had to create armies for the long wars in Wales and Scotland which after 1337 merged into the Hundred Years War against France. The Statute of Winchester of 1285 obliged all free men to keep arms for the defence of the realm. When ordered, they were required to parade with them at the muster of the county militia for the king's service. Such soldiers were rank amateurs and under Edward I the large infantry forces thus recruited tended to melt away through desertion. But increasingly captains concluded indentures or contracts with the crown to supply men-at-arms and archers with all their equipment for a fixed term and recruited these from musters of the militia. As the war after 1337 was fought in France, these companies often stayed there pursuing free-enterprise objectives whose destruction of French resources suited English policy. This gave the English crown access to a regular army of experienced soldiers, without continuously paying all the costs.

The English wars in Wales and Scotland demanded footsoldiers and more particularly showed the value of archers. Continuous warfare made it worth men's while to practise archery, and the most competent of them equipped themselves with the finest longbows. These were made of yew and cut from the tree where the sap and heartwood meet, providing a draw-weight of up to 150–60 pounds. Such powerful weapons, which could penetrate the best armour, presented a major challenge to the armoured men, whether on foot or on horseback. And these archers were usually mounted, increasing their flexibility, and were trained to work with 'men-at-arms'. This colourless term came into use in the fourteenth century to denote heavily armoured men who fought on horseback or on foot. It certainly included knights and nobles who served in the royal armies. But in a more diverse society many other careers were open to the upper class so that those who chose to become warriors were specialists. And they fought alongside humbler men, perhaps often their poorer relatives, who chose a military career. They were not precisely mercenaries, but were paid professional soldiers and formed the leadership of the emerging companies. The continuous warfare of the English crown in the later thirteenth and fourteenth centuries offered to all these soldiers not only pay, but also the prospect of plunder and ransom of enemy prisoners, giving a great impulse to the professionalisation of war.

Commanders who could count on better armies could think more boldly about the conduct of war. One indication of this was the multiplication of manuscripts and translations of the Roman military writer Vegetius, who advocated military training and a systematic approach to war. Edward III of England (1327–77) recognised the power of the defensive position and the value, therefore, of forcing an enemy to attack him. In 1346 he thrust into French territory doing enormous damage, and drew the French into attacking him in a strong position at Crécy. His son, the Black Prince, achieved much the same at Poitiers in 1356. At Agincourt in 1415 the English again succeeded in drawing the French into attacking a strong line of battle. In each case the English arranged dismounted heavily armoured cavalrymen into close-order formations. The archers, sheltered behind hedges or lines of stakes, broke up the momentum of enemy attacks, which were absorbed and defeated by the phalanx of heavy infantry. Thus the notion of marrying the strategic offensive and the tactical defensive was very fruitful. Fundamentally the English were victorious because their soldiers were professionals.

Victories in battle are spectacular and we, like contemporaries, tend to be hypnotised by them. But much of the Hundred Years War was fought by quite different and much more common methods of destruction. The English crown could not afford a standing army capable of conquering France. Instead the royal government raised companies of soldiers whom they encouraged to fend for themselves when there was a lull in the fighting. These independent groups established themselves in parts of France and paid themselves by ravaging and taxing the countryside and towns. The English captain Robert Knolles attacked the area around Orléans:

> In the year of Our Lord 1358 the English came to Chantecoq, and on the evening of 31 October they took possession of the castle and burned almost all of the town. Then they brought the whole of the region around under their control, ordering every village great or small to ransom itself and buy back the bodies, goods and stores of every inhabitant or see them burned, as they had been in so many other places. The people appeared before the Englishmen, confused and terrified. They

agreed to pay in coin, flour, grain, or other victuals in return for a temporary respite from persecution. Those who stood in their way the English
killed, or locked away in dark cells, threatening them daily with death,
beating and maiming them, and leaving them hungry and destitute.[7]

Such actions eroded the wealth of France at little cost to the English
crown. But ultimately, in France and all over Europe, conquest depended
on seizing great cities and fortifications. These were so formidable and so
numerous that it was necessary to invest heavily in the latest machines for
battering them down: cannon.

The military effectiveness of these new weapons was for long very
limited. Saltpetre, the key substance in gunpowder, was expensive because
it had to be imported from the east. Only at the end of the fourteenth
century did Europeans devise a reliable method of making it, by collecting
animal and human dung and urine, laced with calcium-rich materials in
the dry environment of a cellar: a saltpetre plantation. But gunpowder
posed other problems. If shaken about in transit the different constituents
in gunpowder, sulphur, saltpetre and charcoal, separated out, while it was
notoriously prone to damp. This led to the process of corning: the fine dry
powder was mixed with a liquid such as vinegar and the resultant paste
dried into dumplings which held the powder together and resisted damp.
These were then ground up into coarse grains immediately before firing.
This preserved the powder but created yet another range of problems.

European metallurgy was an art rather than a science. Guns were
usually made by forging together iron rods into a long cylinder, and they
were never cheap. In 1375 a single cannon took forty-two days to build
and cost the French crown 5,000 *livres*: an ordinary French knight at this
time lived on perhaps 250–300 *livres* per annum. The uncertain quality of
metals made all guns very dangerous. Corned powder has a granular structure which allows much greater amounts of air in a charge, and is therefore very much more explosive than fine powder. Smiths had to learn to
make guns stronger – and heavier – and loads had to be adjusted to the
likely bursting point. At the same time the consequences of granulation
had to be explored and appropriate types of powder developed for the
various kinds of gun.

Designing cannon was a complicated business. Siege demanded heavy
missiles to demolish walls, and, as powder became cheaper towards 1400,
gigantic bombards were produced. Mons Meg, now in Edinburgh Castle,
was made in Flanders in 1449 and presented to the king of Scotland some
seven years later. It has a calibre of 56 cm (22 in.) and could fire a ball of

180 kg (396 lb) up to 3.2 kilometres (2 miles). This sounds impressive, but it could only be fired 8–10 times a day due to the heat generated and the need to cool the barrel, while moving its 7.6 tons was very difficult. Weapons like this were only good for siege. Loading systems were also a matter of experimentation. Guns often had removable firing chambers which were wedged into the back of the barrel, but the joint tended to leak so that muzzle-loaders came into prominence. Early weapons used stones which broke up against castle walls. By the late fifteenth century iron balls had become the norm. They were more effective on impact and helped to standardise calibres because they could be made in fairly uniform sizes. Soldiers came to realise that guns with long barrels firing balls at high velocity were very effective, and so monstrous calibres fell into disuse. Gradually it was understood that cast bronze provided a good balance between weight and strength. Carriages based on large wheels were devised. By the time the French invaded Italy in 1494, inaugurating a series of wars which would last for half a century, they were able to bring with them relatively mobile cannon which battered down the medieval walls of cities and were sufficiently handy (albeit very clumsy) to be used in battle.

The earliest handguns in Europe were miniature cannon mounted on poles – staff-guns. Such weapons had been used in China, where they were called fire-lances, as early as the eleventh century. Corned powder was much less dangerous when used in small weapons and, as a consequence, by the early fifteenth century long-barrelled weapons of narrow bore were starting to be used. The arquebus, a weapon with a length of about a metre, some forty times the bore, seems to have originated in the rich cities of south Germany, perhaps most particularly Nuremberg. City authorities wanted to protect their independence, but were little interested in conquest and the raising of large armies to besiege enemies. However, they were open to new technologies and they had plenty of good metal-workers. As a result they developed the arquebus, whose name derives from *Hackenbüchse* meaning 'hook gun', which describes how it was mounted on walls. This weapon was simple and cheap to make, about half the price of a good crossbow, consisting merely of the proverbial 'lock, stock and barrel'. In a wooden stock was mounted a simple iron tube closed at the back which was muzzle loaded. The charge was ignited through a small hole at the back to which a burning match mounted in a serpentine fired by a trigger was applied: this was the matchlock whose outstanding virtue was that it was simple to use.

This was the true advantage of firearms. Dependence on 'native skills' had always been a major bottleneck for armies. Modern analysis of the skeletons of archers has shown that key bones used in the drawing of a longbow become deformed, the result of long practice from childhood. Relatively few men would have been willing to train so intensively. Equally, the man-at-arms needed to develop athletic skills through constant practice from youth if he was to be effective. By contrast, the arquebus was a simple killing tool which almost any male could be quickly trained to use, so that unskilled men could be recruited easily to make up for losses. Of course, the weapons were not very accurate, but the quality of archers too must have varied enormously in this respect. More importantly, the rate of fire might be slow, but this was compensated for by greater numbers and, in time, careful tactics and drill. There were also logistical reasons for preferring firearms. Arrows were heavy and voluminous. At the battle of Crécy in 1346 the English archers each carried 24 arrows and drew on a reserve of about five million which weighed 55 tons. Powder and shot were much more compact. In fast-moving steppe warfare these were not great advantages, but in Western Europe where geography, agriculture, climate and fortifications conspired to slow the pace of war, they were substantial. It was, therefore, worth the effort of compensating for the obvious weaknesses: slow loading and inaccuracy.

The slow development of firearms meant that there was no sudden change in the way armies fought, and at times they had much less effect on war than, for example, Edward III's tactical innovations. Cannon came into use in the early fourteenth century and had obvious value in sieges. But although they were employed at Crécy in 1346, they played no part at Nicopolis in 1396 when a western crusader force was crushed by the Ottoman Turks, nor at Agincourt in 1415, when the English defeated the French. In 1420, when the Hussites of Bohemia rebelled against German rule, gunpowder weapons for the first time played a decisive role in field warfare. Jan Zizka, the rebel commander, knew that his untrained and largely infantry army could not defeat the German heavy cavalry. In the open his raw footsoldiers would be ridden down, and the staff-guns and arquebuses were so slow to load that they could offer little protection. He hit upon the idea of putting his men into trains of heavy wagons which were chained together in a *laager* (circle) when the enemy attacked, the famous *Wagenburg*. Each wagon held a mixture of crossbowmen, staff-gunners and conventional infantrymen with swords and spears, while heavier guns were placed between the wagons. Hussite commanders were defending, so that if they chose their ground carefully the Germans would be obliged to attack these mobile fortresses. The firepower of the *Wagenburg* decimated the attackers, and those few who did survive to close could be held off by the conventional infantry, giving the gunners and archers time to reload. In theory the Germans could have destroyed these *laagers* with cannon of their own, but these were so heavy and clumsy as to be of limited value on the battlefield. In the end the Hussite rebellion collapsed in 1434 because of internal tensions, but the *Wagenburg* was widely copied because it enabled raw troops to use their gunpowder weapons very effectively.

In the mid-fifteenth century English dynastic disputes opened the way for a French reconquest of her lost territories by 1453. The French established a regular force the Compagnies d'Ordonnance which numbered up to twenty companies, each of 100 'lances'. These were *lances fournies*, each made up of one experienced man-at-arms and a squire, both with warhorses, together with two mounted archers, supported by two pages. The archers evolved into cavalrymen and the companies in practice became a regular force of heavy cavalry numbering about 9,000. The French crown recognised the value of artillery because the reconquest of lands lost to the English involved numerous sieges. At Castillon on 17 July 1453 the French were besieging the city when an English relief army approached. The French dug in and turned their cannon against the English, achieving an overwhelming victory to which gunpowder weapons made a substantial contribution. But France was subsequently challenged by the dukes of Burgundy, one of whom, Charles the Bold (1467–77), developed the most modern and massive artillery train, forcing the French to follow suit.

The twist in the tale is that the Burgundians were defeated by the Swiss, a people who had virtually no such modern technology. Since the thirteenth century the Swiss cantons and cities had been fighting for their independence from the Hapsburg rulers of Austria. The narrow plains and passes of the Alps were not good territory for the Hapsburg cavalry, and in the long conflict the insurgents reverted to an ancient formation, the phalanx, equipped with long spears or pikes. At Sempbach on 9 July 1386 a tight formation of pikemen held off a superior Austrian force which was then taken in the flank by another phalanx of pikemen who deployed rapidly from their column of march. It was the discipline of the Swiss that was so impressive, and their mobility because they were very lightly armed. The success of their pikes, some 3–4 metres long and simply a long spear like the ancient Macedonian *sarissa*, with an admixture of halberds (a long-handled axe) underlines the limitations of gunpowder weapons. The long wars had imbued the Swiss with discipline, and as a result they were in much demand as mercenaries, which, of course, improved their performance. However, Switzerland had a small population, which meant that Swiss mercenaries were in short supply. But their methods were imitated, especially by the *Landsknechte* of western Germany who became their bitter rivals.

When the French invaded Italy in 1494 in a series of wars which lasted until 1559, they deployed all the latest military developments. Their cavalry were numerous and superb in their plate armour. This offered considerable protection from arrows, crossbow quarrels and even the low-velocity lead bullets of the arquebus. The most advanced type, developed by Milanese armourers, was cooled by immersion in water producing a very hard surface which was cunningly sculpted to deflect missiles. Such armour extended the life of the already heavily armoured cavalryman on the battlefield, but it was very expensive. The French had numerous *arquebusiers*, and employed Swiss pikemen who formed the backbone of their infantry. Their artillery consisted of the latest bronze muzzle-loaders on high-wheeled carriages which could be used in battle as well as against cities. But as yet no tactical system had been worked out to accommodate this mix.

The long wars with England and Burgundy meant that this French army, the most experienced in Europe, at first carried all before it. For a brief moment it seemed as if the age-old pattern of war dominated by fortifications was to be eclipsed, because the tall medieval walls of the Italian cities were battered by French cannon and surrendered quickly, forcing any state that wanted to challenge French domination of Italy to take to the battlefield. Since neither side had much idea of how to deploy their forces, they had to feel their way. At Cerignola on 28 April 1503 a Spanish army, which lacked cavalry, dug a trench manned by 2,000 *arquebusiers*. The French cavalry charge was checked by the earthworks, and shot down by arquebus fire. The use of field fortifications against cavalry was very reminiscent of Courtrai two hundred years before, and it highlighted the need to shield *arquebusiers*; the problem was how to do it with a degree of mobility, for enemies would not always obligingly charge fortifications or fail to bring infantry and artillery to bear. The *Wagenburg* was one means, but it still compromised mobility.

The beginnings of a solution to combining gunpowder weapons with other arms were apparent at the battle of Ceresole, fought between the French and Germans, on 11 April 1544. The infantry on both sides formed squares in which pikemen created defensive hedgehogs. *Arquebusiers* sallied out from these 'moving forts' or fired from within them. The French and German infantry squares closed with one another in a 'push at pike' so that their *arquebusiers* were firing at a range of 5 metres, producing what one eyewitness described as a 'great slaughter'. The bloody stalemate was broken by the superior French heavy cavalry which drove the German horse from the field and exploited gaps in the enemy squares. This combination of pikemen protecting the slow-loading and firing *arquebusiers* was to form the basis of infantry field warfare for over a century.

But the most radical change that arose from the early experience of the Italian wars was the ease with which fortifications were destroyed by cannon. The tall walls and towers of medieval cities and castles kept out enemies on foot and horse, but were vulnerable to cannon. As a result, during the Hundred Years War boulevards were constructed outside the city walls. These were strong-points of masonry, timber and earth equipped with guns which served to keep attackers at a distance from the vulnerable enceinte. The Italian states of the late fifteenth and early sixteenth centuries lacked such defences and capitulated rapidly to French attack. But Italian engineers soon developed the *trace italienne*. Cities were now defended by thick low walls of earth and masonry fronted by deep ditches. The pattern of the perimeter was marked by projecting bastions, usually arrow-shaped, which housed artillery to outrange enemy batteries. Some city walls were entirely rebuilt, and new fortresses were redesigned on this pattern, but this was very expensive, so more often they were updated and adapted. The result was that within thirty years of the French invasion of Italy fortifications once more determined the pattern of war and the slow style of agro-urban warfare reasserted itself.

The greatest army of the second half of the sixteenth century was the Spanish Army of the Netherlands, created to suppress the revolt of the Netherlands (1568–1609) which was also a religious struggle between Catholic Spain and the largely Protestant Dutch. The basic tactical unit of the Army of the Netherlands was the *tercio* of about 3,000 men subdivided into companies of 250–300, further subdivided into squads of 25. About 500 in each *tercio* were equipped with firearms (though the proportion tended to rise), while the rest used pikes to protect them from attack while reloading. Typically the pikemen would form a square. The musketeers deployed on either side or in front as skirmishers, in formations eight deep, enabling the front rank to fire, then retired to reload while the other ranks fired. Under a general threat, the musketeers could retreat into the square of pikes. Both types of soldier needed careful discipline administered by a hierarchy of numerous officers, but units were cumbersome. The drill for loading an arquebus musket was complicated. In his *Wapenhandleninghe*,

written and illustrated for Prince Maurice of Nassau, J. de Gheyn identified forty-two separate movements for the individual soldier. These were
quite different from the drills for wielding pikes, so command and control
were difficult. Moreover the square formations generally adopted by the
tercios were very vulnerable to cannon fire. The arquebus was so inaccurate
and so slow to load that volley-fire was essential, and even this was so
imperfect that the clash with edged weapons continued, as in the ancient
world, to be of prime importance.

The *tercio* evolved as a result of experience, but this stimulated thought
about military matters. Prince Maurice of Nassau, Stadtholder of the
Netherlands, who died in 1625, became commander of the Dutch armies
in 1590 and, therefore, the arch enemy of the Army of the Netherlands
against whom he would fight at twenty sieges and two battles. Like so
many thinkers of this age, he was inspired by the classical past, and established the first military school, at Siegen in 1616. He was deeply impressed
by the discipline of the Romans and insisted on systematic drill for all his
troops. In the interests of control he reduced the size of the basic tactical
unit of infantry down to the battalion of 600–1,000, with a roughly equal
ratio of pikes to *arquebusiers*. Pikemen formed rather shallower files than in
the *tercio*, but still constituted the centre of the fighting unit with the *arquebusiers* deployed on either side in formations eight deep, each line retiring
while the next fired; when a general attack materialised, they took refuge
behind the pikemen. The result was that Dutch armies deployed into
rather thinner lines which were less vulnerable to cannon fire, and their
battalions were more flexible and more mobile than the huge *tercios* of their
enemies. In attack single-shot muskets were of limited value, so that
pikemen normally went first, followed by musketeers using their weapons
as clubs. Maurice won a great victory over the Spanish at Nieuwpoort on
2 July 1600, but he owed his contemporary fame to his siegecraft.

For the Dutch, wars turned on possession of the numerous fortified
cities of the Netherlands which meant that Holland, Zeeland and Utrecht
formed the only solid block of territory held by the rebels. In 1590 most
of the Spanish field army became involved in a war in northern France so
that Maurice's force of 10,000 could operate freely. Maurice adopted
Roman methods, surrounding his target city with trenches, but with the
significant difference that he then pushed forward more excavations
bringing his concentrated artillery onto a weak point; he employed engineers and specialist contractors for this complex work. Such an attack
demanded careful logistical preparations, because an army consumed vast
amounts of money and stores which could only be collected at certain

seasons of the year. Since campaigning in winter was difficult, the 'window of opportunity' for undertaking such enterprises was limited and it was rare for more than one investment to be attempted in a campaigning season. Maurice took endless pains over the details of his sieges and was impressively systematic; indeed, he established the form of siege warfare for generations to come. The ancient pattern of war based on sieges had thoroughly re-established itself and was consolidated as more and more fortresses adopted the pattern of the *trace italienne*.

Fortresses dominated the bitter religious struggle between Protestant and Catholic, the Thirty Years War (1618–48) which devastated much of Germany and Central Europe. Its greatest soldier was Gustavus Adolphus, king of Sweden (1611–32). He favoured battalions (called squadrons) of about 500 men, fairly equally divided between pike and gunners. They were subdivided into companies and grouped in brigades of four to six squadrons according to tactical needs. Each brigade had a dozen light guns, integrating artillery and infantry. His *arquebusiers* were trained to advance first and then to break down into shallow lines, which were best suited to pouring concentrated firepower upon the enemy. They took with them very light 3-pounder guns which could fire their pre-loaded cartridges even more rapidly than the musketeers. Once the enemy had been blasted by this fire, the pikemen in close order could charge into close quarters. They were supported by artillery using standardised calibres, 24-, 12- and 6-pounders. In the battles of the English Civil War (1641–51) the armies usually achieved a ratio of 400–600 men to one cannon, which was about the same as in late eighteenth-century armies.

Infantry tactics were partly shaped by the existence of cavalry. This was why *arquebusiers*, with their slow rate of fire, had to be protected by pikemen. But everybody also knew that dragging cannon around the battlefield was slow, that drill was imperfect, that movement disordered infantry formations, that troops were prone to panic and that in battle opportunities opened up which could only be exploited by speedy action – the strength of the horseman. The trick was, as it had always been, to choose the moment for the attack. Gustavus insisted that his cavalry charge home to exploit gaps and weaknesses in the enemy formations and in this he was followed in England by Cromwell, whose 'Ironsides' were specifically trained to get in amongst the opposing ranks.

At the battle of Breitenfeld, 17 September 1631, a German Catholic army of 10,000 cavalry and 24,000 infantry supported by twenty-seven cannon confronted a Protestant force led by Gustavus with 13,000 cavalry, 28,000 infantry and fifty-one guns. The Swedes deployed in linear formation and destroyed the Catholic squares, fifty men wide and thirty deep, by volley fire. Such a rare and decisive victory echoed throughout Europe, and from this time onwards linear formations firing volleys predominated in all armies. This was very clearly the best way to deliver firepower and it was made easier with the decline of pikemen. From 1650 armies were adopting the plug bayonet, which was jammed into the muzzle of the musket. By about 1670 this had been replaced by the socket bayonet which fitted around the muzzle of the musket, enabling it to be loaded and fired with the bayonet in place. The long musket thereby became a kind of pike. This was important because, given the slow loading sequence of all firearms, infantry needed to have edged weapons to hold off cavalry. Moreover there was now only one kind of soldier and, therefore, one kind of infantry drill, making it easier to manoeuvre. At the same time armies were discarding the matchlock in favour of the flintlock: a flint was driven by a spring onto a steel frizzen to produce a spark which ignited the powder in the flashpan. This was a surer and safer means of ignition than the burning fuse held in the jaws of the arquebus lock. The pre-packaged cartridge, a paper roll containing both powder charge and bullet, speeded loading and further simplified drill. The soldier bit off the ball ('biting the bullet'), emptied the charge into the barrel and rammed it down with the ball. In attack the strongest and fittest men were often grenadiers – picked men strong enough to throw iron balls filled with explosives far enough to hurt the enemy.

Flintlock smoothbore muskets were one-shot weapons, because although loading was simpler than on earlier weapons, it remained painfully slow and effective ranges continued to be very short. Volley fire partially compensated for these shortcomings, so in combat a battalion of about 600 men would be arrayed in a triple line and made to hold their fire until the enemy was about 50 metres away when a high proportion of shot was likely to hit its target. Fighting thereafter was with bayonets and swords. Cannon, of course, were effective at much longer ranges, but linear formations limited the damage they could do and they remained heavy and clumsy. Because firearms were so limited, armour continued to be worn. Infantry often became disorganised or panicked, so cavalry remained very useful for charging into their ranks or pursuing broken troops. In effect, gunpowder weapons had extended the killing ground and become a longsword, but close order remained vital because armies had to come to close quarters (or at least threaten to) to defeat their enemies. This pattern of close-order infantry and limited numbers of cavalry was essentially a continuation of the ancient and medieval experience, but elaborated by the use of firepower which in its primitive form is best regarded as a kind of longsword, a limited extension of the killing ground.

And there were plenty of other continuities in European warfare. Feeding an army was always difficult. In 1536 the Hapsburg emperor Charles V crossed the Alps and invaded Provence with 60,000 men, the largest army he ever assembled against a Christian power. The French response was very traditional – they scorched the earth, burning and destroying everything which could not be carried away, to the extent that local peasants were provoked into a guerrilla war. They then fortified the crossings of the Rhône and the passes to the north so that the imperial army was caught in a trap. The invaders could get little food from their distant Italian bases, so they plundered the land, provoking yet more resistance from the local people, some of whom actually tried to assassinate the emperor. When the French realised that the mills at Auriol had not been put out of action and were providing flour for the enemy, they destroyed them in a daring raid under Blaise de Montluc on 19–20 August. Faced with the prospect of starvation, the imperial army withdrew having accomplished nothing.

Such campaigns had been waged since time immemorial, and they continued because states with limited wealth and administrative capacity could not overcome the formidable problems of supply and organisation. This is one key reason why, although the European population grew in the early modern period, increases in the size of armies for long tended to be episodic. In the later fifteenth century the French monarchy, with a population of 12–15 million, briefly raised about 70,000–80,000 men. In the sixteenth century 50,000–60,000 was a more normal maximum, though population was climbing towards 18 million. At the height of the Thirty Years War when total population was only a little higher the figure rose to 125,000. These are wartime figures – in peacetime they fell away dramatically: between 1600 and 1620 the French supported only about 10,000 soldiers. The reasons for this were both political and economic.

Overall the wealth of Europe was evidently increasing, but the ability of governments to tap into this was limited, so that rulers could ill afford standing armies. In 1588 England mobilised against the Spanish Armada, but as soon as the threat had passed the men were turned out to die of starvation and disease. The Spanish 'Army of Flanders', which waged the 'Eighty Years War' (1568–1648) to subdue the Dutch revolt against Spain, was a standing force with its own elaborate medical and support services. They should have defeated the rebels, but in 1575 Philip II of Spain (1556–98), at a critical stage in the war, went bankrupt and his troops mutinied, enabling the Dutch to revive. Philip actually went bankrupt three times. If the greatest western power of the age, backed by the wealth of its American empire, could barely sustain regular forces, it is hardly surprising that all other states relied on hiring mercenaries for short periods of time.

The fundamental cause of such limitation was nobles' and city elites' dislike of taxation. Since all rulers needed their cooperation for effective rule, such people were in a position to sustain resistance. Moreover, in most states strong elements of the nobility regarded war as their special preserve and source of profit. The monarchy therefore depended upon their nobles to hire, and in part pay, for troops to augment a central core of royal forces. These were 'aggregate contract armies'.[8] The French armies which invaded Italy in the sixteenth century employed Swiss pikemen as infantry and there were plenty of other mercenaries in the ranks, while many of the 'French' units, both cavalry and infantry, were contingents raised by important noblemen. The disparate elements of these composite armies were, of course, very difficult to control, because noblemen expected to use troops for their own purposes and to make money from them. But at least relying on these intermediaries saved costs, and troops paid by the monarchy could be dismissed to fend for themselves. Even so, soldiers were paid irregularly, and tended to despoil even friendly countryside for their own needs.

This European military system was tested almost to destruction in the Thirty Years War. The war was caused by religious divisions in the loose structure of the German Empire whose independent princes and cities, whether Catholic or Protestant, feared domination by the Hapsburg emperors. This inevitably merged with the conflict between the Catholic Spanish Hapsburgs and their rebellious Dutch Protestant subjects. Fear of a strong German Empire prompted foreign intervention by Protestant Denmark and Sweden, and, decisively, Catholic France. Their participation, in turn, dragged in other powers like Poland which feared the Baltic ambitions of Sweden, and even Bethlen Gabor, the Calvinist-Protestant prince of Transylvania who saw an opportunity to throw off the domination of Austria. Germany became a battlefield whose sufferings were exemplified by the Catholic sack of Protestant Magdeburg in 1631.

Yet the war was episodic and often there was little fighting, but this did not diminish the evils inflicted upon the countryside. Wallenstein (1583–1634) was an able general in the service of the German emperor, but he was chiefly important as a kind of military entrepreneur who could put together large armies, up to 50,000 strong, for his master. The trouble was that although the emperor could raise enough money to tempt men to enlist, he lacked the means to continue to support them, so that as a result they became parasites on the countryside of Central Europe. All too often they pillaged wildly, but Wallenstein understood that this could provoke resistance and even flight from the land, and preferred to levy 'contributions', carefully organised levies of food and money from the peasantry, to support his men. In fact on both sides this process became an end in itself. Wallenstein commanded an army whose purpose, in the mind of its emperor, was to destroy Protestantism, but in pursuit of supply and support Wallenstein tolerated Protestants as long as they yielded 'contributions', an outlook so at odds with that of his Catholic emperor that Ferdinand II (1619–37) had him assassinated in 1634.

Given the constraints on royal finances, war had to pay for itself. In 1630 Sweden provided 2,368,000 *riksdaler* for Gustavus Adolphus's war in Germany, but this had fallen to 128,573 by 1633.[9] Contributions on this scale had devastating consequences for ordinary people, as noted by a resident of Allensbach when the village had to support a company of Bavarians:

> A lieutenant, who got 80 florins in cash every month, hay for three horses and wood for his housekeeping: a sergeant 16 florins; a couple of corporals 12 florins each; several lance-corporals, eight florins each; common soldiers six florins per man. Even then we were still pestered by them and had to give them a good few quarts of wine every week. It all amounted to a cash sum of 270 florins every month, and this lasted for 13 weeks.[10]

Because 'contributions' were the real mainstay of armies, war developed a momentum of its own. Victory demanded a great army whose costs quickly outran the wealth of a state, so conquest was needed to sustain a great army. This vicious circle clearly bewildered even the greatest monarchs. Moreover, their dependence on intermediaries to raise forces loosened their actual control over troops, and the pace of the conflict intensified this subjection. Ultimately such depredations became unbearable and in the end the Peace of Westphalia of 1648 was built around the principle that religion would be determined by the rulers of individual states. The internal security implications of the composite or 'aggregate contract armies' led princes to reflect upon their military structures, particularly as they were painfully aware that their armies lagged behind those of their nearest neighbours, the Ottoman Turks, a steppe people whose urge to expansion was threatening to Central Europe and the Mediterranean.

In the period 1300 to 1650 Europeans were very struck by the changes wrought in their armies by gunpowder weapons. In 1598 an English writer explained: 'The wars are much altered since the fierie weapons came up.'[11] And indeed much progress had been made in adapting to the new gunpowder technology, but European armies remained incoherent, ill-organised and ill-disciplined, and there had been little change in the balance of advantage between steppe forces and those of the settled agro-urban world. The Mongol eruption of the thirteenth century had lost its momentum, but a small Turkish principality or *beylik* emerged in western Anatolia ruled by Osman (1281–1321) which attracted recruits from the steppe on a large scale because it was hard up against Christian Byzantine territory. Osman's Turkish light cavalry soon came to dominate western Anatolia, partly because civil strife wrecked the Byzantine Empire and many Christian peasants came to terms with the Turks who offered religious toleration in return for obedience and moderate taxes. Turkish horsemen could not take fortifications, but their hold over the countryside isolated cities, so that Bursa fell in 1326 and Nicaea in 1331. The Turks were then invited into Greece by nobles fighting in a series of bitter Byzantine civil wars, and by 1363 had seized Adrianople.

The Ottoman ruler Murad I (1362–89), seeing the political dangers of relying on Turkish tribal leaders, reorganised the army. In each province or *sanjac* he established a substantial group of *sipahis*, heavy cavalrymen who formed the strike force of his army. Income from land grants (*timar*) supported these men who formed the dominant force within the *sanjac*. At least 50,000 cavalrymen could be raised in this way. In addition the Sultan could raise numerous 'raiders' (*akinjis*), the traditional light horse of the steppe. They were vital for the war of raids and destruction along the Christian frontier in Central Europe and the Balkans, and as counters to the light cavalry of Mamluk Egypt and Safavid Persia in the east. In the fifteenth century some 20,000 were registered for service, but as many as 40,000 might accompany a great imperial expedition. With the extinction of Hungary and the hardening of the Austrian frontier with a line of fortresses towards the end of the sixteenth century, they became less useful, and the sultans preferred to hire light horse at need from the Tatars of southern Russia.

But the Ottomans needed infantry if they were to adapt to European conditions and extend their expansion westwards. The *Azabs* were conscripts, usually fairly lightly armed with spear, shield and sword, often raised from towns. A law text of 1499 explains:

If, for example, it falls to twenty households to provide one *Azab*, from among the twenty people [provided by the twenty households] in that quarter, one suitable should be enrolled for *Azab* service. Expenses for him should be collected from the remaining nineteen households.[12]

In practice there was probably never a total mobilisation of the *Azabs*, but they could provide mass in the field and they were very useful in sieges and as fighters on ships.

But such territorial forces inevitably lacked the discipline and commitment of regulars and gradually they became supplementary to the Palace army, the regular troops of the Sultan who were paid out of taxes and formed the heart of the Ottoman forces. Their cavalry was made up of splendidly equipped *sipahis*, whose numbers rose to a strength of over 10,000. The infantry were the janissaries, a corps of slave-soldiers who belonged to the Sultan, recruited as a form of taxation from the sons of the Christian population. They were founded as an elite force to counterbalance the Turkish tribal leaders who dominated the court and disposed of considerable military followings. Because of this, numbers were at first limited to about 6,000. But they were well paid and organised in regiments which had their own auxiliary functions like medical services. Their status made them very attractive to potential recruits. As the sultans needed good infantry they were expanded by allowing Turks to join, so that by the late sixteenth century they numbered about 12,000. The Palace army also included gunners, engineers and drivers, who in the sixteenth century were formed into regular units, far in advance of European practice where such functions were given out to civilian contractors. By the early sixteenth century this standing army stood at 16,000 and rose thereafter to 26,000.

Europeans regarded Turkish armies as vast, and there was certainly the potential to raise an army of 100,000. But actually, as in Europe, 50,000 was a very large army. What made the Ottoman army so effective was not so much its sheer numbers as the considerable size of the highly disciplined and well-organised soldiers of the Palace army which formed its core. The territorial forces were much less important, and because of this could be more easily controlled. On campaign the Palace army and the provincial troops were supported by special corps which prepared roads, supplied food and established camps. Engineers were an integral part of the army and sappers were enlisted to do the hard work of digging so vital in siege warfare. Campaigns were carefully planned beforehand, and all these fighting elements were brought together as appropriate for the circumstances. Above all, regular payment, an efficient supply system and good facilities resulted in the impressive discipline which underlay the fighting capacity of the Ottoman soldier. In 1665 a European observer commented:

> In the Turkish camp no brawls, quarrels or clamours are heard; no abuses are committed on the people in the march of their army; all is bought and paid with money, as by travellers that are guests at an inn.[13]

This was the key to its effectiveness. Moreover, the Turkish court was highly receptive to new ideas. They recognised the value of firearms, and soon after the capture of Constantinople in 1453 established foundries for the manufacture of cannon and handguns together with gunpowder factories in Constantinople, which became their new capital.

The Ottomans were Muslims, profoundly influenced by Persia whose language was adopted by their court. They retained their steppe traditions and their Turkish culture, but adopted fighting methods appropriate to their new environment in Europe. This is a clear illustration of the importance of material and environmental factors in determining military methods, irrespective of cultural traditions. The Ottomans learned a great deal from their confrontation with the Hungarians. When they attacked Belgrade in 1440 they encountered determined resistance led by John Hunyadi who used the *Wagenburg* to hold off Ottoman cavalry. In 1444 Hunyadi led an allied army 20,000 strong against the Turks who had gathered about 60,000. On 10 November, at the battle of the Varna, the Ottomans were victorious, but only by the narrowest of margins. They owed their victory to the stubborn resistance of the janissaries who fought from behind fortified positions in the centre of the Turkish line. Even so, Turkish casualties were enormous, largely because many of their soldiers had never before encountered gunpowder weapons.

The Ottoman victory at Varna opened the way for the attack on Constantinople in 1453, by which time the sultans had strengthened the janissaries, increased the number of firearms amongst them, and created a corps of artillerymen who were aided by European technicians in the casting of the huge bombards which smashed through the walls of the city. Once they had absorbed the old Byzantine Empire, the obvious line of penetration lay up the Danube valley. Here in the early sixteenth century they confronted the Hungarians who had managed to fight off earlier Ottoman attacks and had enjoyed a long peace. But the Hungarians had not developed a real state bureaucracy and taxation for the army was largely controlled by the aristocracy who were deeply suspicious of crown 'despotism'. As a result the Hungarians had failed to keep up with military developments and their army continued to be based on noble retinues. On 29 August 1526 at Mohács the Hungarians under King Louis II (1516–26), with about 25,000 men including 10,000 infantry, challenged an Ottoman force 70,000 strong under Suleiman the Magnificent (1520–66). Despite initial Hungarian successes, the janissaries, armed with arquebuses, deployed in a *Wagenburg* and triumphed. But the Ottomans made limited gains from the victory. Louis II was killed at Mohács, but he was married to a Hapsburg, and as a result the emperor Charles V claimed as much of Hungary as he could prevent the Ottomans from occupying. Thereafter the Hapsburgs expanded their army and planted modern fortresses along the frontiers. Importantly, in contrast to the Orthodox of the old Byzantine lands, their fiercely Catholic subjects hated the Turks and took arms against them as irregulars. But as German emperors and champions of the Catholic cause the Hapsburgs became deeply involved in the Thirty Years War, and this should have enabled the Ottomans to advance.

However, the Ottomans had other enemies. They were devoutly Sunni and regarded themselves as the leaders of the Muslim world, but the fierceness of their orthodoxy provoked rebellion by the Shi'ites of Anatolia. When some of them were driven out by the Ottomans, they moved eastwards and under the leadership of the Safavid dynasty created a mighty Persian Empire. Their Shi'ite zeal enabled them to foment rebellion in Anatolia, and they conspired with the rivals of Selim I (1512–20) when his accession was contested. In 1513 Selim allied with the Uzbeks on the southern steppe and led a huge Ottoman army, perhaps 60,000 strong, against Shah Ismail (1502–24). In the rough mountainous country it was hard to feed such a force, especially as the Safavids resorted to scorched earth tactics. Discontent was rife among the Ottoman forces, so when Selim heard that Shah Ismail had advanced from his capital at Tabriz and was gathering his men on what is now the Turko–Iranian border, he was eager for battle.

The Persian army was a steppe cavalry force and the clumsy and slow firearms of the age were of little importance in their fast-moving style of war. On 23 August 1513, at Chaldiran, they were heavily outnumbered by the Ottomans with their strong cavalry, infantry and artillery elements. The janissaries, in a *Wagenburg* supported by cannon, cut down the attacking Persian horsemen who were driven from the field by the disciplined Turkish *sipahis*. Shah Ismail was wounded and barely escaped. Chaldiran might seem to signal the triumph of gunpowder weapons over steppe methods, but the real reason for the Safavid defeat was overconfidence; they attacked despite being heavily outnumbered and scorned the option of drawing the starving Ottomans deeper into barren territory. By 1533 the Ottomans had repelled the Safavid bid to dominate Iraq, but conquering Persia was beyond them. This was an ideological war – the Ottoman Sunni against the rigidly Shi'ite Safavid regime. The brilliant Shah Abbas I (1587–1629) promoted the trade of Iran and sought alliances with European powers against the Ottomans. He moved his capital from the exposed frontier to Isfahan which he made into a shining cultural centre.

In military affairs Shah Abbas brought in two Englishmen, Robert Sherley and his brother Anthony, who helped him to create an artillery arm and infantry units with firearms. The wars against the Ottomans which began in 1603 focused on Iraq where Abbas seized Baghdad in 1622. It was this trouble in the east, which continued until 1639, that prevented the Ottomans from intervening while Europe tore itself apart in the religious holocaust of the Thirty Years War. The crucial event in this conflict was the eventual Ottoman capture of strongly fortified Baghdad in 1638. The Ottoman siege was as systematic as any conducted by Prince Maurice of Nassau. Some 24,000 sappers and 8,000 engineers supported the soldiers in digging trenches around the city, from which zigzag trenches were thrown forward towards the fortifications. Cannon were floated down the Tigris and run through the zigzags to positions from which they could be placed on raised gabions to bear upon the walls. For most of the thirty-nine days of the siege there was little actual fighting, but enormous effort was put into digging, clearing and filling by both attackers and defenders. Nearly half a century later such methods would almost deliver Vienna to the Ottomans.

Mamluk Egypt was alarmed by Chaldiran. Its standing army had long been deprived of steppe recruits who preferred the profits and plunder offered by the Ottomans in their successful wars against Christian powers. Moreover, armies atrophy through disuse, and by the time it challenged the Ottomans the Mamluk army had not faced any real enemies for a very long time. Given their cavalry tradition of speed and movement their slow adoption of firearms is hardly surprising. But perhaps the real reason for the Mamluk collapse was the excellence of their enemies. What the Mamluks encountered at the battle of Marj Dabiq on 24 August 1516 was the most modern and experienced army in the Mediterranean.

The Ottomans placed their best cavalry on the wings, while the janissaries held the centre in a *Wagenburg* and in front of them were the

Azabs preceded by the 'Raiders'. The Mamluks obligingly charged the
Ottoman centre where the 'Raiders' and *Azabs* absorbed much of their
momentum, and as they checked before the janissaries the *sipahis* cut
them to pieces. At Raydaniyya in the following year the Mamluks improvised artillery and threw *arquebusiers* into the battle, but it was too late and
they were crushed – armies took time to adapt and the Mamluks had been
slow, in the face of an enemy who moved very quickly. The conquest of
Egypt brought naval matters to the fore for the Ottomans, because sea
routes provided the obvious link between Constantinople and its rich new
dominion in the Nile valley. This is why, in 1522, the Ottomans cleared
the Knights Hospitaller from Rhodes, leaving Venetian-ruled Cyprus as
the last crusading outpost in the eastern Mediterranean.

The creation of a navy is an indication of the remarkable adaptability of
the Ottomans. They saw it as a means to circumvent the formidable
fortresses the Austrians were creating. Oared galleys remained the strike
force of Mediterranean fleets as they had been in the ancient world. Most
Mediterranean trade was carried in large square-sailed merchantmen
called carracks; they had considerable military potential because they
carried heavy guns in broadsides, but they could not manoeuvre well in the
light winds of the Mediterranean. Nonetheless, their size and height and
weight of broadside made them useful. To counter these, by the sixteenth
century galleys were bigger and carried very heavy cannon under the fore-
castle, mounted in wooden slides to absorb the recoil. This combined with
manoeuvrability to revive the galley as a fighting vehicle and even in the
northern seas the English and Dutch experimented with them. So intense
was the naval warfare in the Mediterranean that all the powers resorted to
slaves to man the oars of the galleys, and even mounted raids especially to
obtain them.

By 1540 a Turkish fleet was holding sway in the Adriatic and threatening
Italy, while other Ottoman forces were clearing North Africa of Spanish
bases like Tripoli. But the short-range galley fleets needed bases, and
in 1565 the Ottomans attacked Malta where their old enemies, the
Hospitallers, were established. An enormous fleet of 200 ships conveyed an
army of about 30,000 to seize this small island held by a garrison of some
8,000 in what is known as the Great Siege (May–September 1565). The
Ottoman command was divided between a general, Lala Mustafa Pasha,
and an admiral, Piyale Pasha. The forts of the Hospitallers dominated the
two best anchorages of Grand Harbour and Marsamuscetto, obliging the
fleet to anchor in May at Marsasirocco. Piyale Pasha was painfully aware
that this harbour was very exposed and that if the wind blew from the

south, as it often does, his fleet would be destroyed and with it the whole expedition. Quite reasonably, he insisted that the army first attack Fort St Elmo on the tip of what is now Valletta, so as to open Marsamuscetto for the fleet as a preliminary to an assault on the forts in Grand Harbour. The Turkish army became locked into a terrible siege against very determined resistance, and because it had never cleared the central and northern parts of the island a relief force from Spain was able to land and end the siege.

In 1570 the Ottomans attacked Cyprus which was then held by Venice. To save the island the papacy created a 'Holy League' of Spain, Sardinia, Sicily, Naples and Venice which mustered 208 ships, of which 202 were galleys and the remainder galleasses (very large galleys relying on both sails and oars and capable of carrying much artillery). The fleet carried 12,000 crew and 24,000 soldiers, all under the command of Don Juan of Austria. The Ottomans fielded 222 galleys and about sixty lighter craft, carrying crews of 13,000 and about 24,000 soldiers. The Christians sought out the Ottoman fleet which they knew was gathered at its base of Lepanto in the Gulf of Patras and on 7 October 1571 destroyed it with great slaughter. Some 187 Turkish ships were sunk or captured and 20,000 sailors and soldiers killed, for the loss of seventeen Christian ships and 7,500 men.

Several factors contributed to bring about this result. Many of the Christian ships were rowed by free oarsmen, who were acknowledged to be better than slaves. The Turks had very few janissaries while some 10,000 Spanish regulars proved formidable. Above all, the Ottomans had only some 750 cannon, while the Christians had about 1,800 – and it is known that the heavy broadsides of the galleasses wrought great destruction. Lepanto was the last great clash of whole fleets of galleys, because evolving naval technology made them obsolete. In galley warfare each ship lay alongside its enemy and the crews fought hand to hand. The massive use of cannon on board these relatively light vessels caused carnage. Despite the victory, the western powers were unable to recover Cyprus; the Ottomans, however, could not make up for the losses of skilled sailors at Lepanto and never again threatened the western basin of the Mediterranean. But they were able to drive Spain from her North African enclaves, forcing her out of the war in the Mediterranean in 1580, and in 1640 Crete fell to the Ottomans.

Turkish conquest in Eastern Europe continued. By 1606 Austria had conceded much territory in Hungary and Croatia. The Austrians controlled the better part of Hungary but their clumsy handling of the fractious nobles and their savagery in persecuting Protestants provoked revolts. Many Hungarians were ready to settle for Ottoman tolerance so by 1682 the country had fallen to the Turks. The Grand Vizier, Kara

Mustafa Pasha, persuaded the Ottoman court that this presented an opportunity to end the stalemate in Central Europe.

Vienna was the heart of the German and Slavonic lands which belonged to the Hapsburg family. They had also monopolised elections to the German Empire for centuries. Their dominions were the greatest obstacle to Ottoman advance in the Danube valley. Vienna was defended by modern fortifications and powerful artillery bastions. By the time the Ottoman army under Mustafa Pasha arrived on 14 July 1683 most of its population had fled, leaving about 16,000 soldiers and 9,000 volunteers to man the defences. Attacking a modern fortification was necessarily a slow business, but the successful siege of Baghdad in 1638 showed that the Ottomans were perfectly familiar with the technique. Europeans were impressed by the systematic way in which the Turkish army went about its business and by its strict discipline.

But at Vienna the Ottomans had only about 150 cannon because they were at the utmost reach of their logistics and such weapons were enormously heavy. The city garrison controlled some 260 cannon, though contemporaries believed that their muskets were outranged by those of the Ottomans. To compensate for their lack of artillery, the Ottomans tunnelled under the walls and dug mines whose explosions damaged the city's bastions. Very soon Vienna was short of food and sickness was ravaging the garrison. But by September a coalition of European powers headed by the Poles was on its way. In the fringe of the Vienna woods at Kahlenberg on 11–12 September 1683 the coalition forces, some 80,000 strong, defeated 50,000 Turks and raised the siege. It had been a close-run affair and Vienna was probably saved because the Turks did not realise how quickly a coalition against them was forming. In the war which followed the Ottomans lost Hungary to the Hapsburgs and were obliged to accept this loss by the Peace of Karlowitz of 1699. However, they retained their dominion over Eastern Europe.

The Ottomans were a steppe people who adapted to different conditions and simultaneously fought off the Safavids and dominated the western Mediterranean. From this perspective the European exploration of the Atlantic and the route around Africa, which began in earnest in the fifteenth century, can be seen in part as a reaction to Ottoman power. Portuguese expansion into the Indian Ocean was certainly designed to break the Muslim stranglehold on trade with the Indies. But this still ultimately had to be done by war. By the late thirteenth century the conquest of Muslim Spain had progressed sufficiently to allow extensive trade through the Straits of Gibraltar, creating a single European market.

Shipbuilding expertise developed large ships, the cogs and carracks, which carried bulk commodities like wool and alum. The lure of the profitable trade in African slaves, hitherto monopolised by Muslim traders crossing the Sahara, and a growing knowledge of the islands of the Atlantic, led to exploration of the African coast. The Portuguese used caravels, small handy vessels with fine sailing qualities.

But once in the Indian Ocean they encountered Islamic imperialism in the form of settlements like Zanzibar along the African coast. To seize them the Portuguese brought in bigger ships equipped with cannon and in 1509 their fleet destroyed a Muslim naval force off Diu in Gujarat and laid the foundations for a seaborne empire which for a time dominated the seaways to the Spice Islands. Muslim traders appealed to the Ottoman sultans for protection, but their preoccupations elsewhere prevented any effective intervention. The Spanish conquest of the Americas was another important consequence of the intensification of shipping through the Gibraltar Straits and the desire to circumvent Muslim power in the Mediterranean. The new trading systems were made possible by the great ships with their heavy broadsides of cannon, and in the long run they intensified wealth production in Europe, but for the moment not to the point where the small European states could rival the mighty armed forces at the disposal of the steppe empires.

It was the clash of these steppe empires which settled the fate of most of the world. In 1336, somewhere near Samarkand in what is now Uzbekistan, was born Timur, the child of a Turkish chieftain converted to Islam. By 1369 this warrior, who claimed descent from Genghis Khan, ruled Samarkand. In 1383 he swept into Persia where the Il-Khanid regime had collapsed, and by 1395 he had subjugated the Golden Horde of what is now southern Russia. In 1398 he invaded India and destroyed the Delhi Sultanate in a terrible massacre which he himself recorded:

> In a short space of time all the people in the [New Delhi] fort were put to the sword, and in the course of one hour the heads of 10,000 infidels were cut off. The sword of Islam was washed in the blood of the infidels, and all the goods and effects, the treasure and the grain which for many a long year had been stored in the fort became the spoil of my soldiers.[14]

Shortly after, he captured Aleppo and Damascus, and in 1401 seized Baghdad, massacring all its inhabitants. On 28 July 1402 he destroyed the Ottoman army at the battle of Ankara and captured Sultan Bayazid (1389–1403), who died a prisoner. By this time, however, the Ottoman regime was primarily European and Timur never followed up his victory. He died in February 1405 preparing to attack China. Feuding amongst the various steppe dynasties broke up his Asian empire, and the Timurids, in the person of Babur (1483–1530), were driven into Afghanistan. Babur allied with the Safavids to reassert his Central Asian claims, but their defeat at Chaldiran undermined his position and his Uzbek enemies drove him back to Kabul.

Babur's raids on India to raise funds for more wars in Central Asia revealed the real opportunities there, not least because the Afghan Sultanate of Delhi was divided and had many enemies. Babur raised an army of about 12,000, a tiny force to conquer such a vast area. The Hindu powers of south India used firearms, but the Delhi Muslims were largely ignorant of them. Aware of the lessons of Chaldiran, Babur purchased cannon and muskets and the services of Turkish instructors, though the bulk of his force was made up of heavy and light Asian cavalry. At Panipat, 80 kilometres north of Delhi, in April 1526, Babur confronted the Delhi army of about 100,000 cavalry. He placed a *Wagenburg* at the centre of his line and when this repelled the enemy advance, sent his cavalry to encircle the Delhi forces, causing enormous panic and destruction. Almost immediately Babur seized Delhi and Agra and began a process of conquest which eventually would reach deep into south India, creating the Mughal Empire.

As always, power in India depended on control of the horse supply from Central Asia. The Mughal army was based on horse-archers backed up by more heavily armoured troops, equipped for shock tactics. These men were recruited by important Muslim leaders, *mansabdars* or *amirs*, from the tide of horsemen from the Central Asian fringes and northern India. Zamindars were petty local gentry responsible for recruiting local troops. The soldiers were paid by state taxes, forming a distinct and separate group in the population. Given the wealth of India, the Mughals were able to mobilise huge armies, of up to 100,000 or even 200,000, largely consisting of masses of horsemen, and in the open plains of India such forces were virtually irresistible. Moreover, Mughal emperors down to the time of Aurangzeb (1658–1707) led their armies in person, leaving the centralised bureaucracy to collect the taxes which supported them.

Relatively little attention was paid to fortifications – because the Mughals were expanding until the early eighteenth century and their control of Afghanistan meant that they did not fear attack from the steppe. Because sieges were rare, artillery was not needed, and could only have hindered the fast-moving cavalry armies of the Mughals. Rockets were used, presumably because they were light and could frighten both horses and men. Indian matchlock guns were of excellent quality and musketeers were important because of this – their deployment at Panipat in 1526 showed that they could anchor a line and form a formidable obstacle to sweeping cavalry movement. Mughal India, therefore, resembled Safavid Persia rather more than Ottoman Turkey, in that steppe methods were eminently suited to the environment and required only limited adaptation.

But the greatest empire of the steppe people was China whose Mongol conquerors faced the same dilemma as earlier nomad conquerors. It was apparently suggested to Kubilai Khan that he should either destroy north China and annihilate its population so that the land would revert to grass over which the steppe people could spread their way of life, or adopt the Chinese method of government by extracting taxes. In proclaiming the Yuan dynasty in 1271, Kubilai opted for the second course of action, but not unequivocally. And these equivocations ultimately helped to destroy his dynasty. He was a Mongol Khan as well as a Chinese emperor. He distrusted Chinese administrators, but faced divided attitudes to rule over China amongst the Mongol elite whose control of the cavalry armies of the steppe made them essential to his government.

Within China Kubilai established a pattern of legally defined military households, each of which was obliged to provide a properly equipped warrior in return for tax exemption. This military caste was sharply distinguished from the civil elite. Moreover, across China the local aristocrats and gentry had become ever more wary of imperial service in which the risks of a violent end had always been great. In effect, therefore, they tended to separate themselves from the state and from the conduct of war. At the top, Mongol nobles quarrelled with one another and with Chinese advisers. Factional struggles were especially dangerous at moments of succession, because it was not regulated: Kubilai ruled for thirty-four years, but there were no fewer than nine emperors in the period between his death in 1294 and the collapse of the dynasty in 1355. The regime weakened under the impact of these divisions, and a series of rebellions broke out, amongst which the most important was that of a Buddhist sect, the Red Turbans. Under the leadership of a poor peasant of great ability, Zhu Yuanzhang, the Yuan were destroyed and Zhu inaugurated his Ming dynasty in 1368 as the Hongwu emperor (1368–98).

The Ming kept the Mongols at bay by manipulating tribal divisions with trade and gifts. They maintained the military settlements of the Yuan which became suppliers of manpower for frontier armies. In addition, they hired nomads as cavalrymen, providing another useful lever against their leaders. Although the defensive stance of the Ming prevented serious attack from the north there was always the risk of minor raids. As a result the Ming built the Great Wall, essentially renewing and connecting existing walls which dated back to Shi Huangdi the 'First Emperor'. This fortified line could not resist a major assault, but diplomacy aimed to prevent this. It was, however, very successful in fending off raids, which all too often in the past had created reputations for their leaders and produced a snowball effect. The wall and the accompanying manipulation of tribal divisions formed a management technique which was supported by remarkable Chinese military development.

The long Mongol wars and the conflicts attending the collapse of the Yuan promoted considerable advances in military technology. In the thirteenth century trebuchets had been used to fling explosive missiles whose metal casings caused jagged fragmentation wounds. Smaller versions were used as grenades, while defenders of fortifications sometimes placed mines fired by flintlocks which anticipated seventeenth-century European developments. By the fifteenth century rocket-powered arrows, often launched from special wheelbarrows, were in use but they were probably not very effective, for they were soon superseded by guns. Bronze handguns mounted on poles were noted in Kubilai's expedition to Manchuria in 1287–9 and a bronze cannon in Peking is dated to 1332; surviving examples show that Chinese development paralleled that in Europe. But the Ming held off the Mongols by management techniques, and in the absence of serious attack there seemed no reason to spend more money on the military, particularly as building and maintaining the Great Wall was expensive.

Most field warfare in China consisted of forays into the steppe where cannon were an impediment to movement, though light firearms could usefully help to defend a camp against cavalry attack. For the purposes of internal security, the Ming maintained garrisons within the great cities. Moreover, there was little incentive to improve artillery because of the strength of their fortifications. At Xian the Ming encased a much older rammed-earth rampart in brick, creating a circuit of 13.7 kilometres which was 12 metres high and about 14 metres wide at the top and almost 20 at the bottom. It was studded with 98 towers set at intervals of 120 metres, enabling the defenders to enfilade any attack. Cannon and muskets were important for the defenders, while any attacker could use artillery only to clear the tops of the rampart walls, rather than to batter. As a result, once established the Ming court neglected the military. But then nobody was threatening China and its economy was largely self-sufficient.

The price of this negligence became apparent under the emperor Wanli (1572–1620) during his 'Three Great Campaigns' which were all clearly the result of military vulnerability. In 1591 an able Mongol commander, Pubei, was provoked into rebellion by factions at the Ming court, and it was only after major exertions that his uprising was put down in 1593. In the third and final of these campaigns the Ming had great difficulty in crushing an aboriginal rebellion (by non-Han people) in the south-west. They managed only because big armies had been raised to repel the Japanese invasion of Korea begun in 1592.

Japan had been an empire since about AD 500, but the emperors had lost authority to military men, samurai, who cultivated bushido ('the way of the warrior') and fought one another for power and influence, each aspiring to be Shogun (Supreme Commander), nominally under the emperor. They indulged in a highly ritualised form of cavalry warfare in which the one-to-one duel was supreme. This was essentially an aspect of the jockeying for position that took place amongst the barons, because no major party disputed the supremacy of the imperial court and there was no external threat. In the fourteenth and fifteenth centuries it became apparent that the emperor was a mere puppet and these aristocratic rivalries escalated into greater wars in which ferocious clashes of close-order mass infantry armies supplanted the encounters of bow-armed aristocratic cavalry. In this increasingly savage warfare the competing samurai were ready to embrace any weapon which enabled them to win.

In 1543 a Chinese junk with three Portuguese traders equipped with firearms was blown ashore off Kyushu. The importance of the new weapons was immediately recognised. Oda Nobunaga, the leader of an aristocratic faction whose success began the unification of Japan, ordered 500 matchlocks from gunsmiths in Kunitomo in 1549, and in 1575 his army, numbering 3,000 musketeers in its 70,000, won the decisive battle of Nagashino. In 1582 the armies of his successor, Hideyoshi, besieged Kanki castle using artillery:

Korezumi Gorozaemon and his soldiers from the province of Wakasa were assigned to the eastern gate of Kanki castle. First he had two high towers erected from which cannons were fired. The moat was filled in and artificial mounds were made, and from these the castle was attacked. Takigawa Sagon moved from the southern to the eastern gate where he had labourers erect towers and had the walls and the citadel bombarded with cannon. The citadel caught fire and burned down.[15]

Hideyoshi had established a shaky unity, and it may have been a desire to occupy the enormous armies generated by his rise to power that gave birth to his effort to conquer China via an invasion of Korea. He understood the Ming weakness, but perhaps trusted too much in his new weapons. Japanese tactics certainly adapted well, with the emphasis on defensive positions to protect musketeers from attack by infantry or cavalry. One of Hideyoshi's generals during the invasion of Korea wrote back to Japan:

> Please arrange to send us guns and ammunition. There is absolutely no use for spears. It is vital that you arrange to obtain a number of guns. Furthermore, you should certainly see to it that those persons departing for Korea understand this situation. The arrangements for guns should receive your closest attention.[16]

The Ming mobilised large numbers of troops and the best of their firearms, and allied with the Koreans, but it still took them until 1597 to beat back Japanese forces which never numbered above 60,000. A key factor in the defeat of the Japanese was the Korean admiral Yi Sun-Sin whose 'turtleboats', iron-clad and oar-driven and equipped with heavy cannon, were highly effective in destroying the Japanese navy. Japan turned its back on the world, becoming a 'closed country' and largely abandoning firearms. It was, ironically, in this era of peace that the code of bushido reached its highest development, a process made possible because draconian legislation excluded peasants from owning weapons. For over 200 years the clock was turned back to a highly idealised form of the world of bushido. This was brought to a sharp end by the impact of the western powers in the form of Admiral Perry's 'Black Ships' in 1853.

At the start of the seventeenth century economic conditions in China were so poor that they provoked rebellions which the Ming army was too weak to crush. As noted earlier, the Jurchen of Manchuria had once dominated China as the Jin dynasty, and they had not evaporated. In the early seventeenth century they produced a leader of genius, Nurhaci, who unified them and conquered some of the neighbouring Mongol tribes. He grouped his people into companies of 300, and each set of five companies formed a Banner, of which there were originally four, augmented to eight by 1614. The Jurchen really were not strong enough to conquer China, but the inability of the Ming court to make decisions enabled rebellion to grow and allowed the Jurchen to seize parts of north China. The Jurchen never had more than about 100,000 troops in their Banner army, and they faced fierce resistance. As a consequence of their neglect of the army the

Ming turned to the Portuguese for western-style cannon and muskets, which enabled them to inflict defeats upon the Jurchen in 1626 and 1627. This prompted the nomads in turn to purchase and copy similar weapons. But there was no coordinated Ming resistance, and many Chinese generals and their soldiers went over to the Jurchen, who proclaimed their Manchu or Qing dynasty in 1636. It was with the aid of Chinese armies that the new dynasty conquered China, though it took until 1661 before the last Ming emperor was killed.

The dynamic leadership of the new dynasty and their respect for Chinese institutions won over many who hoped for an end to the cycle of war and rebellion which had been their lot under the Ming. The Manchu's Banner Army became the ruling elite of Qing China, but the purely Chinese Green Standard Armies were far more numerous – perhaps providing over two-thirds of the million-strong army deployed by the emperors. They were recruited from the military settlements established by the Ming. The new dynasty was anxious to maintain the warlike vigour of the Manchu based on the steppe skills of horsemanship and archery and was always anxious about the loyalty of the native Chinese forces. However, their main military problem was overcoming the Mongols and other peoples on the steppe frontier. The cannon and other firearms which the Jurchen had used with great enthusiasm and skill during the conquest of China were of little use in this environment, and so fell out of use. And once the Qing had crushed the nomads in the mid-eighteenth century, China was left without any major enemies. The Qing conquest of China was the last major victory of the steppe people, and their dependence on gunpowder weapons during the conquest period showed that the steppe way of war, hitherto so dominant, was giving way to new forces.

The weakening of steppe domination was even more evident further west. The conquests of Timur had damaged the Golden Horde of the Black Sea steppe, allowing Moscow to emerge as the strongest Russian principality whose annexation of Novgorod in 1462 brought it into conflict with Poland–Lithuania and the Baltic powers of Sweden and the German Hanse. Moscow had to fight in the Baltic, but it also expanded in other directions. Russian colonisation of the forest-steppe and its fringes reached the Urals during the reign of Ivan the Terrible (1547–84) and brought about the annexation of the khanates of Kazan, Astrakhan and Siberia. Very quickly Moscow reached out southwards from the forest-steppe into the open grasslands of the Black Sea steppe. Here it encountered both Poland–Lithuania, which had seized Kiev, and the aggressive Crimean

Khanate which, after 1475, was usually tributary to and acting as a surrogate for the Ottomans. All three of these powers deployed light cavalry as a natural consequence of the environment in which they were fighting. Notable amongst these were the Cossacks in both Catholic Poland–Lithuania and Orthodox Moscow. These were Christian Slavs who had moved onto the steppe and adopted a lifestyle similar to the Mongols'. But new kinds of forces were emerging in this conflict. Military settlements along the frontier provided the means to support soldiers and particularly the *strel'tsy*, musketeer infantry, vital for holding and seizing these strong-points. The leading Russian soldiers were supported by *pomestie*, lifetime grants of land in return for military service which gave the holder considerable authority over peasants who were effectively tied to the soil. Poland–Lithuania established very similar forces.

In southern Russia speed and surprise were important and traditional steppe manoeuvre could count as much as firepower. To fight off their European enemies in the Baltic, Russia by the seventeenth century had developed a European-style army, but it was of limited value on the southern steppe. In 1659 a Russian army over 21,000 strong, based around four infantry regiments supported by dragoons, attacked Konotop in the Ukraine which was held by Poland–Lithuania. But the Zaporozhian Cossacks and their Crimean Khanate allies hid their forces and drew the Russians into a trap in the classic steppe manner. Only a fraction of the Russian force, formed into a *Wagenburg*, made a successful withdrawal. As a result the Crimean Tatars were able to threaten Moscow for the first time in over a century. Moscow proved, however, to be a much more unified state than Poland–Lithuania and as a consequence did not suffer from the extensive Cossack rebellions of the mid-seventeenth century. The Ottomans attacked Moscow again in the war of 1676–81, but the peace concluded in 1682 was generally advantageous to them. In the course of the fighting the Russian regiments organised on the European model in tight and disciplined linear formations and (sometimes commanded by foreigners like General Franz Wolf or Patrick Gordon) showed that they could hold off steppe horsemen with firepower and bayonets. However, it should be noted that they were strongly supported by Cossacks and Russian regular cavalry. Firepower and discipline were beginning to win even on the steppe, but only beginning. It was not until 1696 that Peter the Great reached Azov, and Russian supremacy on the Black Sea littoral came only in the reign of Catherine II (1762–96).

European armies, spared by geography and the screen of Russia and Poland–Lithuania from the need to adapt to steppe methods, lived in an environment where war moved much more slowly and was dominated by fortresses, hence the development of cannon and musketry. In many ways the Ottomans were the leaders in this kind of warfare. Far more radical in the European experience were the consequences of the application of gunpowder to ships. The voyages of discovery were actually voyages of conquest, which is why, wherever there was substantial resistance, as in the Far East, Europeans made only superficial inroads; the development of European land warfare was insufficient to achieve anything more. As late as 1687–90 the Mughals brushed aside a military attack by a belligerent British East India Company.

The contrast with the New World is striking. The conquistador Cortés attacked the Aztec Empire of Mexico in 1519 with eleven ships bearing only 100 sailors, 530 soldiers (including thirty crossbowmen and twelve *arquebusiers*), eight women, many slaves and horses, and a few cannon. The natives were startled by the horses and the new technology, but they adapted quickly. Cortés was besieged and all but overwhelmed by the warriors of the Tlaxcalan Confederacy, and saved only because their leaders perceived the Spaniards as allies against the hated Aztecs. The joint Spanish–Tlaxcalan army was ejected from the fabulous Aztec capital of Tenochtitlan with heavy losses, and Cortés had to concede a generous treaty to persuade the Tlaxcalans to join him in a new assault upon Tenochtitlan, which fell in 1521. The cities of Mayan Yucatan offered a strenuous resistance to the Spanish for 170 years after their first attempts at conquest in 1527, but the defection of Mani from their alliance in 1546 was a crucial stage in their collapse. In North America many tribes saw the tenuous English and French settlements as allies against their local enemies. It was by exploiting divisions amongst the indigenous populations, rather than by the application of superior military technology, that Europeans established themselves in both North and South America. Moreover, the diseases they brought with them further debilitated resistance.

The European conquest of the New World and the establishment of a network of trading bases in the Far East have attracted enormous attention and too often dominate our view of history. They were made possible by naval developments in the late Middle Ages, and ultimately brought about a dramatic change in human affairs. But all this was overshadowed by the great steppe empires in the Middle East, India and China: these were the dominant powers in the world for a very long time and in the period considered here they were virtually unchallengeable.

The Europeans developed gunpowder weapons to a much greater extent than peoples elsewhere not because of any special peculiarity of their culture (or cultures), but because they suited their style of war and meshed with their emphasis on close-order, close-quarter fighting; but these weapons had grave limitations. Outside Europe the speed and firepower of the steppe warriors, with their remarkable capacity to adapt which is best illustrated by the Ottomans, remained dominant over the slow and poorly organised forces of the Europeans. It was not apparent at the time that the New World would generate a new economic system which would surpass those of the steppe empires and enable the small European states to evolve a peculiarly intense form of gunpowder warfare. But in the age of the steppe dominance the methods of land warfare in Europe gave little hint of future development and supremacy.

CHAPTER SEVEN

DISCIPLINE, *c.*1683–*c.*1860

I have throughout my Book, taken every Occasion to inculcate the Necessity of legal Military Subordination. It has been the practice of all nations, even where the people have been blessed with the biggest liberty, never to admit of a military Independance [sic] upon their Military Superiors. I look upon it as the Band which ties the Whole together, and without it, all our rules and forms to be of no Use. Perhaps it is the great distinction between regular Troops and Militia, and the Cause why the Former have always had the advantage over the Latter.[1]

B Y the middle of the seventeenth century it was becoming obvious that, as far as Europe was concerned, a new world economic order had come into being. The conquest of the Americas and the exploitation of their resources created a trading zone across the Atlantic and stimulated economic and commercial growth. The great sailing ships with their heavy broadsides of cannon had reached beyond Islam, so that the new wealth derived from the Americas could be traded for the traditional commodities of the East – silks, jewellery, spices, fine pottery and, later, porcelain. The Mediterranean was no longer the centre of the European world. England set up the Honourable East India Company in 1600, Holland sponsored the United East Indies Company and France quickly followed. Islamic merchants had long monopolised the trade in West African slaves, and they continued to be important. However, Europeans now competed for this human trade to feed labour into the sugar industries of the West Indies and South America, and the plantations of the Carolinas, generating enormous profits. Industrial growth and new inventions multiplied, while improved agricultural techniques enhanced food supply dramatically. By the end of the seventeenth century steam engines were in use in England, and in 1712 the efficient Newcomen model was introduced.

Not all of this was peculiarly European. The Ottomans encouraged their own traders. Chinese products were sought after the world over, while both they and the Indians had trading companies to match anything in Europe. But in some of the states of Western Europe the intensification of economic production, mercantile, industrial and agricultural, was remarkable. This prosperity extended to states which were not directly involved in the Atlantic trade: Scandinavia, for example, supplied France, Holland and England with timber for their growing fleets while Germany traded intensely with the lands of the Atlantic littoral. Peter the Great (1682–1725) imitated western development in order to modernise the economy of Russia. This new wealth enabled relatively small states to create military power to rival great empires.

The European expansion was as violent and competitive as that of other empires. The ruthlessness that in the ancient world produced the smoking ruins of cities and the enslavement of entire populations now applied itself to the exploitation of the native peoples of the Caribbean and North and South America. Successful trading nations tried to exclude others by force from the benefits of 'their' trade or tried to take over their trade. The Portuguese had been the first to break into the Indian Ocean in the fifteenth century, but they were elbowed aside by the Dutch and later the French and English, all of whom were firmly established in the area by the late seventeenth century. Spain and Portugal seized the New World in the sixteenth century, but despite their resistance Holland, France and England had forced their way into the Caribbean by the end of the seventeenth century. In North America, England and France profited from the divisions of the native tribes to establish colonies and then fought one another for supremacy. But as long as the empires of the Ottomans, the Mughals and the Qing remained strong, the European predators were peripheral in Asia.

The overseas ambitions of some European states complicated the intense rivalries of a deeply divided continent which focused on a shifting galaxy of powers. In the seventeenth century Austria, France, England, Holland, Spain, Poland, Sweden and Prussia were all important. In the eighteenth century Russia under Peter the Great established an autocratic bureaucracy to make Russia into a great military power, displacing Sweden in northern Europe. By the mid-century Spain, Holland and Sweden occupied secondary positions while at its end Poland had ceased to exist altogether, partitioned by Russia, Austria and Prussia.

The new wealth had significant political and military consequences. Holland was a merchant republic and her entire policy was dedicated to the interests of trade. The commercial skill of the Dutch created a new means of war finance which enabled a very small country to defy bigger powers like France, while continuing to expand abroad. Holland had a population of less than two million in 1700, but it supported the double burden of a great fleet to protect its trade and an army to hold its frontiers. Like any other state it was driven to borrow, but Dutch merchants understood the need to guarantee payment in order to safeguard future credit, and out of this they developed deficit finance. In England landed aristocrats dominated political affairs, but they recognised the value of its growing mercantile and colonial power. England copied Dutch financial methods with the foundation of the Bank of England in 1694 and the institution of the National Debt, a kind of permanent state deficit which paid a fairly low rate of interest to lenders who were confident of their income. This provided a highly flexible instrument for war finance, because borrowing could be stepped up at need and the costs spread over long periods.

France was an aristocratic state whose leaders saw the need to foster economic development, but without ever acquiring real understanding of how it worked, and this was crucially important for war finance. France failed to develop deficit financing because aristocratic participation and quiescence in the state were much more important in a crisis than satisfying creditors. In this way the needs of 260,000 tax-exempt nobles dominated a population of 19 million. War threw the finances of Louis XIV (1643–1715) into crisis and this influenced military activity. In 1695 Louis wrote to Catinat, his commander in Italy:

> the only difficulty that presents itself for pursuing offensive war is the considerable sum of money it requires . . . and after having examined the state of my finances . . . I have, despite myself, been obliged to resolve to pursue only defensive war during the coming year.[2]

After 1709 during the War of Spanish Succession (1701–14) the French suspended virtually all offensives to save money. More subtly, throughout this long war much French activity was limited to occupying land outside France, upon which they then levied 'contributions' offsetting as much as 25 per cent of military costs. In 1789 war finance precipitated the French Revolution.

The effect of new groups sharing in power or, in the case of some traditional monarchies, being catered for by those in power, was to extend the sense of belonging to the state and having a vested interest in its military success. We speak of 'France' as if it were a monolith, but communications were poor and the reach of government machinery limited, so for many the state was very remote, and some subjects did not even speak French. Further, the military and those who served in it had always been the instruments of the elite, and soldiers were usually separate from the mass of the population and often entirely foreign. The great achievement of the major European regimes between the seventeenth and nineteenth centuries was to create standing armies, establishing a state monopoly on violence. Such 'nationalised' armies were, if not popular, at least bearable and even at times a matter of pride.

The new armies sprang from the security needs of monarchs. The mercenary armies of the early seventeenth century were dangerously independent. The Swedish model of the 'state commission army', a standing force recruited from native peoples and tied to state authority by an articulated command structure, showed the way ahead. Instead of being intermediaries, aristocrats could be drawn into service as officers dependent on royal patronage, while those who remained defiant could be intimidated. These fundamental political developments underpinned the new regular armies. The French monarchy set the pace. It was a dynastic state, but it had always been centralised, so that the creation of a military bureaucracy to control and support its new model army was practicable. The key figures were the *intendants* who supervised military administration and travelled with the armies, controlling all aspects of military infrastructure. There were limits to what the state could do and the *intendants* had to supervise the private contractors, *munitionnaires*, who provided food and dealt with others such as those who managed the artillery.

Monarchs had to compromise with the practices of the old armies. Captains and colonels continued to profit from 'their' companies and regiments so it was necessary to ensure that they were supplying uniforms, or cash allowances in lieu, for the troops. There was undoubtedly much peculation: soldiers were convinced suppliers cheated on both quantity and quality, while there was an obvious temptation for officers to claim to have more men than were actually in the ranks. By modern standards this was a complex and messy system of support, but it was an enormous improvement on what had gone before. Soldiers seem to have been relatively well fed and this motivated them to fight. Monarchs replaced civilian contractors with specialist corps of gunners, engineers and pioneers who were vital in sieges and in the preparation of camps and bridges. Across Western Europe, in response to the needs of trade and industry, roads were improved and bridges were built, thus speeding the movement of troops.

Improved supply and well-organised support had tactical and even strategic implications. Under Louis XIV French armies built up stockpiles of food and equipment over the winter in frontier fortresses, enabling them to take the field earlier than their enemies. Gradually European armies were catching up with the Ottomans.

The most obvious military consequence of the new wealth was an increase in the number and size of forces. Every petty German ruler now had his miniature army. Under Louis XIV France was a superpower with a peacetime army of 150,000, expanded to 279,000 during the Dutch War of 1672–8 and reaching a peak of 420,000 in the War of the Spanish Succession. The Austrian regular force in 1699 stood at 59,000 but under the pressure of war had reached 135,000 by 1705: in 1761 it numbered over 200,000 and by the French Revolution about 300,000. Under the Great Elector in the late seventeenth century, the Prussian army numbered 30,000, rising to 40,000 under his immediate successors, but Frederick the Great (1740–86) had an army of 83,000 at the start of his reign. These are paper figures, but the scale of battles reflects the overall rise: at Breitenfeld in 1631, 40,000 Swedes confronted the same number of imperial troops; at Neerwinden (Landen) in 1693, 80,000 French fought 50,000 Dutch; at Malplaquet, Marlborough's 86,000 defeated 75,000 French.

Armies were still reduced in peacetime, but only on a partial basis: the half-pay officer kicking his heels and hoping for a war which would recall him to the colours is a cliché of eighteenth-century literature. Ordinary soldiers were still paid off in large numbers as quickly as possible, and some of those retained acted as part-time farmers. However, it is very impressive that France could afford a peacetime establishment of 150,000. Of course such numbers never came together in a single force. Many were needed to garrison fortresses and protect roads. But the chief limitation on numbers in armies was different.

Logistics imposed a limit on the size of individual armies. Away from its base, no army could carry all the supplies it needed so 'contributions' were vital. This was increasingly a bureaucratic and orderly process because pillage threatened the discipline upon which all armies depended, and ravaging could drive peasant populations from the land and even convert them into guerrillas. 'Contributions' left the countryside stable, if impoverished. Moreover, armies usually offered credit payment, and generally this produced some compensation in the end. It is difficult to see how else armies could have been supplied with food. Ammunition and guns had to be transported, and officers were permitted to bring lavish amounts of baggage, as befitted their aristocratic status. To carry more than a few days' supplies of food on top of this would have compromised an army's mobility. Forage for horses was so bulky that under almost any circumstances it had to be found locally. On the move an army could feed itself, at least in the prosperous farming communities of Western Europe, though extorting 'contributions' took time and effort, so it was usual to pause to stockpile food in magazines which could then supply the army for the first part of its next advance. An army besieging could not forage, so lines of communication had to be established and guarded. A major siege was labour-intensive and armies were relatively small, so that it would demand all the efforts of a realm for a fighting season, but it was the only way to secure conquest. For example, at the siege of Lille, August to 22 October 1708, Marlborough needed 3,000 horses to drag a siege-train of 80 heavy cannon and 20 mortars, escorted by 2,500 cavalry and 5,000 foot. Half his army was retained to keep open lines of communication.

The pattern of European war which emerged by the end of the seventeenth century and which would endure well into the nineteenth was remarkably like that which had dominated warfare since ancient times: infantry stood in close order and engaged their enemy at very close quarters when, unless one side gave way, the fight with edged weapons became decisive. This at first seems rather surprising after four centuries of gunpowder weapons. However, it was based on the possibilities and limitations of the 6-foot-long, 11-pound smoothbore flintlock musket with its lug bayonet. This was very inaccurate because the ball was smaller in diameter than the bore and so bounced, producing an erratic flight. At 150 metres, in ideal conditions, a carefully aimed weapon would hit a target equivalent to three men six foot tall only five times out of ten shots. But conditions were rarely ideal in the frightening surge of battle, so that soldiers preferred to fire as close as 50 metres. Loading was so slow that a surviving attacker could charge across this distance long before a soldier could prepare his weapon for a second shot, and, of course, a man on horseback could do this even more quickly. The individual infantryman was, therefore, very vulnerable, and needed the shelter of his comrades with their 'porcupine' of bayonets. But at 50 metres volley-fire could inflict appalling casualties on a close-packed enemy. Linear formations two or three ranks deep could bring most fire to bear upon an approaching enemy, so that units formed themselves into line as a prelude to battle, which is why we still speak of 'infantry of the line'.

In attack, infantry formations were usually preceded by light-3 pounder cannon firing canister, a can of small shot which burst as it emerged from the muzzle, spreading a dense and lethal spray effective up to 400 yards.

The infantry fired as close to the enemy as possible before charging in with the bayonet. The consequences of such close-quarter encounters could be ghastly. At Malplaquet in 1709 Marlborough with an army of 86,000 attacked 75,000 French: casualties were 21,000 and 12,000 respectively. To deliver volley-fire like this demanded close control. The characteristic unit of the infantry in this age was the regiment of around 2,000–3,000 men, broken down into battalions, ranging in numbers from 500 to 1,000, which formed the basic tactical unit. These were subdivided into companies of about 200 controlled by officers, with sections under the command of NCOs. Discipline was the key to making men stand and fight – the blast of a close-quarter volley could decimate a battalion. It was widely observed that the unit which fired last usually won any encounter. At the battle of Fontenoy in 1745 a French officer called to his English opposite number: 'Messieurs les Anglais, tirez les premiers!' The assumption underlying this invitation was that his own men were so regimented that they would absorb the shock and casualties of a volley, and then be in a position to deliver their own – all because they were so tightly disciplined. And beyond the volley lay the encounter with edged weapons.

Maurice de Saxe (1696–1750) was a progressive and experienced soldier of German birth who had fought in the armies of Austria, Russia and France, in the last rising to the rank of marshal. He thought that in the clash of battalions, the last to fire would be the victor, and urged attacking units to endure defending fire, to deliver their own volley at point-blank range, and to charge in with the bayonet. To the end of his life he believed that pikemen had their place on the battlefield. In this he was not alone. In 1702 a British soldier of Marlborough's army complained that

> My size made me a pikeman against my will, though indeed I liked that service, and thought it the most becoming and manly of all. There was an encouragement [to induce a brisk and smart motion in charging] of half a crown to everyone that should break a pike in that motion, and I had the good fortune to break two before I left the regiment.[3]

Frederick the Great of Prussia was dismissive of firepower and urged his infantry to move swiftly to close quarters. There was plenty of pragmatic evidence that man-to-man battle at close quarters, or at least its prospect, was the ultimate physical and psychological weapon which broke defenders. In 1745 'Bonnie Prince Charlie', the Stuart pretender to the English throne, won an extraordinary success at the battle of Prestonpans when his Highland swordsmen overran English regulars who were unnerved by their wild charge. As late as the battle of Busaco in 1809, an ensign with the British Guards reported the repulse of a French attack: 'In the centre where at last the enemy made his grand push, we charged when he was within 100 yards, and our fire was reserved until they were flying.'[4]

Infantry were the backbone of eighteenth-century armies, but cavalry usually accounted for about 30 per cent of fighting men, a rather higher percentage than in the Middle Ages when ratios of 1:5 were common. They became increasingly specialised. Light cavalry were used for reconnaissance, to screen the movements of troops and in the business of plundering enemy territory. Heavy cavalry, often still equipped with the breastplate, hovered close to the infantry battalions, ready to use their speed to charge home if gaps opened in the enemy line. At Landen in July 1693 it was a cavalry charge which brought the French victory. In 1745 at Hohenfriedberg a chance charge by the Bayreuth dragoons saved the day for the Prussian army which was hard pressed by the Austrians. Cavalry regiments varied in size but quite normally numbered about 1,000 horsemen, divided into ten companies which were combined into squadrons.

Discipline was the means by which European armies overcame the limitations of their gunpowder weapons and maximised their power. In the eighteenth century armies still fought in phalanxes, but they enjoyed the enhanced killing range of gunpowder weapons which acted as a kind of longsword. But this could only be successful if it was accompanied by sensible organisation and enforced, and this is why corps of officers became vital. France had a numerous petty and often impoverished aristocracy whose cultural inheritance was contempt for labour and even trade. For such young men, commissions in the forces offered what they considered an honourable way of making a living. Pay was not good and often irregular, but officers were provided with servants from the other ranks and enjoyed considerable status in society. Moreover, if a man was promoted to company commander he could expect to make money, taking a cut from the administration of supplies and even charging for promotions. In the messes of regiments these young officers cultivated a warrior ethic centred around the notion of honour and its consequence – the duel. Rising young soldiers became clients of great men at court through whose influence they might hope to buy commissions and become colonels, with far greater hopes of profit from control of a whole regiment. Such patrons often inserted men of birth into these positions, and their wealth supported the troops, thus offsetting some of the crown's costs.

By contrast, the Hapsburg monarchy was a personal union of diverse and separate lands centred on Austria, Hungary and Bohemia, whose rulers had established a claim to the throne of the loose agglomeration of Germanic principalities, lordships and free cities known as the Holy Roman Empire. It did not form a coherent and centralised state like France, but a dynastic dominion, and in each of its lands the Estates, essentially representative of the nobility and Church, were anxious to preserve their own privileges. Service in the regular army never enjoyed great cachet amongst the nobles of the Hapsburg lands, especially those of Austria and Bohemia, partly because they could enjoy careers in local administration under the Estates, which they dominated.

However, the higher nobility controlled all senior commands because they could purchase commissions, and especially colonelcies, for their younger sons, and thus had an enormous advantage in the promotion race. But the lower-level officers were mainly commoners, often drawn from the peoples of the Ottoman frontier for whom war was a way of life. Moreover, Austria was prepared to recruit from all over Europe, as exemplified by its most famous soldier, Prince Eugene (1663–1736), born in Paris and rejected by the French army before moving on to the Hapsburgs. Even in the late eighteenth century foreigners sometimes raised entire regiments for the monarchy. The result was a less homogeneous and coherent officer corps than the French.

The Hohenzollern dynasty of Prussia, like the Hapsburgs, had scattered lands. East Prussia was separated by Polish territory from the family inheritance of Brandenburg, while Cleves and Julich lay far to the west on the Rhine. Frederick the Great Elector (1740–88) was conscious of being surrounded by hostile neighbours. He decided that he needed a standing army to fight off potential challenges and to grasp swiftly any opportunities for expansion which might present themselves. He therefore took steps to centralise government and, because his lands lacked great aristocrats, broke the power of local assemblies and drew in the aristocracy by making them officers. The despotism of Peter the Great similarly drove Russian aristocrats into the army.

The other ranks were filled by the poorest and least educated of the European population, inducted by a number of mechanisms. Service in the French army was voluntary, often stimulated by recruitment bonuses. But this was inadequate for the major expansion during the War of the Spanish Succession, so Louis XIV reinforced his standing army by resurrecting the ancient right of the king to call all free men to arms, creating a reserve force drawn from unmarried men between the ages of 18 and 40 selected by lot. In practice, middle-class people and substantial peasants could easily get exemptions, so most soldiers came from among the poorest in society.

During this war the system provided about half the levies to Louis's armies. It was, however, very unpopular, so in more normal times the state tempted volunteers by offering recruitment bonuses. The legal maximum of 60 *livres* was often exceeded and might, in time of war, reach 500 *livres*, five or six times an annual agricultural wage. But armies were rarely homogeneous. The French royal guard was Swiss, and many regiments recruited heavily from the German principalities.

Prussia, after the reforms of 1733, had a very systematic form of conscription. The whole realm was divided into districts rated by the number of hearths in each. Every regiment drew its soldiers from the district in which it was based, and each company recruited from an allocated subdivision or canton. In principle, every able-bodied man was eligible but conscription on such a scale would have bankrupted the state. As a result, the system was very selective. Exemptions were granted to the economically active and important; in short, the middle class. Since the system was supervised by landlords, in practice they decided which of the peasants were called to war.

The Prussian cantonal model produced highly disciplined soldiers whose service life was spent in groups who had known one another from birth, under the supervision of officers drawn from the landlord families who ruled their families in civilian life. Once they were trained, soldiers were often sent home to support themselves on the land, so relieving the state of the costs of their upkeep. Soldiers enjoyed enhanced status in the community for which they could sometimes speak, and this mitigated the harshness of the system and inculcated a degree of pride in it. This integration of home and service life created a highly disciplined force. But Prussia had a small population, and in time of war recruited soldiers from all over Germany and Central Europe. In 1729 Hanover came near to war with Prussia over the activities of aggressive recruiting officers. More than a third of the Prussian army were foreigners, though such men were retained only as long as war lasted, then dismissed to save money. Prisoners of war were routinely incorporated into victorious armies. In 1760–61 the Prussians were so desperate for men that they inducted prisoners at the point of capture. The regiments of the Russian army were conscripted, theoretically for life, from amongst the serfs. In practice landlords oversaw this process and the result was, as elsewhere, an arbitrary form of selective conscription.

The training of soldiers, necessarily in view of the poor quality and unwillingness of many of those inducted, focused on discipline. The tactics of the age required soldiers to march in column and then, when battle threatened, to deploy into line, a relatively complex manoeuvre. The business of loading and firing in frightening and distracting conditions was dinned into men, and they learned to respond to sudden changes in orders coming from their officers. Drill conditioned soldiers to perform their functions and to obey their commanders. Discipline mattered much more than skill: few infantrymen would have fired more than five live shots from their muskets before going into action. Draconian punishments were the order of the day. Frederick the Great ordered that NCOs should kill any man who turned in flight. Flogging continued in the British army throughout the nineteenth century, and 'Field Punishment No. 1' by which men were shackled to a wheel, into the twentieth. Even so, all armies suffered from appalling levels of desertion, which was in fact so prevalent that it was generally treated very mildly.

Infantry of the line, backed up by cavalry and artillery, were at the core of eighteenth-century armies, but it must not be thought that military development was everywhere the same even within Europe. Russia converted its army to a western model in order to fight the Swedes and others, but on the Black Sea steppe, where it confronted the Crimean Tatars, the Ottomans and other Mongol successor states, cavalry, especially the Don Cossacks, remained very important, supported by military settlements along the frontier. Similar methods underpinned the Russian expansion beyond the Urals and across Siberia, because they were well suited to the task of driving outward the frontiers in the forest-steppe. In Austria the Ottoman frontier was held by fortresses supported by military settlements. Mounted raiding was a way of life for both sides, and as a result Austrian cavalry was good, both on the battlefield and in harassing, and indeed the European vogue for hussars was copied from the *huszár*, a particular kind of Hungarian light cavalry. Frederick the Great of Prussia came to dread the 'Croatians', the generic name for Christians settled along the Ottoman border by the Hapsburgs. They made excellent light infantry who, in broken countryside, could inflict major damage on their enemies. During the eighteenth century skirmishing forces like these became increasingly important.

The British military structure was another variant. British elites were deeply suspicious of a large standing army because they feared the monarchy might use it to deprive them of their privileges and liberties. Accordingly they preferred to pay continental powers, like Austria, to fight against France, whose imperial ambitions conflicted with British interests all over the globe. But others were not always willing to fight Britain's battles, and recipients tended to take the money and use it for their own ends, so that it became important to put armies in the field to influence events. The British filled their ranks with mercenaries, and Hanover, where their royal family originated, was a useful recruiting base. During the American Revolution men were raised from neighbouring lands in Germany; these 'Hessians' were much reviled by the American insurgents, but they were good soldiers. The purely British army was made up of volunteers, but the term voluntary is a relative one, and contemporaries had few illusions about the methods of recruiting officers, as satirised in Farquhar's famous play, *The Recruiting Officer* (1706). Moreover, impressing men from the jails was not uncommon. The duke of Wellington was essentially correct, though perhaps harsh, when he described the British army: 'People talk of their enlistment from their fine military feeling – all stuff – no such thing. Some of our men enlist from having got bastard children – some for minor offences – many more for drink.'[5] British officers were recruited from the younger sons of the nobility and from the gentry; great aristocrats preferred other careers. But officers had to purchase their commissions or find a patron wealthy enough to do so, maintaining a certain social exclusivity. It is notable that most of the military figures of the eighteenth century came from the gentry or impoverished noble families.

British military expenditure focused on its fleet. The rise of the big-gun ship in the sixteenth century meant that temporary use of converted merchantmen was not viable. So, just as standing armies were becoming fashionable across Europe, permanent directly controlled fleets came into being. The ship-of-the-line, which would dominate warfare until the mid-nineteenth century, was a multi-decked wooden box constructed in such a way as to carry the maximum number of cannon while retaining manoeuvrability. By the late eighteenth century, the two-deck '74', named for the number of guns, was the staple of the line of battle. By sailing in line and delivering their broadsides, fleets of this kind could drive an enemy from the seas, exposing his commerce to attack and isolated outposts and colonies to annexation. In many ways the ships-of-the-line and the infantry of the line were parallels, units designed to work together to deliver savage close-range volley-fire against their enemies. And after the cannonade boarding parties armed with edged weapons were vital to seize enemy ships. Lighter ships had their uses, preying upon or protecting trade, but naval domination depended on the ships-of-the-line.

The British, because of their geographic location, quickly appreciated the connection between commerce, industry and naval supremacy, and grasped the notion that force could exclude rivals from these important sources of wealth. An elaborate structure mobilised and sustained maritime power. The Board of Admiralty coordinated the work of many specialist boards like the Navy Board which was primarily in charge of dockyards, the Board of Victualling, the Ordnance Board and the Commission of Sick and Wounded. The fleet was hideously expensive. In 1664 parliament voted £2.5 million for the Dutch War, the largest single tax before the eighteenth century, but even so by 1666 the Admiralty had spent £3,200,516. This debt, and the lack of success, persuaded Charles II (1649–85) to negotiate for peace and to lay up the fleet, but before nego- tiations were finished the Dutch admiral, De Witt, made a great raid on the Medway ports, burning a number of ships-of-the-line and towing away the flagship, the *Royal Charles*. This disaster triggered a parliamen- tary inquiry, but essentially cemented the consensus of support in parliament which continued to vote money for the fleet.

Between 1688 and 1715 the number of cruisers designed to protect commerce rose from eight to sixty-six and ships-of-the-line from 100 to 131. At a time when most armies had only one cannon per 500 men, the greatest of these ships carried eighty. The 3,000 oaks needed for a man- of-war had to come from inland forests, and road transport more than doubled costs. Masts were imported from New England, spars and pitch from the Baltic and hemp from far overseas. When the French wars prevented the import of the best sails from Brittany, a competition, even- tually successful, was held to provide substitutes of good quality. To accom- modate and service such ships, stone docks had to be built and protected with great forts. The new Plymouth Yard, completed in 1700, cost £67,000 and by 1711 the royal dockyards were employing 6,488 officers and men. The navy was by far the greatest single enterprise in the British Isles.

Manning was a major problem because in peacetime many ships were mothballed and men paid off – there were limits to the peacetime navy just as there were to peacetime armies. Ships were relatively complex weapons systems and navigation was a delicate art, so that officers had to be educated. For the younger sons of petty gentry and bourgeoisie the navy offered good training and an honourable career, but one that, unlike the army, did not involve heavy investment in the purchase of a commission. And unlike the Church, the law and the academic life, a long and expen- sive education and a predisposition to scholarly activity were not required. For families, the prospect of unloading a young son at the age of 12 to be a petty officer was attractive. Moreover, such was the demand for special skills that non-commissioned officers and merchant sailors could earn commissions. The distinguished explorer Captain James Cook (1728–79), a farm manager's son, served on Whitby coal ships before entering the Royal Navy in 1755 and, indeed, his famous ship, the *Endeavour*, was a converted collier. Officers were usually paid in arrears but with reasonable regularity, and the commander of a major ship-of-the-line could expect 20 shillings per day. Prize money from captured enemy shipping offered prospects of real wealth. In 1758 Captain Elliot took a French privateer, receiving £2,000 as his share. As against this, periods of half-pay were common when ships were decommissioned after wars.

But recruiting the 'other ranks' was a major problem, because ships ran on human expertise which took time to develop: native skills had always been a brake on military development. In peace, demand for manpower was fairly stable and time could be taken to train, but when war came ships had to be commissioned and men found quickly. The obvious source was the merchant marine, but in time of war this competed with the navy for trained seamen. There was a limit to what the government could afford to pay. As a consequence, conscription was introduced in the form of the 'press-gang' which operated in the streets of ports or at sea by boarding. Its prey was not just anybody – the law allowed 'pressing' only of sailors and the navy wanted skilled men. In a sense 'the press' was a tax on the huge success of British shipping which had been promoted by legislation such as the Navigation Acts of 1660 and 1663. Manning the navy was a perennial problem, but so it was for the main enemies, France and Holland. A substantial navy was bound to be expensive. In the second half of the seventeenth century France poured enormous resources into building a fleet. French ships in the eighteenth century were highly regarded and often used as models by the British, but their fine design gave relatively few additional advantages compared with the brute English drive to build and keep at sea numerous warships.

The battlefleets with masses of ships and great weights of cannon dominate our vision of late seventeenth- and early eighteenth-century naval warfare just as mass infantry formations are central to our view of land warfare. But there was an equivalent to the light troops of the armies of this period. The great ships were clumsy, relatively slow, and could only undertake long journeys with great difficulty and careful preparation. In 1693 an Anglo-Dutch fleet, allied against Louis XIV of France, was ordered to escort through the Channel a convoy of merchant ships from both countries bound for Smyrna. The allies had recently won a substantial fleet action over the French at Barfleur-sur-Hogue in 1692, and this may have inspired the governments to order the departure of this convoy at short order. The great battle fleet, however, was short of provisions and accompanied its charges only beyond Brest. The French ambushed the convoy off Cape St Vincent, capturing or sinking ninety-two ships in a disaster which cost more than the total losses of the Great Fire of London in 1666. By the late 1690s the French realised that they could not match the building programmes of their Anglo-Dutch enemies and so could not challenge them in fleet actions. Instead they resorted to the *guerre de course*, war against commerce, which, as the Smyrna incident shows, could be highly effective. Privateer captains fitted out their ships at their own expense, though with government aid. Prizes, captured ships and cargoes, were divided between the state and the privateer captains. This stimulated the British to build cruisers, later called frigates, fast light ships which could take on privateers.

Seen from the twenty-first century, warfare in the eighteenth century often appears stately, almost ritualistic. Armies in their colourful uniforms were relatively small and moved slowly, often bogged down in sieges of places now regarded as unimportant. Wars were waged for the 'balance of power in Europe'; this has often seemed a very abstract notion, and one appropriately served by limited war. But Louis XIV's ambitions to seize the Low Countries and expand the frontiers of France were very threatening to the real interests of many states which banded together in coalitions against her. The result was a whole series of wars. The War of Devolution (1667–8), the Dutch War (1672–8), the War of the Reunions (1683–4) and the Nine Years War (1688–97) were succeeded by the War of the Spanish Succession. At times the fighting was very intense: at Landen in 1693 there were 23,000 casualties which compares with Malplaquet whose butcher's bill of 33,000 shocked Europe in 1709.

The stakes were high. In the case of the Dutch War, Louis clearly intended to extinguish Holland, which had frustrated his ambitions in the War of Devolution. There was fighting in the West Indies and such was the internal pressure in France that revolts broke out in Brittany and amongst the Protestant Huguenots, which the Dutch sought to encourage. Louis's seizure of Philippsburg in 1688 prompted a Dutch coup in alliance with English opposition forces which overthrew Louis's friend and ally, the Catholic James II of England (1685–8), and replaced him with the Dutch Stadtholder William of Orange (1672–1702). In the resultant war there was fighting in the Netherlands, Germany, Ireland, Spain, Italy, the Mediterranean, Canada and South America. And civilian populations suffered badly. Year by year the French established armies in western Germany, and while 'contributions' were less brutal than ravaging, this may not have been evident to the suffering peasantry. In 1672–3 the

French adopted a scorched earth policy to force the Dutch to surrender, and in 1674 and 1688–89 they devastated the Rhine Palatinate to deny its resources to the enemy. The warfare of the early eighteenth century was slow-moving, but it was as destructive as warfare always is. Louis annexed substantial territory in what had been the Spanish Netherlands and 'rounded out' the frontier elsewhere, building modern fortresses to protect his gains. His success rested on sustained warfare, a grinding attrition over long periods of time, made possible by the growing wealth of the French monarchy.

Louis's wars culminated in the War of the Spanish Succession which was brought on by the death without heir of Charles II (1665–1701) of Spain. His empire extended to most of Italy, the Spanish Netherlands, the Americas and the Philippines. As a Hapsburg he was a member of the family which ruled Austria, but he was also closely related to the French Bourbons. He wanted his lands to pass intact to a single heir, and chose Louis XIV's grandson, Philip of Anjou. Although the will stipulated against it, this bequest raised the prospect of an eventual union of the crowns of Spain and France, and the creation of a gigantic superpower which would dominate the whole continent. Louis did nothing to dispel this fear, precipitating a great general war. Philip was accepted in Spain and Louis enjoyed the support of Bavaria and some other minor German powers like Cologne which resented Hapsburg domination. The duke of Savoy protected his Italian frontier against the Austrians. Louis even encouraged Ferenc Rákóczi to lead a Hungarian uprising against the Hapsburgs. The Hapsburg Emperor Leopold I (1658–1705) was at the heart of the alliance against France and he drew in his wake most of the German principalities. In 1701 he persuaded the Elector of Prussia to join by granting him the title 'King in Prussia', while England and Holland were major allies.

This war exemplified early eighteenth-century warfare in that it was dominated by fortifications. Large numbers of the soldiers on both sides were absorbed in defending these strong-points. At heart they were massively developed and strengthened versions of the *trace italienne*, mounting huge numbers of heavy guns. Louis XIV's great engineer, the marquis de Vauban, is chiefly remembered for his skill in designing some of the most modern of these along the French frontier. But his great contribution to war was the systematisation of siege. At Maastricht in 1673 he surrounded the city with zigzag lines from which trenches moved in to create yet more lines from which the walls could be bombarded or assaulted. As long as the besieger prepared well and fed his army, and could prevent relief, sieges now proceeded with mathematical precision. If the garrison was determined the process was bloody. Lille held out against Marlborough for four months before surrendering on terms, having inflicted 14,000 casualties on his army. Assault was terrifying, as a young officer remembered how he had stormed one of the breaches made by the artillery:

> I went up the ladder and when about halfway up I called out 'Here is the 94th!' I was glad to see the men begin to mount . . . I believe there were not many of our regiment up before me – at least I was up before the commander of my company. I lost him at the heap of slain caused by the grape-shot.[6]

The line of confrontation between France and the coalition lay through the Netherlands and down the Rhine, the most heavily fortified zone in Europe. On the upper Rhine the imperial forces created the lines of Stollhofen, penning in the French around Strasbourg, lest they use this as a jumping-off point to attack south Germany and Austria. There were sieges and battles, but they all failed to achieve decisive results. Then there was a sudden flurry of spectacular movement. In 1703 the French general Villars attacked Landau in the Stollhofen lines very late in the season, catching the allies off guard, and subsequently defeated their poorly commanded relief effort at Speyerbach. In conjunction with Max Emanuel of Bavaria, Villars seized Ulm and Augsburg and threatened Vienna whose forces were distracted by the Rákóczi revolt in Hungary and reduced by the needs of the fighting in Italy. Villars imposed heavy 'contributions' on the German countryside to supply his army, defraying 42 per cent of his costs, including 128,000 *livres* in ransoms. Max Emanuel demanded a substantial slice of the 'contributions' and their disagreements stymied further progress. Ultimately the French general was replaced by Marsin.

Austria was clearly at risk and the English commander, Marlborough, took 20,000 men and feinted towards the Moselle. On 19 May he abruptly marched south, collecting allied forces en route and arriving at Launsheim close to Ulm on 22 June. The crude rate of march of 7.5 miles per day was not especially impressive and the average distance of 13 miles covered on days of actual march corresponded to what ancient and medieval armies had normally managed. What was impressive was that the force arrived in good shape to fight, because Marlborough contracted with his agents, the brothers Medina, to purchase food and threatened the 'friendly' rulers of the territories through which he was passing with dire consequences if they did not help him. By the standards of the age this was a lightning march made possible by careful preparation, but the demands of speed meant that Marlborough had relatively few guns. He therefore had to storm Donauwörth to obtain a bridge across the Danube, suffering 5,000 casualties in the process and lacked artillery to attack a fortress like Ulm. In fact he proceeded to ravage Bavaria in a brutal effort to drive Max Emanuel out of the war. In response, Louis XIV dispatched Marshal Tallard with a formidable French army, but although they made good speed they were exhausted by the effort and harassed badly by German peasants enraged by their ravaging.

On 12 August the allied and French armies faced one another across the little river Nebel on the north bank of the Danube. Each army had roughly 56,000 men, though the French possessed ninety guns to the allies' sixty. The French thought a clash unlikely, with good reason. Battle was chancy, the allied army was far from its bases and the key fortresses in the area were all held by the Franco-Bavarians. Defeat, therefore, would have been disastrous. This misreading of allied intentions probably explains why the French and their allies deployed so badly, with Tallard's purely French forces around Blenheim near to the Danube on his right, and Marsin and the Elector far to the left. Oberglau marked the junction of what were effectively two armies barely linked together. Marlborough made a great thrust at the centre of the enemy line. Some 14,000 Franco-Bavarian troops surrendered and perhaps as many as 20,000 were killed or wounded. The allies suffered 13,000 losses. Such losses are a testimony to the effectiveness of close-range musketry and massed bayonets.

Blenheim was a decisive victory which ended the threat to Vienna and brought all Germany over to the allies, but essentially it only nullified a temporary French advantage, and the whole Franco-Spanish defensive system along the Rhine and into Flanders remained. Marlborough was soon re-immersed in attacking fortifications in Flanders where the French easily held their own. In 1706, however, when Louis changed his strategy and ordered his armies onto the offensive, Marlborough won a great victory at Ramillies and scooped up a number of towns and cities, but was bogged down till September by the formidable fortress of Dendermonde. In Italy, after initial French gains, Prince Eugene relieved the siege of Turin and crushed the French army, forcing evacuation of the Po plain, while the Catalan rebels against Philip of Spain held out and an allied army threatened from Portugal. But nothing had broken the French will to fight on and the coming years failed to produce any decisive result, although Marlborough won a stunning victory at Oudenarde on 11 July 1708 which led to the capitulation of Lille after a long siege in December. In 1709 Marlborough scored another great victory, at Malplaquet, but at a cost of enormous losses in the face of an able defence by Villars whose army suffered much fewer losses and retired in good order. With military momentum lost, political initiatives then took centre stage and by 1713 peace left Spain in Bourbon hands and France virtually undiminished.

Louis XIV, despite losing many major battles, won the War of the Spanish Succession, essentially because he was defending the status quo established at its start. The warfare of this period resembled that of the Hundred Years War in that it was a long-drawn-out contest of wills, spurred on by occasional victories. In the absence of any means to destroy an enemy, victory was a mirage. On land it could only be purchased by casualties which exhausted the victor, and the defeated could repair to his fortifications. At sea it was difficult to achieve a decisive result because fleets depended on the wind and could as easily fly from battle as close for it. As a result war slid into compromise, but it was the compromise of exhaustion, not of intent.

Our eye is taken by spectacular events like Blenheim and the savage warfare in Flanders, but the sheer scale and intensity of the fighting were staggering. In France there were persistent Protestant revolts, and the famine of 1709–10 there caused terrible unrest and brought offensive actions to a halt. In England, Louis tried to foment civil war in order to restore the Stuart monarchy. Hungary rose against its Hapsburg rulers with French encouragement, while Catalonia made a bid for independence from the Spanish crown. Italy was ravaged by the clash of French and Austrians, and Portugal wavered between France and the allies. Navies fought at sea and there was war in the colonies. And appalling damage was inflicted. An estimated 1,251,000 seem to have died in fighting during the War of the Spanish Succession; that does not take into account deaths by sickness, or civilian casualties direct and indirect. On Louis's death in 1715 it was revealed that the French state owed 2.5 million *livres*. In no real sense was this limited war, except, perhaps, for the British who, safe behind their navy, picked up colonies and guarantees which profited them for the future.

European warfare in the eighteenth century was certainly not just a formal parade-ground affair, and it was not static because war was frequent and soldiers and political leaders reflected carefully on their ideas and experiences. The Emperor of Austria, Charles VI (1711–40), had only a daughter, Maria Theresa (1740–80), and the law provided that a woman could not succeed to the throne. Charles persuaded the European powers to agree to her succession by the Pragmatic Sanction of 1713, but when he actually died on 20 October 1740 most of the signatories reneged. Frederick the Great of Prussia had inherited a standing army of 83,000 which could be mobilised quickly. On 16 December 1740 he invaded the rich province of Silesia which he had long coveted; by the New Year he held most of it. This precipitated the War of Austrian Succession (1740–48), in which Prussia, France and Spain allied against Austria, Holland and Britain. This gave rise to the Anglo-French conflicts of 'King George's War' in North America and the First Carnatic War in India. The settlement of 1748 confirmed Frederick's possession of Silesia and all Europe recognised the rise of a new military power based on the best infantry in the continent.

Frederick the Great is the dominating figure in the military history of the mid-eighteenth century. Yet in his first experience of battle, at Mollwitz on 10 April 1741, he fled the field when things appeared to be going badly. All was saved by his senior officers, and above all by the discipline of the Prussian infantry. In the words of an Austrian officer captured in the battle: 'It did not appear to be infantry that was marching towards them, but moving walls.'[7] The price was high – the Prussians lost 4,850 men – some 300 more than the Austrians. Frederick was truly a child of the Enlightenment, the great intellectual current then sweeping Europe which recognised 'reason' as the great source of power and authority. Accordingly, in his *General Principles of War* published in 1753, he tried to systematise what he had learned. He understood the limitations of contemporary infantry volley fire. The king's preference was for skilful manoeuvre and fast and relentless movement which he thought would overwhelm his enemies. He insisted on infantry advancing in very close order with muskets on the shoulder until the very last moment. At his insistence Prussian troops adopted cadenced marching to keep them in step and he developed very complex drills to bring his forces quickly from line of march into line of battle. In battle the enemy would be softened up by artillery preparation and infantry were equipped with light 3-pounder infantry cannon to pave the way for the assault, but it was shock and cold steel which would destroy the enemy, and troops were urged not to hesitate but to press on until victory was complete. His cavalry were also drilled to close order and expected to charge home. He had plenty of opportunity to test these ideas in the wars that lay ahead.

Austria feared Prussia as a dangerous adversary in Germany and formed an alliance with France and Russia whose rulers had ambitions to acquire Poland which Frederick was certain to contest. English rivalry with France in North America was becoming acute. The French claimed the Mississippi, precipitating fighting in Ohio in 1754, and this was followed by their construction of forts in western Pennsylvania. For this reason the English backed Prussia in the Seven Years War of 1756–63. The Austrian commanders had recognised Frederick's fondness for rapid movement and direct assault with cold steel. At Lobositz on 1 October 1756 Frederick attacked an Austrian army in broken country where their Croatian irregulars inflicted heavy casualties before his infantry drove the Austrians into an orderly retreat. In the following year at Prague on 6 May Frederick threw his Prussians against a strongly entrenched Austrian army and suffered 14,000 Prussian dead. At Kolin on 18 June he again attacked the Austrians in a prepared position. His infantry were harassed by the Croatians, disrupting their assault on the Austrians who won an important victory, forcing Frederick to retreat from Prague. In each case the Austrians deployed their fire-power against Frederick's well-known predilection for frontal assault. But at Leuthen on 5 December 1757 Frederick engaged on much more open ground, manoeuvring quickly to strike the enemy where least expected, but his infantry now relied far more on firepower to win a famous victory and he concentrated his artillery, hitherto somewhat ignored, against the Austrian infantry.

Frederick conceived of horse-artillery – light cannon and their caissons of shot harnessed to strong horse-teams, with the gunners riding alongside – as a means of weakening enemy infantry who were an obstacle to the fast and aggressive movement which he wanted from his cavalry. At the siege of Schweidnitz in June 1762 he deployed his cannon carefully, with the very latest howitzers firing explosive shells. His infantry then worked their way into the Austrian positions using the ground skilfully. He was always impatient of engineers, partly because in the open spaces of Central Europe fortresses were much less common than in the west. But at Bunzelwitz in 1761, faced with an overwhelming challenge from Austrian and Russian armies, Frederick was happy to resort to a well-fortified camp. Both Frederick and his enemies learned from experience. As more powers engaged, war grew in scale and became more intense. At Zorndorf in August 1758 Frederick checked the Russian invasion of his lands, but at a cost of 12,000 casualties – the enemy endured 18,000. Armies were increasing in size and Frederick always suffered from a manpower shortage. By 1777 his army was not far short of 200,000, over double the number he had inherited in 1740.

The intense warfare of the eighteenth century produced a new emphasis on the training of officers. Prussia established the Berlin Cadet

Corps in 1717 for officer training. The French School of Engineers was founded at Mezières in 1749, and the following year a similar institution for the artillery appeared. The École Royale Militaire, where Napoleon would be educated, was founded in Paris in 1750. In Austria the Wiener Neustadt Military Academy served the same function while the Russian Cadet Corps had been founded in 1731, and subsequently a number of specialist academies were created. In England the Royal Military Academy at Woolwich opened in 1741. This all owed something to the Enlightenment which was to influence Frederick the Great's *General Principles of War*, but the practical needs of war really drove the trend: calculating artillery fire and siege-works, the difficulties of controlling large armies, now regularly of the order of 60,000. War was becoming increasingly complex and educating officers was therefore vital.

The rise of a more educated officer corps raised the intellectual level of debate on war. France had done badly during the Seven Years War, losing her overseas empire to Britain, and seeing her army defeated by the Prussians at Rossbach on 5 November 1757. As a result, a series of reforms was introduced and vigorous discussion was encouraged. Entry to the officer corps was restricted to nobles; they were very numerous in France and many of them were poor, so this measure helped to bind them to the crown. The abolition of purchase of commissions offered them better prospects of promotion. The staff, responsible for the organisation of war, was strengthened. French commanders debated the value of attack in column, which was quicker than deploying into line and easier to control. Their distinguished soldier and military theorist, Jacques Antoine Hippolyte, comte de Guibert (1743–90), advocated rapid movement and suggested avoiding siege by masking fortresses. He thought that supply trains could be lightened and more emphasis placed on living off the country in the interests of speed.

On the battlefield Guibert favoured experimentation with light troops, even equipping some with rifles which had greater range and accuracy than muskets so that they could harass the enemy line and pick off officers. His greatest innovation, implemented after 1766, was to develop a system whereby troops could deploy quickly for battle as they marched towards the enemy. In addition he recommended that on the offensive a line of skirmishers should be thrown forward to prepare the way for an *ordre mixte* with formations attacking in column (usually battalions split into company columns) or in line, as circumstances suggested. Such thinking about tactics and organisation was by no means confined to the French. The British lined their men up in a double rank and fired by platoon, thus·a battalion delivered rolling fire across its front from the moment the enemy came into range. During the later stages of the Seven Years War, as armies became bigger and more difficult to control, the Austrians seem to have experimented with very large sub-units of all arms led by senior officers which could march and fight independently, but when necessary combine on the battlefield.

Traditionally, because artillery was expensive, guns were made 12 feet long so that if used in fortresses the muzzle would project and the blast would not damage the masonry. This, of course, made them very heavy and clumsy in the field. Frederick the Great's horse-artillery were shorter and had lighter bronze guns whose gunners rode into action to break up enemy formations. In 1776 Gribeauval became French inspector of artillery; he demanded that a regular corps of gunners be instituted, and he standardised calibres. Under his aegis, an infrastructure of state-owned arsenals was developed with their own boring machines. Hitherto cannon had been cast around a clay core which was cut out when the metal had cooled. This produced erratic bores, so that cannonballs could not be made to fit tightly. Boring made calibres much more consistent so that ammunition could be standardised. Under the Gribeauval system there was a sharp distinction between the lighter bronze guns for field use and heavier weapons for fortress and siege.

Although European thinking was dominated by the full frontal collision of regular infantry masses hardened to the ordeal of battle and siege by discipline, Europeans knew very well what they called 'little war' (*petite guerre*), a name which embraced anything outside the mainstream. The Austro–Ottoman frontier saw constant raiding, and the 'Croats' and Hussars who waged it were starting to contribute to the more fluid tactics evident in Europe in the second half of the eighteenth century. In all major campaigns light forces of cavalry and infantry skirmished; this was the inevitable accompaniment of ravaging and levying 'contributions.' In addition, regular armies maintained light forces whose task was to harass the enemy. In 1745 at Fontenoy Marshal de Saxe employed sharpshooters who did great harm to the attacking British and allied forces. During the colonial wars in the dense forests and wastes of North America, both the British and the French employed native tribes to harass their enemies. Famously, a Franco-Indian force ambushed and killed the British General Braddock at the battle of the Monongahela in 1755. In the forest-steppe the Russians advanced by raiding, desisting only when the small native tribes agreed to pay tribute and obey them. Gradually a thin network of forts established Russian dominion over a vast area, but the conquest was very much driven by local initiatives, though supplied with modern weapons and backed, on an occasional basis, by Russian troops. Massacre and the threat of massacre were the methods of both sides, but it was the growth of the Russian population which drove the expansion, until they met Chinese imperialism advancing from the other end of Asia.

In the eighteenth century popular insurgency, people's war, was uncommon in Europe. However, there is a myth that the American Revolutionary War was won by patriots rallying to their militias in a people's war. This was certainly a broadly based rebellion against British rule. In 1776 the thirteen British colonies in North America revolted against the crown. Notable amongst their many grievances was discontent at taxation levied by London to cover some of the costs of protecting the colonies and the anger of the colonial elite at London's decision to halt westward colonisation beyond the Appalachian Mountains. Open rebellion began in 1776, but became serious when the Americans isolated Burgoyne's small army at Saratoga in 1777, provoking France, Spain and Holland to intervene. Thus a colonial dispute became a worldwide war. But far from finding colonials anxious to rally to their cause, the Revolutionary leaders had great difficulty in recruiting troops at all. Washington had few illusions about the colonial militias. Indeed, he would probably have agreed with Clausewitz: 'Insurgent actions are similar in character to all others fought by second-rate troops: they start out full of vigor and enthusiasm but there is little level-headedness and tenacity in the long-run.'[8] His Continental Army of regulars was never really able to fight the British on equal terms, but as long as it existed it gave hope to convinced supporters, rallied the doubtful and served to threaten the hostile. But in the Carolinas campaign of 1780–81 irregular warfare was decisive.

The British, with their increasing distractions elsewhere in the world, could only deploy quite a small army, which made the reconquest of the huge area of the colonies very difficult. One way in which they multiplied the effectiveness of their troops was to use their command of the sea. In 1780 they seized the ports of Savannah and Charleston, and their commander, Cornwallis, shipped in troops and supplies with which to rally the loyalists of the Carolinas and thence to penetrate Virginia. At Camden, on 16 August 1780, he defeated General Gates whose regulars fought well but were deserted by the local militia. However, the British threw away the fruits of victory by scattering their forces to rally the loyalists, and the new American commander, Nathanael Greene, with inferior forces, was happy to engage in guerrilla warfare which became more and more savage, polarising support. When Cornwallis tried to advance northwards, Greene's irregulars harassed the British in support of his few regulars. They fought delaying actions which ultimately made the British advance impossible to sustain.

There were clear signs that the new developments in Europe were changing the balance of power hitherto so favourable to the steppe empires. Nomad warfare, based on speed and light weaponry, did not foster the development of gunpowder weapons. However, the peoples who created the steppe empires had always shown remarkable adaptability. Ottoman armies in the sixteenth century established a real lead in weapons and organisation over their western neighbours, while the Manchu eagerly took up gunpowder in their conquest of China. India produced magnificent firearms. There was no inherent reason why these great empires should not respond to the European challenge. That they failed was due to the chance factor that from the second half of the eighteenth century, for very different reasons, all of them were going into political decline.

The Ottoman standing army was formidable: by 1670 there were about 50,000 janissaries, 14,000 regular cavalry and 8,000 men in the artillery corps. The system of supply was far in advance of any army in Europe. But the Ottomans were challenged by Austria in the Danube valley and the Balkans, by Persia in the east and by Russia on the southern steppe. Their decisive weakness was the decline of the janissaries. By the end of the sixteenth century they had become a praetorian guard, and they overthrew the sultan Osman II (1617–22) when he proposed to replace them. By the eighteenth century they were becoming demilitarised. To save on cost the Ottomans permitted janissaries to undertake civilian work, which gradually dominated their lives. An increasingly small percentage of them were ever mobilised for war, but they were all tax-exempt in respect of their 'military' status. As a result the janissaries became political soldiers whose only military value was ceremonial, but their integration into the political factions at the court made it impossible to destroy them or to reduce their privileges even though their nominal numbers were increasing. Some janissaries were permitted to acquire military lands (*timars*) in the provinces to where they and other gentry increasingly diverted funds from the central government. The decay of the janissaries forced the sultans to raise new infantry and cavalry regiments, but because of the reduction in central income and the burden of paying the janissaries, the new troops did not form a standing force, so that increasingly the empire was dependent on raw and half-trained soldiery. The artillery corps also suffered from under-investment so that it was unable to modernise. These disturbing trends took some time to become apparent and so great was the Ottoman lead in military organisation that in 1711 they routed Peter the Great's army at the Pruth, and as late as 1739 recovered Belgrade from the Austrians and threw back a Russian advance towards the Black Sea, forcing them to abandon their new Black Sea fleet and its bases.

But the decay of the janissaries and the under-investment in artillery weakened the Ottoman army, while the Russians and the Austrians were learning from the European wars. In 1770 a Russian army of about 40,000 destroyed over 100,000 Ottomans at the battle of Kartal and the ensuing treaty of Küçük Kaynarca ratified the Russian advance to the Black Sea and the permanent subjugation of the Tatars. By 1791 Austria controlled Belgrade and the Russians were in Bucharest. As a result, in 1792 the Sultan devised his 'New Order' (*Nizam-i*), bringing in French soldiers to train new regiments on the European model. The janissary opposition was supported by popular dislike of new taxes to pay for the military reforms and by provincial resentments which sparked local revolts. By 1797, however, the French held the Ionian islands and in 1798 Napoleon invaded Egypt, curtailing efforts at military reform. England and France then proceeded to dispute control of Egypt and the eastern Mediterranean with little reference to its nominal ruler at Constantinople. Such was the price of 'asymmetry', failure to keep up with the European arms race.

In India the Mughals, another steppe power, declined sharply after the death of Aurangzeb in 1707. He had rejected the policy of tolerance towards the Hindu majority, and the strength of Islamic fundamentalism embittered tensions at the courts of his successors who were in any case much less capable men, creating widespread discontent. In 1739 Nadir Shah of Persia sacked Delhi with an immense slaughter and in 1756 Ahmad Shah Abdali of Afghanistan repeated the performance. Within India there were plenty of possible successor states, notably the Maratha Confederacy, the Sikh Confederacy and Bengal which had long enjoyed good government under a line of independent nawabs (governors); in the south, Mysore had great potential. Amongst the European trading companies the British were the most powerful with outposts at Bombay, Madras and Calcutta. They were, however, rivalled by the French with stations at Chandannagar and Pondicherry, while the Portuguese and Dutch also had enclaves. All these companies had private armies backed up by fleets, but a strong power could have played them off against one another. What was lacking was just such a powerful local authority, and after the Seven Years War the British were much stronger than the

French. Marathas, and Sikhs, could be militarily dangerous, but they were never really united and were quite distinct from Muslim Mysore. The British, by contrast, displayed a solidarity which impressed locals.

And they had a powerful motive for intervention. The East India Company had very high costs which often exceeded income. As Mughal power declined, the acquisition of *jagirs*, assignments of district revenues, was becoming a major and highly profitable business. So grabbing the right to collect taxes was an obvious path to riches. In 1756 the Nawab of Bengal quarrelled with the British and seized Calcutta: many of his British prisoners, including women and children, were imprisoned in a badly overcrowded dungeon and perished in what became known as the Black Hole of Calcutta. The British under Clive quickly reconquered Calcutta, and then at Plassey on 23 June 1757 their army of 3,000 faced the Nawab with 50,000. Clive bribed many of the Nawab's supporters so that the army melted away, enabling the Company to appoint a puppet ruler. Of Clive's troops, over 2,000 were local soldiers or sepoys and only about 1,000, including the gunners, were Europeans. At Buxar in 1764 a Company army of 7,000 with less than 1,000 British, triumphed over 30,000 enemies because, according to their commander, Hector Munro, they had 'regular discipline and strict obedience to orders'.[9] By 1773 the British had taken over as rulers of Bengal and a number of other small states. This was not a merely military triumph; many of the local notables favoured the stability of British rule, but the recruitment of the local soldiery, and their training in modern methods of war, was the prerequisite for success.

The Indian powers were keenly aware of the need to develop comparable discipline and methods, and as a result the British suffered many setbacks in their path to empire. It took four wars lasting until 1804 to subdue Mysore, while the three Maratha wars ended only in 1818. The Sikhs under Ranjit Singh created a powerful empire of the Punjab centred on Lahore. Their army was trained and officered by experienced French soldiers and equipped with modern artillery which hitherto had largely been a British monopoly. Succession disputes on Ranjit's death in 1839 opened the way for British intervention, but it was only after two costly wars that the Sikhs were finally annexed in 1849. The British domination of India owed much to skilful diplomacy, which resulted in a network of princely states whose rulers agreed to collaborate. The merchants of the Indian cities came to see the Company as a force for stability. The multiplicity of states in eighteenth-century India had created a great market for soldiers, and the Company could offer well-paid and successful service, in effect cornering the market, to create a powerful sepoy army. British dominance rested on victory brought about by successful military methods. The surging armies of light cavalry which had so often been the key to victory in the northern plains were replaced by disciplined lines of infantry supported by artillery and smaller cavalry units. The European way of war had clearly displaced that of the steppe people. The native powers, despite their different culture, espoused these new methods enthusiastically, but Indian political units proved to be fissiparous and no single one of them was quite strong enough quite consistently enough to survive. This was not a case of 'asymmetry' in the military sense, but of political weakness.

Further east the steppe regime of the Qing (or Manchu) made China into a land without enemies. Under three great emperors, Kangxi (1662–1722), Yongzheng (1722–36) and Qianlong (1736–96), the Manchu embraced Chinese patterns of government and culture while yet trying to preserve the character and privileges of their own people. At strategic points in the land, especially around Beijing, Banner garrisons of Manchu troops were established. These were, however, only an elite and the bulk of the army was made up of purely Chinese Green Standard Armies raised from military settlements. The main threats to the Manchu came from the steppe nomad tribes and the eastward advance of the Russians. Kangxi eliminated the Russian outpost of Albazin and concluded the Treaty of Nerchinsk in 1689 which delineated the Russo–Chinese border for nearly two centuries. The Manchu knew the steppe because it had been their home, and they developed highly efficient logistics to supply their armies on its vast wastes. This enabled them to conquer the nomads. Faced with continued Zhungar resistance, in 1757 the Chinese resorted to genocide. By 1750 most of inner Asia and Tibet had been annexed to China, almost doubling the size of the empire whose population by 1800 reached 300 million. With no obvious outside threat the Manchu had little incentive to reform their forces. They were always suspicious of the Green Standard Armies and allowed the system of military settlements which provided their troops to decay. The sheer size and isolation of the empire appeared to make China immune from the consequences of 'asymmetry' in military matters. It was not to last.

The year 1789 is commonly seen as a break-point in European military history because the French Revolution unleashed national feeling and created willing soldiers by admitting all (male) citizens to the political community. Clearly this is a simplification, though with a kernel of truth. The foreign attack on France in 1791 produced a rush of volunteers, eager to defend the state and the Revolution from which many of them had profited, raising the army to nearly half a million men. Their spirit was splendidly encapsulated in what is now the French national anthem, *La Marseillaise*:

To arms citizens!/Form your battalions!/Let's march, let's march!/May impure blood/Water our furrows![10]

But by the time this was written in 1792 the volunteers were going home, and 1793 saw the introduction of conscription with all its inequities and its apparatus of enforcement. There was much rhetoric of national enthusiasm, but conscription provoked rebellion in the Vendée (1793–96) and much resistance elsewhere. However, the appeal to national feeling enabled the French government to extend its power into the provinces and so to create the means to raise and sustain very large forces. Moreover, national fervour ebbs and flows. When the young Napoleon took over the army of Italy in 1796 his appeal to the troops rested on rather more traditional incentives which would have been familiar to Genghis Khan:[11]

Soldiers! You are hungry and naked; the government owes you much but can give you nothing. The patience and courage which you have displayed among these rocks are admirable; but they bring you no glory – not a glimmer falls upon you. I will lead you into the most fertile plains on earth. Rich provinces, opulent towns, all shall be at your disposal; there you will find honour, glory and riches. Soldiers of Italy! Will you be lacking in courage or endurance?

Napoleon inherited conscription, but he preferred to keep men with the colours for long periods of time so that they became experienced soldiers. However, as casualties mounted after 1807 he was driven to take more and more raw recruits, diluting the quality of his army. Under the consulate and empire many of the soldiers were not French at all, but levies extorted from 'liberated' lands like Italy. For his invasion of Russia in 1812 Napoleon had 800,000 men, but less than half were French; 34,000 Austrians, 90,000 Poles, 90,000 Germans and 57,000 Italians with a smattering of others made up the rest. This was exceptional, but French forces at all times contained large foreign contingents. Size was the real secret of Revolutionary and Napoleonic success. Large armies could mask fortifications and seek out battles of annihilation with the enemy. They could sustain heavy losses once engaged and accept the wastage of desertion: on

22 June 1812 about 600,000 troops crossed into Russia, but by the time
Napoleon brought the Russians to battle on 7 September at Borodino he
was down to 135,000 men, largely because of desertion. These great armies
could not be sustained and held together by enthusiasm alone and structural changes were vitally important in contributing to victory.

At the heart of an army are its officers and NCOs. The Revolution
swept away the system of noble preferment and opened the highest ranks
of the army to talent. F.J. Lefebvre joined the royal army in 1763, rising to
the rank of sergeant by 1789. But by 1793 he was a brigadier-general and
in 1804 became one of Napoleon's marshals. This elite group, the 'Swords
around the Throne', epitomised the opportunities which inspired French
officers in this period, and made them not merely gallant but efficient.[12]
Napoleon believed in discipline and training, and these men were ready to
drill their soldiers in pursuit of their own ambitions. Napoleon is said to
have remarked that 'every French soldier carriers a marshal's baton in his
knapsack', and in truth he created a body of officers and NCOs for whom
continual war offered opportunities for promotion untrammelled by rank
and status. They saw the Emperor as their model and patron, and formed
a dynamic force animating the whole French military structure. Discipline
and training did the rest.

The sheer size of armies, of course, presented problems of control which
Napoleon met by dividing his forces into corps of 20,000–30,000, each with
its own infantry, artillery and cavalry. Corps of all arms were armies in their
own right, capable of independent manoeuvre, and the art of battle consisted
in bringing them together at the right moment. Napoleon created a circle of
able subordinates who knew his mind and were capable of independent
action which meshed with his own. Thus he could break his army up into
units which could move quickly and under control, yet be strong enough to
face almost any enemy. At Austerlitz in 1805 Davout drove his III Corps
70 miles in 48 hours to play a vital role in the fighting. On 14 October 1806
Napoleon's 90,000 confronted 40,000 Prussians at Jena, forcing them to
retreat with 25,000 casualties. But at the same time Davout, a mere junior
officer in 1789, with III Corps of 26,000 men, encountered the main
Prussian force of nearly 50,000, and won a great victory at nearby Auerstadt.

Napoleon was the heir to the reforming ideas current in the military of
the *Ancien Régime*. The corps system had already been mooted in the
armies of the eighteenth century. Similarly the tactical system of French
armies also owed much to the past. The attack in column was adopted
long before 1789. It suited ill-trained but enthusiastic armies early in the
Revolution and Napoleon's characteristic fondness for rapid movement,

and was the more effective because his soldiers were well disciplined. In fact Napoleon used the *ordre mixte* of line and column attack as appropriate. French armies preceded their attacks with clouds of light troops, *tirailleurs*, who could be trusted not to run away, and if they did they could be replaced from these huge armies. A modern writer explains what it must have been like to face the French tactics of using skirmishers backed up by a massed column:

> Put yourself in their place. Swarms of skirmishers have enveloped your tight, strictly-dressed formations, firing from behind cover in a most unsoldierly fashion. If you charge them with the bayonet, they drift away – still shooting – and follow you when you return to your original position. Eventually your lines are in tatters. Then suddenly, out of the smoke, comes a howling, trampling, caterwauling rush of battalion columns, the bayonets and bull-weight of twelve fresh men against every yard of your exhausted line (which was only three deep when the action began) at their chosen point of impact.[13]

Napoleon insisted on rigorous training, with steady infantry as the backbone of his army. He also created an exceptional cavalry force whose speed greatly assisted his mobility. Napoleon was an artilleryman by training, and he recognised the virtues of standardisation which Gribeauval had introduced into the French royal army. He often concentrated his guns into great batteries which bombarded his enemies. In battle he generally pinned the enemy by frontal assault, and sent major units around a flank towards his rear.

Speed was at the heart of Napoleon's strategic and tactical practice. In August 1805 Napoleon's army was at Boulogne contemplating an invasion of England, but news that Russia and Austria had agreed to join a third coalition led to a fast march eastwards. Seven corps, some 300,000 men, concentrated on the Rhine which was crossed on 25 September. They moved separately for the sake of rapidity and isolated 23,000 Austrians, including Mack, their commander, at Ulm which capitulated on 20 October. In November Vienna fell to the French. The army then concentrated and on 2 December Napoleon defeated the Austro-Russian army at Austerlitz, forcing a peace on draconian terms.

Such methods were not simply military in origin. The French Republic and Empire never had a satisfactory way of raising war finance, and faced many enemies. Lightning war which aimed to eliminate threats was essential, and a thrust into hostile heartlands would largely pay for itself. Bold action, therefore, sprang from economic necessity. French armies no longer allowed officers vast quantities of personal baggage and their supply trains were trimmed so that their troops were forced to live off the country. Once they enjoyed some success, large areas of Italy and Germany were drawn into tribute and, in effect, paid for French warfare. As Napoleon remarked: 'The basic principle that we must follow in directing the armies of the Republic is this: that they must feed themselves on war at the expense of the enemy territory.'[14] And pay they did. In the years 1806–8 Prussia alone paid out 600 million French francs to support the *Grande Armée*.

Moreover, French success owed much to the divisions of their enemies. The Revolution aroused distaste in the traditional monarchies, but it also created new circumstances which individual states sought to exploit in their own interests. Prussia, Russia and Austria were deeply interested in seizing Polish territory, a process begun in 1772 and completed with further partitions in 1793 and 1795. The major European states wanted to profit from the decline of the Ottoman Empire. The continental countries had noted England's habit of profiting from their wars by seizing colonies and regarded her as a poor ally. This is why, although there were seven coalitions against Revolutionary and Napoleonic France, they were punctuated by periods of peace. The powers could and did make considerable efforts to live with Revolutionary and Napoleonic France.

However, Napoleon's demands for continental dominance in the end drove them into alliance against him, and this was made possible because he over-extended his forces, committing them to an assault on Russia in 1812 while 300,000 men were still labouring in Spain against an Anglo-Portuguese-Spanish army supported by a considerable guerrilla movement. Moreover, states like Prussia, Austria and Russia all learned from Napoleon and imitated his methods. As early as February 1807 the Russians fought Napoleon to a standstill at Eylau where the French lost 14,000 to the Russian 25,000. Napoleon was victorious at Friedland in the following June, but for a loss of 8,000 French. In May 1809 at Aspern-Essling the Austrians threw back a French attempt to cross the Danube, with each side suffering 20,000 casualties. In July Napoleon came again with a huge army of 190,000 which overwhelmed the Austrians, but at a cost of 34,000 casualties. Defeat by Russia in 1812 encouraged his enemies to combine against him. In the subsequent campaigns in Germany and France he was handicapped by the poor quality of his troops and the loss of his best cavalry in Russia. At the Battle of the Nations, Leipzig, 16–19 October 1813, 200,000 French confronted well over 300,000 allied forces. God was distinctly on the side of the big battalions.

1 War before the state: a watchtower manned by a warrior against a neighbouring village. The Grand Valley Dani people of Papua New Guinea (Irian Barat Indonesia) were studied by the Harvard-Peabody Expedition of 1961–3. Despite such vigilance savage raiding was common, sometimes resulting in the extinction of whole settlements.

2 The Stele of the Vultures, Mesopotamian, *c.*2440 BC, depicting King Eanatum's victory over Umma. This is the first picture of an infantry phalanx, the close-order formation which would dominate warfare down to the Military Revolution of the nineteenth century.

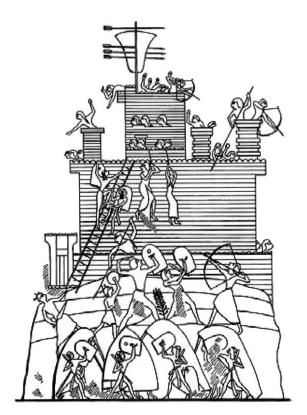

3 The tomb of Inty, late Egyptian Old Kingdom, c.2300 BC: the Egyptians besiege a Canaanite city. Siege was as vital as battle and often more important in agro-urban warfare because rulers controlled their lands from cities and fortresses. Here the Egyptians have seized the outer wall of a concentric fortification and are storming the inner.

4 Egyptian chariot from the tomb of Tutankhamun, Pharaoh of Egypt (1333–1324 BC). Note the light structure and the yoke designed to attach two horses – this would have made it very fast.

5 Real cavalry: Assyrian mounted archer of the seventh century BC. Earlier ninth-century illustrations show them working in pairs, one holding the reins of both horses while the other shoots, but this rider has an assured seat on his horse whose elaborate harness was also protective.

A Greek hoplite. Note how little armour he wears.

7 The Terracotta Army of the First Emperor of China dating from *c*.210 BC. These are figures of very well-equipped regular soldiers, and in this, the first of three pits, they seem to be in order of march.

8 Chinese bronze infantry weapons including two dagger-axes which would have been mounted on poles. The dagger-axe was extensively used from the Shang (1600 BC–1050 BC) down to the Han period (from 206 BC) after which it was replaced by iron spears and halberds. Like the contemporary sword and dagger shown here it was a weapon for close-quarter fighting.

9 A superbly modelled bronze crossbow lock, Chinese, probably Han dynasty (post 206 BC). Chinese armies produced such fine mechanisms in vast quantities because they had ample resources of tin and copper. They were very useful against steppe horsemen.

10 Roman legionary. He wears the segmented armour common during the late Republican and Imperial periods, and is preparing to throw his pilum, a javelin with a long narrow neck which, if it did not kill, bent on impact with the defenders shield, making both useless. The Romans then charged into the enemy ranks using their short swords.

11 Full-size replica of a Roman ballista, a machine for throwing arrows or sometimes stones. It works by torsion – the arms of the machine are buried in a tightly wound skein of ropes providing strong resistance. The string is pulled back by a windlass and secured by a simple trigger mechanism. The Romans adapted the torsion principle to make a whole range of machines, many of them much bigger than this.

12 Tang horseman extracting an arrow, which an enemy has fired into his mount. Ninth-century AD plaque now in Xian.

13 Preparing for battle. The Normans are loading suits of armour on to their ships prior to the battle of Hastings. They may be made of chain mail or lamellar, small plates of metal sewn on to leather or cloth. Worn over a padded shirt they provided great protection against any except the most direct blow or arrow strike from short range. Wine in the barrel was also vital.

14 Crac des Chevaliers in modern Syria, which has survived almost intact since it was built by the Monastic Military Order of the Hospital *c.*1200. On three sides the land falls away very steeply, and on the fourth (south) side the defences are, as this photo shows, massive. The castle is concentric with the inner defences capable of supporting the outer ones. Within each line of defence the garrison works largely in shooting galleries to avoid exposure on the wall-top, and they use firing slits and machicolations, which are carefully tiered. Nevertheless, Baybars's successful siege lasted only from 3 March to 8 April 1271.

15 Steppe horse-archer. His equipment is remarkably light compared to that of the western knights. The bow looks almost fragile, but in fact it was as powerful as the 6-foot English longbow.

16 Medieval handgun. The Chinese had been using these simple weapons since the eleventh century. It took a very long time to develop these primitive weapons into something more effective.

17 Mons Meg, a mighty bombard cast in Flanders and presented to James II of Scotland in 1457. The charge was placed in the removable rear chamber. Note the size of the cannonballs. It was last fired in 1681 when the barrel burst. The Ottomans used weapons like this against Constantinople in 1453.

18 The trace italienne: Bourtange in Groningen was built in 1593 to defend Holland against the Spanish. Earthworks, masonry and deep ditches combined to make fortresses like this very difficult to take, especially if they were provided with ample artillery which was housed in the pointed bastions.

19 J. de Gheyn II described some 42 actions before the arquebusier could fire. Here he has loaded his piece and placed a slow-burning match in the jaws of the serpent which, when the trigger was pulled, was drawn down on to a small pan containing loose powder whose flash ignited the main charge via a small hole in the barrel. He is blowing on the burning match prior to aiming the piece. Note he puts his finger over the pan lest a stray spark should fire the gun. Although heavy it was relatively handy compared to the staff-gun and almost any man could be taught to fire it. Because it was inaccurate, volley fire was important.

20 Battle scene from a manuscript of the memoirs of Emperor Babur (1483–1530), founder of the Mughal Empire of India. Cavalry were dominant in Indian warfare right down to the British conquest.

21 US Civil War: dead soldier in the Petersburg trenches of 9 June 1864 to 25 March 1865. The similarity to the western front of 1914–18 is striking but European soldiers were unimpressed by the quality of American armies and believed they could avoid this kind of stalemate.

4. - Bataille de Sedan. - Un épisode du combat de La Moncelle, 1er Septembre 1870

22 Prussian infantry seen from the French lines on 1 September 1870 at La Moncelle during the Sedan battle. The skirmish line is well within range of the *chassepot* rifle, as witness the falling man on the right. Note the dense column of infantry marching up on the right to strengthen the attack and the bodies littering the ground. This is claimed to be the first photograph taken of actual combat.

23 Hiram Maxim with his machine gun, which he invented in London in the years 1883–5. Weapons like this remained in use until the 1950s.

24 'God the Father, God the Son and God the Holy Ghost', the remarkable French Puteaux 75mm which could fire a *rafale* of 26 shells per minute. Its shrapnel shells created the 'empty battlefield' by driving infantry into trenches where they could be killed only by the indirect plunging fire of howitzers. This shows a US gun crew, probably in 1918, and gives a vivid impression of the rapidity of fire.

25 The glory of war – imagination. Lady Butler's (1846–1933) famous *Scotland Forever!* (1881), portraying the charge of the Scots Greys at Waterloo, shows how Victorians and Edwardians thought of war.

26 The glory of war – reality. French infantry, living and dead, in the trenches around Verdun 1917.

27 French infantry attacking *c.*1914. This is virtually close-order in the face of artillery and machine guns. An English observer remarked that officers thought it 'chic to die in white gloves'.

28 American infantry on patrol in Iraq: even the US with the world's most advanced hardware ultimately has to depend on the foot soldier.

In the warfare of the Revolutionary and Napoleonic periods, grand strategy and tactics take the eye but, as in the eighteenth century, battles were fought by men grappling with one another in bloody contests at close quarters. At Austerlitz it was the bayonets of St-Hilaire's men which cleared the vital Pratzen heights, breaking the allied army into two forces. Steadiness of nerve instilled by discipline was vital if units were to hold together under fire. George Hennell, a volunteer in Wellington's army in Spain recalled at the battle of Vitoria (21 June 1813): 'In another minute a ball struck a close column of the 17th Portuguese . . . about 16 yards from us. It killed a sergeant and took off the leg of each of the ensigns with the colours.'[15] A very junior officer in the same army recalled an enemy attack at Talavera (27–28 July 1809):

> On the left and the right of our positions, where the attacks were most frequent, the men were ordered to remain on the ground till the French came within 40 yards. They then rose, gave the enemy a volley, and repulsed them with the bayonet. The coolness on our part staggered the resolution of the enemy and instead of being the assailants they by it became the assailed . . . in short the enemy in every attack was repulsed with prodigious slaughter.[16]

Fighting on such a grand scale took a heavy toll. It has been estimated that in the period 1806–14 some two million Frenchmen served in Napoleon's armies and that amongst these there were 15,000 officer casualties, while 90,000 enlisted men died on the battlefield, a further 300,000 in hospital, and 625,000 were missing or prisoners. Perhaps 70 per cent of French conscripts aged 20 in 1812 were killed. Officer losses were particularly enfeebling because they reduced the loyal backbone of the army. This kind of attrition could not be sustained, most particularly as the French had become used to fighting wars which were cheap in blood. In 1813 the prefect of the Ariège protested at a new demand for men:

> 'I have taken them all. For the years 1813 and 1814 I swear that there will be no more young men left to have children. This demand is disastrous. It will be done, but it is my duty to tell you that it will deprive us of all the young men capable of working or marrying.'[17]

Little wonder that anti-conscription riots became common, along with sharp attacks on the gendarmerie who enforced it. And things were made worse by the erosion of French dominance over Germany and Italy after

1812, reducing tribute and, thereby, increasing French taxation. All this brought enormous pressure upon Napoleon's political base, forcing his abdication in 1814.

The French had broken the European balance because the Revolution enabled them to create large armies commanded by men who could take risks and recognise the best means of fighting. France was defeated in a long hard wearing-down fight by traditional armies. The Congress of Vienna of 1815, which concluded the peace, wanted to maintain a peaceful Europe by containing France and firmly screwing down the lid on what they recognised as the evil genie of nationalism. Metternich, the architect of the peace, was the foreign minister of the Hapsburg monarchy and he was painfully aware how dangerous nationalism could be to that empire which embraced so many peoples. Moreover, all the states had been appalled by the destructive ambition of Napoleon and the general view was that a balance of power, which could tolerate limited war, was the best way to bring peace and prosperity. This had military consequences: long-term armies closely linked to monarchs seemed a good safeguard against popular explosions. Prussia maintained her faith in short-service conscription with a general reserve, but her system was so clearly centred on the monarchy that this could be accommodated. France preferred a long-service army, but for the moment its size was limited. English liberalism, with its spreading influence, thought mass armies would impoverish states and peoples, and so endorsed such apparently reactionary ideas. But the genie in the bottle was very powerful. Nationalism offered seductive charms to military men especially the potential to provide ever bigger armies and to align public opinion behind them. And other forces were at large undermining the settlement made by the Congress of Vienna.

Clausewitz commented rightly that 'Very few of the new manifestations in war can be ascribed to new inventions.'[18] This was about to change under the impact of new wealth and new technology. 'England,' Napoleon is supposed to have remarked, 'is a nation of shopkeepers.'[19] But in that despised nation a revolution in wealth production was taking place which would also transform the battlefield. Cheap wool and cotton garments, often produced by coal-driven machinery, dressed armies. Iron, and increasingly steel, offered the prospect of mass production of better weapons. In 1809 Napoleon had offered a prize of 12,000 francs to anyone who could invent a good method of preserving food to feed the troops. A Frenchman, Appert, devised bottling, but it was in England that Peter Durand developed the much more robust tin. By the 1850s widespread production was bringing down costs and making tins the practical means to feed armies which had been sought in 1809. On 15 September 1830 the Liverpool MP and former minister, William Huskisson, was killed by the locomotive *Rocket*. This was an accident, but the railway would lead to literally millions of deaths. In 1859 Napoleon III of France chose to intervene on behalf of the nascent Italian kingdom against Austria, whose armies were badly surprised by the speed with which the new French railways transported their army to war in the plain of the Po. Industrial development made it possible to clothe, feed, arm and transport armies in a way hitherto impossible. Moreover governments soon had the means to control them over long distances. In 1844 Morse connected Washington and Baltimore with his electric telegraph, providing instant communication irrespective of distance. By 1875 London was at the centre of a network of over a million miles of electric telegraph and connected to virtually all the major world centres.

The new technology had an enormous effect upon navies too. The application of steam power to shipping had begun in the late eighteenth century, and by 1833 a screw-driven vessel, Isambard Kingdom Brunel's *Great Western*, was plying the North Atlantic, and European navies were experimenting with steam power. A French artillery officer, H-J. Paixhans, invented a high-velocity flat trajectory gun firing a 60-pound explosive shell of 22 cm (8.5 in.). By 1838 this was sufficiently developed to be recognised as a threat to all navies, and in the early 1840s an American, Dahlgren, improved it. On 30 November 1853 a Russian squadron armed with thirty-eight Paixhan guns totally destroyed a Turkish fleet at Sinope, demonstrating the vulnerability of 'wooden walls'. This attack on Turkey was one of the factors which precipitated the Crimean War (1854–6), in which the Anglo-French navies swept the Black Sea clear of Russian ships, but were quite unable to overwhelm the port of Sebastopol whose artillery was reinforced by many of the new naval cannon. This failure gave urgency to the quest to develop iron ships. In 1859 France launched *La Gloire*, a wooden steam screw-driven ship clad in iron, but a year later this was trumped by the British *Warrior*, an entirely iron-built ship of immense strength, capable of more than 14 knots. These ships were still partly dependent on sail, but the end of the long tyranny of wind was now in sight. The Crimean War brought other signs of things to come.

In 1853 the British adopted the Enfield rifle. It had long been recognised that rifling the barrel of a musket to spin the missile increased both range and accuracy. The trouble was that the process of rifling was expensive, and the ball had to be forced down the spiral grooves of the barrel, making loading painfully slow. But the quality of iron and steel improved and new machinery made boring easier, cheaper and more exact. In the 1840s a French officer, Minié, developed a conical bullet with a hollow in its base. This could be pushed down the rifled barrel without effort, but when the charge fired the hollow expanded and the surrounding lead engaged with the rifling grooves, spinning the missile. The Enfield had a range of 1,000 metres and a reasonably accurate practical range of 450 metres. Moreover, it could be fired much faster than a musket because instead of a flint striking loose powder in a pan, the main charge was now ignited by a copper percussion cap. And this system reduced misfires due to rain and damp. The effect of this was that an attacking force could be taken under fire at a distance which allowed for several shots to be got off. During the Crimean War this practice wreaked havoc amongst the dense masses of Russian infantry armed with smoothbore muskets seeking to engage at close quarters. The new rifle was one of the causes of the Indian Mutiny (1857–9) because it was rumoured that its paper cartridges were coated by pig (offensive to Muslims) and cow (offensive to Hindus) grease. However, the Enfield 1853 proved very useful in putting down the revolt because the rebellious native sepoys were still equipped with smoothbores. William Armstrong was struck by the news that at the battle of Inkerman in November 1854 it had taken the British two hours to redeploy two critically sited 12-pounder guns each weighing two tons. Inspired by this he devised his famous 12-pounder breech-loaders which weighed only a quarter of a ton. Armstrong was aware that his rival, Krupp in Prussia, was designing steel guns, but knowing that consistency of manufacture was difficult in this material, he used wrought iron.

Since the late seventeenth century the main thrust of change in European armies was organisational, with discipline as the essential cement of their armies. European armies of the eighteenth century remained in principle close-order forces designed for the close-quarter battle, but they became very tightly organised, well supported and, above all, embraced by an iron discipline which largely made up for the limitations of their weapons. Lesser powers like Holland, Sweden and Poland dropped or were driven out of competition, but essentially there was symmetry between the major powers and even large-scale wars seemed to have a limited overall effect on Europe. Soldiers devised ideas to unpick what they regarded as a frustrating deadlock, and these were applied when the French Revolution, for a whole variety of reasons, introduced a risk-taking mentality. This was not sustained because Napoleon overreached himself.

The greatest change of the period was in the position of Europe in the world and this was largely a matter of chance. The growing military strength of the European states coincided with decline and stagnation elsewhere. The Ottomans and the Mughals in their prime were formidable enemies who could check outside intervention in their affairs, because despite undoubted progress the Europeans enjoyed no obvious military superiority over these powers, except at sea. It was their internal decline which opened the way for the British in India, and for the gradual reduction of the Ottoman Empire's power on the continent where it was seen by 1850 as the 'Sick Man of Europe'. Even the small bases of the Dutch and the Portuguese in the Far East enlarged into colonies as local powers declined, while the French took over the old Ottoman protectorate in North Africa.

Underlying European expansion was economic development. The agricultural and industrial revolutions intensified wealth creation. Their impact was far from uniform in Europe but made itself felt everywhere to a degree. Seemingly small powers, like Britain, could therefore afford military forces which were all the more powerful because of the decline of the steppe empires. But European forces, once separated from the limited modern infrastructure which gave them their power, were very vulnerable. The French suffered many defeats in their conquest of North Africa. In 1839 the British invaded Afghanistan to prevent Russian influence growing there. After a series of defeats a force of 4,500 troops with 12,000 camp followers attempted to withdraw and was totally annihilated, with only a doctor, William Brydon, surviving to tell the tale.

Nonetheless in 1840 European military technological might made its impact upon China, the last great empire which stood outside the European sphere. All foreign trade with China was channelled through Canton (now Guangzhou) and in theory very strictly controlled. The British East India Company had an enormous market at home for Chinese tea and ceramics, but had, for over a century, been in part paying for such imports by illegally selling Indian opium to the Chinese. This was possible because some local authorities in China connived at it and many Chinese merchants shared in the profits. By the 1830s the scale of this trade had become enormous, involving something like 900 tons of opium per annum, and the imperial authorities decided to act.

When they confiscated and destroyed opium in 1840, the economic effects were so severe that the British dispatched an army and a fleet to south China to re-establish the trade. The East India Company ship, *Nemesis*, was an ironclad paddle steamer armed with 12- and 32-pound guns. She and her ilk pounded the Chinese forts, which the infantry then captured. They also wrought great destruction along the coast and penetrated the Yangtze. The result was the Treaty of Nanjing of 1842 by which

China opened more ports to British shipping, paid compensation for the destroyed opium and ceded Hong Kong, prompting France and the United States to demand similar concessions in 1844. What is striking is that this victory was achieved with very little effort. The British demanded no sacrifices from their people to inflict a defeat, with all its far-reaching consequences, upon what had been the world's greatest power.

The fact was that in organisation, technology and logistics, the European style of war was, by the nineteenth century, becoming the international style of war. In the eighteenth century the wealth generated by the seizure of the New World finally enabled the European powers to realise the potential of the limited gunpowder technology which was available all over the globe. This coincided with the decline of the steppe empires, which now became vulnerable to the slow-moving phalanx which they had for so long outclassed. In the nineteenth century this substantial advantage was enormously amplified by technological developments which brought in their train a true Military Revolution.

CHAPTER EIGHT

THE MILITARY REVOLUTION

At one time war appealed to the imagination of man, and the poets and painters found no theme so tempting as depicting the heroism of the individual warrior . . . All that has long gone by the board. War has become more and more a matter of mechanical arrangement. Modern battles will be decided, so far as they can be decided at all, by men lying in improvised ditches they have scooped out to protect themselves from the fire of distant and invisible enemy . . . War, instead of being a hand-to-hand contest . . . will become a kind of stalemate, in which neither army will be able to get at the other.[1]

WAR in the second half of the nineteenth century was transformed by two interacting forces – the French Revolution with its ideas of nationalism and democracy, and the huge surge in industrial development. This last gave rise to an extraordinary technological revolution which utterly changed the conduct of war. In 1854 Britain went to war against Russia with a fleet of 'wooden walls'. In 1906 she launched HMS *Dreadnought*, a steel battleship of 17,900 tons capable of 21.6 knots and carrying ten 12-in. guns with ranges of over 12,000 metres. The science of hydraulics which governed the movement of her guns and the optics which made it possible to aim them barely existed in 1856. In 1900 a single British battalion of 600 had more firepower than all the 60,000 who fought at Waterloo in 1815. The internal combustion engine, though as yet crude, promised quick and flexible road transport. In 1903 the Wright brothers flew the first heavier-than-air machine and by 1912 Russian army field manoeuvres enlisted eight aircraft, bringing an entirely new dimension to war.

Populations grew enormously in Europe from 187 million in 1800 to 400 million by 1900, and in the US for the same period from 5.3 million to 76.2 million. This vast increase created the potential for larger armies, which could be realised because the means to supply and maintain them had radically improved. During the Revolutionary and Napoleonic Wars forces of 70,000 were commonplace and occasionally, in battles like Wagram and Borodino, both sides mustered over 100,000. Leipzig, 16–19 October 1813, was extraordinary in that Napoleon's army of 190,000 faced an allied force of 365,000. At Gettysburg in the American Civil War, 1–3 July 1863, 70,000 Confederates were defeated by 90,000 Unionists. In 1914 the French had a standing army of 823,000 with 2.9 million reserves and the Germans 700,000 with 3.8 million reserves. Such was the scale of armies and so great their firepower that the author of *The Future of War*, I.S. Bloch, was not alone in thinking that war was now so terrible as to be unthinkable. And in fact leading soldiers were at least as confused as anybody else by the new means of war which technology was putting in their hands.

The key commodity of the 'Second Industrial Revolution' after 1870 was cheap high-quality steel which could be drilled, cut and worked by its characteristic product, the machine tool. The dyestuffs and chemical industry became important, along with electricity, optics and hydraulics. The telephone and later the wireless offered ever faster communication. The generals were no longer the force driving military innovation, as entrepreneurs, often by dazzling salesmanship and bribery, imposed their new weapons on armies. In 1849 the Prussian Alfred Krupp, 'the Cannon King', delivered an all-steel breech-loading cannon to the Prussian army, only for it to be left out in the rain to rust for nearly two years. But at the London Great Exhibition in 1851 he exhibited a cast-steel ingot of 2,000 kg, more than twice as big as any yet made, and with it his new cannon. The international admiration and excitement this evoked led to the adoption of his cannon. Thereafter the Krupp enterprise at Essen dominated the manufacture of arms in Germany. In France there were state arsenals like that at Puteaux, but the vast private business of Schneider at St Etienne became the vital developer and supplier of weapons to the French forces. In Britain the Woolwich arsenal continued, but the biggest manufacturer of military hardware was Armstrong on the Tyne – later Vickers-Armstrong. In the US the very small army and navy that survived after 1865 were generally supplied by the Springfield armoury, but private firms like Colt, Smith & Wesson, and Winchester were major innovators and producers of weapons.

Commercial firms could sell arms for profit on the open market, defraying costs; thus in World War I Krupp guns were used by both sides.

These huge firms enjoyed special relationships with government and commanders alike. The result was what in 1961 US President Eisenhower, himself a former general, called 'military-industrial complexes' whose power was such that many feared that they influenced and even dominated the conduct of foreign affairs and war in their own interests.[2] In time these arms-makers would be pilloried as 'Merchants of Death', and even blamed for the horrors of World War I, but men like Sir Basil Zaharoff KBE, Chairman of Vickers, were valued and honoured by governments. By selling guns to the world, they created capital to develop more and better ones, relieving states of massive financial burdens and enabling them to keep up with their neighbours in the arms race.

If the generals and their masters were confused by the technological change, they were appalled by the mass culture which industrial development created. The complexities of the new industrial fabric demanded educated people – technicians to operate its mechanisms and administrators to govern them. An immense growth in the middle class was the inevitable consequence, and this new group did not necessarily accept passively the existing political order of aristocrats and peasants with a small bourgeoisie closely linked to the former. Yet more novel were the 'mechanics', the top rank of skilled workers vital to the functioning of industry, the so-called 'aristocracy of labour'. And below them the mass of the working population was ever more mobile, with growing expectations in a new and wealthier world.

New mass media sprang into existence to feed the curiosity and express the needs and interests of all these people. The Hoe rotary press arrived in Britain from the US in 1856 just as steam power was being seriously applied to printing. By 1868 continuous webs of paper were deployed and after 1889 the linotype was in use. Such technical developments and the rise of advertising revenue made newspapers very cheap and very popular. Newspapers competed for market share by becoming avowedly sensationalist. Press impact upon public opinion was immense. In 1885 General Gordon was killed at the siege of Khartoum by Sudanese rebels, and because the government had failed to send aid Prime Minister Gladstone, hitherto the GOM (Grand Old Man) was denounced as MOG (Murderer Of Gordon). Improvements in communication and expanding education were powerful factors in producing mass political parties, of which the Liberals in England and the Social Democrats in Germany are obvious examples. In the industrial countries trade unions grew despite considerable efforts to prevent them. All these, and myriad other associations, developed views on military matters.

The interplay of all these factors was first clearly visible in the American Civil War (1861–5). On 21 July 1861 news of an impending battle at Bull Run, close to Manassas Junction, drew fashionable crowds in fine carriages from Washington, just 25 miles to the north-east, to see the spectacle. Shot and shell disrupted their picnics and they were caught up in the shambolic retreat of the Union army back to its capital. No one would ever again try to treat modern warfare as a spectator sport. The battle itself was a dismal and disorganised affair. The Union army commander, General Irvin McDowell, had been reluctant to risk his untried army, but President Lincoln reassured him: 'You are green, it is true, but they are green also; you are all green alike.'[3] This was indeed nothing less than the truth. The US army numbered only 16,000 when war broke out in April. Much of it remained on garrison duty in the west, while some officers and men joined the contending armies. So the 30,000 on each side at Bull Run were a barely trained militia in the charge of inexperienced officers. A Pennsylvania soldier remarked of his own unit: 'Col. Roberts has shown himself to be ignorant of the most simple company movements . . . We can only justly be called a mob, and one not fit to face the enemy.'[4]

McDowell's plan was to employ his 30,000 men to attack the 22,000 Confederates under General P.G.T. Beauregard at Manassas Junction, while his colleague, General Robert Patterson, with about 18,000 men, pinned down General J.E. Johnston's 10,000-strong army in the Shenandoah Valley. But Patterson failed to engage the Confederate forces who were taken by train in time to reinforce Beauregard. McDowell's attack on the Confederate left was delayed by the clumsy movements of his raw soldiers, but it almost succeeded against an equally confused defence. Most of the troops on both sides were equipped with muzzle-loading rifles, others with smooth-bore muskets, but in the hands of unskilled men the difference was barely noticeable. The day was saved for the Southerners by the determined leadership of Jackson, commander of the Virginia brigade, and the chance that the blue-coated 33rd Virginia were mistaken by the Union artillery for their own men and so were able to capture a crucial battery. The Union retreat quickly became a rout, but the Confederates were in no state to follow up their victory, for as a Prussian observer remarked, 'Rebel as well as Federal spirits less than stout had been shaken.'[5] Losses amounted to 500 Union killed and 1,200 wounded with 400 and 1,500 for the Confederates, who, however, garnered some 1,300 prisoners in the confused Northern retreat.

It is remarkable that troops so poorly trained fought so hard for so long. This owed much to the reasons why it happened in the first place. The war resulted from the Southern states deciding to secede from the Union in the face of the determination of the Republican-led government to preserve it. The Southern attack on Fort Sumter, in Charleston harbour, on 12 April 1861, meant that the issue would be decided by force, and both sides set to raising armies. But how were they to be used? The Northern General-in-Chief, Winfield Scott, shrank from the costs in blood and bitterness inherent in subduing the Confederacy which covered an area about the size of Western Europe. He wanted to surround the Confederacy by seizing the Mississippi river and blockading its Atlantic coast, as a preliminary to exerting military pressure which would bring it back into the fold. Jefferson Davis, the Confederate President, envisaged standing on the defensive and wearing down the enemy by preventing him from gaining any decisive success.

But both sides were democracies, literate states served by a popular press fed by the new telegraph and distributed by the new railways. This was a war about ideas and it was to be fought out in the minds of men and women as well as on the battlefield. Popular knowledge of the Napoleonic Wars meant that people expected the issue to be settled by a climactic battle. Northern editors scornfully dismissed Winfield Scott's strategy as an 'Anaconda Plan', and demanded a quick and decisive response to the rebellion, which would quell the separatists and save the Union. The *New York Tribune* demanded an immediate attack:

FORWARD TO RICHMOND! FORWARD TO RICHMOND!
The Rebel Congress must not be allowed to meet there on the 20th July.
BY THAT DATE THE PLACE MUST BE HELD BY THE NATIONAL ARMY.

In the South the *Richmond Examiner* was just as inflammatory and decried a defensive posture:

The aggressive policy is the truly defensive one. A column pushed forward into Ohio or Pennsylvania is worth more to us, as a defensive measure, than a whole tier of seacoast batteries.[6]

The outcome was Bull Run which Jefferson Davis, aware that many Southerners feared war, skilfully trumpeted as a great victory, while news of the defeat shocked the North, and many soldiers on short enlistments went home. But opinion hardened, and the South was alarmed to see the swelling numbers in the Union army. Before the French Revolution, war had been the business of military elites; involvement of the masses had been confined to very particular occasions, notably religious wars or resistance to bad government. But now the commanders had to cope with volatile public opinion which was shaped by private bodies such as churches and associations, and informed by organs of mass culture like newspapers. Elites had often been divided about war: Marlborough had to watch the balance of Whig and Tory at Westminster while he fought Louis XIV, and Chinese emperors were usually aware of a peace party amongst their administrators. But divisions within elites were quite different from the clash of ideas and attitudes in whole populations. Dissent in the Confederacy was limited, but in the North the Democratic Party loathed President Lincoln's Republicans and argued for a negotiated peace. Within their ranks elements of the militantly anti-war 'Copperheads' conspired with the South against the government, giving justification for frequent arrests and harassment, but democratic scruples limited the actions that the government could take against them.

Events on the battlefield had a marked impact on popular feeling. The new Northern commander, General G.B. McClellan, created the army of the Potomac and in 1862 launched an attack on Richmond, raising hopes of a rapid end to the war. But his failure and other defeats in the same year depressed Northern enthusiasm. The Confederacy's finest general, Robert E. Lee, staged an invasion of the North, but his defeat at Antietam on 17 September rallied public opinion. At this point Lincoln issued the Emancipation Proclamation ending slavery, the 'Peculiar Institution', to defend which the South had sought to end the Union. In 1863 Lincoln faced both demands at home for peace, and movements abroad to recognise the Confederacy. But after the Northern victory at Gettysburg on 1–3 July 1863 and the capture on the following day of Vicksburg, the crucial fortress on the Mississippi, these pressures subsided. After yet more long months of bitter and inconclusive fighting, the Democrats were hopeful of defeating Lincoln in the presidential elections of 1864 with McClellan as their candidate. But on 2 September 1864 Union General W.T. Sherman seized Atlanta and the whole political complexion changed as Lincoln became the victorious war leader – and went on to win the election.

Throughout the war Lincoln was painfully aware that many people in the North hoped that reasonable elements in the South would force a compromise. But as more and more blood was shed, he and his leading generals, Grant and Sherman, understood that sentiment was hardening. After the fall of Atlanta, Sherman had realised that he could cut through

Georgia to Savannah, feeding his army from the countryside as he ravaged it. He claimed he could 'move through Georgia, smashing things to the sea . . . I can make the march and make Georgia howl.' His rationale was brutal but effective: 'We cannot change the hearts of these people of the South, but we can make war so terrible . . . make them so sick of war that generations would pass away before they would again appeal to it.' His thrust into Georgia was a stunning success, and on 22 December he informed Lincoln of the capture of Savannah in terms undoubtedly phrased for public consumption:

> I beg to present you, as a Christmas gift, the city of Savannah, with 150 heavy guns and . . . about 25000 bales of cotton.[7]

Further north the supreme commander, U.S. Grant, instructed General Sheridan to turn 'the Shenandoah Valley into a barren waste . . . so that crows flying over it for the balance of this season will have to carry their provender with them'. And Sheridan responded: 'The people must be left nothing but their eyes to weep with over the war.'[8]

This kind of war would not have been acceptable to opinion in the North in 1861, nor even for most people in 1862, but by the fourth year of war there was a real impatience to be through with it. Lincoln and his leading commanders showed a remarkable sensitivity to public opinion, and this strongly influenced military strategy. Nor was the South immune from such extremism. On 21 August 1863 Southern raiders attacked Lawrence, Kansas, their commander, Quantrill, ordering: 'Kill every male and burn every house.'[9] A total of 182 men and boys were killed and the town was destroyed. The results of this resort to extremes are divisive in American society to this day. There is still no consensus about what to call the war. For Northerners 'American Civil War' is normal, but in the South it is the 'War between the States'. Even battles often have two names, so that what the Northerners call First Bull Run (there was a second battle on the same site) is known as First Manassas to Southerners.

Public opinion brought about the battle of First Bull Run, and this set the pattern of a war fought in the hearts and minds of people on both sides. In a military sense it also set the pattern – of bloody but indecisive battle in which the defender usually had the upper hand. Most observers noted the dominance of infantry firepower. The muzzle-loading rifle devastated frontal assault. At Franklin, on 30 November 1864, the Confederate commander, General J.B. Hood, hurled 22,000 of his 38,000 men against the 30,000-strong Union Army of Ohio which was well dug in and supported by artillery. The result was losses of 7,000, including twelve generals and fifty-four regimental commanders, fatally weakening his army. In the spring and summer of 1864 Sherman and his Union army were driving south from Chattanooga towards the great centre of Atlanta. The Confederates dug in to block his way, but Sherman simply outflanked them. However, in June wet weather churned up the roads, and to keep up the momentum of his drive Sherman saw no alternative but frontal assault. At Kennesaw Mountain his troops were thrown back from the well dug in Confederate line with 3,000 casualties to 1,000. Overall the new rifles greatly extended and, with their rapider rate of fire of 2–3 rounds per minute, intensified the killing ground. In these circumstances, the men went to earth: 'It is a rule that when the Rebels halt, the first day gives them a good rifle pit; the second a regular infantry parapet with artillery in posi- tion . . . You would be amazed to see how this country is intersected with field works.'[10] Storming such trenches was a bloody business with men thrusting against one another at close quarters. A Union soldier recalled the fighting at Spotsylvania, part of the Wilderness Campaign in May 1864: 'The flags of both armies waved at the same moment over the same breastworks while beneath them Federal and Confederate endeavoured to drive home the bayonet through the interstices of logs.'[11]

The rifle changed the balance between artillery and small arms. At the start of the war both sides deployed the bronze, smooth-bored Napoleon, either 12- or 6-pounder, on its light carriage. Its maximum range firing solid cannonballs was 1,500 metres, but its accurate range was less than half of that. It was capable of firing explosive shell though this was gener- ally used in lighter and shorter-range howitzers. At close range canister was murderously effective against infantry. The accuracy and reach of the infantry rifle made moving these weapons up to the attack very hazardous, so both sides protected their guns with earthworks. Bigger cannon could fire further but they were too heavy to manoeuvre on the battlefield. This stimulated the development of rifled guns with their greater reach and accuracy. The Parrott gun had a bad reputation for bursting, but the 3-in. Ordnance Rifle made of wrought iron was impressive. At the siege of Atlanta a Confederate artilleryman commented: 'The Yankee three-inch rifle was a dead shot at any distance under a mile. They could hit the end of a flour barrel more often than miss, unless the gunner got rattled.'[12]

Fire-power signalled the end of close-order battle. The rifle and the cannon were imperfect in many respects, but they could destroy packed formations with ease. Confronted with this phenomenon, how did the Americans adapt to the end of a literally age-old style of warfare?

Close-order was now hazardous, but close-quarter was still vital: infantry are the bailiffs of war, who must evict enemies from their real estate. The answer lay in the adoption of new tactical methods. A Prussian observer, Scheibert, noted that 'From the chaos of attempts, experiments, tests, thrusts, campaigns and expeditions, infantry tactics developed clear and sharp. Both sides adopted them. They deserve our attention.'[13] Both sides abandoned the attack in column because experience taught them it would be destroyed by artillery, and adopted linear attacks. Their battalions were grouped in brigades and echeloned in waves, and each battalion threw skirmish lines ahead of its main force to minimise casualties. Scheibert noted that in this extended order command and control was difficult and leaders had to trust subordinates to conduct the battle. In fact troops tended to lose all formation and to advance in groups by rushes, creating confusion which generals simply could not control. This was especially the case in the close and wooded country in which so many battles were fought. Scheibert criticised American junior officers, but he understood that their inexperience and lack of military education was a consequence of the way in which American armies were improvised with little opportunity for training.

It was extraordinarily difficult for commanders, especially American commanders who were new to the job and charged with raw soldiery, to cope with this new situation. After three millennia of close-order, the abrupt demise of the traditional pattern of fighting was profoundly challenging. Moreover, the new weapons seemed to strengthen the defence to such an extent that achieving a decisive victory was immensely difficult. Chancellorsville, 30 April to 6 May 1863, is commonly reckoned as Lee's most brilliant victory, for his 61,000 confederates defeated 134,000 Unionists under Hooker. But Hooker's army withdrew intact, despite having suffered 17,000 casualties (12.6 per cent), while Lee, having lost 13,000 (21.3 per cent), was in no state to pursue.

The failure of pursuit was partly because cavalry, the traditional arm of penetration and exploitation, was fatally weakened by infantry firepower. In the western theatre beyond the Mississippi both sides used cavalry to raid long and vulnerable lines of communication. In the irregular warfare which tore apart divided states like Missouri and Kansas, Southern 'Bushwhackers' and Northern 'Redleggers' (from their red gaiters) staged merciless mounted raids. On the main battlefields cavalry were irreplaceable for screening and reconnoitring armies. Lee's army was handicapped in the Gettysburg campaign when the cavalry became separated from the main bulk of his forces. But when large armies clashed, horsemen were frighteningly vulnerable. Cavalrymen increasingly acted as mounted infantry, moving about on horseback but dismounting to fight with pistols and carbines (short rifles). Sabres were little used, as a Confederate cavalryman remarked: 'The only real use I ever heard of their being put to was to hold a piece of meat over a fire for frying.'[14]

The result of this situation was a kind of deadlock because no battle in itself could be decisive. Both sides were becoming convinced of the righteousness of their cause and poured men, money and equipment into seeking a military decision, and so the fighting was very intense. The war broke out in April 1861, and in that year alone there were 34 battles and sieges, followed by 85 in 1862, 79 in 1863, 108 in 1864 and another 28 by the time of the Southern surrender in May 1865. Each clash and each disappointment simply stimulated both sides to pour ever-greater resources into the pursuit of victory. It is not difficult to illustrate the superior resources enjoyed by the North. In 1860, of a total US population of 31 million, only about 9 million lived in the Confederate states, including 3.5 million slaves who could not be mobilised for war. Over 90 per cent of cloth, boots and shoes, pig iron and weapons were produced in the North, which controlled more than two-thirds of the rail network. The South was forced to improvise a war economy, even calling upon women to save urine for saltpetre production. War material was always short in the Confederacy and often poor in quality, though there was enough to sustain the armies.

The mere tally of resources is barely relevant, for what mattered was resources mobilised for the purpose of war, and here the disparity was nowhere as great as first appears. The need to raise men forced both sides to resort to conscription. The Confederacy called 850,000 men to the colours, or about 70 per cent of the eligible white male population. In the North two million served, or some 17.5 per cent of those eligible. This Northern advantage of over 2:1 has to be seen against the task of conquering the Confederacy, an area the size of Western Europe. The South had only to block a Union victory and hold out, knowing of the uncertainties and divisions in the North.

The mobilisation of Northern industry and society was astonishing. The standard rifle of the North was the Springfield of which, between 1857 and 1861, the two Federal armouries at Springfield and Harpers Ferry produced about 60,000. Harpers Ferry was captured by the South, but Springfield went on to make a million Model 1861s. When a shortage of gunsmiths threatened supplies, Springfield adopted production lines, with men working on specialist parts. Even so, the North, like the South, was driven to purchasing foreign weapons, notably the British Enfield

Model 1853. Though it took time, all the necessities of war could be forged, fabricated, woven, packaged or bought, and dispatched to the armies by water or by railway. To prevent the South from purchasing freely on the international market the Union navy blockaded the whole southern coast. This necessitated the creation of a huge fleet which increasingly relied upon ironclad ships as its strike force. This in turn depended on an immense logistical and organisational effort. In the West the struggle for the Mississippi was fought out in a region much of which was barely mapped, and into which the invading Union armies had to bring vast quantities of supplies. But by the summer of 1863 they had seized control of the river and cut the Confederacy in two, enabling Sherman to seize Chattanooga.

Railways were essential to the movement and supply of armies. The Southern network was poorly connected and employed no less than four gauges of track ranging from 4 ft 8 in. to 5 ft 6 in. Before the war the Southern companies depended on the North for supplies of iron rails, rolling stock and engines, so that under the pressures of war their equipment deteriorated. The Union government could rely on a much more developed industry and stockpiled material for rapid building of new routes to supply the armies. Both sides systematically destroyed the lines of their enemies, and this had a crippling effect upon the South with its limited capacity to replace destroyed material. The impact on military fortunes was remarkable. After their victory at Chickamauga, 18–20 .September 1863, the Confederate forces besieged the Union army in Chattanooga. The Northern commanders moved 20,000 men and their equipment from Virginia to Chattanooga, 1,233 miles in eleven days, a feat of organisation and coordination not exceeded until the twentieth century. The skilful use of railways and the telegraph by the Union armies was noted by most observers who were also deeply impressed by the logistical support provided for the armies, which were supplied with ample food, up-to-date medical facilities and ambulances and plenty of ammunition.

Such enormous efforts rested upon highly intelligent war finance, above all the enactment of the Legal Tender Act of 1862 which created a national currency and capitalised upon the North's booming economy to sustain credit. By contrast the South printed money, and disastrous inflation duly ensued. To a modest degree innovative machinery freed up manpower for the war. The reaping machine reduced the need for farm labour, and could be worked by women. The production of uniforms was speeded up by the spread of the sewing machine; shoemaking became quicker with the introduction of the Blake-McKay machine. In these respects the Civil War was a very modern phenomenon, demanding contributions from the whole of society.

The war also stimulated invention in a way not seen before. The principle of the self-contained brass cartridge housing a cap for ignition, the charge and shot, was invented by Ethan Allen in the 1850s, but the gunmaker Christopher Spencer adapted it to create a repeating rifle in which lever action ejected the spent shell and injected a fresh one from a cylindrical magazine in the butt, making possible a rate of fire of 20 rounds per minute. By the end of the war this had been widely adopted in the US Cavalry, strong elements of which fought essentially as mounted infantry. But there was no system to supply ammunition for use on this scale, and generals had not given any real thought to applying such rapid fire, so the weapon was of limited value. Even more striking was the Gatling gun, patented in 1862. This was a continuous-fire gun in which the operator turned a handle to rotate six barrels around a central shaft. The barrels were loaded from a gravity-feed magazine. In final form it achieved a rate of fire of 600 rounds per minute, but it came too late for the war. It is interesting that its inventor thought it would reduce the casualties of war:

'It occurred to me if I could invent a machine – a gun – which could by its rapidity of fire, enable one man to do as much battle duty as a hundred, that it would, to a great extent, supersede the necessity of large armies, and consequently, exposure to battle and disease be greatly diminished. I thought over the subject and finally this idea took practical form in the invention of the Gatling Gun.'[15]

Despite the massive resources and the exploitation of the possibilities of industrial production, there was no decisive breakthrough on the battlefield, and so siege warfare became important. Most forts were around ports, so that the Union navy was able to bring up the heavy artillery vital to smash them and to counter the huge guns mounted in them. For the most part they were of masonry, and these proved very vulnerable to the new artillery. On 10 April the Union navy, equipped with high-velocity rifled Dahlgren guns, attacked Fort Pulaski which guarded the entrance to the port of Savannah, forcing its surrender the next day without the need for an infantry assault. The technique was to use large-calibre rifled guns to batter walls, while mortars lobbed explosive shells into the interior. But earthwork and timber embankments, together with trenches, proved very effective against artillery attack, and where ships could not bring their guns to bear huge siege-trains had to be assembled. At the siege of Petersburg, 15 June 1864 to 25 March 1865, the Federals gathered eighty-seven rifled guns and seventy-three mortars including one mighty rail-mounted 13-in. model known as the 'Dictator', supplemented by the army's field guns. It was a key railway junction close to the Confederate capital of Richmond, and defended by a network of deep trenches and batteries. Photographs show a landscape astonishingly like that of the World War I trenches, with *chevaux de frise*, a log mounted on a portable frame and girt with spikes taking the place of barbed wire.

Decisive battle, the assumed outcome in 1861, was clearly a mirage. The result was stalemate, so common in the eighteenth century, but now that the masses had been enlisted, compromise proved impossible. Attrition was the only path to victory. The 'Anaconda Plan' had been much derided at the outbreak of war, but it proved to be the most appropriate strategy. Under Grant the Union forces pressed forward aggressively on all fronts, overwhelming the South. As Sherman surged towards Atlanta from May to September 1864, Grant launched the Wilderness Campaign of May–June, a thrust towards Richmond which aimed to draw Lee into battle. The Confederates won several individual encounters, but Grant pressed on, recognising that he could afford losses and his enemy could not. 'If you see the President,' he remarked to a journalist, 'tell him from me that whatever happens there will be no turning back.'[16]

Historians distinguish some twelve battles in the Wilderness Campaign, but the reality was continual fighting in which each encounter merged into the next. The price of attrition was horrific; the Union army suffered between 40,000 and 65,000 casualties and the Confederates something approaching 40,000. Grant achieved no decisive victory, but he forced Lee back and put his army into a position to besiege Petersburg. The long siege of this vital railway junction pinned his enemy down and its fall eventually broke the Confederacy. This pattern was a grim portent of World War I. The overall human cost of the war was very high: the North suffered 110,000 battle deaths and about 250,000 from disease, a total of 18 per cent of those who served, while for the South the figures were of the order of 94,000 and 164,000, or 30 per cent of those enlisted. Above and beyond these were the huge numbers of the maimed whose lives were cut short or made miserable by their injuries. Civilian casualties have been estimated at 50,000, but this is probably an understatement.

European soldiers observed the American Civil War with great interest. The brilliant logistics of the Northern armies were particularly closely studied while the clear demonstration of the fragility of masonry forts had an immediate impact on military architecture. But the resort to trenches and the inconclusiveness of battle were discounted as evidence of the poor training of American troops rather than as the consequences of the new firepower. The attrition which resulted could, therefore, be dismissed, and along with it the need to mobilise the economy and to manage public opinion with all its consequences for the conduct of war.

It was not just in America that the difficulties of living with popular culture were becoming apparent. The outbreak of the Crimean War in 1854 had seen war fever whipped up by the popular press in Britain. A music-hall ballad of the time gave rise to the word 'Jingo' for super-patriotism:

We don't want to fight but by Jingo if we do
We've got the ships, we've got the men, we've got the money too.[17]

The expectations raised amongst the general public by such agitation were dangerously beyond reality. The British army had little experience of modern war, indeed was so small that it had to resort to hiring German and Swiss mercenaries. The war was marked by blunders brought home to the public by newspaper reporting from the front via the electric telegraph which had an immediacy and an impact beyond all expectation. On 25 October 1854 at the battle of Balaclava, the Light Brigade, some 670 strong, was launched against Russian guns: 118 men were killed, 127 wounded and 60 taken prisoner. It was an appalling error of judgement because, as Lord Cardigan who led the charge recalled:

'We advanced down a gradual descent of more than three-quarters of a mile, with the batteries vomiting forth upon us shells and shot, round and grape, with one battery on our right flank and another on the left, and all the intermediate ground covered with the Russian riflemen; so that when we came to within a distance of fifty yards from the mouths of the artillery which had been hurling destruction upon us, we were, in fact, surrounded and encircled by a blaze of fire, in addition to the fire of the riflemen upon our flanks.'[18]

It was the reaction of the press and the furore it created, rather than the event itself, which led to the dismissal of Lord Raglan, the army commander who had ordered the attack.

Even worse was the neglect of the wounded before treatment was radically improved by Florence Nightingale and her volunteer nurses. This was a long-running press story in which Nightingale was dramatised as

'The Lady with the Lamp' by the London *Times*. These scandals had enormous impact on British opinion. Moreover the war came to a sudden end in 1856 at a time when the British contribution to it was seen as failing. In response to the sustained outcry in the press, the government established a Royal Commission to consider reform of the army. The middle class was very hostile to aristocratic privilege, which it held responsible for the failures. As a result the immediate focus of the inquiry was the purchase of commissions, which was abolished. Ultimately, under Edward Cardwell, Secretary of State for War (1868–74), recruitment of regiments was made local and men enlisted for six years with twelve in reserve. Regiments were standardised with two regular battalions: one to serve abroad while the other was at home. A third was made up of the local militia and served as a kind of reserve for the regulars. With peace the mood of crisis passed, but the popular reaction to the war had reverberations in the political system.

Events in America also impacted upon British opinion, complicating the management of relations between the two countries. Initially pride in their own abolition of slavery meant that British sentiment favoured the North. The Confederates embargoed British cotton exports in a bid to force diplomatic recognition, and this threat to the Lancashire cotton industry caused outrage. But when the British declared neutrality, this was interpreted in the North as covert recognition of the secession and produced a mood of belligerence and suspicion that annoyed the British. In November 1862 a Union naval ship stopped the British passenger packet *Trent* and arrested Southern envoys travelling to Europe. Opinion on both sides became inflamed, and there was a genuine threat of war. In turn Northerners were angry because the British permitted the construction of Confederate commerce raiders like the *Alabama* in breach of their own neutrality laws. Managing international relations in the face of popular attitudes was difficult and certainly did not become any simpler as time went on.

In 1899 Britain invaded the Boer republics in South Africa. This was from the first highly controversial, but the patriotic appeal of the press, led by the *Daily Mail*, rallied support. Pretoria was captured in June 1900, but the Boers continued to fight a guerrilla war. The British response was scorched earth, destroying farms in order to deny resources to the guerrillas, and rehousing the civilian population in concentration camps. There was nothing unusual in this. Forcible resettlement of hostile peoples was an ancient practice. The US had used such methods against the Indians and in the Philippines. But in Britain a new culture of humanitarian sympathy had grown up, associated with Liberal Party radicals and the new socialist movement, and on this issue their concerns were shared by the wider public, forcing the government to improve treatment of the enemy. The military blunders of the war, which were extensively reported in the press, provoked demands for reform and resulted in the changes implemented by Richard Haldane, Secretary of State for War (1906–12), who created an effective Imperial General Staff to control the army, and a British Expeditionary Force to participate in major wars, backed up by a new Territorial Army.

In France too the new popular culture made itself felt. In 1894 Alfred Dreyfus, a Jewish artillery officer in the French army, was convicted on the most flimsy of evidence of betraying military secrets to the Germans and sent to Devil's Island in French Guiana. In 1896 evidence appeared to suggest that another French officer was guilty, but the army suppressed it and fabricated further evidence against Dreyfus. In 1898 the author and journalist Emile Zola denounced the verdict as a perversion of justice in 'J'Accuse', a letter to a French newspaper. The subsequent scandal divided the army and, indeed, all of France. The anti-Dreyfusards were mainly conservatives and monarchists amongst whom anti-Semitism had been growing, while the Dreyfusards were republicans, anti-clericals and social-ists. Dreyfus was acquitted in 1906, but it was clear that French culture now permeated the French army.

France, Britain and the United States were all democracies with national assemblies, to which their armed forces were responsible. For all of them the ideas of the French Revolution were part of the fabric of life. But the same culture was making its impact elsewhere despite enormous resistance. The Vienna peace settlement of 1815 was primarily intended to prevent France ever again dominating the continent. But its architect, Metternich, foreign minister of Austria (1809–48), understood that it was the ideas of the French Revolution which were most dangerous. Nationalism was deeply threatening to the multinational empires of Austria and Russia, and even to a degree to Prussia, while their absolutist monarchies rejected democracy and their aristocratic elites despised any notion of equality.

The weak spot in the settlement of 1815 was France, because of its revolutionary tradition. The overthrow of its Bourbon monarchy in favour of the Orléanist line in 1832 worried European statesmen. Then in February 1848, France put an end to the monarchy in favour of the Second Republic (1848–51), and the contagion of radical ideas spread rapidly. Across Germany mobs of peasants demanded the end of serfdom while the liberal middle class clamoured for a share in government. In Vienna Metternich was deposed and a constitution granted, and by the end of March much the same had happened in Prussia. The Assembly of the German Confederation, originally created in 1815, now aspired to become the motor of a united Germany. But the revolutionaries were divided amongst themselves, and the armies of Austria and Prussia, loyal to their rulers, crushed them. However, the emancipation of the peasants in Germany could not be reversed, and even the Prussian government saw that a constitution was a necessity. In 1848 thrones trembled. The shock wave was strengthened by the sight of the working masses on the streets, and the knowledge that this terrifying mob, as rulers saw it, was finding a voice. In 1848 Marx opened his *Communist Manifesto* with the bold declaration: 'A spectre is haunting Europe – the spectre of communism. All the powers of old Europe have entered into a holy alliance to exorcise this spectre.'[19] This was, to say the least, an exaggeration, but it threw down the gauntlet to the traditional ruling classes whose monarchies in Austria, Russia and Prussia retained control over their armies.

In Prussia the officer corps regarded itself as the main prop of the throne and separated itself from the liberals who used the new parliament to seek control over the armed forces. This dispute was resolved in favour of the monarchy, but when Bismarck (1815–98) became Minister-President of Prussia (1862–90) he was afraid that his liberal enemies in the parliament would enlist the rising tide of German nationalism and so he banged the nationalist drum, and in creating the German Empire by conquest (as we shall see) annexed patriotism which became an obsession of the military establishment around the throne. The Emperor in the new Germany after 1870, like the king in Prussia before, was the supreme warlord. He presided over a military caste which regarded itself as the true embodiment of the German nation and determinedly maintained its separation from civil society and the apparatus of the parliament (Reichstag).

The trouble with this situation was that civil society in Prussia and later Germany developed along the same general lines as France and Britain. By 1900 socialist and in particular Marxist ideas in Germany had generated, despite severe official persecution, a powerful trade union movement and a Social Democratic Party (SDP) which in 1912 became the largest in the Reichstag. Under the German system ministers were appointed by and responsible to the Emperor (*Kaiser*), but the Reichstag ultimately controlled finance and, as the voice of public opinion, could not simply be ignored. For the German army, the growth of liberalism, socialism and pacifism was a dangerous and threatening development, and like soldiers everywhere they feared its influence upon the mass of the population, and through them on the conscripts who constituted their army. Russia had been largely exempt from the events of 1848 but even she felt the need to change and shortly after the Crimean War emancipated the serfs. Rapid industrialisation fostered the spread of liberal and socialist ideas which erupted in the 1905 Revolution. This failed to overthrow the government, but forced the creation of a parliament, the state Duma. The same coalition of ideas which was exercising other conservative governments and their soldiers in Europe had now spread to Russia.

One characteristic effect of this popular concern with the business of war was to accelerate attempts to impose constraints upon it. The horrors of the Thirty Years War had inspired Grotius (1583–1645) to argue for a common 'Law of Nations' to regulate war, while the practice of eighteenth-century warfare with its focus on professional armies had led to the notion of a clear distinction between civilians and soldiers. The Swiss jurist Emerich de Vattel (1714–67) in his *Law of Nations* declared that 'At present war is conducted by regular armies. The ordinary people take no part and as a rule have nothing to fear from the enemy.'[20] This reflected a consensus amongst the educated classes of the eighteenth century in favour of humane behaviour. The French Revolutionary Assembly laid down rules for the conduct of armies and the fair treatment of prisoners. Soldiers had to pay attention to such ideas, even if they often ignored them in practice. The Paris Peace Conference which ended the Crimean War in 1856 tried to regulate war at sea. The foundation of the Red Cross in 1859, a reaction to the horrific casualties of the Italian War of 1859, was a private initiative but its activities on behalf of the sick and injured were hardly possible without some agreement by the powers. The First Geneva Convention of 1864 laid down that the injured should be properly treated and the Red Cross respected. In the early 1860s the Russians developed an explosive bullet, and, horrified by the mayhem which this could wreak, convened an International Military Commission under the Geneva Convention which banned these weapons. This led to the Hague Peace Conference of 1899 which introduced voluntary international arbitration and banned some of the worst weapons, such as dum-dum bullets and poison gas. A further conference in 1907 attempted to clarify the laws of war at sea. The Hague and Geneva Conventions were significant attempts by the new culture to influence the conduct of war, hitherto the sphere of the military.

These initiatives were not entirely unwelcome to soldiers who were all too aware of the horrors of modern war and this, perhaps, explains why the emergence of 'peace societies', first in Britain and then across Europe, was of surprisingly little concern to military authorities. There had always been a pacifist strain in the Christian Church, notably represented by the Quakers. This was the mainspring of the British peace movement which spread to France and Germany. For the British, with no mass army to worry about, it was merely one middle-class pressure group amongst many which infiltrated the political classes and mobilised opinion through the new media. In 1910 the Peace Society Executive recorded that it needed 'a young educated gentleman with journalistic experience' to ensure that it would 'get into political, religious and social circles where, hitherto, it has had but small influence'.[21] The German movement was even more marginal and in 1914 endorsed the German war effort:

> There can be no doubt about the duties of the pacifists during the war. We German pacifists have always recognised the right and obligation of national self-defence. Each pacifist must fulfil his common responsibility to the fatherland just like any other German.[22]

French pacifism was closely linked to the Socialist Party and hence enjoyed some influence. By and large all these organisations were marginal and bourgeois, advocating arms limitation and international arbitration as means of settling disputes between nations. Perhaps the most important impetus to their influence was the work of J. Bloch, *La Guerre future*, published in 1898 and translated with incredible speed by the campaigning journalist W.T. Stead as *Is War Now Impossible?* Bloch argued that weapons were now so terrible that war was not possible, and that the interdependence of nations meant that it simply could not be sustained.[23] His ideas seemed to express the very essence of progressive capitalist society and he was invited to the first Hague Peace Conference in 1899.

If army leaderships were not greatly disturbed by the middle-class peace movements, they were deeply fearful of the socialists. Marx's 'spectre' of 1848 gained more and more substance as industrialisation increased the urban populations of the major European states and the new proletariats looked to parties of the Left for relief from its worst effects. European socialists were not opposed to violence, but took the view that war was an evil which, like many others, arose from the contradictions of capitalism which, they believed, should be overthrown. The German SDP became by far the strongest socialist movement in Europe; the main plank of its military policy was the demand for the abolition of the standing army and its replacement by a citizen militia which could be used neither for aggressive purposes in the world at large nor for repression at home. As the European crisis deepened in the summer of 1914, the party made contact with the International Socialist Bureau and called for mass demonstrations against the war:

> The class-conscious proletariat of Germany, in the name of humanity and civilization, raises a flaming protest against this criminal activity of the warmongers. It insistently demands that the German Government exercise its influence on the Austrian Government to maintain peace; and, in the event that the shameful war cannot be prevented, that it refrain from belligerent intervention.[24]

This stance was quickly reversed; the SDP accepted the *Burgfrieden* or suspension of party differences to unite the nation, and at the meeting of the Reichstag on 4 August agreed unconditionally to war credits. But the original anti-war declaration was no more than an expression of the spirit of the party. In 1907 one of the SDP's leading radicals, Karl Liebknecht, had published his *Militarism and Anti-Militarism*. At the request of the Prussian war minister, Liebknecht was charged with High Treason:

> Of having set on foot a treasonable undertaking in the years 1906 and 1907 . . . of effecting a change in the constitution of the German Empire by violence, viz: abolition of the standing army by means of a military strike, if needs be conjointly with the incitement of troops to take part in the revolution, by writing the work *Militarism and Anti-Militarism*.[25]

Such attitudes caused hysterical rage amongst the middle and lower-middle classes who feared the rise of socialism and the potential upsurge of the proletariat. They had banded together in the Leagues, ultra-right groups which emerged in Germany at the end of the nineteenth century. The Pan-German League, founded in 1891, regarded socialism as the root of all evil. The Navy League, established in 1898, was highly successful in campaigning for an expanded fleet, largely because Admiral Alfred von Tirpitz manipulated public opinion with the aid of the Kaiser. The Imperial League against Social Democracy was established in 1904 as a reaction to the excellent SDP results in the elections of 1903. The German Army League, founded in 1912, demanded that working-class youth be disciplined in preparation for the army. The bellicose nationalism of the Leagues was bitterly xenophobic and it fed on governmental propaganda which from the 1890s increasingly portrayed Germany as threatened on all sides by enemies. The participation of officers in extreme nationalism was profoundly disturbing to Germany's neighbours.

But the Leagues, just as much as the SDP, demanded influence over military policy, and this was disliked by the German officer corps because they wanted to stay 'above politics', as they would have put it. As 'Swords around a Throne' they exploited popular nationalism not merely as counter to socialism but also as a means of preserving their special position in German society. Officers cultivated a code of honour, breaches of which could be satisfied only by the duel. It demanded courage and was seen as vital to the vigour and morale of the officer corps. Long after it had been outlawed in civil society, officers were dismissed the service for refusing to duel. In 1901 a Bavarian War Office publication stated: 'In the Prussian Officer Corps there should be no room for people who do not accept the duel . . . Anyone can be against duels as much as he likes, but then he should not try to enter the Officer Corps in which he must be fully aware that an unconditional obligation to duel exists.'[26] Young men of the rising middle classes mostly admired the prestige of the officer corps, clamoured for admission and copied its rituals, especially the duel, which became a rite of passage for German students.

This separation of officers from the mass of the population produced a terrible fear of any trend in German society which could be construed as threatening, and in particular a paranoid hatred of the SDP. The German army was a conscript body, and theoretically all young men became liable at the age of 20. However, the army could never have dealt with a genuinely universal intake, and in any case the Reichstag limited its funds. In 1911, 563,024 men were theoretically available, but only 129,070 were actually called up. This surplus enabled the army to recruit from the rural population which was regarded as much more trustworthy. But industrialisation in Germany meant that increasingly the ranks were filled by factory workers infected, as officers saw it, by revolutionary and especially SDP ideas that they regarded as disloyal. In 1893 it was agreed that the command structure of the army should be used to prevent recruits having anything to do with the SDP and this was formalised in a military proclamation of 1896. This had little effect, and repeated efforts to make the army the 'School of the Nation' by a process of indoctrination failed disastrously. Official opinion despaired and there was talk of a coup to smash the SDP and, indeed, democratic pretensions generally: 'Let revolution shake its fist at throne and altar, the German knights assembled round their holy standard, armed with the holy power of God, will be ready with sharpened sword and shining buckler to fight victoriously with God for Kaiser and Reich.'[27]

The German army was unusually separate from civil society. It could maintain this position because its victories in 1866 and 1871 over Austria and France had created the German Reich and conferred upon it enormous prestige. This separation appears extraordinary only because of our modern perspective which assumes that the military are integrated into society and obedient to its norms. Throughout recorded history, with very rare exceptions, armies have been isolated from social culture: 'War is a special activity and separate from any other pursued by man.'[28] The Prussian officer corps was unusual only in that it expected the state to enforce its wishes while it enjoyed a degree of aloofness which was, however, shared by soldiers the world over. Chinese soldiers had formed a distinct element in the empire, while Indian soldiers for long constituted a special society hiring themselves out to the local rulers who succeeded the Mughal Empire. The British army was essentially no different.

In the nineteenth century the British army was commanded by a crown appointee, but represented in parliament by the Secretary at War. This constitutional duality enabled officers to enjoy great autonomy. Waves of reform, occasioned by military failures like the Crimean and Boer Wars, were bitterly resented by officers who regarded change imposed by parliament as an intrusion into their special sphere. And none of the reforms affected the simple fact that officers continued to be recruited from the landed gentry whose living standards demanded that they have a private income. In 1903 an officer of the cavalry needed £700–900 a year on top of his pay, while even an infantry officer in an unfashionable regiment had to find £200–300. By comparison, a skilled labourer could expect to earn £2 per week. Officers were further isolated from civil society because the British army's primary task was policing colonies. Large units were rarely gathered together and men spent their time in regiments, each with its own special milieu; they received very little further training. When, in the early twentieth century, Haldane tried to create a British Expeditionary Force (BEF) which could intervene in a continental war, one of his problems was that few officers were educated and interested. British officers were as devoted as Prussians to the notion of military autonomy, but they lacked the prestige of victory, operated in a political culture intolerant of militarism and accepted that politicians managed British public opinion.

The French officer corps, in contrast, was deeply enmeshed in politics. The turbulence of French politics culminated in the 1871 defeat by Prussia. This unleashed social revolution in Paris which the army crushed.

The dominant republican radicals who controlled the government in the ensuing years launched far-reaching military reforms which established a conscript army on the basis of universal service, organised around a General Staff very much on the Prussian model. Aristocratic, Bonapartist and strongly Catholic families, excluded from power in the new republic, colonised the army where they felt their service was 'non-political'. But republican politicians were suspicious of them and favoured officers known to be republican. The Dreyfus affair in part sprang from the anxiety of the high command to enjoy some degree of autonomy despite this scale of political interference. But its consequence was a long purge of conservatives in which officers were invited to inform on one another. It was possible to lose all prospect of promotion as a result of comments like: 'Goes to Mass . . . His brother is a Jesuit.'[29]

The prestige of the French army declined sharply after this turmoil, and in 1905 military service was cut to two years, with a resulting slump in morale and efficiency. An important underlying factor was the rise of socialism which was at least as marked in France as in Germany, and had the same internationalist and pacifist agenda, sharpened considerably by the frequent use of the army against strikers. In 1896 the Congress of the trade union movement, the CGT (Confédération Générale de Travail) declared:

Antimilitarist and antipatriotic propaganda must become ever more intense and audacious. In every strike the Army is for the employers, in every national or colonial war and in every European war the working class is the dupe and is sacrificed for the advantage of the parasitic, bourgeois employers' class . . .[30]

In 1907 the 100th Infantry regiment mutinied when sent to quell rioters. The French socialists, like the German SDP, were constrained by patriotic feeling in 1914 to agree to a party truce, the *Union Sacrée*, justifying their stance by arguing that France was fighting for the rights of small nations everywhere. The responsiveness of the army to currents within French culture owed much to revolutionary tradition. Officers could not appeal to a monarch 'above politics', as in Germany and England. They were so poorly paid that promotion was essential and this depended upon pleasing their political masters.

In Russia, however, distrust between emerging political movements, the government and the army, was immense. Until their emancipation in 1861 the mass of the army had been recruited for a twenty-year period of service by impressing serfs who were usually selected by their landlords. In contrast, officers were aristocrats. The 1874 conscription law introduced the principle of universal military service; though, because the better-off could purchase exemption, the army remained largely peasant. In 1888 the period of active service was reduced from six to four years, and reserve status extended to fifteen, resulting in a standing army of 800,000, backed up by reserves. Strenuous efforts were made to widen the social range from which officers were drawn, with some success, and equipment was modernised. Army service was brutal, but it provided men with a minimal education in reading and writing, and former soldiers played an active role in popular agitation in countryside and town.

Russian society in the late nineteenth century was plagued by discontent. Serfs had been freed, but only in return for paying compensation to their former owners. Government was autocratic but corruption was rife, and redress for injustice almost impossible. At the same time, Russia was industrialising very rapidly and, as elsewhere, the rise of an urban proletariat produced workers' organisations against which the army and police were frequently deployed. This bred revolutionary underground movements like the Bolsheviks, the Mensheviks and the Revolutionary Socialists. The army played a considerable role in repression, and remained loyal, until the disasters of the Russo-Japanese War of 1904–5 provoked a revolution which nearly brought down the crown.

The forces of nationalism unleashed by the revolutions of 1848 were a particular threat to the Hapsburg Empire, a hotchpotch of Germans, Hungarians, Czechs, Italians, Lithuanians, Poles, Romanians, Slovaks, Slovenes, Croatians, Serbians, Ukrainians and Russians. The army, dominated by Germans, was the most truly imperial unity within this immense variety, and it crushed the revolts of 1848. It fought well in Italy against the Piedmontese who were trying to establish an Italian kingdom. In 1859 defeat in northern Italy by France in alliance with Piedmont prompted much soul-searching and produced a reform and reorganisation of the Austrian army. By the 1860s Austria could raise 400,000 regulars supported by some of the best rifled artillery in Europe. The defeat by Prussia in 1866 forced the Austrian ruler, Franz-Joseph (1848–1916) to make peace, lest the Hapsburg lands fly apart. In the event the Hapsburg state was reconfigured by the creation of the Austro-Hungarian Empire which was, in effect, a coalition of the Germans and the Hungarians to hold down the other nationalities, especially the Slavs. In 1867 the Austrian prime minister remarked to his Hungarian counterpart: 'You manage your hordes and we'll manage ours.'[31]

The Austrian army was reformed on the Prussian model with universal conscription and the formation of a reserve force. This created a multinational force whose language of command was German, though officers were exhorted to learn other tongues. Loyalty to the dynasty was the uniting force, and at the highest level was the key to promotion. But the Hungarians refused to pay their share of supporting the central army and diverted troops from it to the *honvéd*, their national guard. So while the officer corps did their best to modernise, the army was actually smaller in 1912 than it had been in 1866. By the end of the Balkan wars of 1912–13 Serbia had expanded to the extent that it could create an army bigger than that of the Austro-Hungarian Empire. The Hungarians now realised that they had been sawing off the branch on which they sat, because Serbian expansion, supported by Russia, fomented Slav discontent which had been increased by brutal Hungarian repression. A real effort, which would pay off in World War II, was made to modernise and increase the armed forces.

It is hardly surprising that the officer corps of the European powers gave little attention to the management of public feeling. The generals of the American Civil War have been much criticised, but they instinctively responded to public pressures, despite the complexities. This was because they were citizens first and soldiers second, and once they were locked into their long war they understood the need to work within the limits of popular feeling. European generals were bred from aristocratic elites contemptuous of the mass of the population, and they put their faith in a narrow professionalism which they believed could win wars quickly and cheaply. This enabled them to discount the disquieting experience of the American Civil War which seemed uncomfortably to reinforce Bloch's message that war 'will become a kind of stalemate, in which neither army will be able to get at the other'. And for a time they were proved right.

Because of this professionalism, however much they chose to discount some of the wider lessons of the American Civil War, the leaders of European armies recognised the problems presented by the new firepower. A French officer, Colonel Ardant du Picq, more than most, perceived that the high rates of fire and long range of modern weapons meant that close-order battle was no longer possible:

Ancient combat was fought in groups close together, within a small space, in open ground, in full view of one another, without the deafening noise of present-day arms. Men in formation marched into an action that took place on the spot and did not carry them thousands of feet away from the starting point. The surveillance of the leaders was easy, individual weakness was immediately checked. General consternation alone caused flight.

Today fighting is done over immense spaces, along thinly drawn out lines broken every instant by the accidents and obstacles of terrain. From the time the action begins, as soon as there are rifle shots, the men spread out as skirmishers, or, lost in the inevitable disorder of rapid march, escape the supervision of their commanding officers. A considerable number conceal themselves, they get away from the engagement and diminish by just so much the material and moral effect and confidence of the brave ones who remain. This can bring about defeat.

He drew the conclusion that the old ways of the close-order battle must be replaced, arguing that

Combat requires today, in order to give the best results, a moral cohesion, a unity more binding than at any other time. It is as true as it is clear, that, if one does not wish bonds to break, one must make them elastic in order to strengthen them.

His tactical conclusion was that infantry should fight in open order in which they could maximise the effectiveness of their weapons and take shelter from enemy fire:

Riflemen placed at greater intervals, will be less bewildered, will see more clearly, will be better watched (which may seem strange to you), and will consequently deliver a better fire than formerly.

He had seen men under fire, understood their actions, and argued that their instinct to seek shelter from the firestorm was right, but that it needed to be controlled and organised:

Why does the Frenchman of today, in singular contrast to the [ancient] Gaul, scatter under fire? His natural intelligence, his instinct under the pressure of danger causes him to deploy. His method must be adopted . . . we must adopt the soldier's method and try to put some order into it.[32]

Du Picq, who was killed in 1870 at the very start of the Franco-Prussian War, offered a brilliant analysis of the problems posed by the new firepower. But European powers found their way to a solution to the problem via hard experience, particularly in the wars of German unification which pitted Prussia against Austria (1866) and France (1870–1). In 1815 Germany had become a confederation of thirty-nine individual states and cities, dominated by Prussia in the north and Austria in the south. The year 1848 raised the prospect of a full union of the German people, and while Austria and Prussia united against the spectre of liberalism, they became rivals for leadership in Germany. The subsequent tensions were inevitably of deep concern to France whose rulers feared a strong state on their eastern frontier. Under Bismarck, Prussian Minister-President after 1862, Prussia played the national card. In 1866 the tensions between Prussia and Austria broke into war.

The Prussian military system had been thoroughly reformed after Napoleon had crushed it at Jena in 1806. The crucial development was the growth of a Great General Staff, embodied in law in 1814. Bright officers were selected to what was effectively a military brotherhood, charged with continuous study of the art of war and the drawing up and review of plans. Essentially a managerial system, in the long run it proved brilliantly suited to control large complex armies. Because it was successful in the wars of 1866 and 1870–1 the General Staff developed enormous prestige and decisive influence in military affairs. General Staff officers formed specialised groups, such as that dealing with railways, and were skilful at spotting ways in which new technology could be adapted for military use. Ultimately every general in command of an army had a chief of staff who had a right of appeal if he did not like his superior's plans. To prevent these officers losing touch with military reality they were rotated through regular periods of service in line regiments. The Prussian General Staff presided over an army of 300,000 raised by a highly selective form of conscription. These were backed up by 800,000 reserves, each of whom at the age of 32 passed into the militia or *Landwehr* which would only be called up in emergency. In 1859 Prussia had tried to move to support Austria against France, but mobilisation had been a fiasco. As a result the General Staff paid careful attention to the use of railways to get troops quickly to the front. At the same time reserve and regular battalions were firmly attached to local military districts so each got to know the other.

In 1866 the tensions between Prussia and Austria over the leadership of Germany led to war. Prussia had only half the population of its adversary and the Austrians had a long-service conscript army of 400,000 which, in theory, could strike first into enemy territory. But the Austrian army could not concentrate quickly because its units were used for internal security, scattered in such a way that the men were always strangers to the people whom they garrisoned. Prussia thus had time to summon its reserves and to take the initiative under Helmuth von Moltke. Moreover, the Austrian advantage in numbers was partially nullified because Prussia allied with

Italy, forcing Austria to dispatch an army there. In Italy in 1859 Austrian forces had failed to implement firepower tactics, and had been overwhelmed by direct (and very costly) French attacks. They were now armed with a good muzzle-loading Lorenz rifle, but thought that they should hold their troops together in large units that were trained to deliver bayonet charges. Also, aware of the inadequacy of their cannon in Italy, the Austrians had bought excellent rifled breech-loading artillery.

Moltke sent three armies along five railways to attack Austria through Bohemia, with the intention of concentrating them against the enemy's main force. In the event, two of these armies confronted the Austrians in their strong and partly fortified position at Sadowa/Königgrätz on 3 July 1866. Each side had about 220,000 men. Fighting was ferocious but the Prussians held on until their third army arrived to bring victory. Prussian infantry tactics were the revelation of Sadowa. In 1846 the Prussian army had adopted a breech-loading rifle, the Dreyse needle-gun. This had a potential firing rate of about five shots per minute and it could be loaded and fired from the prone position. The Dreyse was scorned by other armies: it lacked range because the gas seal on the breech was inadequate and it was feared that such a high rate of fire would encourage soldiers to waste their ammunition before charging the enemy, so overburdening supply lines. At Sadowa the Austrian artillery did much damage, but the rapid fire of the Dreyse at close range cut down the Austrians whose forces were gathered in large close-order units highly vulnerable to this kind of firestorm. The British Colonel G.F.R. Henderson commented that the Prussians did not charge with the bayonet until the enemy had been destroyed by musketry: 'The Germans relied on fire, and on fire alone, to beat down the enemy's resistance: the final charge was a secondary consideration altogether.'[33]

Important as the Dreyse was, the real key to victory was tactical and organisational. Moltke, like Clausewitz, understood the fluidity of battle and the problem of control:

> Diverse are the situations under which an officer has to act on the basis of his own view of the situation. It would be wrong if he had to wait for orders at times when no orders can be given. But most productive are his actions when he acts within the framework of his senior commander's intent.[34]

He developed what would later be called the doctrine of mission tactics (*Auftragstaktik*), under which subordinate officers, even down to platoon level, were instructed in the intentions of the overall commander, but left to find their own way of achieving this end. At Sadowa the Prussians made their infantry firepower count by closing with the enemy in forest land where the strong Austrian artillery could not bear upon them. This enabled them to shoot into the packed Austrian ranks as their junior officers led them around the enemy flanks. Fire and movement was the solution to the conundrum so ably propounded by du Picq.

This was possible because junior officers in the Prussian army were thoroughly trained, and understood the need to accept responsibility for the progress of their soldiers, and staff officers rotated through the fighting units communicated what senior commanders wanted. In addition, at the core of the Prussian army was an excellent corps of long-term NCOs well able to support their officers. At Sadowa the Austrians suffered 6,000 dead, over 8,000 wounded and about the same number missing, and conceded 22,000 prisoners. The Prussians lost 2,000 dead and 6,000 wounded. Austria made peace almost immediately and Prussia took over all the north German states, enormously enhancing her military capability. The obvious lesson of Sadowa was firepower. The Austrian Field Marshal Hess articulated another very clearly: 'Prussia has conclusively demonstrated that the strength of an armed force derives from its readiness. Wars now happen so quickly that what is not ready at the outset will not be made ready in time . . . and a ready army is twice as powerful as a half-ready one.'[35] Strike first would become an article of faith amongst the general staffs of Europe in the years down to 1914.

The rise of Prussia threatened the France of Napoleon III. The nephew of the great Napoleon had taken advantage of the turbulence of the Second Republic to seize power and declare the Second Empire in 1852. He stood, above all, for the dominance of France in European affairs. The Prussian victory in 1866 was therefore a blow to the very foundations of the regime, and all parties in French public life thereafter regarded war with Prussia as inevitable. This focused attention on the French army, a long-term conscript body very like the Austrian but with far more fighting experience. However, it lacked a reserve force, while French officers and NCOs enjoyed low pay and status and suffered a constipated promotion system. There was a General Staff, but its officers formed a tiny elite who had little to do with the army as a whole. At all levels there was an absence of initiative, partly because Napoleon, though lacking real military grasp, cultivated the 'Napoleonic myth' of the heroic and omnipotent leader.

In reaction to Sadowa the French adopted a new breech-loading rifle, the chassepot. This had an excellent breech mechanism which doubled both the rate of fire and, at 1,200 metres, the effective range of the Dreyse.

Remarkably the mitrailleuse, a crude machine-gun, was developed, but it was surrounded by such tight security that the troops were never able to integrate it into their tactics. Because these weapons were costly, the smooth-bore Napoleon cannon of 1859 remained the dominant artillery piece. In 1868 legislation was passed to create a reserve whose members would ultimately pass into a territorial militia, the *garde mobile*. But Napoleon was unpopular, the Legislative Assembly obstructed the law and so the system was barely operating by 1871.

The French decided that tactically the new weapons favoured the defensive, so they grouped soldiers in large solid units to produce massive firepower, denying any flexibility to local commanders and laying units open to the risk of being outflanked; indeed, the French system was highly centralised and dependent on the will and capacity of the emperor. Even worse, despite bellicose intentions and pronouncements, no real plans were made for war against Prussia. This negated the key advantage of a standing army, that it could strike first before an enemy dependent on conscription could gather his forces. Moreover, the French army was very dispersed. Its troops were used for internal security, so units were spread out and not allowed to serve in their areas of origin.

When war came in 1871 the French planned to mobilise and concentrate their armies on the frontier at Metz and Strasbourg, but Staff planning was hopeless. Choked roads and railways and poor attention to logistics turned this process into a nightmare. At the end of July, when Napoleon arrived at Metz to assume command, barely 100,000 of 150,000 troops had arrived, and only 40,000 of 100,000 had reached Strasbourg. The reserve system worked so slowly that there was no support for the regulars, while the *garde mobile* was wholly untrained, unequipped and, in places, openly disloyal. Supplies of bread and other essentials failed, while there was indiscipline and even explicit grumbling against the regime. But perhaps the key factor in spreading demoralisation was that in the absence of plans Napoleon was vacillating.

The French had originally projected a thrust into the sensitive junction between north and south Germany. Then the notion of a defensive stance to repel a Prussian attack came to the fore. The hope of Austrian intervention, perhaps supported by the south German states who loathed Prussia, led to the establishment of strong forces at Strasbourg. This force, under Marshal Maurice MacMahon, was rather cut off by the Vosges mountains from Napoleon's main force around Metz. It was unclear to Napoleon's senior commanders which, if any, of these options, none of which had been properly thought through and planned, was to be taken.

Such hesitancy quickly communicated itself to the soldiers, for armies are highly sensitive to this kind of doubt. Here, then, was an army without a strategy, led by a vacillating ruler tormented by painful illness but keenly aware that his regime needed military success.

By contrast, the Prussians were devout believers in speed and their planning enabled Moltke to deliver three armies to the frontier where French inaction permitted them to organise themselves at leisure. They were backed up by a steady flow of reserves, so that Prussian forces quickly outnumbered the French. The process of concentration was by no means perfect, and moving troops and supplies away from the railhead caused congestion. For both armies the frontier with its hills and rivers posed considerable problems. Moltke directed his superior forces to converge on the French. Since Sadowa he had systematised tactics so that the standard attack force was now the 250-man company. Moreover, Moltke had noted the heavy losses inflicted upon his infantry by Austrian artillery, and had bought Krupp rifled guns. There was uncertainty about how best to deploy these, but they were mostly brought up close to the front to support the infantry. Late on in the Sadowa battle the Austrians had launched a charge of their heavy cavalry to cover their retreat, but it was cut to pieces by rifle fire. As a consequence the Prussian cavalry was now trained very thoroughly for an active role in reconnaissance which it discharged very effectively.

The first encounter of the war, at Wissembourg on 4 August 1870, set the pattern. The Crown Prince of Prussia with 60,000 men and 144 guns bumped into a single division of 8,000 French with twelve guns, well entrenched and sheltered by the buildings of the town. Frontal attacks against intense fire from the chassepots of the well-entrenched French infantry cost the Prussians dearly. However, Prussian artillery moved up to blast the French positions; the few and outranged French guns could make no reply. This enabled the Prussian infantry to work around the French flanks and to force a retreat. But against a single division, the Prussians suffered 1,500 casualties, almost as many as against a vast Austrian army at Sadowa, though they inflicted 2,000. Ultimately they were victorious in five major battles.[36] The failure of French command is all too evident, in that even on the one occasion they were not outnumbered, they still failed to win.

It cannot be said that the generalship on either side was of a very high standard. At Gravelotte on 18 August 30,000 Prussians attacked rows of trenches rising to St Privat: they advanced in what was virtually an eighteenth-century formation, a thin skirmish line succeeded by half-battalions backed up in a third line by massed battalions. Too many senior officers were just plain old-fashioned or distrusted the new methods of *Auftragstaktik*, which Moltke had applied at Sadowa. Within minutes of launching their assault they had lost 5,000 men. Gradually small units under junior officers fanned out, extending and thinning the line of attack, while twenty-six field artillery batteries bombarded the French positions which were seized at a cost of 8,000 casualties. Some 70 per cent of German casualties were caused by rifle fire, but about the same proportion of French casualties were inflicted by explosive shell. The French never really adapted their tactics to the aggressive Prussian artillery attack. Their commanders were hamstrung by tight central control and reluctant to take any initiative which at times could have snatched victory. At Mars-la-Tour on 18 August General Cissey saw an opportunity to destroy the Prussians and ordered his men into columns of attack but they refused, reflecting their distrust of the high command which had failed to develop sensible methods of attack.

The Prussians isolated Napoleon III and his army in Metz, then arrived before Paris on 19 September where Napoleon had been overthrown and Gambetta had formed a new French Government of National Defence which refused to surrender. As a result the city was bombarded and after the capitulation of Metz on 29 October, a close siege was set. Large numbers of French reservists had never reached the active front. Concentrated on the Loire, they threatened the Prussian army there, and even managed to reconquer Orléans on 10 November. But ultimately Paris starved and on 28 January 1871 an armistice was agreed which led to peace. The new Republic tried to wage a people's war by calling every man to arms, and the Prussians suffered some casualties from a motley assortment of *francs-tireurs*, civilians, deserters and irregulars, who sniped at the invaders. But the French people saw no point in continuing a lost war, and refused to support it, so a guerrilla war never developed.

The Franco-Prussian War effected a dramatic change in the balance of power in Europe, symbolised by the proclamation at Versailles of the German Empire on 18 January 1871. The new Reich now became the dominant European power. This was apparently a triumph for the professionalism of the Prussian army and its aggressive tactics. On the face of it a well-trained European army had shown twice within five years that it could bring war to a rapid and successful conclusion. The role of the General Staff had been vital and as a result it was widely copied. But the logistical problems of the German army in 1866 and 1871 had been quite substantial and soldiers had often ended up foraging, with evil results for the countryside at their mercy. But these wars were fought close to bases on a continent with good communications and over short periods of time.

More seriously, while Napoleon III's armies had been destroyed in roughly six weeks, the population of Paris really mobilised against the invader, and the siege of that city dragged on for nearly five months. The refusal of the new interim government in France to surrender was deeply frustrating for the German army which wreaked a terrible vengeance on the civilian population wherever *francs-tireurs* appeared or were imagined. Casualties were appalling: France suffered 138,871 dead and 143,000 wounded, and Prussia something approaching 50,000 dead and 90,000 wounded. The war exposed the stresses within France, triggering a social revolution as Paris rose in the famous Commune of 18 March–21 May 1871, a communist revolution which was destroyed by provincial France in a bloodbath. Modern war was deeply threatening to the structure of the state and could unleash unknown forces. War was no longer simply a matter for armies.

In terms of the way in which war was fought, the end of close-order should have been very evident: it was destroyed by rifle fire and the new artillery. But if war was to continue, armies still needed to attack in order to get to close quarters where infantry could fulfil their immemorial role as the bailiffs of war. The most rational response was open-order small unit assault, *Auftragstaktik* or something like it, of which Ardant du Picq had been the great prophet and the Prussians the great practitioners. The problem was that even senior German generals did not altogether trust their soldiers. As du Picq had shrewdly observed, one of the advantages of close-order was that 'The surveillance of the leaders was easy'. This meant a great deal to those in authority, especially after the Paris Commune of 1871, and was reinforced by the Russian Revolution of 1905.

In Germany conservative officers tried to undermine the new tactics of small-group attack enshrined in the field regulations of 1872, because they wondered if soldiers would attack without the 'surveillance of the leaders' and doubted if random fire would be as effective as volley-fire at the command of officers. Most German officers understood that in the face of modern firepower attackers needed to advance in small groups using fire and movement to confuse the defence, and making best use of the ground. By 1914 official German infantry doctrine favoured company attacks by columns of platoon, though officers were urged to be flexible in the light of terrain and circumstance. But this had been imperfectly adopted by 1914, partly because the German military system left a great deal of latitude to commanders at army and even battalion level where there were many who were unconvinced of such methods.

German military conservatives were not just sceptical of novel infantry tactics. They even tried to revive mass cavalry charges, though the Austrian and French wars showed that these were suicidal. The Prussian general and war minister, von Schellendorf, refused to purchase new artillery in 1887, saying that 'one can have too much artillery', and preferred to emphasise the moral qualities of his soldiers. In much the same mode, in the 1860s the British adjutant-general Sir Thomas Troubridge had devised a mechanism to be attached to rifles to limit the firing rate of soldiers. In a conservative profession the notion of the soldier as simply an exporter of lead was deeply repugnant. This is why, despite the example of the American Civil War, armies were very imperfectly adapted to the new firepower by the turn of the twentieth century.

And by then officers were having to work out how best to use whole ranges of new weapons put into their hands by ever rapider industrial development. One of the key military applications of the new technology was the magazine rifle. The Dreyse showed the potential of bolt-action and the rubber sealing ring of the chassepot remedied its chief weakness. American Spencers and Winchesters were magazine rifles, but their lever action was awkward for a man lying down, while the mechanism was not particularly robust. One key factor held up the development of magazine rifles, continuous-fire guns and better artillery: black powder was the only known propellant. Gunpowder is fast-burning, so its explosion exerts tremendous pressure on the barrel of a weapon. Moreover, 55 per cent of the product is solid, visible in dense smoke and sooty deposits which foul barrels and mechanisms and give away the location of the firer while obscuring his vision.

In 1884 the French developed pyrocellulose and three years later Nobel in England produced cordite, which was more stable and would become the normal propellant worldwide for small arms and artillery. The new powders were more powerful than gunpowder, so calibres could be smaller and bullets lighter, enabling the soldier to carry more ammunition. But most importantly, they produced much less smoke and residue, hence they were called 'Smokeless', and this enabled new and more complex weapons to be developed. Magazine rifles then became a must for all armies and they remained in service for very long periods of time. The French introduced the Lebel Model 1886 magazine rifle specifically designed for their new powder. Russia adopted the 7.62mm Mosin in 1891 and used it throughout World War II: the Germans finally opted for the 7.92 Mauser 1898 which was still in service in 1945; the British .303 Lee-Enfield was the standard infantry rifle from 1895 to 1957. The new metallurgy, and particularly machine-tools, made it possible to manufacture these machines in vast quantities. They all had adjustable sights and used self-contained brass shells which were bound together, usually in fives, with self-stripping clips for rapid loading. By 1914 regular British infantry could fire thirty aimed shots per minute.

But even this rate of fire would be eclipsed. In 1884 Hiram Maxim, an American, came to the UK to build a machine-gun. He, like many others before him, worked on the notion that the recoil from the explosion of a self-contained brass cartridge could eject it, cock the gun and feed in the next bullet – the recoil principle. The new techniques for working steel made such a weapon more practicable, but the great problem was that gunpowder clogged mechanisms and obscured the operator's vision. Smokeless powder disposed of these difficulties. The Maxim could fire 600 rounds per minute, and it entered British service in 1888. During the First Matabele War (1891–3) a detachment of fifty British soldiers with four Maxims fought off 5,000 warriors, prompting Hilaire Belloc's couplet:

> Whatever happens, we have got
> The Maxim gun, and they have not.[37]

The machine-gun had arrived, though at first armies were uncertain how to use it.

Artillery was now made of steel and rifled. The new machining techniques created the interrupted screw which provided a gas-proof breech-loading mechanism. But its fire-rate was relatively slow because the explosion of the charge and the throwing of the missile blew the weapon back from its position, necessitating a relaying of the gun onto its target. Fortress guns could employ recoil brakes, but these were too bulky for field use. The new science of hydraulics pointed the way to a possible solution, by using a cylinder of liquid (typically oil) to absorb the shock, but bulk was again a problem and seals frequently failed. In 1896 the French adopted a new field gun, the Puteaux 75mm, the famous *soixante-quinze*, which incorporated a lightweight hydraulic recoil mechanism and used self-contained cartridges which were ejected by opening the breech. It was equipped with its own sight, an automatic fuse-setter to determine the range at which the shell would explode, and a nickel-steel shield to protect the crew. The weapon could fire twenty shots per minute in its famous *rafale*. Little wonder that it was revered as 'God the Father, God the Son and God the Holy Ghost'. The *soixante-quinze* was essentially designed to kill infantry using its explosive (or shrapnel) shells in open ground. By 1914 all armies had developed similar pieces, and were also deploying heavier weapons. But enemy formations could shelter in broken ground and reverse slopes which could only be swept by the plunging fire of howitzers. Trenches, it was noted, protected soldiers from shrapnel, so high-explosive shells were needed to blast them out, necessitating even heavier guns.

The result of all these developments was to extend and intensify the battlefield. The magazine rifle had a range of 2,000 metres, field-guns like the *soixante-quinze* were accurate up to 6,000 metres, while heavier guns and howitzers were good up to 10,000 metres. The Waterloo battlefield was 4 kilometres wide; at Gravelotte in 1870 the armies had faced one another strung out over 13 kilometres. The lethality of the new weapons was clearly revealed in two wars at the turn of the century. The Second Boer War (1899–1902) in South Africa pitted the British army against an alliance of the Transvaal and the Orange Free State which could raise barely 25,000 troops. These were, however, equipped with the latest Mauser magazine rifles and both Krupp and Le Creusot 75mm field-guns, with heavier weapons like the 120mm Krupp howitzer. The Boers opened the war by besieging key fortresses. In November the British sought to relieve them and in 'Black Week', 10–15 December 1899, suffered three major defeats culminating at Colenso when 16,000 British confronted 12,000 Boers in an effort to relieve Ladysmith. The British suffered 145 killed and 1,200 wounded, captured or missing, and lost ten guns, inflicting only forty casualties on their enemies. This was largely the result of faulty training and tactics, because the British were used to fighting peoples who lacked modern weapons, and they formed up in mass columns of attack. A contemporary commented:

> The officers and men were absolutely untrained for that kind of warfare; they were unable to use their eyes, they did not know how to use their rifles, they did not know how to take cover; in every possible way they were unfitted for that kind of work, but they very rapidly acquired the powers.[38]

Moreover, their Lee-Metford rifle had been designed for black powder and was inferior to the Mauser, while the British 15-pounder howitzer was less good than the Krupps models used by the Boers. The South African War taught the British the lessons of the 'empty battlefield', empty because everybody took to the earth for protection, and they applied them in 1914 to some effect.

The same lesson was hammered home by the Russo-Japanese War. On 14 July 1853 a squadron of 'black ships' appeared in Yokosuka harbour under the command of US Commodore Perry, and forced the Japanese Shogunate to agree to open the country to foreign traders. This precipitated a civil war after which all power, though actually exercised by a clique of powerful nobles, was formally returned to the Emperor by 'the Meiji Restoration'. The new rulers recognised that the country risked foreign domination if it did not change, and set in train a far-reaching programme of modernisation and industrialisation which made it a formidable power by the end of the nineteenth century. Universal conscription was introduced and imported foreign advisers, first French and then Prussian, trained the army. British officers helped create a navy. Although there was a constitution, senior officers were directly responsible to the Emperor who was the focus of a cult of obedience. In 1894–95 Japan fought China for control of Korea and took Port Arthur – a clear sign of its emergence – but it was subsequently forced to cede the port to Russia. The completion of the Trans-Siberian Railway encouraged Russian ambitions to control Korea, and it was this which precipitated war in February 1904.

The central act of the war was the siege of Port Arthur, 1 August 1904 to 2 January 1905. Its fortifications were deeply entrenched and strengthened by concrete emplacements, barbed-wire entanglements, machine-gun nests and minefields. Both sides illuminated night operations with searchlights and were equipped with the latest artillery while telephones, radio, and even radio jamming, appeared. Assaults on such fortifications produced appalling casualties: in October the attack on 203-metre Hill cost the Japanese 124 officers and 3,611 men. The Japanese used every device possible, including mines, but it was the fire of 280mm Krupp mortars with their 500kg shells which proved decisive. In all, the siege cost the Japanese 58,000 casualties, while the Russian garrison of 50,000 lost about 30,000. Subsequently the Japanese army defeated the Russians in a series of battles at Mukden, over an 80-kilometre front, which raged from February to March 1905. The Russian Far Eastern Fleet had been neutralised in Port Arthur during the siege, but in May 1905 the Baltic fleet reached Korean waters and was destroyed at the battle of Tsushima, 27–28 May 1905, bringing the war to an end by the Treaty of Portsmouth (New Hampshire) of 5 September 1905. This costly failure precipitated violent revolution in the Russian heartlands, and led to the establishment of a constitution for the first time. Hitherto Europeans had often explained their dominance in terms of racial and cultural superiority, but the Japanese victory revealed that economic development, military technology and military competence were not racially or culturally specific.

Firepower very evidently strengthened defence, but many argued that modern developments would actually assist attack. The English commentator, Henderson, remarked:

> Neither smokeless powder nor the magazine rifle will necessitate any radical change. If the defence has gained, as has been asserted, by these inventions, the plunging fire of rifled howitzers will add a more than proportional strength to the attack. And if the magazine rifle has introduced a new and formidable element into battle, the moral element remains the same.[39]

'The moral element' became the key to military thinking. Military men recognised firepower, but they also knew that in battle there came a point at which infantry had to close with the enemy and they urged the need to inculcate moral spirit into troops so that they would disregard losses and press on. A vital part of this process was keeping men together under the eyes of their officers to steel them for the assault with bayonet. Despite the horrors of Colenso and other battles, Winston Churchill, who was an eyewitness to the South African War, in 1900 urged the bayonet charge:

> Battles nowadays are fought mainly with firearms, but no troops, however brave, however well directed, can enjoy the full advantage of their success if they exclude the possibilities of cold steel ... The bayonet is the most powerful weapon we possess out here. Firearms kill many of the enemy, but it is the white weapon that makes them run away. Rifles can inflict loss, but victory depends, for us at least, on the bayonets.[40]

This emphasis on moral qualities had a certain logic. Ultimately infantry had to seize and occupy ground, and soldiers needed to be convinced that even in the new conditions this could be done. The rhetoric of war in the late nineteenth and early twentieth centuries emphasised dash and spirit, the moral qualities which, it was thought, could carry troops through the firestorm. Such ideas were at their strongest in France where the high command was infused with the notion of the *attaque à l'outrance* as preached by Lieutenant-Colonel Louis Loyzeaux de Grandmaison, the head of the Third Bureau of the General Staff. But the same sentiments could be found in all armies, and this was reinforced by the observation that in the Russo-Japanese war the offensive had actually triumphed. By contrast, the French in 1870 had been defensive, had lost and had suffered terrible casualties. In an age which was not infused with the notion of the sanctity of human life casualties were something that had to be accepted, because otherwise how could war be fought?

Yet at the same time there was a deep distrust of the conscripts who would have to do the attacking. This was partly fear of left-wing ideas and partly a widely shared conviction that the process of industrialisation was producing poorer human material. A German military theorist expressed this in the widest terms:

> The steadily improving standards of living tend to increase the instinct of self-preservation and to diminish the spirit of self-sacrifice . . . the fast manner of living at the present day tends to undermine the nervous system, the fanaticism and religious and national enthusiasm of a bygone age is lacking, and finally the physical powers of the human species are also partly diminishing . . . We should send our soldiers into battle with a reserve of moral courage great enough to prevent the premature moral and mental depreciation of the individual.[41]

The distinguished French soldier Lyautey proclaimed: 'France is dying less from '70 and its regime than from internal contradictions and atrophy in which everyone grows complacent from material comfort.'[42] Such attitudes go far to explaining the distrust of small-group tactics in all the conscript armies and the reluctance to trust ordinary men to go about the business of war without 'the surveillance of the leaders'.

The cult of the offensive with its emphasis on moral qualities, which reached its zenith in the early twentieth century, came at a time when tensions between the European powers were mounting. Germany was the single most powerful state in Europe, yet it was also the most restless. Her economy was highly advanced, her people enjoyed the benefits of a nascent welfare state, Austria was virtually a dependent power, Italy was an ally and Turkey was friendly. Since 1892 this triple alliance had confronted a pact between France and Russia. The German emperor and the German elite seem to have been convinced that they were thus encircled. But their resentment focused on the issue of colonies. Because Germany had joined the circle of great powers late in the day, and because Bismarck had subsequently been quite indifferent to them, Germany had few colonies.

A colonial empire was the 'must-have' status symbol of the early twentieth century, and the need for it could be rationalised by reference to acquiring strategic places and materials. How far the mass of German people worried about this is uncertain, but the Leagues waxed indignant, and they operated with the sympathy of ruling powers. The new Kaiser Wilhelm II (1888–1918) was easily influenced by this atmosphere and lacked the strength to direct policy. One unfortunate consequence was the Anglo-German naval race. In 1897 Admiral Alfred von Tirpitz became naval secretary. He established the Navy League in 1898 and in that year an ambitious naval construction campaign was begun. The British Empire, whose very basis was naval supremacy, perceived this as a threat and reacted very strongly. After the failure to resolve the tensions by negotiation in 1901, the British accelerated their building programme. Even more seriously, in 1904 Anglo-French negotiations launched a series of understandings known as the *Entente Cordiale* which gradually drew Britain into association with the Franco-Russian alliance, giving them the name of the Entente powers. Tirpitz achieved naval expansion by exploiting German political culture, but the costs were high.

Because the warship is a specialised weapons system it has always been extremely expensive. The wooden ships of the Nelson era had at least lasted a long time: HMS *Victory*, Nelson's flagship at Trafalgar, was commissioned in 1765 and remained in service until 1812. But by the 1840s the pace of change was accelerating. Steam power was introduced, and the experience of the Crimean War prompted the British to produce the iron-built *Warrior*. But for the world's premier navy technological progress produced conundrums. Big, inefficient engines needing vast quantities of coal were hardly suitable for a fleet whose ships had to travel to far-flung imperial stations, so sails continued to be necessary. Iron armour and muzzle-loading guns were immensely heavy and made ships clumsy, but they were essential. In 1862 the Confederacy had built the *Merrimack*, a steam-driven iron-plated ship with ten guns, which threatened to destroy the Union fleet in Chesapeake Bay. But to the rescue came the USS *Monitor*, a small iron steamship with two heavy muzzle-loaders in a rotating turret. The two fought out a drawn battle, but demonstrated that iron vessels with heavy guns were deadly against other ships.

The problems arising from all this became clearly visible in 1870 with the sinking in the Channel of the *Captain*. This British battleship had 8-in. armoured sides, and mounted four 25-ton 12-in. guns in two turrets protected by 10-in. armour, and although she was steam-powered she also had a full rig of sails. Her freeboard (distance above water level) was only a little over 6 feet. The committee of inquiry established that she had failed to trim her sails in a rising wind. Gradually the problems were overcome. Steel offered greater protection for lighter weight, commercial developments like the triple expansion engine used less coal and drove ships faster, while the establishment of a worldwide network of coaling stations made refuelling easier. Recoilless rifled breech-loaders made of steel using smokeless powder were lighter and easier to work.

The naval race came at a bad time for Britain. Until the 1870s she had dominated the world's tropics cheaply with a dispersed fleet of assorted ships. But the onset of 'colonial mania' in the late nineteenth century meant that European powers like France carved out numerous colonies, effectively reducing Britain's inexpensive and informal dominion and forcing costly conquest in competition with other empires. At the same time the growth of railroads cut the advantages of sea-power and enabled continental states like America, Germany and Russia to develop their economic potential. The British share of world trade fell from 25 per cent in 1860 to 17 per cent in 1898. British firms failed to invest in the new technology, and as a result Britain fell behind in steel production and machine-tools. In the booming chemical industry her pre-eminent firm was Brunner Mond (later Imperial Chemical Industries) whose founders, significantly, were German. In optics and many other fields Britain lagged badly behind Germany and the United States. It is not difficult to perceive the sense of ebbing power. In 1897 Kipling chose to celebrate Queen Victoria's Diamond Jubilee in 'Recessional', a poem replete with this sense of failure:

Far-called, our navies melt away;
On dune and headland sinks the fire: Lo, all our pomp of yesterday
Is one with Nineveh and Tyre![43]

But at governmental level this simply reinforced the determination to dominate at sea.

On 1 October 1906 the Anglo-German naval race entered a new dimension when the British launched HMS *Dreadnought*. The Germans responded to this challenge by launching dreadnoughts of their own, and technology developed apace, so that by 1910 Superdreadnoughts were mounting 13.5-in. guns. In 1912 Britain laid down the first of the *Queen Elizabeth* class of 27,000 tons firing 15-in. guns and powered by oil. The world went dreadnought-mad and the British became the primary builder of such monsters. By the start of World War I she had conclusively won the naval race, with 32 battleships and 10 battle cruisers to Germany's 21 + 8, but at a price. *Dreadnought* cost £1.79 million but *Queen Elizabeth* raised this to £2.5 million and the naval estimates went up from £18.7

million in 1896 to £40.4 million in 1910, inevitably limiting what Britain
could afford to spend on her army. This mighty battle fleet brought little
assurance because the floating mine, fast torpedeo-armed gunboats and,
above all, submarines, threatened the behemoths. The pressure of the
naval race forced Britain into an alliance with Japan in 1902, enabling her
to withdraw ships from the Pacific, while also leaving the Mediterranean
to France. By 1907 a series of understandings with Russia ended tensions
over imperial ambitions with that power.

In 1871 France had been demoted in the European power standings by
German unity, and had lost the important province of Alsace-Lorraine,
but she was hardly thirsting for revenge. Much military effort was
spent on the overseas empire. The alliance with Russia was not aggressive,
and general military policy was to keep the army sufficiently strong to
balance German power. The French army and intelligentsia were happily
engaged in the bitter internal conflict between republicans and conservatives which afflicted the army in the form of the Dreyfus affair. France
at the turn of the century was famous for its culture and good living,
the epitome of civilisation, a huge contrast with the modern Sparta to the
east. But the rise of socialism in the early twentieth century frightened the
republicans and radicals into a reconciliation with their conservative
enemies.

In 1904 a traitor in the German General Staff revealed the extent of its
war plans against France. As a result, a major reform of the army was set
in train. The enormous military spending, inevitably contested by the
socialists, led to a propaganda battle whipping up fears, promoting
national pride and revealing deep uncertainties. Underlying everything
was French consciousness of numbers. In contrast to almost all the major
European countries, France in the nineteenth century had a very low birth
rate, and in 1910 had a population of just 40 million compared with
Germany's 65 million. In 1912–13 the Reichstag approved changes which
expanded the German army, and in response the French increased the
term of service to three years. In 1914 the French pitted 823,000 troops
against 700,000 Germans, but while they could raise only 2.9 million
reserves, Germany could mobilise 3.8 million. It was, therefore, of the
highest importance that in 1912 Russia promised to put 800,000 men in
the field against Germany within fifteen days of mobilisation.

Criticising the generals of the early twentieth century as bumbling fools
playing with men's lives is a long-established and popular blood sport. But
during their lifetime war had been transformed, and nobody fully understood the consequences of the new technology. As late as Bull Run in

1861 people expected battle to be a spectacle, and all the major commanders of the 1914 war were born in the year of that battle or earlier.[44] Down to about 1860 military leaders worked within the highly stable framework of agro-urban warfare, depending on close-order mass formations of infantry supported by cavalry fighting at close quarter. The obvious rival system of war was that of the steppe peoples, but their effectiveness was overwhelmed by European firepower. Leading soldiers traditionally operated within narrow elites where debate might be fierce, but was always confined. By the early twentieth century leading soldiers were largely estranged from the mass of the population and fearful of 'Red Revolution', whose standards were everywhere raised.

But they were the servants of competing states in which strident nationalism was everywhere seen as a way of countering the forces of the Left. Political Darwinism preached struggle through which the fittest would survive, offering a rationalisation of the situation and even an encouragement to conflict. Emergent social science was strongly influenced by eugenics and the notion of purity of the race which converged with Darwinism and nationalism. Many of the soldiers saw all too well that war between major states would be of unprecedented horror and could very well produce deadlock. But soldiers were expected to plan for victory, and it was in their very instincts to do so. The US Civil War had shown the risks of attrition, but the German experience of 1866 and 1870–1 appeared to indicate how to avoid it. Strike hard, strike fast, strike first was the lesson of the German wars adopted by all the states of Europe in their planning. And they put their trust in the moral qualities and training of their infantry to overcome the firestorm. In this way the terrible casualties which they knew modern firepower could inflict would be acceptable because the war would be short. Above all, they all knew that if attrition set in the risks to the stability of their states would be enormous. The plans they made for war were designed to avoid it.

Germany, faced by the Franco-Russian alliance of 1892, planned for war on two fronts, and this became more pressing as French military power revived in the early twentieth century. Count Alfred von Schlieffen, Chief of the Imperial General Staff from 1891 to 1905, understood clearly the terrible risks of deadlock. Commenting on the Russo-Japanese war he remarked:

They may face each other for months on end in impregnable positions. In Western Europe we cannot allow ourselves the luxury of waging war in this manner. The machine with a thousand wheels, upon which millions depend for their livelihood, cannot stand still for long . . . We must try to overthrow the enemy quickly and then destroy him.[45]

Schlieffen calculated that if Russia was attacked she could exchange space for time, in which France could attack in the west. Moreover by the time he drew up his 1905 'Deployment Plan West I' Russia had been crippled by the revolution of that year which, it seemed, would weaken her for years. Therefore he proposed to destroy France before turning on Russia. The plan was to outflank his enemy by invading Belgium, Luxembourg and Holland with an enormously strengthened right wing. Since France's frontier with Belgium was not fortified, the Germans could sweep across and trap the French armies against their eastern frontier. This represented a strategic application of the German tactical preference for flanking attack. The basic idea formed the bedrock of the plan implemented by his successor, Helmuth von Moltke the Younger (nephew of the victor of 1871 of the same name), in 1914, although he narrowed the 'right hook' by cutting out the attack on Holland and strengthened his left wing against French attack. By and large this was sensible, because Schlieffen's plan had paid almost no attention to logistics and Moltke's, to a degree at least, took them into account. Any attack on the Low Countries risked making an enemy of Britain, which regarded their independence as vital to her interests. However, the Kaiser sanctioned the plan, probably because he regarded the *Entente Cordiale* between France and Britain signed in 1904 as an alliance which would bring the British in anyway.

The French Plan XIV, formulated in 1898, called for a defensive stance with the army's weight in Lorraine. By 1910 France had a good idea of German intentions. The Chief of the General Staff, V.C. Michel, wanted to stand on the defensive with a view to an ultimate counterpunch against German attack. He believed that the French reserves could be mobilised quickly and incorporated into the army for this purpose. But most of his colleagues were sceptical of the early use of reserves they regarded as second-rate soldiers. They put their trust in the active army and an aggressive thrust into Alsace-Lorraine to defeat the Germans. The lure of decisive victory, and the political importance attached to the recovery of Alsace-Lorraine, led to Michel's dismissal. His replacement, Joffre, adopted Plan XVII which aimed to snatch the initiative away from the Germans by invading Lorraine. Russia promised to mobilise within fifteen days of a declaration of war and planned to attack East Prussia from Poland at the same time as fighting the Austrians in Galicia. The Austrian commander, Conrad von Hötzendorf, envisaged a rapid destruction of Serbia and a simultaneous thrust into Russian Poland in concert with Germany.

All these plans made some sort of sense in the light of national priorities and recent military experience, but not all armies were well prepared to execute them. The Germans knew that they would need to destroy the Belgian fortifications, especially Liège, if they were to achieve this mission. This is why they borrowed eight Skoda 350mm siege-guns from their Austrian allies, and commissioned heavy howitzers, of which the greatest were the two 'Big Berthas' of 420mm calibre which threw a 2,200-pound high-explosive shell up to nine miles. Their plan depended on speed, and because entrenched infantry could delay them the Germans devised the mobile 150mm howitzer whose 93-pound high explosive shell could blast trenches up to a range of 10,000 metres. They provided two machine-guns for every battalion (the same number as the British). But the German air service, created in 1912 for use in reconnaissance, was poorly organised and limited attention was paid to radio communication. French preparations depended on the dash of their troops supported by the fire of the *soixante-quinze*. But the broken terrain of Alsace-Lorraine was well suited to defensive warfare and the Germans had improved it by fortifying key points. The French army lacked heavy artillery to smash concrete and they had no howitzers, whose plunging fire was vital against entrenched defenders. They were, moreover, deficient in machine-guns. Yet French generals developed radio communication and were imaginative enough to start training pilots as early as 1909, establishing the Aéronautique militaire in 1910. The Austrian army was handicapped by political problems and poorly equipped, while the Russians lacked adequate supplies of war materiel.

The late nineteenth century witnessed the first Military Revolution in human history. In the space of a very few years rapid technological development in Europe and the US had brought about staggering changes which can only be described as revolutionary. This bestowed upon soldiers an immense firepower which meant that close-order, the way in which armies had fought since time immemorial, was suddenly and sharply out of date. At the highest level soldiers were well aware that this made any kind of offensive strategy very difficult, because a defender, especially one dug in, could unleash a firestorm capable of sweeping the attackers away. This introduced the deeply disturbing prospect of war turning into long attritional struggles which would cripple the economies of the participants and might even precipitate social revolution, as in 1871 in France and 1905 in Russia. *Auftragstaktik*, fire and movement in small groups taking maximum advantage of terrain, offered a way of sustaining the offensive. However, many senior commanders were very slow to adjust to this, and many were fearful that their soldiers would not truly attack unless they were under the eye of their officers, and therefore distrusted such a system.

These fears were reinforced by the fact that the industrial development which had created the new weapons had also created a popular culture in which the masses had started to take an interest in the conduct of military affairs, often in a strongly anti-militaristic sense. From the military perspective middle-class meddling, as exemplified by the German Leagues or the debates in the British parliament, was bad enough, but the spread amongst the masses of 'socialism' seemed to threaten army discipline and the will to fight and it seemed likely that this would increase if war was allowed to drag on. In these circumstances generals put their trust in plans for a short war. They knew that any conflict between first-rate powers would be bloody, but they believed that it could at least be made short and so acceptable. This is why relatively little attention was paid to sensible infantry tactics and so much wind was spent in a rhetoric which praised the moral qualities of soldiers who had to be steeled to face the firestorm of modern war. Thinking about war took time to catch up with technological progress – reality outstripped intellect.

The American Civil War demonstrated the incredible difficulties which would arise if war dragged on. Few generals understood the need to manipulate and control the mass culture which had accompanied the industrialisation of the advanced countries in the later nineteenth century. Officer corps almost everywhere stood (or tried to stand) outside the reach of this popular clamour. Most senior commanders had been born into a world where war was, as it had for so long been, the business of the professionals and removed from widespread scrutiny. The American experience showed a new dimension to war before which they instinctively recoiled – and so, while they knew the risks of a stalemate, they put their faith in victory through a short, violent and bloody conflict. This was the driving force of all the plans which would be put to the test in 1914. The military planners were ready to accept heavy casualties in expectation of a short war. But there was no provision for failure and no notion of mobilising nations on the American model. In 1914 all the hopes of the military planners were to be dashed and all their worst fears realised.

CHAPTER NINE

INDUSTRIAL KILLING

'This western-front business couldn't be done again, not for a long time. The young men think they could do it but they couldn't. They could fight the first Marne again but not this. This took religion and years of plenty and tremendous sureties and the exact relation that existed between the classes. The Russians and Italians weren't any good on this front. You had to have a whole-souled sentimental equipment going back further than you could remember. You had to remember Christmas, and postcards of the Crown Prince and his fiancée, and little cafés in Valence and beer gardens in Unter den Linden and weddings at the mairie, and going to the Derby, and your grandfather's whiskers.'

'General Grant invented this kind of battle at Petersburg in sixty-five.'

'No, he didn't – he just invented mass butchery. This kind of battle was invented by Lewis Carroll and Jules Verne and whoever wrote *Undine*, and country deacons bowling and marraines in Marseilles and girls seduced in the back lanes of Württemberg and Westphalia. Why, this was a love battle – there was a century of middle-class love spent here. This was the last love battle.'[1]

THUS Scott Fitzgerald's alter ego, Dick Diver, mused as he and his friends walked around the old Somme battlefield in the aftermath of war. This was an imaginary excursion, but the author's reflections on why men stood and fought in such appalling conditions are highly perceptive. For this was a war begun in illusion.

In 1914 most people expected the war to be over quickly, and it nearly was because the German plan, based on that of Schlieffen and implemented by von Moltke, almost succeeded. Von Moltke's scheme was greatly assisted by Plan XVII, the French plunge into Alsace-Lorraine, which was poorly conceived and badly executed. In the teeth of recent experience, the French threw forward mass formations of their infantry, in sky-blue uniforms and red trousers, carrying outdated Lebel rifles. They relied on the *soixante-quinze* to soften up enemy formations, but had no howitzers to tackle the broken ground and prepared defences to which the Germans retreated. By the end of August, after twelve days of fighting, France had lost 4,478 officers and 206,515 other ranks, and very soon the Germans actually pushed them back, threatening Nancy and Verdun.

In 1914 swift German mobilisation deployed 200,000 men against Russia and 1.8 million against France. Five huge German armies pivoted on Luxembourg and thrust through northern France and Belgium. The wide sweep of the attack surprised the French because they had refused to believe that reserves could be smoothly incorporated into the active army. Joffre, therefore, failed at first to grasp the scope of the threat developing through Belgium. Ultra-heavy German guns blasted the Belgian fortresses and howitzers blew infantry out of trenches. But Liège resisted for eleven days, not the expected two, and the Belgian and British armies, though defeated, further upset the German timetable.

The plan called for von Kluck's First Army, on the right wing of the German forces, to march 300 miles, at a rate of 15 miles per day, to sweep around Paris and pin the French forces against their eastern frontier. The infantry drove on, but other frictions delayed the advance. For all the innovations of late nineteenth-century industrial development, beyond their railheads, armies depended upon horses for transport, as they had since time immemorial, especially as their enemies destroyed rails and bridges. Von Kluck's army had 84,000 horses, each needing 24 pounds of grain and hay per day, a daily total of 2 million pounds of fodder. This was not possible; animals died or slowed down, the guns fell behind and supplies faltered. Soldiers could forage, but the huge numbers involved slowed the advance. The German General Staff's traditional focus on planning for victory, with little regard for the troops, was to blame here. Moreover, it was impossible to improvise supplies of ammunition, especially artillery shells, which were used in vast quantities, so resupply inevitably slowed progress. Concerned by all this and at the gap opening up between his own and the Second Army to his left, von Kluck turned east, moving north of Paris as part of a general realignment of the German armies. This highlighted the increasing problem of communications.

Wireless was still very primitive and German planning had made no real attempt to establish a wireless network, so the flow of intelligence to Moltke, the supreme commander, was poor and his orders reached his army commanders only after long delays. Moreover, the exhaustion of their cavalry, and the poor liaison with air reconnaissance, meant that individual German army commanders were increasingly operating in a fog of confusion. As Moltke tried to adapt his plans, the movements of the German armies became increasingly ill-coordinated. By contrast, French lines of communication were shortening and Joffre kept his nerve. He moved onto the defensive in Lorraine and used the excellent French rail network to rush reinforcements westwards. By 3 September French and British air reconnaissance was reporting that von Kluck was moving south-east, exposing his flank. The Allies attacked the Germans on the Marne, 5–12 September, throwing back the German advance. Overall casualties in this series of battles were about 250,000 on each side. Each army then tried to move around the enemy flank, and the fighting moved north-westwards until it reached the sea, establishing a line which would endure until 1918.

Moltke's plan focused on the west. When, in 1913, Conrad, the Austrian Commander-in-Chief, proposed a joint attack on Russian Poland, Moltke brushed him off in unmistakable terms: 'The centre of gravity of the whole European war, and consequently the fate of Austria will not be decided on the Bug, but definitely on the Seine.'[2] But the Russians invaded East Prussia with two separate armies, and on 20 August defeated its defenders at Gumbinnen. The Prussian commander, von Prittwitz, was replaced by General Paul von Hindenburg who had served in the wars against Austria and France and retired in 1910. Erich Ludendorff, who had choreographed the attack on Liège, became his Chief of Staff. They went on to crush the Russian attack, greatly aided by mutual dislike between the two enemy commanders and poor communications within their armies. But the invasion compelled Moltke to transfer two full corps to the east. This, and the heavy losses suffered in the advance through Belgium and France, weakened the German army in the grand test of the Marne battle. As Moltke remarked: 'I admit this was a mistake and one that was fully paid for on the Marne.'[3]

Austria's plan for a twofold attack to destroy Serbia in the south and the Russians in Galicia failed miserably. Attacks on Serbia in July and September brought limited success, but a third led to the capture of Belgrade on 2 December. However, on 15 December the Serbs recaptured it and by the end of the year the front line was back on the frontier. This failure was not altogether surprising because the initial Austrian forces amounted to less than 300,000 against 350,000 Serbs, many of them veterans of the Balkan wars. The Serbs tried to oblige their Russian ally by invading Hungary, but were beaten back. In all, the Hapsburg army lost 220,000 in a disastrous campaign, inflicting about 1.4 million casualties on the Serbs. The Austrian assault on Galicia was defeated decisively with 350,000 casualties by a Russian offensive, and by 11 September the vital centre of Lemberg had surrendered. But the Russians had suffered heavy casualties, delayed pursuit, and became sucked into the siege of Przemsyl, enabling the Austrian survivors to reorganise and dig in. They were helped by a new German army under Hindenburg and Ludendorff which struck the Russians somewhat inconclusively in southern Poland. The Austrian war plan failed because it involved a hopeless division of forces. Similarly, dispersal of effort in Prussia and Galicia compromised the Russian plans, and their total losses were probably not far off one million by the end of 1914.

This was a European war, but it spread to the colonial empires of the contending powers, drawing in Britain's allies in the Far East, the Japanese, who picked off German colonies in the Pacific. Fighting in German Africa went on throughout the war, diverting British resources. German determination to attack British commerce produced naval clashes across the oceans, notably the destruction of the German East Asiatic Squadron off the Falkland Islands in December 1914. The really important extension of the war came with the accession of the Ottoman Empire to the German–Austrian pact. Turkey feared that the Entente powers, and especially Russia, were bent on dismembering their empire. And not without reason; in April 1915 France and Britain agreed that Russia should have Constantinople and the Straits.

Turkish accession to the central powers in November 1914 was a considerable blow to Britain because their dominion over Syria and Palestine enabled the Ottomans to threaten the Suez Canal, which was Britain's vital link to India. Further afield, control over Mesopotamia enabled the Turks to challenge the British hegemony in Persia long seen as important to the security of India. At the same time the Turks attacked the Russians in the Caucasus, opening yet another front. In 1915 a small British force of 8,000 men, based at Basra, tried to seize Baghdad and was driven to surrender. Ottoman agitation, backed up by German supplies, incited the Senussi of Libya to raid Egypt, and they were not crushed until 1916 at the battle of Agagiya, while strong Turkish forces threatened Egypt via Gaza. By 1918 the British had deployed an army of over 400,000, mostly Indian, to Mesopotamia, suffering some 92,000 casualties. It was only in 1917 that Allenby, with 92,000 men based in Egypt, defeated the Turks, seizing Jerusalem on 9 December.

The Middle Eastern war encouraged British politicians who disliked the commitment on the western front and in France created the suspicion, not without foundation, that the British were aiming to carve up the area for their own benefit. In April 1915, a strong Anglo-French naval force attempted to seize Constantinople and the Straits and was repelled; this was followed by a badly handled invasion of Gallipoli involving nearly a quarter of a million allied troops, whose losses amounted to 220,000 by the time of the withdrawal in January 1916. From the German viewpoint the 300,000 Turkish losses in this fighting mattered little. For a limited investment in economic aid and armaments, Germany reaped a rich reward from the Turkish alliance.

The price of the failure of the war plans of 1914 was enormous. The French lost 265,000 dead alone in 1914, while British losses totalled over 80,000, more than the whole army sent in August. The generals had anticipated heavy casualties, but they thought the war would be short. The French had never developed a real doctrine for infantry attack in the age of the firestorm, and trusted to sheer spirit to overwhelm their enemy. The result was a tragedy, as noted by an English liaison officer:

> the sense of the tragic futility of it will never fade from the minds of those who saw these brave men, dashing across the open to the sound of bugles and drum, clad in old red caps and trousers which a parsimonious democracy dictated they should wear, although they turned each man into a target. The gallant officers who led them were entirely ignorant of the stopping power of modern firearms, and many of them thought it chic to die in white gloves.[4]

Joffre tacitly recognised the mistakes which had been made in the 'Battles of the Frontiers' in his *Bulletin* to commanders of 21 September 1914: 'The French soldier has lost none of the military qualities of his race; he retains all of his courage and all of his offensive ardour, but these same qualities need to be wisely directed on the modern battlefield or they will lead to a rapid wearing out of forces.'[5]

The British had learned all about firepower and the empty battlefield in the Boer War. A German officer commented on a British attack: 'It was noticed that a shell, however well aimed, seldom killed more than one man, the lines being so well and widely extended. The front line had taken cover when the shelling began, running behind hedges or buildings nearby, but the second line kept steadily on, while a third and fourth line now appeared. It was magnificently done.'[6] But by spring 1915 continuous combat had virtually wiped out the old British regular army.

German infantry doctrine encouraged soldiers to advance in small mutually supporting groups – fire and movement – making the best use of ground. Erwin Rommel, an infantry lieutenant, exemplified the kind of initiative expected of junior leaders. Finding his platoon without orders, 'Since I didn't want to remain inactive with my platoon, I decided to attack the enemy opposite us.'[7] But even in the German army the quality and equipment of units varied a great deal, and the French soon learned to attack less well-trained German reserve divisions. At the first battle of Ypres, October–November 1914, the Germans flung men fresh from the training camps into a battle remembered still as the *Kindermord bei Ypern* ('The Massacre of the Innocents at Ypres'). A German officer noted: 'There is no doubt that the English and French troops would already have been beaten by trained troops. But these young fellows we have, only just trained, are too helpless, particularly when the officers have been killed.'[8]

In any case, how was one to outflank a fortress with all-round defences, set in a landscape deliberately denuded of cover and swept by carefully sited and well-protected artillery and infantry equipped with automatic weapons? A Belgian officer describes an attempt by German infantry to rush the fortifications at Liège on 4 August:

> They made no attempt at deploying, but came on, line after line, almost shoulder to shoulder, until, as we shot them down, the fallen were heaped one on top of the other in an awful barricade of dead and wounded men that threatened to mask our guns and cause us trouble.[9]

'Shoulder to shoulder', 'line after line', we could almost be talking about the Greek phalanx, the English foot at Hastings or the charge of the Old Guard at Waterloo.

The deadlock on all fronts was a profound shock to the peoples of Europe; breaking it was the great problem for their governments. This involved enormous efforts in a series of directions, all of them interlocking. There was a scramble for allies. Germany acquired Turkey and somewhat later Bulgaria, while the Entente lured Italy into the war in 1915 by the offer of Tyrol, Dalmatia and Istria at the expense of Austria. In August 1916 Romania acceded to the Entente to gain Transylvania, but was quickly eliminated by German attack. The only power whose allegiance could make a substantial difference to the military balance was the US, but she had almost no army, was remote, and was apparently determined to stay out of European entanglements.

The immediate task, therefore, was the maintenance of and, in the case of Britain, creation of huge armies. This obviously demanded the mobilisation of the economic resources of states on a scale never seen before. Initially there were severe material shortages. In Britain and France contractors sometimes signed agreements in the knowledge that they could not deliver, but feared losses to competitors if they did not sign. Shortages of raw materials developed and blind spots in economies became painfully manifest. Before the war Britain had depended heavily on Germany for optics which were essential for gunsights, and chemicals vital for munitions, and now had to create industrial capacity for them or buy supplies elsewhere. Machine-tools, the key to mass production, were in enormous demand. As a consequence the New Armies created by the British war minister, Kitchener, were poorly housed and fed, and obliged to train with broom handles for lack of rifles. France lost her most productive industrial areas to German occupation in 1914, and she had to create new industries. She and Britain accordingly turned to the US to supply war material and in the process developed complex credit systems to pay for the war.

In Russia the war impacted upon an economy which was suffering all the dislocations of rapid development, and the bureaucracy of the state was simply not designed to solve the consequent problems, much less to do so while paying attention to popular feeling. The result was a supply system in chaos and a scandalous shortage of rifles. For this reason many units surrendered to the German offensive of 1915 because they were unarmed. One reason for shortages in Russia was that at the start of the war her government was swindled on a huge scale by western arms contractors. The Italians had introduced conscription in 1907 and by 1914 had an army of 300,000, but it was poorly trained and the country lacked an adequate industrial base to sustain modern warfare, becoming heavily dependent, therefore, upon the other Entente powers.

The prodigious expenditure of ammunition and supplies had been anticipated up to a point, but all armies had assumed they were embarking on a short war. As a result, in 1915 there was a 'shell shortage' amongst all the powers, though this was often used by the generals as a convenient excuse for failure. All the combatants reorganised their economies for war. The British created a Ministry of Munitions under the ambitious Lloyd George, which set the economy on a war footing. In Germany there were already great industrial cartels, and this made reorganisation of the economy comparatively easy. Everywhere the impact of conscription or mass volunteering created a labour shortage at home so that the state had to balance manpower demands.

But, despite many problems all the powers managed, as in the American Civil War, to provide a sufficient material base for the conduct of the war. Bloch, in his *Future of War* (1898), had foreseen the horrors of the new battlefield and the strains imposed on what was essentially an international economy, but he had failed to understand how effectively state power could be mobilised to overcome these problems. Germany's highly developed industrial base gave her an obvious lead in 1914–15. However, the British naval blockade limited German supplies of raw materials and this became progressively more severe. It was made worse because Germany's allies, Austro-Hungary and Turkey, lacked modern industry and became increasingly dependent upon German support.

One of the blockade's most dangerous effects was on food supply. By winter 1914 most German families were living on *Kriegsbrot* (war bread) which was largely made of potatoes, and rationing had been introduced. In 1916 the potato crop failed and there followed the bitter 'turnip winter'. The result for ordinary Germans was increased death rates, and in particular rising infant mortality. Britain, by contrast, imported food, and the shortages first felt in 1916 only became acute with the German submarine campaign of 1917 which forced the introduction of rationing in 1918. Working people in Britain profited from the labour shortage to improve earnings, and overall their standard of living rose, with infant mortality falling.

All this had an obvious impact on what for governments became the central problem of the war: maintaining the will to fight. All governments cultivated patriotism, but they were painfully aware of the questioning attitudes which had been developing amongst the newly educated masses with their growing consciousness of the world. The challenge of justifying the war and its conduct, especially as the toll of battle deaths mounted, was formidable and it was complicated by the widespread ignorance of the realities of war.

Professional soldiers had always recognised that war between the great powers might become long and intense, but they did little to educate their public and fostered older perceptions of glory which dominated art and literature until 1914. They were assisted in this by the long peace which Europe had enjoyed since 1815. The educated people of the liberal states of Western Europe had little real knowledge of military affairs, and such as they had was powerfully influenced by romantic images and notions. This mixture of ignorance and idealism underlay Rupert Brooke's famous sonnet, 'Peace', one of a sequence of five hailed at the time as 'an important document of national preparation for war':

Now, God be thanked Who has matched us with His hour,
And caught our youth, and wakened us from sleeping,
With hand made sure, clear eye, and sharpened power,
   To turn, as swimmers into cleanness leaping,
Glad from a world grown old and cold and weary,
   Leave the sick hearts that honour could not move,
And half-men, and their dirty songs and dreary,
   And all the little emptiness of love!

Oh! we, who have known shame, we have found release there,
Where there's no ill, no grief, but sleep has mending.
   Naught broken save this body, lost but breath;
Nothing to shake the laughing heart's long peace there
But only agony, and that has ending;
   And the worst friend and enemy is but Death.[10]

In England, ordinary people thought war at sea meant the clash of fleets and Nelsonian victories. They would have been shocked by Admiral Beatty's disinclination to risk a confrontation with the German fleet because, 'Being already in possession of all that a powerful fleet can give a country, we should continue quietly to enjoy the advantage.'[11]

The illusion of glory in part explains the outbursts of enthusiasm which greeted the outbreak of war in 1914 in France, Germany, England, and even to a degree Russia. Photographs of popular celebration in 1914, like that at Munich which included Hitler, have assumed a terrible poignancy in the light of our knowledge of the horrors to come, and this has been augmented by constant repetition in print and on television. But contemporaries observed few signs of rejoicing in the countryside of the belligerent nations. These celebratory manifestations were dominated by the urban middle classes, precisely the people educated and deeply marked by the new sensibilities, not to say official propaganda. There were, in fact, occasional demonstrations against the war, in Germany and elsewhere, and in Russia there were riots, but by and large the spirit of national solidarity prevailed. It was hardly surprising that assurances of a short war were welcomed, and continued to be believed even as things dragged on, for accepting the alternative was for long unthinkable.

But by 1915 it was obvious to both military leaders and politicians that the war might drag on for a very long time. Populations had to be given hope and reasons for carrying on with the war, because governments needed them to fight and to produce while enduring inevitable hardships.

States, therefore, created propaganda machines to shore up the 'Home Front'. Obviously military events would have an impact on attitudes, and in this respect Germany began the war with a clear advantage. By 1915 her armies were everywhere on foreign soil. The German government conjured up the glorious past, citing their victory over the Russians at Tannenberg in East Prussia in 1914, suggesting that this was a reversal of the defeat of the Teutonic Order by the Poles in 1410. This set the tone for much German propaganda about fighting back the 'Asiatic hordes' of the Russian Empire. It also made Hindenburg and Ludendorff into national heroes untarnished by failure, promoting their influence in the counsels of the great. But in reality it was a convenient smokescreen for failure in the west. Moltke was dismissed and replaced by Falkenhayn, while Germans celebrated Tannenberg which was a great tactical success with no strategic consequences. It was convenient to forget that Hindenburg and Ludendorff's subsequent plunge into Poland was a failure – such was the power of propaganda.

Within Germany, as in all the warring powers, the years before the war had seen major trade union and political action by elements of the working class. It was essential to limit industrial disruption and the German government, which had always hated 'socialism', embarked on a process of repression, taking draconian powers to control workers' organisations. As living conditions worsened, industrial unrest and protest followed, with notable demonstrations in Berlin on May Day 1916. The SDP was regarded with deep suspicion by government despite its loyal support for the war, but its members in the Reichstag could hardly watch such events with indifference. A strong left-wing breakaway movement subsequently split the SDP, and on 19 July 1917 the Reichstag passed a motion calling for peace without annexations, to the great embarrassment of the government.

But the German government had to take a very different attitude to the middle class because if they became alienated it would decisively undermine the regime. Middle-class anxieties about the war were increasingly expressed by such bodies as the Pan-German League which became ever more vocal as the war dragged on. War eroded the living standards of the middle class, and most particularly the comforting gap which separated them from the working class. The League demanded some reward for the sufferings of the German middle class. Their demands encouraged those in government who wanted to seize territory in Europe. Parts or even the whole of Belgium, together with select portions of France, were earmarked for annexation, while the notion of an empire in Central and

Eastern Europe became firmly rooted. The German middle class was offered the promise of future plenty and profit as a reward for enduring present pain. Because of this German propaganda to the end maintained the image of ever-victorious armies.

The Russian imperial government was far more impervious to public opinion and popular culture, and deeply fearful of the socialists. The Tsar, Nicholas II (1894–1918), was nominally all-powerful, but his first concern was to maintain control of the army. This was contested by the parliament, the Duma, which he had been forced to create after the 1905 Revolution. Partly because of his personal incompetence, the court was divided by factional struggles, and these were replicated in the Russian high command, the *Stavka*, some of whose officers were deeply concerned about the effect of shortages on the army. Because of this perpetual strife in government nobody paid much attention to such obvious problems as bureaucratic corruption and transporting food to the cities, where by 1916 hunger and discontent were taking hold.

In Britain and France maintaining the will to fight took a rather different form. Governments feared that trade unions would profit from the labour shortage, and passed very severe legislation to prevent this, but in practice they negotiated. British trade unions were highly resistant to 'dilution', the use of machinery with the consequent replacement of skilled with unskilled labour and, even worse, women. In the end workable compromises were reached and war production was amply sustained. In France, the German threat was patent and the French Socialist Party was leaderless and divided after the assassination of Jean Jaurès in 1914. In left-wing circles there was much opposition to war, but this lacked focus and was later extinguished with the appointment of Clemenceau to head the government in 1917.

The Entente powers made much play in their own countries and beyond with German 'frightfulness', a charge which gained currency from Germany's invasion of neutral Belgium and brutal treatment of its civilian population. During the Franco-Prussian War the French had tried to recruit *francs-tireurs* to wage guerrilla warfare against the invaders. The effort failed, but the Prussians tended to blame every loss on these shadowy figures and summarily executed those they caught. This stuck in the German memory. At Dinant, on 23 August 1914, German soldiers mending the bridge in the city were fired on, almost certainly by retreating allied forces; they blamed *franc-tireurs*, sacked the city and executed 612 men, women and children. On 19 August Leuwen (Louvain) was occupied by the Germans, and on 25 August they were attacked by Belgian forces based in Antwerp, causing great confusion. In retaliation for their supposed involvement, citizens were shot, the city was burned and the university library destroyed in a five-day rampage. Later, without ever mentioning her neutrality, Ludendorff, proudly boasted of the rapid advance of German troops through Belgium, 'In spite of the national uprisings which took place upon the instructions of the Belgian Government.'[12]

There was no government instruction and no 'national uprising', but everywhere Germany took a very hard line on the least resistance, and while the Allies undoubtedly exaggerated, their propaganda had a real basis in fact and was consequently effective amongst neutrals. The parallel between Germans and past barbarians, embodied in the word 'Huns', certainly stuck. At sea Germany was tempted to use her submarines against British trade. But while the International Law of the Sea recognised blockade as a legitimate means of war, it insisted that civilians should be saved before ships were sunk. This was clearly impossible for cramped and tiny submarines, and sinkings lent further credence to the allied charge of 'frightfulness' against the Germans.

The propaganda war in fact paralleled the real war. In October 1914 over 4,000 German intellectuals (including Einstein) signed a manifesto declaring that their government was defending European culture. In response French intellectuals issued their own statement, emphasising the allied commitment to defend small nations against aggression. An Oxford don, J.C. Powys, contended that 'The German "Idea" is therefore the Idea of the primary importance of the state . . . Against the state no individual has either rights or claims.' By contrast he claimed, the 'Idea' which bound together the Allies was 'The Idea of the rights of individuals against the State-Machine'.[13] Out of such thinking both sides came to believe that this was a war between irreconcilables. In 1911 Friedrich von Bernhardi had published his *Germany and the Next War*, a militarist tract profoundly influenced by popular Darwinism, which proclaimed that war was a biological necessity. Such ideas had an enormous impact upon German official propaganda. German *Kultur*, it was asserted, was not merely different from but superior to the materialistic liberal democracy of the British and French. In response the Allied powers asserted a belief in international law, the freedom of peoples (though not of colonial peoples) and the 'War for Democracy'. Ultimately a strong ideological hatred developed between Germany and Britain, while Germany's belief that it stood for civilisation against the Slavic hordes injected a similar strain into events in the east. Such ideas sustained the notion that this was war to the knife to which only unconditional victory could bring an end.

All this conspired to prevent people asking an ever more pertinent question: what was the war about? The truth was that this was essentially a highly traditional European conflict about the balance of power. Internal stability meant that Austro-Hungary could not afford to be seen to be weak in the face of Serbia, while the Russians felt the need to support their fellow Slavs. Each feared that any sign of feebleness might open them to attack. Germany was conscious of the growing power of Russia, where new railways, and the army reforms begun in 1912, enhanced military effectiveness and the speed of mobilisation. Her alliance with France surrounded Germany whose military leaders had a sense that the crisis of August 1914 was an opportunity, and perhaps a last opportunity, to preserve their dominance in Central and Eastern Europe. France, with her falling birth rate, feared she would be engulfed by the giant to the east, and clung to her alliance with Russia. The British, aware of their political and economic decline, wanted to check the rise of Germany with her strong fleet and colonial ambitions.

Similar fears had often enough provoked European war, but balance had in the past been enshrined in the particularities of territorial extent. Obvious exceptions were ideological wars. The Thirty Years War ended in exhaustion, while the Revolutionary and Napoleonic Wars terminated only with regime change. Gradually the Entente powers made this their purpose, though it was far beyond their original intentions in 1914. But the military role was engulfed in popular culture. No European statesman cared to trust to 'Preserve the balance of power' as a rallying cry. This had to be a war to destroy the enemy, and any compromise was exceedingly difficult, not least because propaganda and official ideas about the war drew upon popular culture and were, therefore, deeply implanted. A British soldier echoed the sentiments of many in 1915: 'We didn't make the war, the blame doesn't rest on us, Germany forced it and will undoubtedly be punished by God.'[14] In effect the war was taking on a momentum of its own.

All governments were badly embarrassed when, in late 1916, US President Woodrow Wilson asked the belligerents to formulate their war aims. Most talk of peace at this time was really aimed at influencing the US as the only major power not yet involved. Germany refused to reply to Wilson's request, but the allies responded by proclaiming the rights of all people to 'national self-determination', though their note skated around some allied claims which clearly breached this – notably the Russian demand for Poland and the offer they had made to Italy of parts of German Austria. The Entente response had to consider very carefully popular opinion in France and Britain as well as that of the US.

But if propaganda could help to rally national feeling, the will to fight depended above all on success, or at least something that could be presented as success. For this an effective army was a prerequisite. Here, again, Germany had at first an obvious advantage. The German army had an efficient General Staff, good officers and a highly effective system of training. It also possessed a hard core of about 100,000 NCOs who made the army work. Of course, many of these, along with their officers, had perished in 1914, but the machine of which they formed a vital part was able to replace them, and training diffused through the new ranks. Their Austro-Hungarian allies on the other hand had suffered irreplaceable losses of officers and men, which diluted the fighting quality of the army. Much the same was true of the French. General Franchet d'Espèrey, watching his Fifth Army prepare for battle on the Marne in September 1914, was heard to lament: 'Mais où sont mes officiers, où sont mes officiers?'[15] The Russian army had always been short of officers, and the loss of 40,000 in 1914 was crippling.

The problems of training an army were very considerable for the British. There was eagerness enough: in Britain 2.25 million men had volunteered by the autumn of 1914. But they were totally untrained and, therefore, of little use. It was vital to kick them into shape quickly, but this in itself posed enormous problems. Regular troops were self-selected and their training extended over a long period at the hands of experienced men. But these expert and hardened men were already fighting in France in 1914 and by the spring of 1915 had virtually been wiped out. Officers, NCOs and trainers, therefore, could only come from the ranks of the untrained, and they would have to learn their trade in the rough school of action. Raw recruits had to be taught the rudiments of soldiering: to understand their position in units and the chain of command. In defence, soldiers had to learn how to lay out trenches and the basics of hygiene and self-protection. It was particularly important that they learned how to attack because the Allies wanted to evict the Germans from French soil. After the initial clashes most soldiers in most armies attempted some form of fire and movement, but for these to work units needed experienced leaders down to the level of corporal who could take responsibility for leading their comrades. In Britain they simply did not exist, and even in France the losses of 1914 meant they were in very short supply.

At higher levels regular British officers knew little about handling large forces, because their entire experience was in colonial policing. Such fighting involved operating in hostile and remote places; as a result the British recognised the importance of logistics, and throughout the war the army was very well supplied and supported by a first-rate infrastructure. But the generals had to learn how to manage armies whose size was far beyond their experience. They needed to have an appreciation of weapons and tactics and to be able to appoint and work with staffs that could coordinate the different arms like engineering, transport, infantry and artillery. Technology was constantly advancing so that innovations like poison gas, air power and wireless had to be understood and integrated into military usage. And, of course, many generals brought to the task much mental baggage, especially a belief in decisive battle, a concept which faded very slowly.

Even at the lowest level, new weapons were appearing, so that training had to be a constant and constantly changing. The grenade was essential in the trenches, while the Germans introduced the trench mortar and the flame-thrower. Because they were clumsy and heavy, machine-guns had always been seen as essentially defensive weapons. In 1915 the British concentrated them in special units, providing the infantry with the lighter Lewis gun which could be carried to give attack new firepower. The tank, first used by the British on the Somme in 1916, offered great possibilities. Above all, artillery was quickly perceived as the key to any breakthrough, but its methods needed enhancing and its limitations needed to be understood. A flood of new ideas and devices demanded an elaborate system of education and training so that they could be spread quickly, and integrated into plans of attack. Creating armies was an enormously difficult business in which the Entente powers for long lagged far behind the Germans, who started with better trained troops and could therefore assimilate the newest techniques more rapidly.

The overwhelming memory of World War I amongst Europeans is of the trenches, and indeed this is hardly surprising. For four years they stretched some 475 miles from the Channel to the Swiss border. British soldiers called the trench system the 'sausage-machine', because without ever moving it chopped up men and material. Trench warfare took its daily toll of casualties, but it was the battles, the attempts to end trench warfare, that created the real death toll. But this is not the whole story of the war, for in the east, while men just as readily took to the earth for protection, the vast open spaces allowed for mobility. The western front was the accidental and unforeseen outcome of the failure of the plans of 1914, but it was frozen in place by the strategic decisions of the German war leaders.

After the failure of Moltke's attack in 1914, the German high command had no 'Plan B' and to a degree circumstantial pressures took over. Falkenhayn was impelled to turn east by the problems of his

Hapsburg ally. Austrian armies in Galicia were collapsing, and the situation worsened when Italy joined the Entente in April 1915. The qualitative superiority of the German army was now at its zenith. Its equipment was superb and production was rising steadily. The reserve divisions were blooded and new recruits were being smoothly incorporated. The Germans were so confident that they reduced the size of their divisions in the west by about 25 per cent, creating new forces for an attack on the Russians. Simultaneously with this eastward movement, Falkenhayn threw seven divisions at eight French, Belgian and British in an effort to snuff out the Ypres salient in the Second Battle of Ypres (April–May 1915). The attack had limited success, but for 35,000 German losses they inflicted 70,000 on the Allies, partly because of the German use of poison gas. This was an ominous example of technological development under the pressures of war.

In the east Mackensen's Eleventh Army attacked in Galicia at Gorlice-Tarnow (May to September 1915). By September the Germans had advanced up to 300 miles, occupied Brest-Litovsk and faced Russia on a front extending from Riga in the north to the eastern end of the Carpathians in the south. Russia suffered a million casualties and lost as many prisoners. Serbia was now annihilated by an army under German command, and Bulgaria, eager to share in the spoils, joined the central powers. It was a triumph, but also a failure: the Russians still had 1.3 million men in arms, and they defeated Ludendorff's thrust to Riga in the north and an Austrian assault in eastern Galicia. Indeed, the Austrian army, which had begun the offensive half a million strong, was reduced to 200,000 by the autumn. The Russian armies, though depleted, were still formidable and the Germans were vulnerable on a long front.

Why was decisive victory so difficult? In the east there was so much space that no army could be strong everywhere, so there were opportunities to outflank or to pierce at a weak point. German armies were coherent, while the Russians had poor internal communications and failed in any war of manoeuvre. Many Russian soldiers were badly equipped – some reserve divisions surrendered because they had no weapons at all. But the space which made possible the German victory could be traded by the Russians for time. Their huge manpower and great industrial resources meant that losses could be made good. A British observer recognised:

> The further the Russians have retired, the slower has been their retreat and the more difficult has it been for the enemy to follow up their strokes with anything like the same strength and energy. In other words,

the Russians are pretty nearly beyond the reach of enemy blows which can hurt them fatally.[16]

Conversely, as the Germans advanced from their railheads, supply depended on the muscles of men and horses, using very bad roads which were in many cases unsuitable for trucks, of which the Germans had relatively few. This slowed the advance and allowed the enemy to recover. This was the friction which had fatally slowed the German attack on France in 1914, and it exerted its baleful influence on the movements of all armies. Equally limiting was the lack of an effective arm of exploitation. Traditionally this was the role of the cavalry, but small-arms fire made it impossible for them to fulfil it because horses made easy targets. After the victory at Gorlice-Tarnow pursuit was necessarily slow and the Germans could not reach any really critical point after the breakthrough, with the result that fighting petered out in September. Many of the same considerations were at work on the western front, despite the obvious differences in space available.

On the western front in 1915 the Germans incorporated the improvised field fortifications of the autumn into a triple line defended by barbed wire and machine-gun emplacements, communicating with command to the rear by buried telephone lines. Deep shelters, and in some places concrete pillboxes, protected troops from shelling, while German artillery pre-registered its targets in their defence-zone. Allied trenches were less elaborate because their commanders were anxious to eject the enemy from French soil. Over this bleak landscape the artillery ruled, forcing men to huddle in holes. Any frontal attack on such obstacles risked appalling casualties, and before they could be penetrated the defenders could rush up reserves to prevent any breakthrough. The British achieved a partial success at Neuve Chapelle in March 1915, which revealed many of the problems of attack.

Neuve Chapelle was an assault by 45,000 men, mostly regulars, on a front of only 2,000 yards, intended to seize the town and the railway to the east, thus cutting a major supply route and forcing an extensive German retreat. The attackers gathered secretly as British aviators swept the air clear of German reconnaissance and strafed road junctions and communications. The assault, under cover of a short bombardment, was a complete surprise and Neuve Chapelle fell within thirty minutes. But because there was no method of rapid communication between the leading infantry and the supporting guns, the British artillery had to timetable its bombardment of enemy lines. This meant that infantry units which had broken quickly through the outer defences often had to wait while artillery engaged targets, even when there was no resistance. Conversely if infantry failed to gain their initial objective, the guns would lift to the next at a fixed time. And even if holes opened in the German lines, there was no means of telling commanders and so opportunities were lost. The Germans rushed up reserves and forced the British to retreat. Losses were heavy – some 13,000 British to about 15,000 German. The problems of artillery support were made worse at Neuve Chapelle because anxiety over supplies of shells led to clumsy central control of this arm, which increased the inevitable delays. But the problem was that even when infantry broke into a defensive system, there was no way to make a rapid breakout. Cavalry had to wait until infantry had cleared through the battle zone, and by that time enemy reserves were in place.

Air power was an entirely new dimension of war which generals now had to master. Both sides used spotter aircraft to find targets for their artillery. This led to fighters, specialist aircraft for shooting down others. At Neuve Chapelle the British planes strafed ground targets and made a series of determined attacks on railways, in one incident killing seventy-five soldiers at Courtrai and closing the line for three days. But bombs were small, and aircraft light, and it took time to evolve more suitable machines. As a result, a technological race ensued. The Germans developed a synchroniser which allowed forward-facing machine-guns to fire through the propeller disk, so that in late 1915 the Fokker swung the balance to the Germans. However, by Verdun in 1916 the French were deploying masses of fighters, depriving enemy artillery of spotters. The Germans then reorganised their squadrons into specialised fighter, bomber and reconnaissance units, and took the initiative in early 1917 with the new Albatross, in turn countered by the British Sopwith Camel and the remarkable SE5. In essence German airframes were superior, but the French Gnome engines were superb. Gradually France and Britain organised assembly-line methods to turn out vast numbers of simple and standardised airframes with ever more powerful engines, and this turned the air war in their favour.

Much publicity was given to 'knights of the air', outstanding individual flyers like the Germans Boelcke, Immelmann and Richthofen, the Frenchman Guynemer, the English Mannock and the American Rickenbacker. But in reality it was numbers and quality of aircraft that counted. The Somme battle in 1916 witnessed a determined attempt by the British to dominate the skies, at an appalling cost. Between 1 July and 17 November 1916, 369 German aircraft were destroyed, but the Royal

Flying Corps lost about 800 aircraft with 500 crew, necessitating the deployment of trainees from the air schools. These heavy losses were partly the result of mistaken tactics. The air commander, Trenchard, demanded patrols over enemy territory throughout the daylight hours, but this allowed the Germans to pick and choose when to attack the small numbers of British aircraft in the sky at any one time.

From the technological competition over the western front strategic bombing emerged. German dirigibles, Zeppelins, carried out the first raids on civilian targets in Britain in 1915, but raids on London were beaten off by strong gun and aircraft defences. In 1917 the Germans tried again with the much more effective Gotha IV bombers carrying 300 kg of bombs, whose tight formations and heavy machine-guns warded off fighters. Elaborate air defences were created around London, so that the last attack on 19/20 May 1918 by forty-three machines cost the Germans eight aircraft. The British then tried to bomb targets in western Germany. None of these raids had much material effect, but the moral impact of the first attacks on London for hundreds of years was considerable, and led directly to the formation of the independent Royal Air Force (RAF) in 1918.

The main use of air power was to spot for the artillery, the only arm which could create the conditions for a breakthrough. But designing and building heavier guns took time, and required the creation of new industries. Once these were available, armies had to set up an enormous infrastructure of dumps, railways and battery positions and to devise methods of transportation. All this was hard to conceal, especially as guns had to register on their targets. This process signalled where the major bombardments would fall and enabled the enemy to prepare accordingly. In time predicted shooting enabled the gunners to calculate range precisely, doing away with registration. Flash-spotting and the new technology of sound location enabled the gunners to find and destroy enemy batteries. This was made even more precise by calibrated screening which made allowances for the idiosyncrasies of individual guns. The new British No. 106 fuse was effective at cutting wire while gas shells proved very successful. All this made possible valuable short surprise barrages. By 1915 artillerymen were developing the creeping barrage which moved just ahead of infantry, keeping enemy heads down till the last moment and masking them from his guns. But each change took time, and it had to be accommodated and understood by the gunners and the staff, and coordinated with other arms. And until the very end communications remained a problem because infantry breaking into multi-layered defences needed to be able to give the guns new targets.

Simply assembling a lot of guns was not enough. At Festubert in May 1915 it became clear that shrapnel did not cut wire. Partly as a result the raw British troops in mass formations suffered 12,000 casualties in a single day. At Arras the French assault, even with 300,000 shells, failed at a cost of 100,000 casualties. In the autumn at Loos the British lost 60,000, while in Champagne, despite the heaviest artillery barrage ever known, the French attack suffered 100,000 casualties. The Germans dug ever deeper and more elaborate fortifications, so that breaking into trench systems was becoming more difficult. And beyond break-in lay the problems of breaking through multiple lines of resistance, because advances moved at the speed of the infantry and even if a gap was made communications were so poor that commanders could not be quickly told. Armies resembled great beasts with inadequate nervous systems.

In these circumstances, some generals like the British Rawlinson suggested a policy of 'bite and hold'. A carefully prepared assault with limited objectives could break into the enemy trench system and be rapidly reinforced, attracting enemy counter-attacks which could then be destroyed. Systematic repetition would gradually crumble the enemy defences. But this patient long-term strategy flew in the face of the political imperative to free French territory and the need to maintain the fiction of a 'short war'. Its adoption would have seemed too much like an acceptance of that dreadful word, attrition, with its ghastly prospect of long, slow and deadly bloodletting. Moreover, senior commanders like Joffre and Haig continued to believe that a breakthrough victory was possible.

In December 1915 at Chantilly the Allies agreed on a series of coordinated attacks for 1916, but in February Falkenhayn launched a massive thrust towards Verdun. So secret were his preparations that 155,000 Germans fell upon only 30,000 French whose forts had been denuded of guns. The artillery preparation was massive but brief, and ferocious counter-battery fire destroyed the few French guns. Special Assault Detachments led the attack, equipped with flame-throwers and accompanied by sappers to deal with French fortifications. By 25 February Fort Douaumont had fallen and Verdun was threatened. The assault petered out, in part because of disorganisation. The French poured in reinforcements and appointed Pétain to direct the defence. He reorganised the army and its supply system, rotating units through the 'Mill on the Meuse' so that none became totally exhausted. He also introduced massive artillery forces which gradually turned the battlefield into an appalling killing ground for the Germans. An estimated 162,000 French and 142,000 Germans were killed, but total casualties were respectively

378,000 and 330,000. Falkenhayn was relieved in August, but his successors, Hindenburg and Ludendorff, did not break off the battle because they felt that too much German prestige rested on success. As a result it dragged on until December. The holocaust on the Meuse had frightful consequences elsewhere.

As a result of Verdun, the French asked the Russians to advance their plans for a thrust against the Austrians in Galicia, the Brusilov offensive named after its commander. Verdun forced the Germans to thin out their troops in the east, leaving Austro-Hungarian armies to hold southern Poland and Galicia. The Austrians thought that the Russians were defeated, and in May attacked Italy from south Tyrol, with some success. Brusilov planned an assault over 300 kilometres of front, quietly reinforcing his troops and artillery. Saps were dug forward to prepare for a close-range attack on enemy lines led by special shock troops who identified weak spots. A lightning artillery bombardment surprised the defenders, and the Russians broke through on a front so wide that it simply could not be reinforced, thus collapsing the entire Austro-Hungarian position. Brusilov's men were in the Carpathians by September, but they were exhausted and Russian forces further north failed dismally. The cost of this victory was high – at least 500,000 Russian casualties, but Austro-Hungary lost about 1.5 million and its army was shattered. Romania joined the Entente in the hope of territorial gain, but strong German intervention stabilised the Austrian line and quickly conquered the Romanians. It was now clear that the Austro-Hungarian army was completely dependent on German support, imposing a vast burden upon the Kaiser's forces.

The British had also agreed to undertake an offensive at Chantilly and chose the Somme where their troops and those of the French met and could attack together. Rawlinson had originally designed a large-scale 'bite and hold' operation to sap German manpower, but the British Commander-in-Chief, Haig, altered the scope of the operation in the hope of forcing a breakthrough: 1,500 guns and limitless shells were concentrated to support an attack by eleven British divisions (with more in reserve) on a front of 24,000 yards with an intended maximum penetration of 4,000 yards. But of the British guns only thirty-four were of large (over 9.2-in.) calibre, while 60 per cent of the shell was shrapnel which had little effect either on wire or the well dug in German troops. Some 30 tons of explosive fell per mile of British front, but the effect of changing the focus of the operation to that of a breakthrough was to spread this too deeply, so that overall the barrage lacked the intensity to smash the German defences. The infantry had been assured that the massive bombardment would pulverise the enemy, but on 1 July the British attack was itself pulverised with 19,240 dead out of a total of 57,470 losses, more than half the troops committed in the initial attack. By contrast, the French, south of the Somme, deployed eleven divisions with their own artillery, producing a massive and concentrated barrage, and gained all their objectives. The only British units to enjoy any success were those that had planted mines beneath the enemy lines or who advanced behind a creeping barrage.

It is often asserted that on the Somme British infantry marched forward in dense lines which made easy targets for German artillery and machine-guns. In fact British training encouraged open order and fire, and movement in attack. But individual battalion commanders were allowed to make their own decisions about tactics in their sectors, and there were enormous differences in the state of preparation between units. German sources commented on the clumsiness of the British infantry compared to the French, and it is likely that inexperienced officers, and heavy losses of junior leaders, resulted in clumsy huddled masses. But if this made casualties worse, infantry tactics probably had little effect on the actual outcome of 1 July which was due to the impossible task given to the artillery. On 1 July their barrage had been far too dispersed, but on 14 July the British attacked Bazentin Ridge with four divisions on a narrow front of 6,000 yards. A brief surprise artillery attack gave way to a creeping barrage ahead of the infantry who captured all their initial targets, though they were unable to exploit their limited victory.

Despite the level of casualties and many setbacks, Haig persisted on the Somme until November, when the battle finally died away. The same syndrome was operating here as at Verdun and Galicia: initial successes simply petered out in the face of battlefield frictions and enemy resistance. The blood-price was huge: the British and French lost over 620,000 in all. But it was a horrific experience for the Germans too, for their casualties were of the order of 500,000, mostly incurred in the 340 counter-attacks which they launched. On the offensive they were no more successful than their enemies. Even their massive counter-attack on 5 July, intended to take advantage of British disorganisation after 1 July, got nowhere.

The trench line was not invulnerable. Surprise and artillery support, preferably both, could enable an attacker to break in. But the Germans were elaborating defence in depth, meaning that the breakout, always difficult because of the efforts of break-in, became more difficult and costly. New methods like air supremacy and the tanks Haig used at the Somme were useful, but at no stage was a breakout achieved. Sensible generalship allied to good Staff work was needed if all arms were to be combined to maximum effect, and this took time to achieve. Even at sea the stalemate seemed to be continuing. On 1 May 1916 the German fleet had at last challenged the Royal Navy at Jutland, but although they sank more ships, they fled back to port never again to emerge in force, leaving the British blockade intact. In Germany shortages of food and material caused much suffering and dislocated the economy, imposing terrible burdens on the government.

Everywhere the war placed enormous strain on the political systems of the belligerents. The hardships of life and the constant news of casualties at the front threatened to undermine the will to fight. In consequence European politicians suppressed peace movements. This was very obvious in Germany, but the British government acquired sweeping powers by the Defence of the Realm Act (DORA) of 1914. Its first victim was one John Maclean, a Clydeside revolutionary, who was fined £5 for protesting against recruitment to the army. He refused to pay and spent five nights in prison. In Britain in December 1916, David Lloyd George overthrew Asquith in an act which divided the Liberal Party, and ruled as Prime Minister in coalition with the Conservatives. He was later to compare himself and Asquith:

> There are certain indispensable qualities essential to the Chief Minister of the Crown in a great war . . . Such a minister must have courage, composure, and judgment. All this Mr. Asquith possessed in a superlative degree. . . . But a war minister must also have vision, imagination and initiative – he must show untiring assiduity, must exercise constant oversight and supervision of every sphere of war activity, must possess driving force to energize this activity, must be in continuous consultation with experts, official and unofficial, as to the best means of utilising the resources of the country in conjunction with the Allies for the achievement of victory. If to this can be added a flair for conducting a great fight, then you have an ideal War Minister.[17]

There is truth in this typically boastful passage if we add that these are the qualities which a war leader must be perceived to have. For projection was essential if the mass of the population was to have confidence in the direction of the war. Lloyd George would maintain that harmony by enforcing political will, and he impressed the public with a sense of purpose and achievement.

In pre-war Germany the army had honoured the Kaiser as their supreme warlord, while simultaneously denying him any practical role because he was incompetent. But he still had influence, so power was divided between the court, the Chancellor Bethmann-Hollweg, and the General Staff, with the SDP members of the Reichstag watching closely on the sidelines. In 1916 Bethmann-Hollweg suggested concessions which might well have taken Russia out of the war. But Hindenburg and Ludendorff had become supreme commanders and they wanted to hang on to their conquests in Poland and middle Europe. Effectively they became the dictators of Germany, relegating the Kaiser and the Chancellor to marginal roles. Their determination to hold Germany's new empire in Europe endeared them to the Pan-German League, further strengthening their dominance. In Russia Tsar Nicholas was as useless as his cousin Wilhelm, but his General Staff remained bitterly divided and tensions with the Duma and its ministers were extremely sharp. In due course France, after a military crisis in 1917, was delivered over to the rule of Clemenceau. Although sceptical at first, the French army and people were won over by his careful projection of determination, particularly by his frequent visits to the trenches. His soubriquet, 'the Tiger', sums up the popular view of him.

But after the slaughters of 1916 public support for the war was everywhere becoming frayed. Popular discontent and demonstrations in St Petersburg in February 1917 brought down the Tsar, though under Kerensky the new government carried on the war. Despite this, there was optimism in the West. General Nivelle, who became French Commander-in-Chief in December 1916, thought he had the solution to the military deadlock. Massive surprise artillery attacks and creeping barrages, co-ordinated with onslaughts by picked troops, had enabled him to recapture forts Douaumont and Vaux in the later stages of the Verdun battle. He exuded confidence, and this chimed with a new mood of hope in France generated by the US entry into the war on 6 April 1917, largely as a consequence of the German declaration in January 1917 of unrestricted submarine warfare.

Nivelle proposed to unhinge the 70-mile-long German salient between Arras and Craonne, which at its greatest bulged some 40 miles into France, by an attack over the Chemin des Dames at its southern end. This was to be coordinated with a British assault in the north near Arras which would draw away enemy reserves. But between 16 and 20 March the German high command withdrew from most of the salient to the Hindenburg Line (which they called the Siegfried Line) of very well-planned and hardened defences. Nivelle insisted that his methods would work just as well against these and pressed on with the attack. In the north, where the Royal Flying Corps seized air superiority, the British attacked at Vimy Ridge and Arras with some success, partly because the Germans were focused on the Chemin des Dames. Whatever the virtues of Nivelle's strategy and his tactical methods, the implementation was immensely sloppy. Nivelle talked a good offensive, too often and too widely. Security was weak and by 16 April, when the attack was launched, the Germans knew exactly what was intended because they had captured a complete plan of the assault. Within a week the French had lost 30,000 dead and 100,000 wounded.

The tide of expectation built up by Nivelle and the American entry into the war produced an intense reaction in the form of the mutinies which for a time paralysed the French army. In some units there was open demand for peace, the Internationale was sung and red flags waved in emulation of the February Revolution in Russia. But most units simply refused to attack any more, while still resolutely defending France. The government hastily put Pétain in charge because he was known to be trusted by the men whose treatment, in terms of food, support and leave he immensely improved, letting it be known at the same time that France should wait for the Americans. In fact he demanded more modern weapons, improved communications and managed successful small-scale but well-prepared offensives by autumn 1917. Clemenceau's appointment as prime minister soon after firmly extinguished the peace movement. The whole sad story of the French mutinies illustrates the new conditions of war. It was no longer simply a matter of leading troops. They formed only a part of mass culture and its manifestations confined what generals and politicians could do. By 1917 all the participants were painfully aware of the fragility of mass opinion and its intimate connection with military morale.

This prompted new methods of attacking the enemy. As early as 1915 the British had contacted the Hashemite Sharif Hussein bin Ali, Emir of Mecca and king of the Arabs, with a view to fomenting an Arab revolt against Turkish rule. They were even persuaded to back Arab insurgency against their Turkish rulers, supplying weapons, explosives and advisers like T.E. Lawrence. In July 1917 Lawrence managed to create an Arab force which seized the port of Aqaba, and this seems to have convinced the British commander in Egypt, Allenby, of the value of the Arab revolt. The Allies also started to support Slavonic aspirations to break away from Hapsburg rule.

Germany was hopeful that the fall of the Tsar would force Russia to a peace, and this was indeed a real prospect. Out of the chaos of the February Revolution there had emerged in Russia a system of dual power, with Kerensky dominating a government based on the Duma, while popular but very mixed parties ruled the Soviets, councils elected by the 'people'. But Germany's price was a vast empire in Eastern Europe and the Kerensky government recoiled from this. In April 1917 Germany sent Lenin and other agitators into Russia in a sealed train. They fanned the disillusion caused by the failure of the new Russian offensive of July 1917 and ultimately carried out the *coup d'état* of November 1917 which placed them in power in St Petersburg and ushered in the Russian civil war.

Encouraging subversion was just one sign of the desperation felt by the warring powers. The British blockade was strangling Germany, arousing demands there for unrestricted submarine warfare which would impose similar sufferings upon Britain. The problem was that this created great hostility in the US. In February 1915 Germany had declared her intention of attacking enemy merchant shipping (though not neutrals) without warning, but the sinking of the British *Lusitania* with the loss of 128 American lives caused an enormous outcry in the US. The German government was divided on submarine campaigns, but gradually recognised that it was losing the propaganda drive in the US because the scale of British and French arms purchases increasingly bound the US to the Entente cause. In these circumstances Hindenburg and Ludendorff became convinced that the US would side with their enemies, and in 1917 launched unrestricted submarine warfare anyway. They knew that the Americans did not have a real army and assumed that it would take months if not years to create one, and that German submarines would block its transport to Europe. This ignored the reality that in 1917 Germany had only 111 submarines rather than the 222 which the naval staff had calculated would be necessary to bring Britain to her knees. Because of the need to refit vessels and to rest crews, only about forty-six could be active at any one time and, while these did much destruction, the British responded with the convoy system which kept losses in check. In April 1917 the US declared war on the central powers, largely as a result of the submarine policy.

The Russian collapse in the summer of 1917, culminating in the November coup by the Bolshevik Party, should have handed an enormous advantage to the Germans because Lenin's slogan 'Peace and Bread' effectively meant peace at any price. But even the Bolsheviks were shaken by German demands and strung out negotiations; the Germans therefore advanced into Russia and at Brest-Litovsk, 3 March 1918, Lenin agreed to a treaty by which Russia lost a third of her population, about half of her industry and most of her coal mines. The slow death of Russia prevented the Germans from taking advantage of the French mutinies and left the initiative in 1917 with the Allies.

In a series of battles culminating in Passchendaele fought between April and November 1917 the British worked out the way to make progress against a determined opposition, though at a price. The key development was coordination of all arms and careful preparation. Massive artillery pounded enemy strongpoints and laid down creeping barrages behind which the infantry could advance right up to the enemy front line. This was accompanied by counter-battery fire which prevented an enemy response in kind. The dangers of enemy counter-attack were appreciated and troops were held in reserve against it. Communications were improved between infantry, artillery and air. Engineer and Pioneer units were briefed to make roads and bring up the guns to support advances. Tanks were used with some success but limited numbers were available. On balance these battles were a British victory and it might have been greater if the weather had been less appalling. But such progress came at a heavy cost – losses of about 250,000 on each side. And while much had been learned, there was still no breakthrough.

But late in 1917 a battle was fought which was to demonstrate new methods of opening up the front. At Cambrai the British commander, Byng, secretly gathered a large concentration of tanks in a dry area with good going, and launched them on 20 November after a short barrage which then lifted to the enemy rear areas. The result was to open a five-mile gap in the German line. But the advancing tanks soon broke down and none had been held in reserve to exploit success. Insufficient infantry were available to follow up the initial advantage. Cavalry had been brought up but their horses proved vulnerable to small-arms fire even when opposition was minimal. Politicians like Lloyd George, appalled by the blood-toll of earlier battles, saw mechanised warfare as a way of avoiding casualties and many of the generals could see value in such tactics. But for a relatively short battle (20 November–7 December) with only two British corps and one German committed, casualties were heavy – about 44,000 on each side.

Too little attention was paid to the German achievements at Cambrai. They improvised well, using their artillery to stop the tanks and sending in aeroplanes for low-level attacks. But the decisive factor in throwing back the British advance was the introduction into the battle of stormtroopers. Several armies had experimented with infiltrating specially trained troops into enemy lines as a means of disrupting them. At Riga in September 1917 the Germans brought their system to maturity. Lightly armed squads went forward under cover of a surprise bombardment of enemy lines. Equipped with light carbines, the new Bergmann machine-gun and grenades, they avoided strong-points, caused confusion and isolated command posts. They were then followed up by fast-moving infantry with plenty of mortars, flame-throwers, machine-guns and even light 77mm artillery pieces. Later, radio stations in the front lines called in air strikes on key points. In many ways this was the German tradition of *Auftragstaktik* applied to trench warfare.

The system worked on a grand scale at Caporetto, 24 October–9 November 1917. Between June 1915 and September 1917 Italy had fought no less than eleven battles on the Isonzo, the vital gateway into the Hapsburg lands, at a cost of some 300,000 casualties. But at Caporetto in October 1917 a German–Austrian attack headed by stormtroopers made a clean breakthrough, routing the Italian army. They lost 11,000 dead, 20,000 wounded and 275,000 prisoners, together with 2,500 guns, in a chaos immortalised by Hemingway in *A Farewell to Arms*. The Italian army fell back 100 kilometres and was re-formed on the line of the Piave only with British and French assistance. But the Italian example was ignored and even the experience of Cambrai, despite the fact that General Maxse of XVIII Corps urged Haig to draw attention to these new methods.

Undoubtedly one reason for this disregard was Haig's need to prepare his army to face a German offensive. Brest-Litovsk theoretically freed Germany to transfer forty-five divisions to the west, giving it numerical superiority there for the first time since 1914. But the British naval blockade was starving Germany, whose armies consequently pillaged Eastern Europe to feed their people. The hatred this aroused meant that the new German Empire needed strong garrisons, so that in the end only thirty-three divisions left for the western front, where American participation did not yet compensate for the loss of Russia. In 1917 the US army did not have even one formed division. Moreover, so much US industrial capacity was tied up in supplying the British and French that equipment shortages were inevitable. And because the US insisted that her forces be deployed as an autonomous army and not under the command of the British or French, the American soldiers in France were not deployed for battle.

After three years on the offensive, the British and French now had to adapt to defence. Haig wanted to copy the German pattern of defence in depth, which called for a lightly held forward zone, a main battle zone and a rear zone. But on much of the British front these lines simply did not exist. And the German system assumed that local commanders would use their initiative to relieve isolated units by counter-attacks. British command was highly centralised and few officers were imbued with such ideas. Moreover, Haig believed that the German attack would be a frontal assault which his armies would repulse with heavy losses, leaving the enemy weaker than before. The French were little better because they left defensive arrangements to local commanders who continued to pack men into the first line of resistance where they were vulnerable to artillery fire.

Hindenburg and Ludendorff knew they now had a window of opportunity. Russia was out of the war, but the US was not really in it. On 21 March 1918 the Germans launched their 'Peace Offensive', codenamed Michael, which struck the junction between British Third and Fifth armies, though principally the latter under Gough, which formed the link with the French on the Oise. The Germans had made their preparations in secret and brought into play 6,473 guns whose initial whirlwind bombardment, in which gas shells figured prominently, destroyed the forward British units. On a 50-mile front, elements of seventy-six German divisions had been massed for the assault against twenty-eight British. The stormtroop units, for which the British were almost entirely unprepared, were amazingly successful, as a British soldier later recalled:

We got a brew going but, damn it, we hadn't been in the dugout for more than about ten minutes when the Captain popped his head in the dugout door. He said, 'You can all come up. You won't want your rifles.' He said it quite calm, like. Anyway, we came walking up the dugout steps, and there was all these Jerries round us! Of course, we realized what had happened. This was a mopping up party coming. They'd never attempted a frontal attack. That was the strategy, you see; they went through on the right and left. Our whole battalion was caught. A Company was back in Essigny-le-Grand. They were just cooking their breakfast for the Company, because they hadn't had a chance to have any, and Jerry walked in just as they were starting to dish up breakfast for the troops. Fried bacon and bread.[18]

Many British battalion commanders found their HQs overrun before they had even realised a serious attack was developing. Once the outer shell had cracked, a phase of semi-mobile warfare began in which the British command system simply collapsed, just like that of the Italians at Caporetto. The result was a highly confused and expensive retreat back to the Somme. The Germans advanced 40 miles in eight days, but by early

April the British had stabilised their front. The great attack had gained territory, but failed. And at vast expense. The Allies had lost 255,000 men, mostly British, 1,300 artillery pieces and 200 tanks, but Germany lost 239,000 men, amongst them many of the highly trained stormtroops.

On 9 April Ludendorff then tried again with 'Georgette', a thrust to seize the key railroad junction of Hazebrouck and thus to break through to the Channel ports; however, British resistance on the Lys was ferocious and by 29 April when the attack was ended each side had suffered over 100,000 casualties. On 27 May Ludendorff turned south with the Blücher-Yorck offensive on the Aisne, hoping to draw allied reserves so that he could renew his assault in the north. His attack fell upon six British divisions which were being rested from the fighting in the north, in a sector where the French commander had packed the men into the front line. They were wiped out by the bombardment and the French were forced back to the Marne, but by July they were counter-attacking and driving the enemy back. It was an ominous sign for the Germans that they were supported by very substantial American forces. Each side suffered about 200,000 casualties.

Why had the 'Peace Offensive', also called the *Kaiserschlacht* (Emperor Battle) failed? The Germans had long identified the British as their most formidable enemy. In 1916 at Verdun they had sought to smash the French army, as England's strongest sword. Now they tried to drive a wedge between the British and French armies and to force the former back to the Channel ports. This was eminently sensible, and in the early stages the apparent British collapse intensified Pétain's distrust of his allies. But on 3 April the allied Supreme War Council confirmed the French general, Foch, as Supreme Commander of all armies, though Haig remained in charge of the British and Pétain of the French. Allied coordination improved, and this was particularly important in holding back 'Georgette'.

At this point German strategy deteriorated, for the unexpected scale of success of Blücher-Yorck, originally intended as diversionary, drew Ludendorff into more and more attacks pursuing the mirage of Paris. This opportunism undermined the whole strategic thrust of destroying the British, especially as the advance ran into the general problems of attack which the war had thrown up. The rapid progress had to be supported by logistics and guns, and in the case of 'Michael', transporting them across the wilderness of the old Somme battlefield resulted in a loss of momentum which allowed the enemy to recover. The British, with an over-centralised command structure, found it difficult, as had the Italians, to cope with the sudden onset of mobile warfare, but they were well equipped and disciplined, so that their resistance was never negligible, and stiffened as the advance lost momentum. The French were pushed back, shortening their lines of communication and extending those of the Germans. Hindenburg and Ludendorff had embarked on their offensives without any weapon of exploitation. The official Reichstag inquiry into the causes of the German collapse of 1918 concluded that military conservatism and industrial problems had prevented construction and use of tanks:

> the importance of tanks was not at first estimated as highly as was proved necessary by later experience . . . Our industries were capable of producing them. On the other hand, the great difficulties with regard to the provision of material and labor must not be underestimated.[19]

In fact early use of the tank, starting on the Somme in 1916, had produced poor results, and the stormtroop method seemed to hold such potential that a vast industrial effort must have seemed redundant. The Germans also lacked armoured cars or other road-bound fighting vehicles, while their cavalry divisions were policing the new empire in Eastern Europe. Without them, infantry set the pace of the advance, giving defenders time to recover and to harden important targets. So, despite the impressive operational skill of the German General Staff in assembling and training men, they were never able to overcome the general conditions of warfare. But there were other factors at work.

During the German counter-attacks at Cambrai in December 1917 Crown Prince Rupprecht of Bavaria commanding the First, Second, Sixth and Seventh armies, complained: 'The looting of enemy dugouts, depots, and baggage of food etc. weakens the front quicker than the enemy fire and attrition.'[20] This became a major problem as the 'Michael' offensive overran rich magazines and dumps. A German captain recalled:

> When I got to the town [Albert] the streets were running with wine. Out of a cellar came a Lieutenant of the second Marine Division, helpless and in despair. I asked him, 'What is going to happen?' It was essential for them to get forward immediately. He replied solemnly and emphatically, 'I cannot get my men out of this cellar without bloodshed.'[21]

Such problems were indicative of two interrelated factors: the deterioration of the German army and the effects of the British blockade on it and the homeland.

German soldiers were fighting in the Middle East, in Central and Eastern Europe and in Italy. But the bulk of the army by 1918 was concentrated on the western front – by the time of 'Michael' 187 divisions, rising to 208 by the summer of 1918. But the German army was wasting away. Ludendorff remarked that

> As our best men became casualties, our infantry approximated more nearly in character to a militia, and discipline declined . . . Skulkers were already numerous. They reappeared as soon as the battle was over, and it became quite common for divisions which came out of action with desperately low effectives to be considerably stronger after only a few days. Against the weight of the enemy's material the troops no longer displayed their old stubbornness.[22]

Although the Allies never formally undertook attrition as a strategy, they recognised German manpower problems. Haig often spoke of the 'wearing down fight', though most of his battles were designed with break-through in mind. Politicians in all fighting nations were horrified by the blood-toll. But the German army too was unnerved by 'Somme fighting' and its casualties were severe. In the offensives against the British in March–April 1918, total German losses amounted to 348,300. The fact was that there was no cheap way of winning the war and that casualties on a large scale were inevitable. The French General C.M.E. Mangin was called 'the Butcher' by his men because they thought he cared little about casualties, but his comment, 'Whatever you do, [whether attack or defence] you lose a lot of men,'[23] was really no more than an accurate observation. Although the German army inflicted more casualties than it suffered overall, it simply could not afford losses on the scale of 1918.

In fact the stormtroop method adopted by the Germans was in part a reaction to the falling quality of the German army as a whole. The stormtroops were recruited from young single men who were concentrated in particular battalions or even smaller units. They formed a cutting edge to open the way for others. But there were simply too many 'others', older, tired men with family responsibilities, and as a result the Germans resorted to designating and training good-quality divisions with substantial proportions of elite soldiers as attack divisions, while the remainder were called trench divisions, with consequent severe effects on morale. Equally importantly, however, the best storm elements in these divisions suffered disproportionate casualties, while the less good were often poorly organised and presented their enemies with easy targets. A British soldier noted that on 21 March the initial enemy formations were widely spaced, but thereafter: 'We saw infantry advancing in mass on our right front and we managed to do considerable damage with Lewis Guns amongst this horde.' A British officer remarked: 'They were hardly close formations so much as thick waves of men almost shoulder to shoulder following one another at short intervals.'[24] 'Shoulder to shoulder', 'line after line': once again we could almost be talking about the Greek phalanx, the English foot at Hastings or the charge of the Old Guard at Waterloo.

As the various thrusts of the 'Peace Offensive' ground to an inconclusive halt, morale in the German army plummeted. Little had been gained for huge losses. The official Reichstag inquiry into the causes of the German collapse noted that at the start of the spring offensives infantry battalions had on average about 807 men, but by the end of September the figure was below 600 and in many cases as low as 400.[25] The troops knew about the sufferings of their families at home, and as they came across American units the failure of the submarine campaign became all too evident. At home socialist organisations were mounting agitation for peace and publicising the Bolshevik Revolution in Russia as pointing the way to peace.

Hindenburg and Ludendorff had held out the prospect of victory and plenty to the German people, but by July 1918 their offensives had petered out. At this point the German army began to disintegrate, as military failure interacted with civilian suffering. The mass armies of industrial warfare shared the same ethos and culture as the population from which they were drawn. And, as in 1914, the high command had no 'Plan B'. Their gamble had failed and, indeed, even accelerated the American build-up.

Foch sensed the change, and on 18 July launched a vigorous counterattack which drove the Germans back. He was determined to sustain a war of movement which alone could bring decisive results. His strategy was to pummel the enemy in a series of short sharp attacks to keep the Germans off balance, spread their reserves and drive them back. In pursuit of this aim he called on all commanders to attack before German positions consolidated. The result was a series of blows on the German line. The main thrust of the offensive was carried by the British because the French were exhausted and the Americans were only just starting to deploy their forces.

On 4 July four divisions of Australian infantry with some American support attacked the powerfully fortified village of Hamel. Extreme secrecy was preserved. The Australian infantry had been trained to work with tanks whose movement up to the front was concealed by bombing attacks. Aerial and ground observation was used to locate enemy strong-points and batteries. The massive but short artillery preparation pulverised many of these and silenced their batteries, all of which were also attacked from the air by bombing and strafing. Extra ammunition was air-dropped to the infantry. The Australians under General Monash achieved all their objectives in ninety-three minutes, killing about 2,000 Germans and capturing 1,600. Surprise, careful preparation and coordination brought success, but victory came at a price: 900 Australian and American dead and over 300 injured. This was a small-scale battle, but the losses indicated the size of the task which the Allies faced.

But the German army was weakening. On 8 August Rawlinson began the main British offensive at Amiens with twelve British divisions, twelve French and one American. Surprise was achieved by maintaining secrecy, and in particular by restricting radio chatter. Four Canadian divisions were quietly moved into the sector, but their radio signals units were left behind – a form of radio deception. Air superiority was obtained by concentrating almost 2,000 aircraft against less than 400 enemy. A huge mass of artillery, some 3,676 pieces of which nearly a third were 'heavies', was assembled. Of particular value was new equipment for the sound-locating of enemy batteries, a technology which the Germans had simply never developed. Every means was employed to enable the British artillery to dominate the Germans, although there was no real barrage because the German troops were in field trenches and reliance was placed on 400 tanks to drive them out and set in train a battle of movement. Instead the guns were directed to counter-battery fire using substantial amounts of gas shells, which in the event was accurate and highly effective. The results were dramatic – a 7-mile advance on the first day against generally disorganised resistance. But heavier weapons like trench mortars and machine-guns found it diffi-cult to keep up with this movement and many tanks broke down or were knocked out by the improving German artillery. Critically, artillery had to catch up with the infantry. By 13 August an advance of 13 miles had been made. German losses were very heavy – of the order of 74,000 while the British had suffered 22,000.

The tanks had proved a success, but they were mechanically unreliable and liaison with infantry was poor. As a result the high command was divided on their use. But of the excellence and sheer weight of the British artillery, there was no doubt. In support of the assault on the Hindenburg line, 26 September to 4 October, they fired 1.3 million high-explosive and gas shells, 943,847 in the 24 hours from noon 28 September to noon 29

September. German artillery was suffering shortages due to the blockade, and they had failed to keep up with the new technologies which aided their enemies. But the real significance of these battles was the revelation of German morale. Trenches had not been properly dug, and there were large numbers of prisoners, though it was noted that machine-gunners almost invariably held out with remarkable persistence and their fire was sufficient to destroy all efforts to use cavalry. Ludendorff called 8 August 'the black day of the German army', largely because as many as 30,000 German soldiers surrendered. And this became the pattern of the war as the Allies advanced, driving the enemy before them. Some German units fought hard, and in all there was a core of stiff resistance, focused on the machine-gunners. But the German army as a whole had ceased to be dependable and no major counter-attacks were mounted. On 3 September a British brigadier watched the enemy retreating:

> I could see with my glasses every evidence of confusion on the part of the enemy . . . Guns, lorries, Convoys moved Eastwards on the roads and parties of the enemy infantry were everywhere in flight toward BOURLON WOOD. Enemy mounted officers could be seen galloping hither and thither, endeavouring to rally their men but apparently without avail. I noticed, however, a very singular thing. In many places there came moving Westwards through the retiring infantry, parties of enemy Machine Gunners, trudging stolidly forward to the Canal Bank, apparently oblivious to the retirement going on about them.[26]

The fall of the Hindenburg line in September was a crucial event, for the Germans had pinned great hopes on holding this carefully prepared position. The Germans now fell back slowly in short hops, but there was no decisive break-through. Cavalry were occasionally useful in panicking enemy infantry, but it was the general experience of the war that they were much too vulnerable to small-arms fire. Tanks were very slow and broke down frequently because they were mechanically unreliable. There was still, therefore, no really effective weapon of exploitation which could have transformed the retreat into a rout. Moreover, the British army lacked the drive and flexibility to exploit the opportunities offered by the war of movement. British troops had not been trained for this kind of fluid warfare. Crucially, the British army had a highly centralised system of command, so that officers tended to ask for instructions from above, and this had a stultifying influence upon officer initiative: 'an army which was prepared to stand enormous losses uncomplainingly, but was practically devoid of real tactical sense'.[27]

The Americans were learning, and their great courage and dash won some victories, as at St Mihiel 12–15 September 1918. But when 106 Regiment attacked outposts of the Hindenburg position on 27 September they were virtually wiped out, partly through inexperience and partly because they had only eighteen officers to 2,000 men. The French army advanced, but with great caution. Pétain was sceptical of early victory and knew his men were tired. Further, to get US troops across the Atlantic quickly it had been agreed that the divisions would arrive without heavy weapons, which would be provided by the French. The result was that many French divisions lacked fighting capacity because they could gather nothing like the great masses of artillery employed by the British in the north. Pétain was probably working within the practical limitations of his forces, and the heavy casualties the French suffered in the autumn of 1918 argue against any charge of inactivity. The Americans were assigned the difficult Argonne sector, where poor Staff work as much as German resistance checked their advance, thereby also holding up French movement on their flank.

Elsewhere there was even more bad news for Germany. On 1 October Allenby captured Damascus, making Ottoman capitulation inevitable. In 1915 the defeated Serbian army had sought refuge in neutral Greece and the Allies had established a base at Salonica where their army vegetated for years. Bulgaria had joined the central powers in 1915 and with their backing dominated the Balkans, but the German alliance was unpopular. On 15 September 1918 a mixed allied force under General Franchet d'Espèrey struck into Bulgaria, precipitating a revolution in which the pro-German monarch, Ferdinand III (1908–18), was overthrown before six German divisions could render aid. On 24 October the Italians attacked at Vittorio Veneto and by 30 October Austria-Hungary had asked for an armistice. The military situation was clearly crumbling. As early as 11 August Ludendorff had offered his resignation, reporting demoralisation amongst soldiers and angry scenes between reinforcements accused of being 'war-prolongers' by retiring units.

Ludendorff's resignation was refused. On 14 August an imperial conference agreed to put out peace-feelers via Queen Wilhelmina of the Netherlands (1898–1948), but nothing was done. Nobody wanted to be responsible for admitting publicly to defeat, so the army fought on. This was rationalised as providing a stronger negotiating position, but the reality was precisely the opposite of this. On 1 October, Ludendorff and Hindenburg agreed that peace must be sought and instructed the foreign ministry to 'make immediate peace overtures'. The troops, they said, 'are still holding on, but no one can predict what will happen tomorrow . . .

the front could be pierced at any moment'.[28] They suggested the negotiations could best be handled by a new government representative of the parties in the Reichstag.

But Ludendorff and Hindenburg both shrank from any realistic assessment of the terms Germany might expect. At the time of the great offensive many senior military men had felt that outright victory was now beyond reach, but they had hoped that the armies would establish a strong negotiating position. Nobody, however, had thought through what that might mean. Supreme political authority rested with the Kaiser, but he was a broken reed and the Chancellor, Georg von Hertling, was a mere cat's paw of the military. Ludendorff and Hindenburg had filled the vacuum of power in the *Reich*, but they lacked diplomatic antennae and demanded that the basis of the peace should be German annexation of much of Belgium and even parts of France, while they simply assumed that the *Reich* would be allowed to enjoy its new empire in the east. The idea that a triumphant Entente would agree to what would amount to a German victory was sheer fantasy.

When the Chancellor, von Hertling, explained the facts of defeat to the Reichstag representatives, they were astonished and appalled. The majority Social Democrats had backed the government, and now were seen to have failed, to the delight of the breakaway Independent Social Democrats and their left-wing Allies like the Spartacists, who saw in this news of defeat the possibility of revolution. A new Chancellor, Prince Max of Baden, formed a government and decided to approach the American President on the basis of his celebrated 14 Points set out in a speech on 8 January 1918. In this Wilson declared that the war was being fought for free trade, open agreements, democracy and self-determination for all peoples and argued for the creation of a League of Nations. On 5 October Prince Max announced to the Reichstag that he was seeking peace terms. German opinion was totally unprepared for this. Until the very last minute censorship had fed them a diet of lies and half-truths, based on the simple fact that their armies were still everywhere on foreign soil.

Prince Max read hope of a peace of reconciliation into the 14 Points. But the British and French had not been consulted on the 14 points (Clemenceau is said to have remarked that 'God himself only had 10') and they insisted upon the removal of the Kaiser and the unconditional surrender of the German army and navy. Moreover, Prince Max's approach coincided with the torpedoing of the passenger ship *Leinster*, with the loss of 450 lives, mostly women and children. Once the secret of defeat was out, the fighting spirit of the German armies sagged. Ludendorff was dismayed by the stiff terms insisted upon by the Allies, and suddenly decided that the army could fight on after all – at which point he was dismissed on 26 October. The army was holding together, but nobody could know when it might break up under the strain of constant withdrawal, debilitating desertion and the frightening effects of the influenza epidemic.

The sense of defeat finally exploded in the navy. The officers of the battle fleet were deeply ashamed, because while light cruisers and destroyers had skirmished with the British, and submarines were fighting a grim war in the Atlantic, they had done nothing. With no sanction from the new government they proposed to make a grand sally against the British, and the fleet gathered on 28 October. The demoralised crews mutinied at the prospect of a 'death ride' and by early November Kiel and other bases were in a state of revolutionary uproar, igniting discontent across Germany. This gave the parties of the far Left their opportunity to give a revolutionary direction to the discontent. 'Bread and Peace' was an alluring slogan, and their demand for the abdication of the Kaiser provided a focus for the masses. In the face of this, the majority Social Democrats in the government had to move leftwards and on 9 November forced the abdication of the Kaiser. Fear of revolution then obliged the new government to ally with the army to put down the Left.

In the midst of these upheavals in Germany, a delegation crossed the lines on 7 November, and on 11 November signed the armistice agreement in a railway car at Compiègne. This was a capitulation: Germany had to evacuate all occupied territory, surrender huge quantities of war material including the navy, and concede bridgeheads across the Rhine to allied forces. Because it was only an armistice pending a wider settlement, the Allies, fearful that Germany might resume the war, maintained the British naval blockade. It is difficult to see what else could have happened. A full peace would need time, because the collapse of the Hapsburg, Russian and Ottoman Empires had created a complex situation which could not immediately be resolved. And there was nobody except the leaders of the great powers who could restore stability to a shattered continent.

The war of 1914–18 witnessed the implementation of the potential created by the Military Revolution of the late nineteenth century, but the war itself also accelerated technological change. This had been foreshadowed in the American Civil War, but the intensity of development in 1914–18 was unprecedented. By 1918 aviation produced the strategic bomber, wireless was much more reliable and more transportable than ever before, artillery had gained amazing accuracy and was immensely more effective especially with the use of gas shells, while at sea a sound detection system, ASDIC, threatened the submarine. But the new technology had grave limitations. The relatively heavy equipment enhanced the defensive, while the absence of any means of rapid movement away from railheads and the lack of an effective arm of pursuit all made fluid offensive action very difficult indeed. The new weaponry should have rendered close-order, the ancient pattern of war, dead long before 1914. But commanders were fearful of the consequences of the new technology, hence the bayonet-charges and mass infantry formations of 1914 and the belief that the warrior spirit could overcome the firestorm. Slowly the new armies adapted their tactics, but the blunt fact was that without the means for break-through and surprise, the war became one of attrition with, inevitably, massive casualties, though these were largely limited to the fighting men.

Attrition brought into play another consequence of the technological development of the nineteenth century – the rise of popular culture. The new industrial development which made possible the well-armed mass armies of the advanced states also created a new culture which embraced fighting men and civilians alike in a giant war machine. The technical chal-lenges of breaking the enemy line were matched by the enormous effort needed to maintain the will to fight. The revelation of 1914–18 was the immense strength of the modern state. It commanded the loyalty of its people, and governmental structures were so well articulated that almost every aspect of their lives could be bent to its ends; up to a point, at least, it could coerce the unwilling and the doubtful to its cause. In these circum-stances unless one side behaved with catastrophic stupidity (and the French came very near in 1914) a close and protracted struggle was the outcome.

In the end it was Germany that fell victim to attrition. Her economy was sapped by the blockade and by the demands of her weaker allies. Her population was threatened by starvation and her magnificent army was eroded by the sheer number of tasks which it was forced to undertake. But there was nothing inevitable about this process and there were times when the military conflict could have developed in quite different ways. In 1916 and again in 1917 there were serious prospects for a Russo-German peace which would have fundamentally altered the military balance, yet they were scorned and the war in the east continued until 1918. The German collapse was not the result of impersonal forces of nature or simply her own mistakes, and credit must be given to the determination, skill and intelligence of the allies. Above all, the Allies responded skilfully to the challenge of maintaining the support of their populations. The collapse of Russia and the French mutinies of 1917 illustrate how difficult this was and how civilian and military morale were both finely balanced and inti-mately connected. The French and British politicians lived in more or less democratic societies, and although they exercised considerable influence over the press, they enjoyed nothing like total control. Thus something like the reality of what was happening at the fronts seeped into civil society and had to be interpreted by the politicians. For all its excesses, allied propaganda bore some relation to fact, and this was very important in maintaining the will to fight. By contrast the Russian state saw little need to consider public opinion and its sheer inefficiency alienated the masses. The German armies in the west were defeated in 1918, but because of the strength of the defensive and the absence of any rapid means of pursuit, they were never routed. Their defeat paralysed the will of the German state long before there was a total military collapse, although that was very close by 11 November 1918. Because the German government had peddled a vision of inevitable victory for so long, the revelation of defeat shattered the political structure of the Reich and all but overthrew the fabric of German society. War, at least war between the advanced powers, had become total in the sense that it embraced all human activities and, once set in train, was beyond compromise.

By 1918, however, there were clear signs that basic military conditions which had made for attrition were changing in favour of the offensive. After all, great forts and strongly fortified zones had fallen to the enemy. British Major-General J.F.C. Fuller, who had planned the Cambrai attack in 1917, produced 'Plan 1919', according to which highly mechanised forces would penetrate the enemy front and smash the command structure. In the light of the limitations of the tanks of 1918 this was probably more visionary than practicable, but at least such ideas promised a return to war of manoeuvre. And Fuller's was only one of many allied plans, the key characteristic of all of which was coordination of all arms to a common end. Technology was delivering better tanks, more effective aeroplanes and more lethal artillery. New methods of communication, above all wireless, could bring these together and had the potential to penetrate the age-old 'fog of war'. The potential for yet more and more novel technology suggested that the human intellect could find different and better means of waging war. For the experience of 1914–18 clearly placed a high premium on the application of intellect to military problems. This emphasised Clausewitz's conviction that education and perception were vital for the successful conduct of war:

> War is the realm of uncertainty; three quarters of the factors on which action in war is based are wrapped in a fog of greater or lesser uncertainty. A sensitive and discriminating judgement is called for; a skilled intelligence to scent out the truth.[29]

CHAPTER TEN

CULTURE AND WARFARE IN THE AGE OF TOTAL WAR, 1919–1945

Therefore, he who desires peace, let him prepare for war. He who wants victory, let him train soldiers diligently. He who wishes a successful outcome, let him fight with strategy, not at random. No one dares challenge or harm one whom he realises will win if he fights.[1]

'THE war to end all wars' left the peoples of the victor powers clamouring for peace and a better world. At the Versailles Peace Conference, January–June 1919, their statesmen did not do a bad job of rebuilding their world. They took precautions against German revanchism by limiting her army to 100,000 long-term soldiers, prohibiting her from having tanks, aeroplanes, heavy guns or warplanes, and severely restricting the navy, which was allowed neither big ships nor submarines. The Rhineland was demilitarised, making Germany very vulnerable to attack from the west. Reparations, to pay for war damage, caused great indignation in Germany, yet she had imposed a 5 billion franc ($1 billion) charge on France in 1871, guaranteed by German occupation of strategic territories. Moreover, after 1914 Germany had ruined the Belgian economy, shipping 106 iron and steel factories to Germany, and ruthlessly exploited occupied northern France to the distress of its inhabitants. Pending settlement of reparations, the Saar was placed under League of Nations administration. Germany lost Alsace-Lorraine which she had stripped from France in 1871, and substantial territories in the east, but in most of them there were large non-German populations so this accorded with the principle of the self-determination of peoples on which the Allies attempted to base their settlement in Europe.

The victor powers were never all-powerful, especially after the US refused to ratify the Versailles peace treaty in 1920, leaving France and

Britain as its guarantors. Their intervention against Bolshevik Russia failed in 1920, though the Japanese persisted in Siberia until 1922. They could do nothing about the appalling civil war in China or the havoc which marked Germany's reluctant withdrawal from her eastern empire to the Versailles frontiers. The Polish–Soviet War of 1919–21 was essentially about control of Belarus and Ukraine and ended with a partition of these provinces which stood quite outside the Versailles settlement.

Many criticised Britain and France because they were certainly not disinterested, acquiring 'League of Nations Mandates' to extend their empires, and encouraging the Greek invasion of Turkey which ended in complete failure in 1922 as Turkey recovered under Kemal Atatürk. But the real weakness of the Versailles settlement was that it had powerful and numerous enemies. Germans could never accept that their army, which still stood on foreign soil in November 1918, had been defeated and they clung to the notion of the 'stab in the back', that it had been betrayed by the 'Left'. This belief was reinforced by the nation's impoverishment and inflation in the 1920s. The Reichstag inquiry of 1925–8 into the causes of the German collapse gave official endorsement to this fantasy:

> Thus the possibility of the continuation of the war by Germany cannot be disputed. It was prevented only by the revolution which broke the sword in the commander's hand, subverted all order and discipline in the Army, above all behind the front, and rendered all further resistance impossible.[2]

Thus a poisonous myth was allowed to flourish, drawing its toxins from the detritus of defeat. Russia, torn by civil war, was not invited to Versailles and its eventual Bolshevik rulers wanted to overthrow the whole capitalist world. Hungary, stripped of half its territory, nursed deep grievances, while Austria protested that although the Versailles settlement claimed to be based on the self-determination of peoples, she was forbidden from joining Germany. Romania and Italy, both former allies of Britain and France, felt insufficiently compensated for their sufferings. Poland harboured ambitions upon Slovakian territory, while Yugoslavia housed a collection of peoples with diverse interests. Japan was angered by the frustration of her imperial ambitions in the Pacific and the contempt with which she was regarded by the US.

Versailles was a flawed settlement, but how could it have been otherwise? The peacemakers knew this and could only hope that time would heal many wounds. The French still feared Germany, and so they tried to safeguard their position by a system of alliances. Belgium became a close ally while the 'Little Entente' of Czechoslovakia, Romania and Yugoslavia formed a substitute, albeit a poor one, for the old pact with Russia. When the German government encouraged galloping inflation as a means of devaluing reparations, France occupied the Ruhr in January 1923 to ensure payments were made in goods and not worthless currency. This was perfectly legal under the Versailles settlement, but the soldiers were heavy-handed and the encouragement of a puppet Rhenish Republic in October 1923 was widely seen as extreme.

Britain and the US feared that French *realpolitik* was alienating the Germans, and in 1924 forced through the Dawes Plan which moderated reparations and ended the occupation of the Ruhr. The French compromised, signing up to the Locarno treaties of October 1925 by which the leading states, including Germany, agreed to a system of collective security in Europe. But France maintained her alliances against Germany and stood somewhat estranged from Britain on the German issue. Thus the two main props of the Versailles settlement could not act together, and neither felt confident enough to act on its own. The French felt they would not be supported if the need for determined action arose. Britain had purchased victory at the expense of her huge overseas investments, and her rulers were uneasily aware of the stagnation of many parts of her industrial base. Unrest in many colonial territories was becoming endemic and the value of all those patches of 'red on the map' was in doubt. Above all, they did not want to be drawn into another continental imbroglio by the French. And Britain's rulers, much more than the French, were powerfully influenced by an idealistic vision of keeping the world's peace which was beginning to exert a considerable hold on international affairs.

The most obvious manifestation of this vision was the League of Nations, established as part of the Versailles settlement in 1919 in an attempt to make the conduct of nations subject to the rule of law. This reinforced the principle of the self-determination of peoples (though not colonial peoples) which had been so important in the settlement of Central and Eastern Europe. A very practical result of the desire to avoid war was the Washington Naval Treaty of 1922. A major naval arms race had seemed likely after the war, but Britain, France, Japan and the US were persuaded to limit their fleets. The Geneva Protocol of 1925 banned the use of poison gas. And idealism was starting to influence the use of violence.

India, the jewel in the British crown, had made great sacrifices during the war, notably in the form of 43,000 dead. It had been anticipated that in return the imperial authorities would offer a real share of governmental responsibility. The Government of India Act of 1919 disappointed this expectation and led to unrest. In April Indian troops under General Dyer perpetrated the Amritsar Massacre, opening fire and killing over a thousand demonstrators. The British and Indian governments tried to cover up the whole affair, but the outcry in Britain, fed by strong press interest, was enormous. By contrast, during the Indian Mutiny many rebels had been tied across the mouths of cannon and blown to smithereens without the least protest. These new attitudes had tremendous effects on the way the British controlled India.

Even more telling was the case of Ireland. Irish rebellion and subsequent repression had been a commonplace in the nineteenth century. In 1919 the Irish insurgency against British rule profited enormously from the firepower of magazine rifles, machine-guns and grenades. Michael Collins directed his men against the police and intelligence officers who were the eyes and ears of the British administration. The British authorities were experienced in counter-insurgency warfare and by 1922 were enjoying considerable success against the rebels. However, they were themselves under pressure from British public opinion which, informed by an active press, reacted very badly to the violence of the authorities in Ireland, notably the burning of Cork on 11 December 1920 as a reprisal for an attack in the city. The result was a compromise, the Anglo-Irish Treaty of 1922, by which Britain relinquished control of southern Ireland but not the north.

Public reactions of this kind were by no means universal or consistent. The French faced a very major rebellion against colonial rule in the Rif mountains of North Africa, but the area was very distant from the homeland and their army controlled newspaper access to the rebels, who were destroyed in 1925 with minimal agitation in metropolitan France. Britain crushed rebellions in India and Iraq, while her suppression of the Arab revolt in Palestine, 1936–39, resulted in 5,000 Arab deaths without any strong public condemnation. But the debates in the League of Nations set the tone for world affairs, and there the new sensitivity and hostility to violence were very important.

In addition, in Britain popular culture was assimilating the experience of 1914–18, and the way in which this happened had an immense impact on policy. Before 1914 Britain had never fought a war in which she fielded an army large enough to take on the main force of a first-class continental enemy. The price of victory in 1918 was 1.1 million British and empire dead, and huge numbers maimed. These are horrific figures, but what matters is to understand how they and the war were viewed. In 1918 the shock generated by the losses was balanced by real pride in British achievement, but this was in time obscured by developments which had nothing to do with the war itself. Politicians failed to keep their promises, symbolised by the 1918 election slogan 'Homes fit for heroes'. The industrial strife and subsequent unemployment of the 1920s merged into the great slump after 1929. By the late 1920s individual deprivation was starting to eclipse the sense of national achievement. The long wrangles in the early 1920s over German reparations, the revival of Germany after 1933, and the new risks of war, encouraged a sense of futility.

In 1927 Captain P.A. Thompson published *Lions Led by Donkeys*, which was subtitled *Showing how Victory in the Great War Was Achieved by Those Who Made the Fewest Mistakes*.[3] His savage criticism of the British high command was given wide currency, not least by the striking title. In 1929 Robert Graves published *Goodbye to All That*, an autobiography which exemplified the mood of disillusion. This book was an important element in a tide of angry literature produced by intellectuals who had experienced the horrors of the trenches. They were not particularly well informed about strategy and certainly not representative of the attitudes of those who fought, but they propagated with great literary skill a vision of the war as a pointless waste presided over by incompetent generals.

This disenchantment was magnified by the dominance of left-wing opinions amongst British intellectuals who were highly responsive to criticism of the 'establishment', and their influence spread across the Labour and trade union movements and beyond. On 9 February 1933, and in a blaze of publicity, only a few days after Hitler had been sworn in as German Chancellor on 30 January, the Oxford University Union passed the resolution: 'This House would under no circumstances fight for its King and country' by 275 votes to 153. At the same time, amongst the ruling class, the self-regarding myth of the 'lost generation'– that so many public schoolboys had been killed that the country was deprived of leadership – emerged. The traditional British elite of the aristocracy and upper middle class seem to have lost their nerve and with it that drive to power which had created a mighty empire. Casualties had much to do with this, but so had the creation of a mass democracy after 1919. Britain was no longer 'theirs' and they were forced to bow to the winds of change embodied in popular culture. The memory of 1914–18, the 'casualty myth', as it might be called, was an important factor in inhibiting any serious consideration of intervention in Europe.

The sense grew that the war had been futile, a terrible bloodletting which had solved nothing and should never be repeated. And British politicians were deeply unwilling to confront the grave strategic problems which they faced. Britain was pledged to protect the security of Australasia, but she had agreed to the Washington Naval Treaty of 1922 which established a 5:5:3 ratio between the British, American and Japanese fleets. This meant that in the Pacific both Japan and the US, who kept their main battle fleets there, were stronger than the British whose forces were concentrated in European waters. Before 1914 Britain had an alliance with Japan, but subsequently had developed a preference for friendship with the US. Because the US was deeply hostile to Japan and especially her ambitions in China, the British spurned the Japanese alliance. However, the Americans strongly disliked the British Empire and would do nothing to support it. All this had implications for the defence of India and the Far Eastern territories. The Royal Navy's response was the creation of the massively fortified Singapore base on which it had spent £60 million by 1939. But actually using the base would involve stripping the fleet in home and Mediterranean waters. This, of course, was only possible if there was peace in Europe, a dubious assumption in view of the seething resentments across the continent.

In these circumstances, British politicians failed to look into the face of war, to consider realistically the European and worldwide threats to the peace, and they put their trust in the League of Nations. To use it as a forum for settling disputes was quite reasonable, but it was a new body with an uncertain future. The idealism which created it was not widely shared, and even the British and their friends were reluctant to allow intervention in their own imperial matters. At heart British politicians clung to the League as a means of avoiding hard decisions about British and imperial security. And they were the more anxious to trust the League because in Britain a new and expensive system of social security was emerging which could be paid for by cutting the increasingly unpopular realm of defence. The result was constant demands for economy and the Ten Year Rule, the 'advice' given annually to the services between 1919 and 1932, to prepare their budgets on the assumption that there would be no major war within the next ten years. In the absence of any real threat in the 1920s this was not unreasonable, but it provided no solution to the problems of imperial defence which were simply put aside. The result of these attitudes was that at the strategic level Britain suffered from an intellectual vacuum, because of a deep unwillingness to confront the military choices the country faced, and this became even more apparent in the bracing international situation of the 1930s.

For the British nothing in the Treaty of Versailles was more crucial than the limitations on the German navy. Yet the German Weimar Republic demonstrated its discontent with such restrictions by commissioning *Deutschland, Admiral Scheer* and *Admiral Graf Spee*, 'pocket battleships' which were launched between 1931 and 1934. Their speed meant that only cruisers could catch them, but no cruiser could match their 11-in. guns. They were over the limits imposed by Versailles and clearly commerce-raiders, but even such a direct threat to British interests evoked no response. By 1931 the First Sea Lord was reporting that the navy was not strong enough to defend both the homeland and the distant parts of the empire. In that same year the Mukden Incident provided Japan with the excuse to seize Manchuria from China, ratcheting up tensions in the Far East. The League of Nations condemned this invasion, but the only result was that in 1933 Japan left that body. In the same year the Nazis, sworn to German military revival and the dismantling of Versailles, came to power.

Hitler's rise to power inspired no reformulation of British policy. Any suggestion of the obvious, that Britain would have to give priority to homeland defence, risked shaking British prestige and damaging the empire irrevocably. The refusal of successive governments to consider the implications meant that as government had no clear sense of priorities, the individual services lacked guidance. Without a lead, the intellectual vacuum in government communicated itself to the services where internal pressures and vested interests became very important. This was particularly disastrous because technological development was proceeding apace. Above all, the forces also lacked money, because governments were anxious about economic weakness and determined to keep down taxes and this crippled any attempt to modernise, especially in the army.

It is not difficult to see the problems which this new cultural atmosphere presented for the army. Recruitment became difficult and its official strength declined from 231,062 in 1922 to 207,537 in 1931; even the onset of the Depression after 1929 did not improve matters. The army had suffered the massive casualties of the war and these were increasingly seen as the result of blundering at senior levels. Colonel Blimp was created in the early 1930s by the cartoonist David Low in the *London Evening Standard*. His pompous pronouncements amused a generation, and reinforced the notion of army incompetence. Low is said to have conceived Blimp after hearing two officers in a Turkish bath arguing that officers should wear spurs in their tanks. While the British saw the navy as their traditional protector, and the air force had real glamour, the army bore the burden of the new memory of World War I and the ridicule associated with it.

The British army conducted a careful examination of the experience of 1914–18, though it avoided any real criticism of the high command. It came to the conclusion that fluid and highly coordinated actions by all arms were the key to future warfare. Whilst appreciating the importance of air power in attack and defence, it was widely accepted that tanks would be of overwhelming importance in land battle and a real interest in armoured warfare developed, especially under Lord Milne, Chief of the Imperial General Staff 1926–33. As the inventors of the tank the British Royal Tank Corps had a lead over all other armies in 1919, and this was sustained throughout the 1920s. By 1923 the British Vickers tank could reach 20 mph and the mobility of armour was clearly demonstrated in a series of annual manoeuvres. In 1927 the Experimental Mechanized Force was established, demonstrating the extraordinary effectiveness of tanks, especially after 1928 when they began to be fitted with wireless. But the British failed to communicate the central ideas of an integrated approach to the army as a whole, and never laid down, as the Germans did, a doctrine of war and a set of drills by which to implement it. This was partly, no doubt, due to British pragmatism and dislike of wide-ranging doctrine. But it was also due to the fact that the British army had little real corporate existence. As the great historian of the British army, Sir John Fortescue (1859–1933), remarked, 'The army was, and within my own lifetime continued to be, not an army at all, but only a collection of regiments.'[4]

The main reason for this remarkable state of affairs was the need to find troops for the Empire, especially for India where 60,000 British soldiers were usually present to balance the 190,000 native troops under British officers. All these units spent much time supporting the civil power or fighting the tribes of the North-West Frontier. Battalions were also in constant movement to other posts in the Empire. In 1927 a large force was rushed to Shanghai to defend the International Settlement. The Arab revolts in Palestine in 1929 and 1936–9 imposed enormous strains. Officers had little opportunity to look beyond day-to-day commitments. When not in transit or action they spent many hours in the routine activities of a garrison, whiling away their time in obscure places where they had little contact with ideas and where sport and hunting were the approved leisure activities. There were thinking and ambitious officers, like Montgomery, but they existed in a curious vacuum where ambition was deprecated and intellectual ability denigrated. Indeed, many battalion commanders regarded applying for the staff as a kind of treachery.

By contrast the German inquest on the war was conducted by the *Truppenamt* (Troop Office) which was a disguised form of the General Staff which had been prohibited by Versailles. This intellectual elite came to much the same conclusions as the British about the need for the integration of all arms and fluid attack and took a keen interest in British tank manoeuvres, matching the data so obtained with their own secret experiments in Russia. However, they spread their conclusions throughout the army and formulated ideas for implementation. In essence they reasserted the value of *Auftragstaktik*. In their view attack should be ruthless, fast and made with total concentration of strength. The result was *Kesselschlacht* (cauldron battle) which required formations to move into weak points to outflank and surround strong enemy units. Rapid advance was to be spearheaded by armoured vehicles, facilitated by radio communications and road transport, and supported by air action, creating an intense pattern of war. This was to apply at all levels, so that even NCOs would be expected to show flexibility in order to achieve the ends laid down for them.

The low-level initiative demanded by this tactical system was possible because very soon after the war the decision was made to train every man in the 100,000-strong force to a level which would enable him to assume the responsibilities of two ranks above, in order to cater for future expansion. This created a lively and well-educated army, in which there was every encouragement to seek professional betterment. The various branches of the German army bickered over resources, and plenty of German generals were deeply suspicious of new technology. But the basic doctrine of swift and coordinated attack represented a consensus, and all subsequent debate about means and weapons took place upon that basis.

By contrast, British officers were prohibited from 'talking shop' in the mess and their intellectual level was poor. The British valued the high morale and coherence of traditional battalions which had served them well in the trenches of the war. But the British army, even at its best in 1918, had lacked coherence, drive and initiative and had relied on a very centralised command system. Class prejudice was important. Officers and men inhabited different worlds. Wellington famously regarded the rank and file as 'the sweepings of the earth' and this attitude had persisted during the war with a refusal to adapt and use the considerable skills of an educated conscript army. Nothing was done to improve this.

In the absence of any clear view of the demands of modern war and the direction of military development, the army found itself quarrelling endlessly over limited resources. In 1921 the Committee on National Expenditure chaired by Sir Eric Geddes reduced the army estimates from £75 million to £55 million; not for nothing was it remembered as the 'Geddes Axe'. But government also imposed a long-lasting regime of economy. From 1923 to 1933 the army's allowance for maintenance and purchase of weapons averaged only £2 million a year, and this sharply limited its ability to experiment. In these circumstances cavalry, infantry, engineers, artillery and tankmen all argued for resources. With no common agreement on doctrine, or even a common view that doctrine was necessary, there was nothing to hold them together. They could agree on, for example, the need for technical corps to provide motor vehicles and signals, but these served them all. Tanks were expensive and raised fundamental questions about priorities.

The debate was all the more bitter because it became very public. General J.F.C. Fuller had been a great champion of armour within the army, but in 1927 had refused command of the tanks when offered it by Lord Milne. He then left the army and became the public advocate of tank armies, polarising opinion between tankmen and others. In parallel with this, the rather wider ideas of the journalist B.H. Liddell Hart, who had served as a captain during and after the war, caused enormous offence. His frequent attacks on the generals scandalised opinion within the forces, especially when it was noted that politicians were strongly influenced by his ideas. The army's leadership, repelled by the new popular culture, failed to understand the need to lead public opinion and fumed when others stepped into their place. In all this confusion and bitterness the central lesson of the war – coordination of all arms – was forgotten. In particular the Experimental Mechanized Force was disbanded, which ended the only real effort to coordinate infantry and tankmen. As a result these two arms of the land battle tended to go their own separate ways.

The debate about tanks in Britain was not dissimilar to the disagreements across Europe, because they were new and there was, therefore, a good deal of uncertainty about what sort of tanks to produce. Weight of armour increased the tank's protection but reduced the speed which enabled it to strike quickly and to avoid artillery attack. High-velocity cannon were needed to knock out other armoured vehicles, but guns of a different type and calibre were required to support infantry. Decisions on such matters were of course influenced heavily by national strategies. The French took a broadly defensive stance, and while they had light cavalry tanks for reconnaissance, they developed super-heavy vehicles to support their infantry, the Char B1, an infantry tank of 28 tons, massively armoured against enemy artillery, but with a maximum speed of just 17 mph, and the Char 3C weighing 81.5 tons.

The Germans and Soviets were developing extremely aggressive strategies, and were increasingly drawn to the mediums which represented a compromise between protection, speed and hitting power. The early German tanks were very light, but by 1940 the Panzer Mark IIIs and

Mark IVs were entering service with their sturdy carapaces and effective guns. In the Soviet Union the T34, a simple and robust design with sloping armour, a powerful diesel engine and a 76mm gun with impressive hitting power, was under development. The French knew that in the end they too would have to take the offensive and produced the excellent Somua S35. None of these armies was truly certain how to deploy their tanks in relation to other arms of their forces, but notions of coordination were very strong in Germany and the Soviet Union.

The British ultimately produced light tanks for reconnaissance and by 1936 were putting into service the heavily armoured infantry tank, the Matilda, with its low maximum speed of 11mph. The British medium, the Valentine, entered service only in late 1940. None of these tanks had been properly trialled and in all of them the guns were clearly inadequate. Even worse, coordination with infantry was barely considered, with the obvious consequence that anti-tank guns were not used to support and protect armour. The situation was further bedevilled by the fact that in the 1930s the British mechanised their cavalry, giving tanks to people who had no real belief in them and who had not studied their use. The Royal Scots Greys did not go over to tanks until 1941. Cavalry officers were permitted to retain two chargers at army expense, as a kind of compensation for being lumbered with these smelly mechanical monsters. The officers of these socially exclusive regiments looked down upon the Royal Tank Corps, creating a sharp division amongst the tankmen themselves. What was astonishing about the British was that they threw away the real lead in tank design and use which they had enjoyed in the 1920s. This was essentially the result of the intellectual vacuum at the heart of the army, which reflected that in government.

If coordination within the army failed, it was almost non-existent between the different forces. The Royal Navy, like its counterparts in the US and Japan, was focused almost entirely on fleet action, at the heart of which was the confrontation of battleships. But it was extraordinary that despite the experience of the submarine threat during the war, the navy sacrificed anti-submarine warfare to the demands of economy. Trust was placed in ASDIC but insistence on secrecy meant there was little realistic testing of this device. In 1918 the Royal Navy had twelve aircraft carriers and ambitious plans for more, some for submarine detection and commerce protection. The interest in a possible war against Japan in the Pacific should have inspired progress in naval aviation, but in 1918 government merged the Royal Naval Air Service into the Royal Air Force, and though the Fleet Air Arm was re-established in 1924 it was under

dual control with the RAF until 1937. This was an unsatisfactory situation, especially as many senior airmen remained in the RAF. This meant
that the navy lacked a body of air-minded officers to balance those
wedded to the battleship who regarded all new technology with disdain.

Because debate over such matters was not encouraged and because the
navy too suffered from cuts in expenditure, the Royal Navy failed to explore
new possibilities. The US and Japan pioneered new aircraft and other developments like catapults, arrester wires and deck storage of aircraft. In 1934
Ark Royal was laid down, but launched only in 1938. She could carry fifty
modern aircraft: by contrast the Japanese *Shōkaku* launched in 1939 took
just two years to build and accommodated over seventy aircraft while the
USS *Lexington* could carry ninety-one. Moreover, because of the pressures
for economy and the attitude of the RAF, British naval aeroplanes were
outmoded, especially compared with those of the Japanese. The US and
Japan regarded one another as potential enemies and each saw the necessity
for naval aviation in the vast open spaces of the Pacific, even if they thought
battleships would ultimately be the arbiters of any conflict there. The Royal
Navy had no comparable view of its task to act as a stimulus. In Britain the
experience of radio interception in the war underpinned the maintenance of
an important intelligence branch, but the navy failed to develop radar.

The RAF in 1918 was the world's first independent air force.
Trenchard, its first commander, argued that strategic bombing, by striking
at enemy cities and industries, could bring victory without a costly clash
of armies. The leaders of the RAF focused on strategic bombing because
it provided for their new force a unique and uniquely important role
which would enable it to protect its independence. The idea had considerable appeal to politicians because it offered both a way of avoiding the
slaughter of the war and a means of deterring possible enemies. It gained
credibility because bombing proved quite effective against Afghan attacks
in 1919, a Somali revolt in 1920 and the Iraqi revolt of 1922–5, greatly
reducing military costs. And the RAF also tapped into popular culture.
Aeroplanes fascinated people in the 1920s. Air shows were immensely
popular, and children were allowed to run out of school to see any flying
machine that passed over.

The romance of the 'air aces' had been cultivated by governments
during the war, but it took on a life of its own in endless novels and
comics, most notably with Biggles, the character created by W.E. Johns in
Britain in 1932. In 1921 the publication of G. Douhet's *Command of the
Air* with its apocalyptic vision of air attack reducing modern states to
chaos had seized the public imagination. In 1933 H.G. Wells's novel, *The*

Shape of Things to Come portrayed the destruction of civilisation by aerial warfare, and in 1936 its impact was amplified by an immensely popular film, *Things to Come,* for which he wrote the screenplay. It was on the basis of such ideas that in 1932 British Prime Minister Stanley Baldwin proclaimed:

> I think it is well also for the man in the street to realize that there is no power on earth that can protect him from being bombed, whatever people may tell him. The bomber will always get through . . .[5]

This was the mantra of the RAF where the bomber barons reigned. But the RAF refused to carry out careful studies to ascertain what it could actually do and what it could hit with reasonable accuracy. And the airy assumption that simply scattering bombs would cause enormous terror excused the RAF from gathering intelligence which could locate vulnerabilities in potential enemies. By 1939 the RAF had no satisfactory bombsight and only the most limited ways of navigating and finding targets. The RAF had signally failed to think through the needs of the strategic mission which it so loudly trumpeted. Above all, its leaders annoyed the army by refusing to take seriously attacks in aid of the ground forces – effectively flouting the principle of military coordination in favour of strategic bombing.

But by the mid-1930s the notion that the bomber would always get through was being seriously challenged. New and faster fighter aircraft were emerging. In 1937 the Hurricane, with its 300mph top speed, was the first modern fighter to enter RAF service. It was of traditional frame construction covered in cloth, but the Spitfire which followed it into service in 1938 was monocoque (metallic stressed skin construction), and, paired with a superb Merlin engine, matched anything then flying and proved capable of great development. The bomber barons resisted the building of fighter fleets, but the experience of the Spanish Civil War (July 1936–April 1939) told against them because the Russian Rata I–16, capable of nearly 300 mph, proved highly effective against bombers whose attacks on cities often had limited effects. This encouraged the development of anti-aircraft defences.

The air raids on Britain during the war had brought home to the British their vulnerability to aerial attack and in 1925 the Royal Observer Corps, staffed by civilian volunteers, was established. Gradually a nation-wide network of watching posts emerged linked by telephone to the RAF. Experiments with sound detection resulted in the construction of acoustic mirrors along the east coast, especially in the south. Faster aircraft rendered these outmoded, prompting the government in 1933 to set up the Committee for Scientific Survey of Air Defence under an exceptional scientific civil servant, H. Tizard, to oversee the search for some means of air defence. The priority accorded to this committee's work reflected deep anxieties about the threat to Britain posed by the ever-changing technology of air war, which resulted in the creation of Fighter Command in 1936 despite the objections of the bomber barons. Ultimately the Committee instigated a string of radar stations, called 'Chain Home', around the British coasts. British radar was far behind German experiments with short-wavelength sets. Even so, radar would prove to be an outstanding success because it was integrated with the Observer Corps into an air defence system with raid plotting and control of aircraft under Fighter Command. This was possible because Tizard and the new chief of Fighter Command, H.C.T. Dowding, worked well together. But this was a very isolated example of coordination and it was not part of any formal strategy of giving priority to home defence.

By 1934 Britain was starting a limited rearmament as the international climate had worsened, but this brought about no real formulation of British defence policy, which remained fragmented. With no clear lead coming from the politicians, the services prepared piecemeal and with little reference to one another. In this situation appeasement of Nazi Germany was a logical policy. Paying Danegeld was a classic way of meeting a threat and by and large the British were able to pay in other people's coin.

The Anglo-German naval agreement of 1935 was a betrayal of Versailles, but it was seen as safeguarding Britain's naval security at a time when Germany was rearming. Acceptance of Hitler's militarisation of the Rhineland in 1936 weakened France, but on the face of it affected Britain little, and the same was true of the absorption of Austria in 1938. Appeasement bought time for some military and economic preparation. A notable example of the creation of an economic infrastructure for war was the building in 1938 of a huge shadow factory at Castle Bromwich specially to produce the Spitfire. Its creator, Supermarine, was a small Southampton firm which only now acquired real manufacturing capacity. But at the heart of British policy was an intellectual vacuum. In the event of war what were the priorities, and how should Britain fight?

In 1932 Liddell Hart, in *The British Way of Warfare*, devised the notion of 'limited liability'. He argued that Britain should never again commit to a continental land war, but should rely on its traditional shield, naval supremacy, augmented by the air force, to strike at any enemy. This had an obvious appeal, especially to Neville Chamberlain, Chancellor of the

Exchequer 1931–7 and Prime Minister 1937–40, who adopted this position as a coherent argument against the costs of army expenditure. In May 1937 Chamberlain appointed L. Hore-Belisha to the War Office, and he in turn made Liddell Hart his unofficial adviser, effectively adopting 'limited liability' as official policy. Thus the very idea of committing an army to a continental war became unthinkable, though there had never been any real testing of 'limited liability' by debate in army circles. In September 1938 Chamberlain, in an ultimate payment of Danegeld, agreed at Munich to the German occupation of much of Czechoslovakia. Hitler's annexation of the rest of the country in direct contravention of that agreement on 15 March 1939 led to the British alliance with Poland signed on 31 March. On 22 February 1939 the British government had authorised the formation of a British Expeditionary Force (initially of four divisions) to support the French. In April 1939, under the pressure of circumstances, a sudden decision was taken to introduce conscription, causing chaos in the army.

In the event, in 1939 the British army could only muster four poorly equipped divisions for dispatch to Europe. One of these was a mobile division, but there was little idea of how the infantry, tank, artillery and other elements within it should be employed. Six more divisions arrived by the spring of 1940, many of them poorly equipped and trained. It is a mark of how hastily improvised the British Expeditionary Force was that its commander and Chief of Staff were not appointed until after war was declared. Because the British government had so long resisted the creation of an expeditionary force the British had no strategy and simply had to fit in with the French. It was a sad end for the triumphant army of 1918, and it represented at all levels of power not just an intellectual failure, but even an inability to recognise that as war became more complex the intellect mattered in military affairs.

In this Britain was not alone: the American army had a similar experience. In the 1920s America was gripped by a violent reaction against intervention in European affairs. The navy was traditionally seen as the bulwark of defence, while there was widespread fascination with aeroplanes. So it was the army which bore the brunt of economy, and it was dispersed across the huge continent and its overseas empire. But the US army did examine the war in detail and drew from this an interest in mechanisation natural in a nation obsessed with industrial development. As the army expanded in 1940, so a United States Armoured Force evolved, and new tanks were developed. But there was no coherent doctrine of all-arms warfare and the technological obsession resulted in the infantry receiving poor leadership and training, with the assumption that it would be machines that would really defeat the enemy. One small part of the US ground forces evolved a specialised doctrine of war. The US Marines in the nineteenth century had been used as a rapid intervention force in broadly colonial situations, and played a spectacular, if minor, part in the war. But as the US considered the Japanese challenge, the leaders of the Marine Corps saw here a distinctive role for their force. They began to work on the problems of amphibious assault and developed ideas for specialist equipment and, above all, the techniques of all-arms attack.

The US Army Air Force (USAAF) was deeply envious of the independence of the RAF and espoused strategic bombing as the key to acquiring its own autonomy. Although part of the army, the airmen neglected close air support in favour of the strategic role. The sheer size of the United States was an incentive to the growth of the civilian aero-industry which could thus support the development of military aviation. New internal combustion engines provided power, and new processes reduced the price of aluminium, making possible monocoque construction. By 1935 the Douglas DC-3 Dakota, a twin-engined all-metal monocoque airliner had appeared. It proved to be a marvellous air transport and remained in regular service until the 1970s.

In 1934 the Martin B-10 was the first all-metal monoplane bomber to enter US service, but in that year tenders were invited for a four-engined bomber capable of a top speed of over 200 mph and an altitude of 10,000 feet with endurance of ten hours: the B-17 Flying Fortress entered service in 1936. Its size and range reflected the expectation that it would be used in any war with Japan across the vast Pacific distances. Roosevelt backed the rapid expansion of US airpower in the late 1930s because bomber forces offered a deterrent which, it could be argued, would help to defend 'the western hemisphere', and this avoided confronting isolationist sentiment among his electorate. Roosevelt's policy readily embraced fighters, which would be needed to defend the Philippines and the fleets in the Pacific. In 1936 the Curtiss P-36, a metal and fabric plane capable of 300 mph, was introduced, but quickly supplanted by the all-metal P-40. For naval use the Wildcat and the Hellcat, introduced into service in 1939, were robust fighters. By 1940 Roosevelt was floating the idea of a 10,000-plane air force as industrial capacity increased to supply Britain and France.

Germany, by contrast, had a very focused view of modern aerial warfare. Her ground forces aimed to mobilise and attack with all branches in fluid movements made possible by mechanisation and modern communications. To this end, when the Luftwaffe came into being in 1935 it was closely integrated with the army from which many of its senior officers were drawn. The most obvious manifestation of this was the Stuka (Ju 87), a precision dive bomber which entered service in 1936 and acted as flying artillery for the army. It was effective because of good army liaison arrangements and wireless communication. But the Luftwaffe was equipped for far more than mere close support. Its medium bombers, like the Do-17 and the Heinkel 111, available by 1937, were well adapted to strike at targets in the enemy's rear and at his centres of production. The Ju 88, introduced in 1939, served as a fast bomber, heavy fighter and dive-bomber. The Luftwaffe recognised the importance of strategic bombing, but development proved difficult because the long Versailles prohibition had crippled German engine development. The He 177 Ural bomber had much potential, but development was painfully slow, not least because of the attempt to make it capable of dive-bombing. The Messerschmitt Bf 109, which entered service in 1938, was an all-metal monocoque fighter of brilliant design, but Rolls-Royce Kestrel engines had to be bought to power the earliest versions. By 1940 the Luftwaffe could muster a formidable air force of over 1,000 twin-engine bombers, a similar number of modern fighters, and 300 dive-bombers, backed up by transport, trainer and other specialised aircraft. Moreover, the German 'Kondor Legion' had given air support to Franco in the Spanish Civil War, providing practical experience of modern aerial combat. Luftwaffe research and development was impressive, establishing a lead in radar and in radio navigation aids which lasted far into the war. The price of this focus was neglect of the navy. Battleships like *Bismarck* and *Tirpitz* were impressive, but they absorbed vast resources and were never numerous enough to challenge the British. Astonishingly, after their successes in the war, Germany had only sixty-five submarines by 1939.

The Japanese army also developed an aggressive doctrine and appropriate tactics. By 1937 it was 300,000 strong, rising to five million by 1945. But although its artillery and infantry weapons were excellent, maintaining high levels of equipment supply as the army expanded was difficult and tanks were very primitive because Japanese industrial capacity was limited. Japanese generals, therefore, emphasised the fighting quality of their men and imposed strict discipline and formidable battle drill which made their infantry highly efficient and adaptable, and inspired a strong sense of self-sacrifice for the imperial cause. For the most part the army was focused on the fighting in China which had broken out in 1931. This was a low-technology struggle against a divided and ill-equipped enemy in which the air arm was not especially important, though the army's Mitsubishi G4M1 Val medium, a bomber, was very useful.

The material shortages of the Japanese army owed much to the heavy demands made upon the limited national industrial base by the navy. This service envisaged a high-technology struggle against the US which would culminate in a giant fleet engagement fought out by battleships. To this end they produced the *Musashi* and the *Yamato*, both of 68,000 tons and equipped with 18.1-in. guns, the biggest battleships ever built. Their carriers resembled the American models, but their planes were better. The Zero, which entered service in 1940, was the best naval fighter at the time. It was complemented by the excellent Aichi D3A 'Val' dive-bomber and the Nakajima B5N torpedo bomber.

At the start of the 1930s the Soviet Union had 1.4 million men under arms, fairly equally divided between the regular forces and the reserves. Artillery was excellent, and there were no fewer than eleven regular and three reserve cavalry divisions, but tanks were relatively scarce and there was no established doctrine for their use. A considerable investment in planes had produced a substantial air force. In theory the army was the instrument of support for world revolution, but in practice its stance was defensive and Russian leaders were acutely aware of its limitations. At every level of command the military leader was supported by a political figure, the Commissar, in a system of joint control. The situation was transformed by the success of the first Five Year Plan (1928–32) in establishing a strong industrial base. This coincided with the rise of Nazi Germany and Japanese aggression in the Far East, stimulating the Soviets to expand and reform their forces.

In 1933 Stalin encouraged the remarkable Marshal M.N. Tukhachevsky, a former Tsarist officer of aristocratic origins, to reform the forces. The standing army was raised and a system of officer training institutions was created, so that the Commissars were eclipsed. Mechanisation of all arms began, a substantial tank force was created and superb artillery provided. In 1934 three airborne divisions emerged and in the summer exercises at Kiev in 1935 a regiment of troops with artillery support was air-dropped. The air force examined issues of strategic bombing, but tended to focus on supporting the army. In 1934 the new Rata I-16 was one of the most advanced fighters in the world, capable of nearly 300 mph, and proved its worth in the Spanish Civil War. Powerful anti-aircraft artillery countered hostile air power. By 1937 the Soviet Union could muster three million men in arms supported by new roads and railways. Its doctrine increasingly emphasised deep penetration attacks by fast-moving mechanised units supported by all arms. In many ways its thinking was the most advanced in the world.

But in 1937 Tukhachevsky was arrested and the military commands were decapitated by the great purges which restored the power of the Commissars. As the scale of the purges became apparent, other countries began to discount the Soviet Union as a military power. But in May–August 1938, in a series of battles culminating in Khalkin-Gol, the Japanese attempt to penetrate Soviet Mongolia was thrown back with disastrous losses. The Soviet commander, General G.K. Zhukov, a former Tsarist cavalryman, created a force of 2,600 trucks to supply his forces, and mustered nearly 500 tanks with which he won a great victory, forcing the Japanese high command to a ceasefire on 15 September. This effectively ended Japanese ambitions against Soviet territory. This battle, fought far from the centres of Russian production, was a demonstration of military power of a very high order indeed.

The French were highly conscious that the war had been decided by attrition and they concluded that in any future conflict a wearing-down process would be the inevitable prelude to victory. They planned to use the new technology for a sustained defence which would erode the enemy forces while France and her allies built up their strength for an attack. Artillery would be the crucial arm, supporting infantry and providing overwhelming firepower to destroy enemy attacks in preparation for the offensive. The Maginot Line, built between 1930 and 1939 and named after a French minister of war, was a deep fortified belt extending along the German frontier from Switzerland to Luxembourg, virtually impregnable to any army of the period. It permitted the army to economise on manpower along much of the frontier with Germany, allowing most of it to concentrate along the vulnerable Belgian border. Here the fortifications were lighter because after 1918 France was pledged to a military alliance with Belgium. When the Rhineland was demilitarised in 1935 the French lost an easy route to attack Germany, and in the face of this fundamental shift in the balance of power Belgium abandoned the alliance and proclaimed neutrality in 1936. This prevented joint measures against Germany, although military conversations continued.

Despite the weakness created by the Belgian defection, there was much to commend the French stance. The next war eventually did develop into a kind of attrition, as they had envisaged. But the massive casualties suffered by France in 1914–18 created an unwillingness to consider risks and, therefore, a focus on the defensive. French commanders believed in systematic battle, in which the enemy should be met only in carefully prepared circumstances. Battles of encounter, where fluid conditions prevailed, were to be avoided. The concomitant of this was a highly centralised command structure and the discouragement of initiatives at lower levels. This became a mindset rather than simply a doctrine, and the high command strongly discouraged debate. As a doctrine it failed to exploit the speed, reliability and flexibility of modern armoured vehicles and the possibilities of using them in conjunction with air power.

In this French vision of future war, holding the line was crucially important, which is why massive infantry tanks, Char B1 and Char 3C, were developed. But these vehicles, in common with other French tanks, rarely had wirelesses, which made concerted movement difficult. However, the main problem was the rather clumsy ideas about how they were to be organised. By 1940 France had three mechanised divisions (DLMs), but they were seen as modern cavalry, limited to screening and reconnaissance. Real armoured divisions (DCRs) began to form in 1940 but there was no consensus on how to use them. Most French tanks were embedded in the infantry and dispersed in order to support a static line. The French air force was not made independent of the army until 1934. A poorly implemented nationalisation of the aircraft industry in 1936 created production difficulties, though some good aircraft, like the Dewoitine and the Morane-Saulnier MS-406 fighters were produced. The task of the air force was support of the army, but for this they were badly organised, with units earmarked for particular armies. Supporting linear defence, which was integral to French military thinking, made concentration problematic and exposed the squadrons to local enemy supremacy. Despite this, overall the French had a pattern of war which made sense. Armour was subordinated to infantry, but the actual experience of the war suggested that tanks found it hard to make progress in the face of artillery.

All the powers were in the end guessing in preparing for war, and nobody got it entirely right. The weaknesses of the Germans and the Japanese were the consequence of their industrial bases and political systems. In Germany much war output depended on craft methods rather than mass production. Sloppy control and direction by the Luftwaffe and by Nazi politicians failed to ensure adequate supplies of replacements and spare parts. It was only in 1942 that the industry truly converted to mass production, and by then it was difficult to develop new aircraft. Raw material and industrial shortages limited Japanese output. As a result the capacity to replace and develop was poor. Neglect of radar and its associated technologies proved a massive handicap while the sharp tension between navy and army prevented the coordination of all arms. By contrast, what was impressive about British and US policy was the creation of industrial capacity which gave them great strength in the long run. All countries failed to foresee the massive casualties of air warfare, the consequence of accidents almost as much as action. But the British and Americans were very quick to introduce flight schools to provide replacements, while the Japanese and Germans badly neglected training establishments.

But in the short run, both Britain and America signally failed to prepare their peoples for war. In particular a belief emerged that future wars would be fought by machines, and that men would be spared the horrors of 1914–18. In his study of World War II, P. Fussell remarks that 'At first everyone hoped, and many believed, that the conflicts would be fast-moving, mechanized, remote-controlled, and perhaps even rather easy.'[6] Mechanisation seemed to offer a means of fighting conflicts without massive casualties, and as a result British and American leaders invested in it to the neglect of the infantry who, consequently, were in short supply by 1944–5. Not all nations shared this belief. An intimate perception of the horrors of the war informed the muted French response to the outbreak of hostilities in 1939. France went in to battle under the dour slogan 'We will win because we are the stronger', intended to unite a republic which had been deeply divided between left and right almost to the point of civil strife throughout the 1930s. The hope in Britain and America that mere machinery would do the fighting was an illusion, for numbers were vital. And the machinery which had developed in the 1920s and 1930s was very labour intensive. A Wellington bomber had a crew of six, a Do-17 five, the Ju 88 between three and five depending on its role. The Lancaster Bomber needed seven men and the B17 ten. The Mathilda tank had a crew of four, the Sherman and the German Panther each had five. The emphasis on technology tended, in Britain and America, to obscure the simple fact that in the end infantrymen had to be got across no-man's-land and into enemy positions, and in large numbers. As a French officer put it in 1944:

The standard infantry action consists of a body of attackers seeking hand-to-hand combat . . . In an attack, no matter how powerful the artillery and heavy weapons, there comes the moment when the infantryman gets close to the enemy lines, all support ceases, and he must mount the charge that is his last argument, his sole *raison d'être*.[7]

The gigantic infrastructure of war, on land, sea and air, was ultimately directed to this simple end. This was an unwelcome truth for the developing culture of inter-war Europe and America, especially because by any calculation there was no way in which it could be achieved without massive losses, for at the sharp end, the firestorm, so remarkable during the war, was now intensified.

Air power and tanks were spectacularly obvious manifestations of this. The huge stocks of magazine rifles and ammunition held by the powers inhibited the introduction of new infantry weapons. Only the American M1 Garand semi-automatic represented a step forward here. But in all armies units were now equipped with much higher ratios of machine-guns. The Germans regarded the excellent German MG34 (later superseded by the MG42) capable of 600–1,000 rounds per minute (rpm), as the primary infantry weapon around which riflemen worked. The Bren, 450–500 rpm, the British equivalent, was seen as an infantry support weapon. The American Browning automatic of 1918 was heavy and had a fast rate of fire but was limited by its small magazine. The Japanese Types 96 and 99 suffered from machining problems which made them less dependable. For short-range work armies adopted sub-machine-guns, like the German MP38. Heavy machine-guns, often of 0.5-in. calibre, like the American Browning, could be used for close support, mounted on vehicles or deployed in an anti-aircraft role. Mortars provided infantry with their own artillery in defence and attack, and ranged from 50mm up to monstrous 120mm models whose missiles had the same explosive charge as a 155mm howitzer shell. Grenade launchers provided a similar service in a smaller way, while flame-throwers were good for very close range work.

None of these weapons were new, but they were lighter and more reliable than World War I models and used in much greater quantities. Artillery was now more manageable and in most armies guns were more mobile because they were pulled and supplied by trucks, though the Germans and Russians continued to use horses throughout the war. Radio communication between artillery and other arms facilitated concentration of fire, improved liaison with spotters on the ground and in the air, and speeded up deployment. The outstanding field-gun was the British 25 pounder of 3.45-in. calibre, which could provide very rapid fire, both direct and indirect. High-velocity weapons were needed against aircraft and tanks, and in this range the German 88mm was highly effective against both targets. To counter low-level air attack 40mm and 20mm automatic types were used, notably the Swedish Bofors and the Swiss Oerlikon. Both the French and the British produced limited numbers of AA guns and in 1940 were deeply impressed by the effectiveness of those deployed by German units.

This array of killing machines should finally have ended close-order. Armies trained their infantry in fire and movement, making particular use of machine guns as a means of suppressing defensive weaponry to get to close quarters. In the German army the basic unit was the platoon of 50–60 men, which was provided with a light mortar and an MG34 for every ten-man rifle squad. Companies (x 3–5 platoons) and battalions (x 4–6 companies) had further support weapons such as concentrations of heavy machine guns, flame-throwers, heavy mortars, light artillery pieces and anti-tank guns. This represented, however, the equipment of the very best units, to which others only approximated. Even so, German infantry had good equipment, were highly trained and led by very expert NCOs.

To act aggressively in the face of this immense firepower took high morale and good training. This was why Hitler attempted a 'Cultural Revolution', developing a militaristic ethos which was calculated to steel young Germans to the tasks of war. The cult of manliness, the deliberate brutality of both the Hitler Youth and the Labour Service, and the harshness of military training when conscription was introduced, with the concomitant subordination of women, were all deliberate policies. Germany, from 1933 to 1939, advanced some way towards becoming a nation in arms. This was much more than mere thuggish violence, for it was underpinned by the regime's notion of racial superiority which it instilled into its young people. This sprang from a clear recognition that modern war was bound to cost lives on a substantial scale. The Nazi Cultural Revolution was an immensely successful part of the preparation for war. It was accompanied by a coercive state apparatus which pervaded all aspects of national life, because the Nazis were determined that there should be no failure of will in the face of enemy action such as, they believed, had happened in 1918. In Japan the increasing influence of the military created a similarly harsh militaristic ethos. Mussolini made attempts to do the same in Fascist Italy, but his government lacked the single-minded drive of his German allies. In the Soviet Union a brutal regime imposed appalling hardships on its people, and developed a cult of sacrifice for socialism which was not dissimilar to that of the Nazis. No comparable effort was made in either the US or Britain to prepare people, and particularly young men. Indeed, the anti-military culture in Britain and the US, founded on a distorted view of the war, meant that young men were poorly prepared when conflict broke out.

World War II was truly global, an amalgam of several conflicts. Japan ended World War I with control over many Pacific islands, Korea and Taiwan, but coveted the raw materials of Manchuria and feared Soviet expansion into this area. Japan seized Manchuria in 1931, and extended its authority into north China, taking advantage of the weakness of the Nationalist (Kuomintang) government based at Nanjing which faced independent warlords and a communist revolt. In 1937 the Japanese forces in Manchuria, the Kwantung army, against the wishes of their own General Staff and the home government, engineered a war with the Chinese. By 1941 Japan controlled virtually the entire coastline of China. But the task of conquering China was far beyond Japanese resources.

They may have been hoping to replicate their success in Manchuria where in 1934 they set up Pu Yi, the last Manchu emperor of China, as a puppet, but agreement with the Chinese proved impossible. For all its imperfections the Kuomintang government was strongly patriotic and its resistance reflected hatred of the invader. Further, its leaders knew that the US was deeply hostile to Japanese intervention in China and traded space for time in which they hoped that the US would enter the war. The Japanese made rapid advances, but controlling the vast countryside was very hard. As the Chinese armies retreated, they devastated the land, making supply difficult. Then there were guerrilla movements which caused major problems. The Japanese response was to set up native governments in conquered areas, but these lacked authority because they were seen to be puppets. Moreover the Japanese policy of terror, exemplified by the massacres which followed their occupation of Nanjing in December 1937, fired many Chinese to resist. By 1941, 1.5 million of the Japanese army of 2.08 million were sucked into the Chinese quagmire. Japanese losses, while only a fraction of those of the Chinese, were high. The Nanjing campaign of 1937 cost the Chinese 367,000 casualties, but the Japanese lost 70,000 dead alone. Japanese generals paid little attention to their soldiers' welfare, and this neglect caused heavy losses due to disease and starvation.

Japanese conquests were regarded with great hostility by Britain and the US which had their own empires in the Pacific. But after 1939 Britain was increasingly preoccupied with Europe and American isolationism made coordinated action difficult. However, their hostility annoyed Japan sufficiently to prompt her formal accession to the Axis alliance of Italy and Germany in September 1940. By that time the fall of France and Holland and the likelihood of a German invasion of Britain had opened obvious prospects for Japan.

The outbreak of World War II in Europe came as a surprise to all parties. Hitler had no plan for a general war, and while he believed that one would eventually be necessary he did not anticipate it before the period 1943–5. Diplomacy had given him a series of coups culminating in the Munich agreement of 1938 which allowed him to occupy the Sudetenland; only a remnant of Czechoslovakia, which had been an important French ally, remained independent. Hitler then began to float the issue of the Polish Corridor. This gave Poland access to the Baltic, but necessarily included many ethnic Germans and divided East and West Prussia. On the face of it Germany here had a good case for some adjustments, and Poland was so inaccessible that Britain and France could hardly provide her with effective aid. But the German annexation of the remaining part of Czechoslovakia in March 1939 was directly contrary to the promises Hitler had made at Munich. Moreover it was clearly not a German land. As a result of this piratical act, Britain and France guaranteed Poland's frontiers. But neither they nor Poland would seriously countenance an alliance with the Soviet Union, and they assumed, in the light of Hitler's hatred of the Bolsheviks, that Germany would equally regard them as beyond the pale. In August 1939 the Nazi–Soviet pact partitioned Poland and divided northern and eastern Europe into spheres of influence. This alliance left Britain and France with no real means of making good on their promise to Poland, but nonetheless they clung to it. On 1 September Germany invaded Poland.

Germany went on to triumph with spectacular speed in three major campaigns. These victories were the result of the German army's careful consideration of the lessons of the war, thoughtful recognition of the possibilities of the new technologies, and realistic acceptance of the need for casualties. The German army invaded Poland with 2,758,000 men, organised into 103 divisions of which 6 were armoured. Poland mustered 37 infantry divisions and 750 armoured vehicles, supported by 900 aircraft. The attack came in the form of a pincer movement by two army groups. The northern force thrust through the Polish Corridor, then turned south towards Warsaw to link up with the main advance from the south. The relative weight of these onslaughts was determined by the greater railway network in the south, for armies basically depended on trains for movement. The Poles tried to defend all their frontiers, but they were destroyed by a series of brilliantly directed cauldron battles (*Kesselschlachten*) in which fast and powerful thrusts broke through their front and isolated their units by main force and speed of movement. For about 15,000 dead and 30,000 wounded, the Germans killed 70,000 Poles and captured nearly ten times that number.

These casualty figures cast an interesting light on the predominantly defensive mindset of the leaders of the western powers. Aggressive deep penetration attack, flexible tactics at all levels, rapid resupply of lead elements by lorry and, above all, close coordination of all arms including low-level air strikes, created this staggering success. By 14 September the Germans were at Brest-Litovsk, and six days later they met their Russian allies advancing into eastern Poland on the Dneiper. German generals noted the excellent progress of their tanks in the fluid stages of the campaign, but worried about the tremendous wear and tear of battle and the heavy losses encountered in the attack on Warsaw, begun on 9 September, which lasted until its surrender on 27 September.

On 9 April 1940 Germany invaded Denmark and thrust on to Norway. The attack was precipitated by fear of allied influence in Norway which threatened German iron-ore supplies from Sweden. When Oslo's maritime defences resisted, German paratroopers seized the airport and quickly took the capital and the major cities. An Anglo-French expedition to help the Norwegians was badly mishandled and by June Norway was conquered, though the German surface fleet had suffered heavy losses. Apart from guaranteeing ore supplies, Norway gave German submarines useful bases on the North Atlantic. The seizure of Norway was a hastily improvised undertaking which demonstrated the operational planning of the German General Staff and the flexibility of their forces. In particular, their attacks had been carried out and supplied by the air force which often acted as flying artillery, demoralising allied troops which had no such liaison. Even before Norway had surrendered, these qualities were being demonstrated on a bigger stage.

Attrition was Hitler's nightmare. He and his paladins remembered the stranglehold of the British naval blockade in World War I. His alliance with the Soviet Union, and his dominion over Poland, together provided enough food supplies to reduce that risk, and victory had given him enormous confidence. His generals, fearful of French strength, responded to his demands for an offensive in the West, *Fall Gelb* (Case Yellow), with rather cautious plans for an invasion of Belgium and Holland which essentially repeated Moltke's plan of 1914 and aspired only to push the enemy back into northern France. But a triumvirate of generals, Gerd von Rundstedt, who was very senior, Erich von Manstein, who was the main planner, and Heinz Guderian, the tank specialist, had bolder ideas based on the new Panzer divisions which had performed so well in Poland.

Panzer divisions combined tanks with fast-moving lorried infantry, specialised combat engineers, ample anti-tank and anti-aircraft guns and their own rapid moving artillery. Commanders were expected to move with these forces and to coordinate their movements by highly developed radio networks which could also summon air support. The mix of arms was intended to keep the force moving at all costs, reflecting German insistence on speed and thrust, reinforced by close observation of the Spanish Civil War. These were elite units. Only ten of the 135 divisions which faced France in spring 1940 were Panzers, but the triumvirate planned to use their speed and strike power against the Allies, leaving the rest of the army to catch up. A typical German infantry division of 17,000 men had 73 motor and 210 horse-drawn vehicles, demanding a pool of over 5,000 animals with all their veterinary and other services.

No assault on the Maginot Line which formed the French right was possible, but of course the garrison units in these fortifications were incapable of making any sally, so they could safely be masked with small forces. The triumvirate argued that the proposed attack on Belgium and Holland should fix the allies, while the main thrust would come through Sedan to achieve what Churchill later called a *Sichelschnitt* (sickle cut) across the rear of allied armies to the Channel. The German armoured divisions should form the spear-point of this attack, relying on speed and shock to disrupt the enemy and prevent coordinated action against their exposed flanks. Close support from the Luftwaffe would, in part, act as a substitute for artillery. Certain difficulties were evident: the roads through the mountainous Ardennes were poor and narrow, while the main line of resistance would clearly be the formidable obstacle of the Meuse. The French in 1935 had considered the possibility of an enemy thrust through the Ardennes and concluded that it was possible, but would founder on this river. However, the plan appealed to Hitler because it offered the prospect of victory avoiding the dreaded effects of attrition, and he pushed it through. Allied plans for 1940 played into his hands.

The French had always supposed that the Germans would take the offensive. Their intention was to draw the Germans into a wasting battle in which the Allies would prepare their position for the offensives to come. It was this last point that unhinged their whole strategy. The order of battle favoured the Germans, whose 135 divisions included ten Panzers. France fielded 79 divisions including six partially mechanised (plus 13 fortress divisions), supported by ten British, one of which was armoured. The French, with about 2,900, had about the same number of tanks as the Germans. Their machines enjoyed a qualitative advantage because the enemy had no equivalent of the heavy B1 and C3, and because the Somua S35 was a better medium than the Panzer III. French artillery at 11,000 pieces outnumbered the Germans who had just under 8,000.

There were grave weaknesses on both sides. The Panzer force had risen to ten divisions by using captured Czech tanks and transport. But the Germans were acutely short of trucks, and requisitioned civilian vehicles had enormously high wastage rates because they were never intended for military use. This jeopardised any Panzer thrust which depended on rapid resupply of petrol and ammunition and fast follow-up by motorised infantry. As a result, ordinary infantry divisions were deprived of motor vehicles and the regular army grudgingly accepted the Nazi Party army, the Waffen SS, into their motorised elite because they had vehicles. But there was a real risk of ordinary infantry divisions falling badly behind schedule, and the whole plan had to depend on elite units. The bulk of the British divisions were Territorial Army and very poorly equipped, though all were motorised, which at least facilitated supply. Neither the French nor the British had any very coherent doctrine for the use of tanks and their armies had inadequate numbers of anti-aircraft or anti-tank weapons. Their airforces were outnumbered by the Luftwaffe and had no way of coordinating air cover. The British Advanced Air Striking Force (AASF), under Bomber Command, was intended for strategic operations against Germany and had no obligation to the BEF, let alone the French. But the gravest problems for the Allies related to Belgium and Holland.

Despite the expectation of a German assault, Belgium would not allow the Allies to advance into its territory, although plans for joint defence were made. This meant that the Allies would have to wait until Germany crossed into Belgium, so that their movement forward would necessarily be rushed. The initial E Plan was to move about 40 kilometres to the line of the Scheldt anchored on Antwerp to the north and the French border to the south, bringing about a junction with the twenty divisions of the Belgian army. An alternative, the D Plan called for an advance to the Dyle. This involved a longer progression, 96 kilometres at its greatest, and a need to secure the Gembloux Gap between Dyle and Sambre, but would facilitate the junction with the Belgians and secure a shorter line protecting much more of Belgium. A variant on D Plan was to extend the line even further, to Breda to link up with the Dutch whose army of twelve divisions could then be added to the Alliance.

The real attraction of the Breda variant was that it would establish a strong position for a future allied offensive into Germany. Gamelin, the French commander, chose this last and most ambitious plan and implemented it when the Germans attacked Belgium and Holland on 10 May 1940. But this aggressive act fitted badly with the general French stance of avoiding encounter battles, because it would definitely precipitate one. Moreover, in order to provide the weight for the northward advance Gamelin stripped his reserve, sending Giraud's Seventh Army, with some of the best French mechanised units, north to Breda. This left Hunzinger's Second Army guarding the gap between the Meuse and the Maginot Line, directly in front of the German axis of advance through the Ardennes. Many of his units were of poor quality, but the real problem was that once the Germans had struck, limited reinforcements were available.

In 1940 the German General Staff demonstrated its mastery of operational method by launching a series of large-scale and very closely coordinated attacks. The Belgian line of defence on the Albert canal was shattered by a parachute assault on Fort Eben-Emael. Airborne troops, strong bomber forces and even seaplanes smashed Dutch resistance, forcing the retreat of Giraud's forces. However, the French still held the Dyle and defeated a powerful German assault through the Gembloux Gap in a carefully prepared battle which illustrated the underlying sense of French doctrine. But the main attack came through the Ardennes. A huge force of 134,000 men and 1,600 vehicles made their tortuous way through the difficult terrain and reached the Meuse on 12 May. This campaign is usually referred to as *Blitzkrieg* (Lightning War).

There could be no rapid movement until the Meuse had been crossed, and this task was given to the infantry. Surprise was the key to their success. Rommel, commanding 7th Panzer, was only able to get his men across by taking personal command of the infantry, while massive bombing opened the way for the vital attack by Guderian at Sedan. The French were spread thinly along this sector, and while some fought well, they had no answer to German airpower whose moral effect was enormous. On 13 May, after much hard fighting, the Germans established bridgeheads across the Meuse. French counter-attacks ought to have destroyed some of these precarious positions, but such French reserves as became available were committed piecemeal, largely because of poor communications, and were defeated in detail. By 17 May the Germans were driving west and north to the coast. Each Panzer division tried to spread its forces over at least three roads, while the spearhead avoided collision with strong enemy forces by seeking a way around them. Reconnaissance aircraft reported back constantly and Stukas were called up when needed.

But there were many doubts and hesitations, and some Panzers had to rely on French garages when their fuel failed to come up. The Germans, having learned from the Polish campaign that close support aircraft like the Ju 87 were very vulnerable, provided strong fighter cover. When this failed the results could be disastrous: on 12 May a single French squadron of Curtiss Hawks shot down all twelve of a flight of Ju 87s near Sedan and turned back others without loss to themselves. Allied attempts to bomb German columns and destroy bridges were crushed by fighter attack and the highly effective anti-aircraft weapons of the German army. By 12 May the RAF's AASF had lost 63 of the 135 aircraft it had committed to the battle. On the ground successive French counter-attacks were never in great enough strength. On 21 May at Arras light French armour and two British tank battalions rattled Rommel's 7th Panzer but lacked the strength to halt the advance, which reached the coast at Abbeville on 20 May. All attempts to recover the situation failed, the British evacuated their soldiers, but not their equipment, through Dunkirk, 26 May to 4 June, and France surrendered on 25 June in the very rail car at Compiègne in which Germany had surrendered in 1918.

Poor intelligence was a major cause of the French defeat. In fine weather, with clear visibility, an enormous army had passed through narrow roads in total secrecy to strike the main line of resistance on the Meuse. This must be connected with the disorganisation of the French airforce and the disdain of the RAF for any kind of army cooperation. But the French then underestimated the speed of the enemy attack, and reacted sluggishly. This was made worse by the generally inadequate wireless communication in the French army. None of this need have been fatal except for the extraordinary decision of Gamelin to act against his own doctrine and risk an encounter battle in Flanders, which stripped the reserves needed to sustain a long line. On 16 May Churchill demanded of the French command: *'Où est votre masse de manoeuvre?'* (Where are your reserves?) and received the response *'Il n'y a aucune!'* ('There are none'). In fact they were in Belgium. Of course, if the British had created a substantial and modern expeditionary force instead of the improvised and ill-equipped force actually sent, Gamelin would not have needed to strip his reserves. It is all a very sad story, reflecting painfully the intellectual failure of the British.

Hitler expected the British to come to terms after their defeat and evacuation from Dunkirk, but Churchill and the war party controlled government and refused. Hitler dithered before issuing his directive for *Seelöwe* (Operation Sea Lion) on 16 July. The whole enterprise depended on the Luftwaffe achieving air supremacy so that it could fight off the Royal Navy which was much stronger than the German navy, and so enable an invasion fleet to put an army ashore. No airforce had ever attempted such an ambitious gambit; moreover in the battle of France the Luftwaffe had lost 30 per cent of its strength, with 240 planes destroyed in the attempt to stop the evacuation of Dunkirk; the RAF lost 177. The Ju 87 was very vulnerable to fighter attack and was quickly withdrawn, leaving the German medium bombers to carry the assault. Their small bomb loads placed a high premium on good targeting and accuracy, but this depended on establishing careful priorities for the attack. Clearly the main thrust of the offensive should be to destroy the RAF by bombing its bases, but how important was this as against targeting the aircraft industry, radar installations and coastal defences? German intelligence knew about 'Chain Home' but took a long time to grasp the very effective command and control system organised by Dowding.

The Luftwaffe was not very well equipped for the task before it. The bombers, attacking in daylight, would need strong fighter escorts. The Me 109 was good, but it had limited endurance, and fighting a determined enemy would inevitably be costly. Replacement of aircraft was slow because of the poor organisation of German industry, which did not improve during the battle. The British could hope to recover pilots of destroyed planes, and acquire reinforcements from the Dominions: the Germans, over enemy territory or the Channel, could expect heavy casualties of these trained men. So the Luftwaffe faced sharp attrition and it was difficult for them to gauge success. If the British suffered losses they could pull their fighters back, ready to support bomber and naval attacks on any invasion.

But the Luftwaffe came very close to establishing air supremacy over southern Britain. Losses on both sides were reaching critical levels: between 10 July and 31 October the Germans lost 1,733 planes and the British 915. German intelligence consistently underestimated the capacity of British industry to replace losses, but it was loss of pilots which most worried the RAF. Ultimately the failure to achieve any decisive success and the approach of autumn brought about the cancellation of *Seelöwe* on 17 September. The Luftwaffe night bombing of 1940–41 profited at first from their research on radio beams for target location. On the night of 14/15 November 550 German bombers attacked Coventry using an advanced radio-beam system, *X-Gerät*. The first wave used high explosives to de-roof, while the main force carried vast loads of incendiaries. Because German bomber loads were limited to 2,000–4,000 pounds the raiders had to fly back and forth to restock, and as a result the attack lacked the intensity which might have set off a firestorm. Even so, they destroyed 60,000 buildings and killed 568 civilians. This was the shape of things to come, but it stimulated British scientists to ever greater efforts, taking the war into the realm of a high-technology contest.

By the end of 1940 Hitler held the initiative in Europe. He could choose to renew the assault on Britain in 1941. Alternatively, by supporting the Italians in North Africa, he could drive the British from the Mediterranean and dominate the oil-rich Middle East. Such a course of action would, incidentally, menace the Soviet Union on its southern flank. In the event he chose the third option: to attack the Soviet Union directly.

This has often been portrayed as an ideologically motivated mistake. Hitler, it is argued, obsessed by his hatred of communism and his conviction of Slav inferiority, exposed Germany to war on two fronts. But in fact it was quite a rational decision. Britain was defeated though she had not surrendered. To carry on the war her government adopted a threefold strategy against Germany: to tighten the naval blockade, to foment resistance in the conquered lands, and to build a strategic bomber force to attack Germany. None of this posed much of a threat. The blockade had nothing like the effects of the similar action in World War I because Germany controlled the resources of Europe. The conquered lands in the west to which Britain had access were not keen to revolt. German occupation in Western Europe was orderly, and harsh punishments for resistance were an effective deterrent. In Eastern Europe, where German occupation had a quite different face and resistance movements were growing, Britain had little purchase. British bombing was almost entirely ineffectual. Moreover, fairly minimal support for Italy in North Africa diverted limited British resources which were already stretched by the Japanese threat in the Far East.

Added to this Germany adopted unrestricted submarine warfare, helped by seizure of the French and Norwegian coasts. Long-range Kondor aircraft found convoys and relayed their location and course to submarine groups, 'wolf packs', arrayed across likely routes. The submarines then gathered and launched mass attacks, usually by night and on the surface to circumvent ASDIC. Such tactics inflicted heavy losses in 1940–1. But submarines were essentially submersibles which had to travel on the surface and could move only slowly under water. Air patrols and radar were essential in spotting them. For both sides breaking enemy signals was vital, and the British effort was expanded by Ultra which tapped into enemy communications at all levels. Germany knew it needed new U-boats, but overall pressure on its industrial base made their production a slow business. In 1943 the highest priority was accorded to the production of advanced Type XXI submarines, but they did not go into service until April 1945. About 830 German submarines went on operations and of these the Allies sank 696, a loss of 83.9 per cent. About 40,900 men served in these submarines and of these 25,870 died, a total of 63 per cent fatalities, to which should be added 5,000 POWs for an overall casualty rate of 76 per cent. In all, Germany sank 14.5 million tons of shipping, and killed over 30,000 sailors. This was a high-technology war, but at a high human cost.

For Hitler the Soviet Union had always been a racial as well as a political enemy, and he wanted its lands as *Lebensraum* for the German people. In 1940 he observed that the Soviet Union was recovering from the Great

Purges and exerting substantial influence in Northern and Eastern Europe. His army was at the height of its powers. To postpone the inevitable conflict would, therefore, be dangerous. Hitler was confident. He despised the Slavs as racially inferior and exaggerated the weaknesses of the Soviet regime, commenting: 'We have only to kick in the door and the whole rotten structure will come crashing down.'[8] But kicking in the door demanded 'Operation Barbarossa', the largest single military operation in human history, involving 151 German divisions, with 14 Finnish and 13 Romanian, in all 3.6 million troops attacking on a front of 1,800 miles with the operational goal of seizing European Russia to the AA (Archangel to Astrakhan) line. They were supported by 3,350 tanks and about 2,000 aircraft. The Soviets had about the same front-line manpower and even more tanks, amongst them the famous T-34 which was superior to the best German models. Although the Soviet airforce was immense, most of its planes were old and lacked radios. However, Barbarossa was a gamble, because while the forces assembled were enormous, Germany could not replace heavy losses of men and materiel. And the plan assumed that logistics could be improvised at need since German supply capacity was unlikely to be able to support the army beyond Smolensk. On 22 June Barbarossa was launched. Stalin had refused to believe intelligence reports of a forthcoming attack, so the Germans achieved complete surprise. Moreover, Soviet forces were right up against the frontier and under orders to stay and counter-attack, enabling the Germans to trap them in gigantic pockets like that at Minsk which yielded 310,000 prisoners and Kiev which produced another 665,000. The Luftwaffe quickly established air supremacy.

But for all their enormous losses, the Soviet armies fought well. Their autocratic regime, which was even more savage than its Nazi counterpart, was able to mobilise replacements and to improvise successive lines of resistance which created an effective defence in depth. It greatly helped that Hitler could never quite make up his mind as to the main thrust of Barbarossa. He wavered between taking Moscow or making gains further south which would give him control of the rich lands of the Ukraine. Ultimately he set the focus on Moscow, but his wavering had caused delays which were made worse by increasing logistical problems. Moreover, strong Soviet resistance was imposing a heavy attrition upon the advanced German units. Stalin had recalled Zhukov's army from Siberia, and this launched a successful counter-offensive on 5 December 1941.

The German generals had not planned for failure and simply did not know what to do. Hitler resolved the matter by ordering the troops to stand

and fight. Whatever the virtues or vices of this order, it certainly worked and it was better than nothing, which was what the generals had to offer. But the failure of Barbarossa meant that Germany was committed to a war of attrition which was exactly what the operation had been designed to avoid. The Germans were astounded by the damage they had inflicted upon Russia – enormous quantities of materiel and, above all casualties, including 800,000 dead and well over three million prisoners. But their own casualties amounted to 918,000, including 250,000 killed. These came disproportionately from the elite troops who bore the brunt of the fighting. In addition, formidable quantities of equipment had been destroyed.

A similar pattern of events unfolded in the Far East. Japan, trapped in her Chinese quagmire, used the fall of France to extend her power over Indochina. The US imposed an oil embargo in the summer of 1941, sent war materials and a Military Mission to China, and intensified discussions with Britain about cooperation in the area. But on 7 December 1941 Japan attacked the American Pacific Fleet in Pearl Harbor, crippling the battleship force but missing the carriers, and on the 23rd they seized Wake Island. They then went on to attack the Philippines, defeating US and local forces and taking Manila on 2 January 1942. A landing in British Malaya suffered heavy initial casualties, but provoked a sally from Singapore by 'Force H' which consisted of the battleship *Prince of Wales* and the battlecruiser *Repulse*. They had no air cover and both were sunk on 10 December 1941 by eighty-six Japanese aircraft operating from bases near Saigon. On 15 February 1942 Singapore surrendered to the Japanese, although from first to last their army had been outnumbered by the defenders. The oil-rich Dutch East Indies fell on 8 March 1942 and by mid-May a Japanese army had occupied Burma and reached the Indian frontier. By this time Japanese attacks had driven the British from the Indian Ocean and for a time it seemed as if the whole British position in the region was collapsing, but in the event the Japanese carriers moved south to support a far-reaching strike towards Australia.

These successes owed much to the weaknesses of Japan's enemies. At Pearl Harbor the US was caught napping, and losses there undermined all her war plans. The British Indian army was the primary prop of her power in the East, but its main purposes were internal security and border skirmishes. It was simply not equipped or trained to fight a strong and experienced enemy, while the British units were as poorly formed and equipped, and as badly led as those in Europe had been. The Japanese army had been fighting in China since 1937, and its highly disciplined troops adapted quickly to the novel circumstances of jungle warfare. The sheer quality of the Japanese troops was a major shock to Europeans with their easy assumptions about racial superiority.

The Japanese revealed remarkable naval skill in the battle of the Java Sea on 27 February 1942 against an American–British–Dutch–Australian fleet, while the destruction of two British cruisers and a carrier in the Indian Ocean in April 1942 for no losses was outstanding. The Japanese profited from aerial supremacy, for the British, heavily engaged at home and in the Middle East, sent only obsolete planes, and few enough of them. But perhaps what is most astonishing was the shamefully poor leadership of British forces in Malaya, Singapore and Burma. This was indeed the pay-off for a popular culture so at odds with military necessity and its consequences for the army. Effectively the loss of Malaya and Singapore sounded the death knell of the British Empire, for British prestige could not survive the surrender of 130,000 troops.

The fighting quality of their troops and careful exploitation of enemy weaknesses won both Germany and Japan great early successes, but both failed to win a decisive victory over a major power with enormous industrial potential and huge manpower resources. In this way both were committed to a war of attrition, in which the long-term odds were stacked against them. Hitler remained confident, because although it was obvious that Stalin was mobilising large numbers of troops, he was sure German forces were better than the Soviets, and he had little knowledge of the massive relocation of factories to the east which would sustain their army. And he retained the initiative. On 28 June 1942 he caught the Soviets by surprise, attacking in the south rather than against Moscow as anticipated, with the intention of seizing the oilfields of the Caucasus. But this campaign ended in disaster at Stalingrad, where, by February 1943 the Russians had destroyed the Sixth Army's 330,000 men. At the same time the Germans lost air supremacy as a result of cumulative erosion of the Luftwaffe's fighting strength.

In 1942 US forces checked the Japanese advance in the Pacific. The battle of the Coral Sea, 4–8 May 1942, the first naval battle in which the opposing ships never sighted one another because it was fought between carrier-based aircraft, blunted the Japanese thrust towards Australia. More importantly, the Japanese attack on Midway was defeated with the loss of four aircraft carriers. On land the Japanese advance across New Guinea was thrown back in hard fighting from July 1942 to January 1943, and in August US marines attacked Guadalcanal, which they had captured from the Japanese by January 1943.

The entry of the US into the war and the determined resurgence of Soviet industry tilted the balance of production and innovation heavily against the Axis powers. The Willow Run plant in Michigan which eventually could produce over 400 B-19 Liberators per day, was a single plant. No less than 12,700 B-19s were produced elsewhere. By 1944 the Americans had developed the gigantic B-29 with its pressurised crew compartments and remotely controlled guns, and were using it to pound Japanese cities. New fighter planes, notably the P-51 Mustang which became a highly successful bomber escort in Europe, and Hellcats, Corsairs and Cutlasses which dominated the skies of the Pacific, were built. After the fighting to relieve Guadalcanal there were no major fleet engagements in the Pacific until the Marianas in 1944. In that time only one big carrier, *Taiho*, and a handful of smaller vessels entered Japanese service, though progress was made on the gigantic *Shinano*. By contrast, the US built ten Essex class large carriers and numerous escort and light carriers. By the end of hostilities the US had built more than twenty fleet carriers, ten new battleships and a host of other vessels.

But perhaps the most astonishing achievement was the construction of 2,751 'Liberty Ships', cargo vessels, typically of about 14,000 tons, which were mass-produced using prefabricated sections. Methods became so refined that each took just forty-two days to build and launch. Such ships enabled the US to build up its forces in Europe despite the submarine threat and to supply its vast fleet and army in the Pacific. By 1944 the US had 600,000 ground troops, 410,000 air force men and 390,000 supply corps in Europe. By 1945 it was planning to land 2.5 million troops on the Japanese home islands. In addition, it also largely sustained the British war effort and supplied the Soviets with immense quantities of war materiel and food – 450,000 motor vehicles alone, although Soviet logistics were still heavily dependent on the horse.

Soviet industrial production focused on simple and easily produced weapons like the T-34 tank which was highly successful, though it had few refinements. Katyusha rockets were not very accurate but they were very easy to manufacture, and swarms of them launched from the backs of trucks deluged enemy positions and were in fact so effective that they were copied by the western Allies. The PPSh-41 was a crude but robust submachine gun introduced by the time of Stalingrad which was so good and so frequently picked up and used by German soldiers that the Germans copied it. Interestingly, they also copied the British Sten, a simple 9mm sub-machine-gun, as the MP 3008. The war on the eastern front was not a high-technology conflict. The Soviet airforce was not very sophisticated and lacked a strategic arm, but the IL-2 Sturmovik was a very successful low-level support fighter-bomber produced in huge quantities.

Mass production of relatively simple weapons enabled the Soviets to arm their huge armies, and the brutal discipline of the regime drove them into battle. At the same time the high technology imposed quite different demands on the German economy and its armed forces.

The war of attrition prompted Hitler to take steps to prepare German industry for a long war. While things were going well he seems simply to have assumed that German industry had been organised to deliver whatever was needed, but gradually he had come to realise that this was an illusion. His economic supremo, Goering, had tried to control the economy by a process of political supervision which alienated businessmen, many of whom strongly resisted attempts to impose mass-production methods. The army's own supply people shared this distrust, demanding that equipment should be excellent and failing to understand the need for efficient mass production. Thus the MG42, for example, was a magnificent machine-gun, but manufacture required much expensive and time-consuming close machining. By contrast the Soviet and British sub-machine-guns, which the Germans copied, used stamped metal which made them much easier to produce. Moreover, the German armed forces constantly demanded modifications in equipment, which they felt small businesses would implement better. Local Nazi officials often objected to the centralisation of enterprises if it deprived their bailiwicks, while other senior Nazis tried to nibble away at Goering's power. All these factors combined to make German industry wasteful and inefficient.

The appointment first of Fritz Todt and then, on his death, of Albert Speer in February 1942 as armaments minister with sweeping powers was a major new departure. Speer divided the armaments industry by weapons system, and made committees of businessmen responsible for each, demanding rationalisation and mass-production methods which enormously increased output. Aircraft production remained in Goering's remit in theory, but in practice his deputy, Milch, worked very closely with Speer. In 1940 Germany had produced 10,000 aircraft, but by 1944, using broadly the same amount of raw materials and energy, her industry built 36,000. Before rationalisation businesses had been immensely wasteful. Messerschmitt had so much spare aluminium that it took to selling ladders and barrack-huts as a sideline. This concentration on production, however, was at the expense of innovation; Speer had no control over research, which was highly politicised. The Luftwaffe's last major new fighter, the FW-190, entered service in 1941, while the Allies were constantly introducing new machines. But the introduction of new mass-production methods needed time to take effect and it was hampered by rivalries within the Nazi hierarchy and by the conservatism of the army and many industrial firms.

As a response to the T-34 the Germans devised the Panther. It was a superb design, but production was delayed by numerous changes required by the army, and, most critically, by a shortage of machine tools. The production target was 600 per month but the quantity manufactured actually never exceeded 380. Early models were unreliable due to haste in getting them through the factories. It was 1943 before regular deliveries began. Another response to the T-34 was the Tiger, a huge and much older design which sacrificed mobility for heavy armour protection and an 88mm gun. It was costly and difficult to build, so that in the end less than 2,000 were produced despite consuming vast quantities of raw materials and tying up massive industrial capacity. Although Germany produced more steel and coal than Russia, the complicated nature of these machines and the often old-fashioned production facilities kept output relatively low. In 1943 the Soviet Union produced 24,000 tanks to 19,800 by Germany. Hitler had feared attrition with very good reason but the failures of 1941 committed him to it. His industrial base was improving, but not in time for the campaigns of 1942 and 1943.

In July 1943 the German army mounted an operation to pinch out the Kursk salient where something like 20 per cent of all Soviet forces were concentrated. The attack was mounted at the behest of the generals rather than Hitler. The salient was a very obvious target for *Kesselschlact* and the Soviets anticipated the assault, so that 1.3 million infantry, 3,600 tanks and 2,700 aircraft were ready to face an onslaught by 900,000 German infantry, 3,000 tanks and 2,000 planes. The German attack on such a carefully prepared position failed and was thrown back, permitting a Russian pursuit which captured Kharkov to the south and Orel to the north. This was a major victory for the Soviets, but the German withdrawal was skilfully conducted especially by the Luftwaffe whose operations, guided by advanced radar, simply destroyed the Soviet air fleet. German losses were significant – 50,000 casualties and perhaps 250 tanks – but the decision to break off the engagement reflects the inadequacy of German resources coming on top of the casualties already sustained. Moreover, new equipment rushed into battle proved unreliable. One Panzer division at Kursk reported that of its original 200 Panthers, by 10 July it had only 38 serviceable and 131 awaiting repair. The Tiger had even worse problems.

Kursk gave the Soviet army confidence. Attrition was taking away the Germans' initial qualitative advantage and eroding their numbers. Soviet planners were becoming better at mounting operations. And the multiplicity of German commitments diverted resources. In late 1942 Hitler had dispatched substantial German forces as the British advanced from Egypt and the Americans landed in Morocco, undermining the whole Axis position in North Africa. This was reinforcing failure, particularly evident because a year before he had refused to support Rommel when Egypt appeared to be within his grasp. In the event, in May 1943, 230,000 Axis troops surrendered in Tunisia. In July of that year the Allies invaded Sicily, and the fall of Mussolini on 24 July meant that a whole new front in Italy became the sole responsibility of the German army. One reason why Hitler broke off the Kursk attack was so that he could send troops to Italy, notably SS Panzer Division *Leibstandarte*, an elite unit. All these efforts increased pressure upon the German industrial base which became more stretched.

Nonetheless, German innovation continued with surprising success. For the low-tech war on the eastern front, good tanks and weapons like the Nebelwerfer and its sister the Panzerwerfer, accurate rocket-firers, were made available. In the west there were different challenges. The bomber barons of the RAF had conceived of strategic bombing on an immensely ambitious scale, and this was realised after 1940 when Churchill needed some means of striking at Germany and this was the most obvious. In February 1942 the RAF adopted area bombing, simply because a whole city was a target which the RAF could hit. New aircraft like the Lancaster were available in large numbers and they carried massive bomb loads. Tactics focused on setting cities ablaze by means of huge numbers of incendiary bombs, interspersed with high explosive to de-roof buildings and deter the emergency services. They were backed up by increasingly sophisticated radar and radio technology, devices with their litany of code-names: H2S, Fishpond, Monica, Gee, Gee-H, Boozer, Oboe, Village Inn, Cigar. This bombing offensive imposed a heavy drain on Germany which had to deflect men, planes and guns on an enormous scale. By and large, however, German science kept up. Radio interception, radar and radar-equipped night-fighters inflicted heavy losses which, in the end, the British could not have sustained. But other factors came into play.

In late 1942 the USAAF entered the fray with daylight bombing. They disregarded RAF advice that German defences would destroy them, placing faith in heavy armament and close-formation flying. On 14 October 1943, 291 bombers attacked the Schweinfurt ballbearing works. In all, seventy-seven were lost and just thirty-three returned without battle damage. Deep penetration raids over Germany were suspended. But by early 1944 the USAAF was equipped with a long-range fighter, the

P-51 Mustang, which had the endurance to fight the bombers all the way to Berlin. With this the USAAF carried the battle to the enemy, quickly realising that the quality of the fighter was such that it could win air supremacy over Germany. 'Big Week', 20–25 February 1944, saw the bombers stage a series of raids upon aircraft plants which the Luftwaffe had to protect. In six days, the USAAF flew more than 3,500 sorties from Britain and Italy, dropping over 10,000 tons of bombs. Operations on this scale were costly, some 247 bombers and 28 fighters; but German losses amounted to about 350 planes, with about 100 pilots killed. On 4 March a major raid on Berlin cost 69 US bombers, but 160 German fighters. The Luftwaffe simply could not replace these pilots and machines, but the Americans, with their huge production facilities and efficient flight schools, could.

In many respects German technical advances were remarkable. German radar was as good as that of their western enemies and far superior to the Soviets'. The Me-262 entered service in April 1944 as the world's first turbojet fighter, but it was unreliable and fuel was short. The British Gloster Meteor did not go into service until the summer of 1944. The advanced German submarine, Type XXI, was fast enough underwater to outrun escorts and evade their ASDIC, while its own sonar array could track up to fifty ships at a range of 7,000 yards and send data direct to its torpedoes. But production was disrupted and the first boats appeared only in the very last stages of the war in 1945. The difficulty of targeting ships which were increasingly well defended from air attack resulted in development of glide-bombs equipped with radio direction which allowed aircraft to launch attacks well out of anti-aircraft range. Fritz X and Hs-292 claimed several victims, including severe damage to the British battleship HMS *Warspite*. There were even experiments using television guidance. But the weakness of these weapons was that allied air supremacy made it difficult for their mother-craft to approach targets.

The V-weapons were the most spectacular evidence of the capacity of German science and the degree to which it had been mobilised for war by the Nazis. The V1 was a cruise missile carrying an explosive charge of something over a half ton (850 kg) with a range of 150 miles. Over 9,000 were launched at Britain, mostly directed at London, which was hit by 2,515: more than 6,000 civilians were killed and about 18,000 were injured. In response the British deployed new and much more powerful radars to direct anti-aircraft guns. These were also given the new proximity fuse which exploded in the general vicinity of its target. This combination did major damage to the V1 offensive, but the onslaught on London was halted by the progress of the allied armies after they invaded France in 1944; however, many were subsequently fired at Antwerp, whose port became vital to allied progress. Even more remarkable was the V2, a ballistic missile which reached sub-orbital heights and descended upon its target at a speed which made it immune to attack. With a range of 200 miles and a warhead of 1 ton this was a lethal weapon whose moral effect was enormous. But it cost as much as a four-engined bomber, delivered a smaller payload, could not be re-used, and was less accurate. We know that this was the technology of the future, and indeed the V1 is the ancestor of all modern rocketry, but Germany needed weapons for the here and now. On average each V2 fired at London killed just over two civilians, a poor return for such a massive investment.

It is certainly true that the US and UK leaders were constantly pursuing success through technology. But technology alone could not deliver victory. Night bombing, the speciality of the RAF, demanded enormous technical expertise simply to locate the target, and right through to the end of the war this proved very difficult. The British attacked cities because that was the scale of target which could be hit, and the measure of success was devastation. The attack on Dresden on 13–15 February 1945 was highly successful in these terms because it created a firestorm which destroyed most of the city and killed around 35,000 citizens.

This result was possible only because by 1945 the RAF had become expert in the careful orchestration of advanced technology and detailed planning of attacks. But it succeeded in hitting its target so accurately only because the weather was good and the anti-aircraft defences were weak. And it inflicted massive losses in part because air raid precautions had been badly neglected by the local Nazi leadership. Shortly after, Leipzig was targeted for a similar assault, but due to bad weather the raid was a total fiasco. In the Far East the Americans established bases within reach of the Japanese home islands and B-29s wreaked havoc on their wooden cities. Tokyo was almost destroyed in a great fire-raid on 9–10 March 1945 which devastated something like 16 square miles of the city and killed 100,000 people. Greater accuracy was now becoming possible. The RAF was redeployed to support the invasion of France in June 1944, and was highly successful in striking bridges, railways and other small targets. Late in the war US precision raids on oil targets almost brought enemy movements to a halt, but were not persisted with long enough. Bombing inflicted horrific mass destruction, and the atomic explosions at Hiroshima and Nagasaki were its culmination.

The really critical damage to the Axis powers was done by ground confrontation on the eastern front and in China. In Europe the intervention of the western powers was marginal until the landings in France on 6 June 1944. When they broke through into Germany in early 1945 about a third of the German army faced them while the remainder opposed the Soviet Union. Losses on the eastern front were incredible: 34,476,700 served in the forces of the USSR, of whom 8,668,400 were killed. This was a one in four chance of death amongst those serving, with risk of injury on top of that. The figures for the German army were directly comparable: 13,600,000 served, of whom 4,202,000 were killed; this is 30.9 per cent (34.9 per cent for the Waffen SS) or roughly a one in three chance of death, with, again, injury an additional risk. In the Japanese armies, 6.3 million were enlisted of whom 1,526,000 were killed, 24.22 per cent or just under one in four. Japan killed over three million Chinese soldiers and 17 million civilians and itself lost over two million military personnel.

At first glance, overall losses for the western powers appear derisory in comparison: for the British, only 5.2 per cent of soldiers were killed, and for the US army 2.8 per cent (Marine Corps, 3.66 per cent) but these figures hide some harsh realities. In their armies very few men served in the front line. The highly mechanised western armies needed numerous support troops who far outnumbered fighting men. In a typical British infantry division there were 17,000 men, but only about 4,000 of these served in the front line, and they suffered almost all the casualties. In the Pacific it was calculated that eighteen men were needed in support services for every rifleman. It is hardly surprising, therefore, that casualty figures amongst fighting units were very high: of the order of 13 per cent dead and 36 per cent wounded, approximating to those of World War I. Individual actions could incur enormous casualties. In November 1941, 2nd Battalion Black Watch lost 440 men and 24 officers in a single attack in North Africa. Tarawa, an atoll three miles long and half a mile wide, cost US Marine 2nd Division over 1,000 dead and 2,000 wounded in a four-day battle in November 1943. These figures, of course, did not approach the Axis and Soviet figures in absolute terms. But they make the point that casualties were heavy amongst the men in the front line, with consequent fears of desertion.

This was a real problem for all armies. Despite a ruthless bureaucracy of terror, supported by visceral hatred of Germany, deserters were a major problem for the Soviet armies. As late as April 1945, 300 Soviet soldiers defected to a single German division. Like the Germans they adopted punishment battalions for 'shirkers' and they executed many simply to 'encourage' others. Some 30,000 German soldiers were shot for various kinds of desertion or cowardice. Japanese troops, subjected to a severe discipline, were made to choose suicide in preference to surrender. The British are said to have had 100,000 deserters during the war as a whole, while about 40,000 deserted from US forces in Europe, almost always infantrymen. Because of the severe sentences attached, the US army tried to avoid trying men for desertion by bringing lesser charges. Even so, 20,000 US soldiers were found guilty of desertion, though just forty-nine death sentences were passed and only one man, Private Slovik, was shot, on 31 January 1945. He probably met his fate because by then high levels of desertion were a worry to allied commanders.

The mass execution of deserters by both sides was only one aspect of the barbarism of the eastern front. When Hitler ordered Barbarossa, he deliberately launched a destructive ideological war: 'The war against the Soviet Union will be such that it cannot be conducted in a knightly fashion: the struggle is one of ideologies and racial differences and will have to be conducted with unprecedented, unmerciful and unrelenting harshness.'[9] The army was urged to be savage, for the soldiers were assured they were fighting racially subhuman creatures. Behind came *Einsatzkommandos* charged with killing Jews, gypsies and Soviet Commissars, and their work was seen as a continuation of that of the front-line troops. This encouraged ferocious fighting, as indeed was intended. On the Russian side killing and mutilation of prisoners quickly became customary under the impact of propaganda which asserted that this was what the Germans would do. Such attitudes were strengthened as soldiers became aware of German massacres of civilians, including women and children. During the war the Germans captured 7.5 million Russian soldiers, of whom 3.3 million died in captivity. The collision of two ideologically inspired armies exceeded the horrors of the Thirty Years War in what both sides came to see as a crusade, with all the overtones of fanaticism that the word implies.

The Soviets had few qualms about sacrificing their troops. Even at the start of Barbarossa when bad strategy, poor leadership and limited communications led to disaster, her soldiers fought on stubbornly, often reverting to the simplest of tactics. 'Bayonet charges are dreaded by the Germans and they always avoid them. When they counter-attack they shoot without aiming.'[10] German soldiers spoke of waves of their enemies hurling themselves at their lines. But the self-sacrifice of the Russians, however ill-directed, held up the Germans and saved Moscow. Gradually the Soviets recovered and after Stalingrad their confidence grew. The Red Army outnumbered the *Wehrmacht*. German strength, including their allies, peaked in July 1943 at 3,933,000, as against 6,724,000 Russians, but by October was down to about three million and by September 1944 had fallen to 2.5 million.

But the Soviet success was not simply due to numbers. The bulk of their army lacked mechanisation, and relied on horse-drawn transport, as did something like 75 per cent of the German divisions. But increasingly the Soviets created highly mobile tank armies. These avoided the elite *Wehrmacht* and mounted deep penetration attacks through the less mobile forces, isolating strongpoints which could be mopped up later. Soviet commanders became adept at masking their intentions and increasingly obtained better intelligence. Deception drew off German forces to the south in preparation for Operation Bagration, 22 June–19 August 1944: this overwhelmed Army Group Centre, which suffered casualties of about 500,000, and propelled the Red Army to the Vistula. Of course the Soviets also suffered the same scale of loss – nearly 700,000 in Bagration, but they had larger reserves of manpower. Moreover, they could replace lost materiel because industrial output was increasing: production of tanks and self-propelled guns rose from 4,700 in 1941 to 29,000 in 1944. And they received enormous quantities of US and British aid. Coercion and propaganda whipped up fanaticism in the Red Army, and its Russian commanders were the readier to sacrifice troops in that most of the 'other ranks' came from subject peoples. This was attrition, in the bluntest sense of the word, but it was an intelligent attrition informed by a cultivated fanaticism.

A similar fanaticism permeated the war in the Far East. Japanese society venerated authority and hierarchy, and was inured to hardship; even in good years the home islands could not feed their growing populations. The Japanese saw themselves as the leading race (*shido minzoku*) and regarded the Americans as *Ebisu* or savages.[11] Such attitudes were cultivated in the army. Officers were aloof from their men, and enforced a harsh discipline which fed a sense of racial superiority. A deliberate brutality towards defeated enemies and, especially in China, the civilian population, reinforced this. When the Americans assaulted the perimeter of defence which the early Japanese successes had established around the home islands, they brought with them deeply racialist attitudes to the Japanese. Even before Pearl Harbor American contempt for the Japanese was very strong, so that when war came it was regarded as part of a 'perpetual war between Oriental ideals and Occidental and the enemy was designated a racial menace'.[12] The result was an embittered conflict in which neither side took prisoners. Japanese officers cultivated a code of honour which saw surrender as shameful. At Attu in 1943 the commander, waving a sword, led his surviving 1,000 men in a banzai charge against the Americans – only twenty-eight survived. At Okinawa, April–June 1945, virtually the whole defending garrison of 100,000 was wiped out at a cost of 12,000 US dead and 38,000 wounded. Here the Japanese, defeated in the air war, sent barely trained pilots on kamikaze missions to crash their planes on the decks of US ships.

There is a notable parallel between the Japanese and their German allies. Both took on enormously powerful enemies and dissipated initial advantages, dooming them to the attrition which they had sought to avoid. The early German superiority owed much to better equipment, but this was not really true for the Japanese. Essentially German and Japanese soldiers were victorious because their front-line troops were very well trained and this in turn owed much to cultural factors. Young Germans emerging from childhood in 1933 would have been indoctrinated in the Hitler Youth and the Labour Service with Nazi ideas of *Volksgemeinschaft* (Folk Community), of which the army was one expression. Of course not all units were equally fanatical, but German fighting power was heavily concentrated in elite units and they certainly were profoundly influenced by Nazi doctrine. And the war in China meant Japanese were battle-hardened by the time they confronted western forces in 1941.

By contrast British and American soldiers were raised in societies whose culture disdained the military virtues, distrusted military leaders, and prized individualism. 'Combat Fatigue', the 'shell shock' of World War I, became an accepted fact of life in the allied armies and a major cause of casualties especially amongst their infantry. Undoubtedly it happened in the Soviet, German and Japanese forces, but its incidence was overridden by other factors like official coercion. Its prevalence in western armies arose from the sense of entitlement to life so characteristic of British and American culture. Unsurprisingly, therefore, almost all observers noted the curious lack of motivation of allied troops. They were even exhorted to fight hard so that they could go home, a curious nega-tivism which contrasted greatly with the ideological conviction of the armies of the Germans, the Soviets and the Japanese. Western soldiers were generally very cautious, and officers sometimes found it difficult to get men to follow them. An American captain of 7th Armoured Division reported: 'A few guys carry your attack, and the rest of the people sort of participate and arrive on the objective shortly after everybody else',[13] while a general urged his officers to convince their men 'that we have got to fight for our country as hard as the Germans are fighting for theirs'. And an American war correspondent commented:

in comparing the average American, British or Canadian soldier with the average German soldier, it is difficult to deny that the German was by far, in most cases, a superior fighting man. . . . The average American . . . is not a soldier, he is a civilian in uniform.[14]

Organisational factors were also at work. American officers were often very remote from those they led. British army officers took their tone from public school boys, valuing bravery, disdaining professional expertise and lacking initiative. Later in the war the British army placed a much heavier emphasis on professional training, but this took time to work its way through. Moreover, the RAF bled off much of the best of British manpower. US policy directed the most educated officers and men into the technical services, leaving the infantry with the rest. Thus even when training and experience improved, allied units were fairly inflexible.

In an infantry assault, a battalion of 600–1,000 men would attack on a front of about 400 metres, with two companies forward and a headquarters group immediately behind, followed by the last company as a reserve. There was chronic distrust in the western armies between infantry and armour because they were not trained to work together. Tanks were very vulnerable because their crews could see very little and they needed infantry to work with them to locate targets and anti-tank weapons. But allied infantry often expected the tanks to clear the way for them. This was in sharp contrast to the close liaison between tanks and *Panzergrenadiers* in German armoured divisions. If objectives were reached allied troops tended to stop instead of seeking to exploit enemy disorder. A German soldier said of the Americans fighting in Normandy: 'We could not understand why they did not break through. The allied soldiers never seemed to be trained as we were, always to try to do more than had been asked of us.'[15]

Night attacks were very rare, and as a result the *Wehrmacht* could generally use the hours of darkness to resupply and reorganise, undoing much of the value of allied air supremacy. German infantry in attack used infiltration tactics which were virtually unknown in the allied forces, sending small units into enemy lines to surround and overcome their enemies. This hesitancy and clumsiness are hardly surprising in view of the cultural background of allied troops. However, it perhaps owed something to the reluctance of western armies to create elite units. Those that existed, the Paratroops and the US Marines, showed an aggression usually lacking elsewhere. But in Western Europe such forces were very small – the Germans managed to form elite units on a much larger scale.

It is indicative of their neglect of the ground war that neither the British nor the Americans built a really good tank or developed an infantry anti-tank weapon as excellent as the German *Panzerfaust*. But both the British and the American armies were highly mechanised, enjoyed lavish logistical support and were provided with excellent artillery. A German prisoner of the Americans in 1944 remarked:

> We drove past kilometer after kilometer of Allied artillery positions, thousands of guns. With us it was always 'Sweat saves Blood', but with them it was 'Equipment saves Men'. Not with us. We didn't need the equipment did we? After all, we were heroes.[16]

But air power was decisive in the allied victory. After the Normandy landings the allied air forces were in the ascendant, and they could be called upon to clear the way for the ground troops. Communications were improved until in Normandy tank commanders could call up air strikes, though even with complete command of the air such missions were very dangerous and losses were heavy.

For the most part allied generals had little experience and inadequate preparation for handling large armies. The German General Staff had served as a nursery for such skills and produced a whole range of very able generals amongst whom Guderian, Model and von Manstein rank high. Soviet commanders learned to be efficient or fell victim to the terror which drove their whole system. Zhukov was probably the greatest commander of World War II, displaying a real flair for handling huge masses of men and material, but several of his Soviet colleagues ran him close. Amongst the Allies only the American General Patton displayed anything like such ability, while the British Montgomery was a dour but effective technician. Undoubtedly allied generals were hampered by the certain knowledge that they would be criticised for losses rather than praised for gaining ground or killing Germans: that was the result of the cultural context in which they worked. When Churchill told him that the Americans felt the British were unduly wary of taking casualties, Montgomery snapped back: 'It was you, Prime Minister, who told me we must not suffer casualties on the scale of the Somme.'[17] As a result they feared to sustain attacks in the face of casualties. A German general commented on the consequences of this fear in Normandy:

> I cannot follow the reasoning that these tactics were supposed to have helped avoid bloodshed, as I was told by captured American officers. For although losses on the day of the attack could be kept low, on the other hand total losses suffered through continuous minor attacks launched

over a long period, were surely heavier than would have been the case if a forceful attack had been conducted.[18]

Once the Anglo-Americans had broken out of Normandy, their pursuit of a scattered enemy was cautious and they proved very reluctant to press on the line of weakest resistance if this meant exposing their flanks, even when the German forces there were virtually immobile. This meant that the line had to advance at the pace of the slowest, to the frustration of bolder spirits like Patton. Such a strategy was in direct contradiction to one of the primary lessons of the war, that deep penetration into the enemy's rear areas paid the highest dividends. Their concern to avoid casualties came at a considerable price when Hitler counter-attacked in what has become known as the Battle of the Bulge, which inflicted 80,000 losses upon the Americans and delayed the end of the war.

But every general makes mistakes, and for all the splendid human material at their disposal the Germans, Japanese and Soviets made major strategic and tactical blunders. The German generals launched Barbarossa with insufficient attention to logistics, which imposed a series of halts on their drive to Moscow. This was a general weakness of German planning epitomised by Rommel who, on being asked how he could supply his army in the North African desert in 1941, responded, 'That is quite immaterial to me. That's your pigeon.'[19]

The presumption of victory against Russia in 1941 and their belief in the inferiority of the Slavs left the Germans with no Plan B when the attack on Moscow was driven back. The Soviets ignored all warnings of Barbarossa and were taken by surprise with their armies in disarray. Even at the end of the war in the final assault upon Berlin the two Soviet armies involved were so poorly coordinated that they got in each other's way and fired upon one another. The Japanese army and navy fought very separate wars, the former obsessed with China and the latter enmeshed in a far-flung war with the US. Once it was clear after Midway that they could not drive the Americans from the Pacific, the navy simply adopted a defensive stance which depended on scattered garrisons on islands which US naval and air power for the most part simply isolated. They were focused on a fleet action, and neglected communications across their vast defensive perimeter, allowing US submarines to destroy their merchant fleet and cut the home islands off from their sources of raw material.

On top of these military errors, the Axis powers committed political mistakes with serious consequences which were clearly the result of their dominant cultures. As the Germans advanced into Eastern Europe they were often greeted as liberators, especially in the Baltic and the Ukraine. Hitler was not wrong in his perception that Stalin's regime was deeply hated in much of the USSR. But such was German disdain for the Slavs that they dismissed any cooperation. Planning for Barbarossa required the conquered lands to feed the German army, even though it was calculated that this would cause some six million of the Russian people to starve to death. As hatred of the occupier grew, so did resistance, fuelled by a sense of hopeless rage.

Nationalist resistance groups emerged in the Ukraine and Belarus, some of whom would carry on their war against the Soviets long after 1945, while refugee Jews armed themselves in desperation. Russian soldiers left behind by the German advance were very important in Belarus, and were supplemented by infiltrators and supplied by air. These official forces often deliberately provoked the Germans into reprisals in order to create enmity between the occupiers and the local population. Gradually Central and Eastern Europe became a charnel house and by 1943 German rear areas were becoming highly dangerous, forcing the *Wehrmacht* to withdraw troops from the line to carry out sweeps to safeguard communications. Attempts were made to cultivate local populations, but they foundered on the demands of the conquerors for food. Even so, by 1944 there were a million Soviet deserters in German uniform, and Hitler, fearful of treachery, ordered many to be transferred to the west where they fought against the western Allies. Vlasov was a Soviet general who defected to the Nazis and urged the formation of a Russian liberation army. Only one division actually fought against the Red Army on the Oder in April 1945, but its men acquitted themselves well, an indication of what a more prudent policy might have achieved. But Hitler was not interested in supporting Ukrainian and other nationalists – he wanted his Slavs as slaves.

The Japanese too enjoyed a welcome as liberators of eastern peoples from western colonialists. After the fall of Singapore some 40,000 out of a total of 45,000 captured Indian troops volunteered for the Indian National Army which, after reorganisation under the political leader, Subhas Chandra Bose, served against the British. Although the Indian Congress Party was never pro-Japanese, these men enjoyed much sympathy in India. But they were poorly armed and rather too obviously served as Japanese stooges; by contrast 1.5 million Indian troops served with considerable distinction under the British in Burma.

The Japanese established puppet governments in their conquered lands under the banner of the 'Greater East Asia Co-Prosperity Sphere' which stood for 'Asia for Asians', a simple slogan with much appeal. They

dismantled the Dutch government of Indonesia, encouraged the emergence of local forces and promoted national leaders like Sukarno, later the
first president of Indonesia. But the Japanese navy and military brutalised
civilians, many of whom were carried off for forced labour in the Japanese
Empire. As Burma's President under Japanese occupation remarked:

> The militarists saw everything only in a Japanese perspective and, even
> worse, they insisted that all others dealing with them should do the same.
> For them there was only one way to do a thing, the Japanese way; only one
> goal and interest, the Japanese interest; only one destiny for the East Asian
> countries, to become so many Manchukuos or Koreas tied forever to
> Japan. These racial impositions . . . made any real understanding between
> the Japanese militarists and the people of our region virtually impossible.[20]

The very cultures which produced excellent soldiers in Japan and
Germany also fostered this kind of unbending arrogance and racial pride.
And in turn this stimulated insurgencies against them.

In Europe the British tried to foment uprisings against the Germans.
In July 1940 Britain formed the Special Operations Executive (SOE), its
mission, in Churchill's words, being 'to set Europe ablaze'. In this it was a
failure until it had become very evident that Germany faced defeat. After
the German attack on the Soviet Union, Communist parties everywhere
were active in resistance and as the tide of war turned against the Axis
their partisans were very obviously jockeying for power in post-war
Europe. In Italy, Greece and Yugoslavia this produced civil wars as the
Germans fell back. But it was not until the very late stages of the war that
these resistance movements became more than an inconvenience for the
Germans. The main value of these networks was to provide intelligence to
the Allies. In France the collaborationist Vichy regime enjoyed considerable support, and as late as August 1944 its President, General Pétain, was
welcomed with enormous enthusiasm in Paris. The German occupation
in the west was orderly, and it could count on bitter hatred of the communists to keep local populations in line.

But under the impact of the Normandy invasion and the insurgency
which hope of deliverance generated, eastern methods were imported into
the west. In June 1944 2nd SS Panzer division *Das Reich* was moving from
Montauban to Normandy. Harassed by resistance fighters, one of its units
burned the village of Oradour-sur-Glane killing 642 people, including 247
women and 205 children, who were burned to death in the church. One of
its officers later remarked that they did such things weekly in the Soviet

Union. This kind of savagery, and the mounting scale of the forced recruitment of young men for labour service in the *Reich*, fanned resistance. Even so, before the D-Day landings the French resistance was not a problem for the Germans, who regarded the west generally as a very soft posting.

Guerrilla warfare was most important in China. The Japanese army fought the Nationalist regime of Chiang Kai-shek based in the south with its capital first at Nanjing and later at Chungking. This was very much the same kind of war as fought by the great powers, but at a more primitive level. The greatest asset of the Nationalists was the sheer size of China and the inability of the Japanese army to control its vast conquests. In the north the Communist Party fought a quite separate war from its mountainous enclaves. There the communists destroyed the power of the landlords and imposed a strict discipline on their followers. This 'Yan'an Way' was able to flourish because the Japanese focused on the nationalist south. But the communists used their secure bases to foster a substantial guerrilla movement against the invaders. This war was marked by a systematic attempt by Mao Tse-tung, the communist leader, to formulate the idea of 'People's War'. His ideas were not particularly original, and indeed they bear the stamp of Clausewitz's comments on the same subject, but they provided a new blueprint adapted to notions of revolution. And in time they came to be associated with success – the triumph of communism in China in 1949.

World War II was a truly global conflict in which almost no area of the world except the Antarctic was spared. The death toll is almost incalculable, but something in the region of 60–70 million died, of whom at least two-thirds were civilians. It was a war rooted in the European experience and in European ideas. Hitler proclaimed that he was fighting for *Lebensraum* and he certainly evoked memories of the short-lived German Empire in Eastern Europe of 1915–18. The Japanese were deeply preoccupied by access to resources. Yet this was not merely a war for territory. Nazism was an ideology which owed much to the experience of empire. The European world-empires, which appeared in the eighteenth and extended into the nineteenth century, were an astonishing phenomenon, and it was hardly surprising that they were explained in terms of racial superiority. For the most part this was casual and assumed but it gave birth to systematic racialist theory. Houston Stewart Chamberlain (1855–1927) was an Englishman whose *Die Grundlagen des neunzehnten Jahrhunderts* (The Foundations of the Nineteenth Century) profoundly influenced Hitler. Chamberlain proclaimed the supremacy of the 'Aryan' peoples, whose finest expression was in the Germanic races – the British and the Germans. This notion, that race could be identified with nation, was appealing and dynamic, and posited the notion of a hierarchy of states. Chamberlain's was a highly explicit assertion of ideas which were circulating all over the advanced world, albeit in a very crude and barely articulated way. 'The British race' and the 'white man's burden' were clichés of the age, and the notions of superiority embodied in them justified rule over a vast empire, while Manifest Destiny was the same sentiment in American guise. Racialist thinking drew its strength from the vulgarisation of scientific ideas like the natural selection posited by Darwin and it was buttressed by eugenics and even notions of public health which urged the sterilisation of the unfit and the insane. Japan stood in a quite different cultural tradition, and indeed was often the butt of European racialism. Its leaders were deeply anxious because their huge population and growing industry were sustained by few natural resources and their island lacked even the capacity to grow food. The militarist option of conquering resources was, therefore, highly attractive and was in the ascendant in domestic politics in the late 1930s. Notions of racial superiority were not at all foreign to their outlook, so that alliance with Germany and Italy was both opportune and, in an ideological sense, congenial.

Racialist ideas were very strong in Central Europe where politics were dominated by ferocious competition amongst numerous peoples, all of whom despised the Jews. In the period after 1918 these notions served yet another purpose in that they provided a set of ideas to counter the ideology of the new nightmare in the east – the Soviet Union. Her regime was founded on the ideas of Karl Marx which arose very directly from analysis of the changing conditions of nineteenth-century capitalism. Marx's ideas were inherently more rational than the mishmash propounded by Hitler, but the communist regime, as established by Lenin and Stalin, was scarcely less irrational in its brutal repression and massacre of its own peoples. Nor was it without a strong racialist tinge, for the Soviet Union was actually a Russian empire dominating many peoples whose role within the Soviet Union was strictly subordinate.

Yet the soldiers of both these states, for all their perversity and horror, fought for them with a will never mustered by the men of the western democracies. Their soldiers butchered one another and any civilians who happened to get in their way with an eagerness which far outstriped that of the crusaders and jihadis of an earlier age. Out of the welter of ideas produced in the nineteenth century these regimes successfully distilled a common essence, the subordination of the individual to the collective: the race in Germany, the notion of universal revolution in the Soviet Union. Never has the idea of a connection between democracy and military success been more loudly and convincingly refuted. The Industrial Revolution of the nineteenth century generated a mass culture which embodied a plethora of ideas, out of which arose the competing systems that fought for world domination in 1939–45. The liberal democracy of Britain and America signally failed to inspire its subjects with martial spirit, and indeed never really tried to do so. Their cultures, to which their war leaders had to be responsive, emphasised the sanctity of human life and the primacy of the individual. This forced their governments to plan and organise in a way that promised to minimise casualties. As a result these states planned and organised brilliantly for war, creating large arsenals and highly effective elite units, like RAF Bomber Command, which harnessed high technology to give them a destructive power out of all proportion to their numbers. But without underestimating their contribution, it must be recognised that war remained a matter of men killing men at relatively close range, and in this process technical innovation had limited success. It was the ferocious ground war in Eastern Europe which destroyed the Nazi regime, and the Chinese conflict which enfeebled Japan.

Ultimately World War II, like World War I, was decided by attrition. It was fought by rapid movement on air, land and sea and over vast spaces, but this should not be allowed to disguise the simple fact that Germany and Japan were defeated by weight of numbers and materiel. This is not to decry the skill, determination and bravery of the Allies – but such qualities were apparent on both sides and in the end numbers and industrial production told. In Germany there was no collapse as there had been in 1918. Hitler's 'Cultural Revolution' and his apparatus of state terror ensured that resistance continued until his own office was all but overrun. Over a third of all the German troops killed in World War II died in the first four and a half months of 1945 before the surrender in May. Millions of civilians died or were displaced in this chaotic *Gotterdämmerung* of the Nazi regime. But until Hitler died they went on fighting, such was his hold over the German people. The Japanese authorities, by 1945 stripped of their empire and under threat of invasion, demanded that the whole population should resist to the last. It was against this background that the Americans dropped the atomic bomb, forcing a surrender which probably saved millions of Japanese lives. This nuclear wonder emphasised the technological aspect of World War II which has stayed in the public mind, but without murderous ground fighting there would have been no victory. The machinery of states enabled governments to mobilise whole peoples more intensively than ever before, so that the outcome could only be decided by attrition. And so it would be with the next great war: the Cold War, fought in very different ways.

CHAPTER ELEVEN

A NEW AGE OF WAR

It is only the dead who have seen the end of war.[1]

WORLD War II destroyed the great European empires, but set in their place a no less western-dominated world order. This was because the amazing military technology revealed by that war was largely monopolised by the two victor powers, the US and the Soviet Union. They were rivals but this should not be allowed to obscure their essentially western nature and common dependence on technological warfare. They were rather different from the preceding empires amongst whose dying remains they were contending.

The Soviet Union portrayed itself as the embodiment of egalitarian socialism, and declared its ultimate purpose to be to spread the socialist revolution. This concealed the reality of a Russian empire dominating the unwilling peoples of Eastern Europe like Belarus, the Ukraine and the Baltic States, and to the east the Turkish and Mongol peoples of Western, Central and Northern Asia. Her western frontier was buttressed by satellite states annexed after World War II when they were 'liberated' by the Red Army from German rule, notably Poland and East Germany, which acted as bases from which the Soviet army confronted the West. The US was a rather more homogeneous state, and exerted enormous power across the globe through the reach of its economy and direct control of critical military facilities, though these were not usually in the form of colonies. The US claimed to stand for democracy and free-market capitalism, even though within its frontiers there were large minorities, especially blacks, who did not enjoy full rights. Beyond its borders, US economic and military power enabled it to dominate many states and patronise almost any regime which would stand against communism, whatever its methods or ideology.

The conflict between the two was never direct because both parties had too much to lose. The US invented the atomic bomb which it used against Japan in 1945, and subsequently developed the even more powerful hydrogen bomb in 1951. In 1949 the Soviets tested an atom bomb, and by 1955 had the hydrogen bomb. The US launched the first nuclear submarine in 1955 and this was matched by the USSR in 1958; subsequently each side equalled the other in the production of stealthier and more effective vessels. In 1955 the first launch of a ballistic missile from a submarine was achieved by the USSR, though it struggled to match the later Polaris, Poseidon and Trident systems deployed by the US. In 1957 the launch of the world's first artificial satellite, Sputnik 1, betokened Soviet advances in space and ballistic missiles. Subsequently the two superpowers expanded their missile arsenals in a way that maintained the balance of terror.

The emergence of nuclear weapons introduced the terrible prospect of world destruction. By about 1960 each side had the power to wipe out the other, but, because there was no defence against missile attack, only at the price of its own annihilation. As a result the notion of Mutually Assured Destruction (MAD) created a stalemate which neither side dared to break overtly. In general the US had superior air and missile power, was dominant at sea, and clearly maintained a technological lead. But Russia, with her allies, had a huge nuclear capacity and a massive conventional supremacy which effectively meant that they held Western Europe as a hostage against US power.

This equilibrium was far from stable. The line of demarcation between Soviet-dominated Central and Eastern Europe and the West lay through Germany. But by wartime agreement Berlin, though in Soviet-controlled East Germany, was administered by the US, Britain, France and the Soviet Union. In June 1948, in an attempt to seize total control of Berlin, the Soviets cut off all supplies by land. The Allies responded by a massive airlift which went on till May 1949. In April 1949 the US and some of the countries of Western Europe formed the North Atlantic Treaty Organization (NATO). This was later countered by the Soviet-inspired Warsaw Pact of 1955 which embraced all the Soviet satellites in Eastern Europe. In June 1953 demonstrations against the Soviet occupation in Berlin were put down by tanks and troops. In summer 1961 Soviet-occupied East Germany, the German Democratic Republic (GDR), with the backing of its Soviet masters, built the Berlin Wall to prevent its citizens leaching westwards, precipitating a crisis in which tanks faced one another at the Checkpoint Charlie crossing, causing tension around the world. Thereafter, conflict in Europe was covert, but it was nakedly apparent in less sensitive parts of the world.

The Soviet Union lent its support to colonial peoples trying to throw off their European rulers, and its greatest success was the triumph of communism in China in 1949. The victory of the North Vietnamese communists over the French colonial forces in the Indochina War in 1954 owed an enormous amount to Russian and Chinese support. The 1959 revolution in Cuba moved quickly from its native origins into the Soviet sphere of influence, forming an outpost for agitation in South America, traditionally seen as America's backyard. A colonial revolt against Portuguese rule in Angola broke out in 1961 where the Soviets backed the left-wing MPLA. After independence in 1975, however, they were drawn into its civil war against rival parties which dragged on until 2002. In 1965–6 the simmering conflict in Indonesia between the communist PKI and the Muslim parties exploded in a wave of violence in which 500,000 to a million people died:

> The murder campaign became so brazen in parts of rural East Java, that Moslem bands placed the heads of victims on poles and paraded them through villages. The killings have been on such a scale that the disposal of the corpses has created a serious sanitation problem in East Java and Northern Sumatra where the humid air bears the reek of decaying flesh. Travelers from those areas tell of small rivers and streams that have been literally clogged with bodies.[2]

In 1974 a left-wing coup in Abyssinia received Soviet support, precipitating a series of grim and bloody wars in the Horn of Africa involving Ethiopia, Eritrea and Somalia, each of which was at one time or another backed by the US or the Soviets.

Thus the world was divided in its allegiance between the eastern and western blocs, with a 'Non-Aligned Movement' emerging, largely made up of former colonial states. Neither bloc seriously accepted this neutrality because non-aligned countries almost always leaned to one side or the other. The blocs were not monolithic. Some of the new countries owed little to either side and tried to exploit their non-aligned status to extract concessions from both. Algeria emerged from French colonial control after a long struggle from 1954 to 1962, owing little to the Soviets who had given barely more than rhetorical support. From 1959 onwards there was tension between China and the Soviet Union focusing on the 4,000-kilometre-long border between the two states which China regarded as the legacy of the 'unequal treaties' of the past. In 1969 fighting erupted over possession of islands in the Ussuri and Amur rivers. Thereafter, relations between the two communist powers were very cool. Although China had atomic weapons by 1964, her relative weakness meant that no tri-polar world emerged. Many states were highly equivocal in their attitudes to the main confrontation. France was western and nuclear-armed, and after 1958 had a right-wing government, but defected from NATO in protest at its domination by the US. Communist Yugoslavia was expelled from the Soviet bloc in 1948. Its communist partisans, led by Tito, had seized power after the German retreat in 1945 before the Red Army could arrive, and they objected to Stalin's attempt to dominate their country. Western aid enabled them to sustain their independence. Nevertheless, the polarisation of the two blocs was the central fact of world politics from 1945 to 1989.

The Cold War was in part a war of cultures and in a sense a European civil war on a global scale. Ultimately Karl Marx and George Washington were both Europeans with ideas rooted in the history of that continent. The Soviet Union offered a vision of an egalitarian future and in practical terms provided struggling new regimes in ex-colonial territories with a model of development linked to national ownership and the prospect of a disciplined and orderly population. In Europe, Communist parties were the legacy of the tensions in industrial society. They were especially strong in Greece and Italy where their command of substantial votes caused much unease in the NATO alliance. In France, however, the failure of the communists to oppose General de Gaulle's coup in 1958 weakened them. More generally, as Europe became richer, class conflict lost it attraction, Europeans became conscious of the nightmare states of Central and Eastern Europe, and elec-torates preferred the notion of personal freedom strongly propagated by the US. In fact, the US cultural impact was enormous: Japan, a traditionally isolationist society, was transformed, at least superficially, into a member of the 'western' bloc. American music, fashion, clothes and language were adopted, even in the states of its enemies. This was because, despite the obvious inconsistencies, the US was an open society. Moreover, US domi-nation of world communications focused the attention of millions far and wide who were deeply impressed by her wealth and the accompanying culture of plenty. 'Coca-Cola culture' was sneered at by intellectuals, but the history of the second half of the twentieth century was played out to a distinctively American rock music accompaniment.

Actual fighting in this grand conflict was largely done by the surrogates of the two great powers, but on particular occasions it involved one or the other in fighting (though never both at the same time) and threatened the uneasy stability assured by MAD. These events shaped military development in the twentieth century. War in Korea (June 1950–July 1953) came close to pitting the two superpowers against one another in a conventional war. At the end of World War II Korea had been divided on the 38th Parallel between a communist North and a southern republic under American protection. In 1950 the Soviet Union and China conspired with North Korea to invade and annex the South. This act of naked aggression produced an entirely new response of great political importance for the future. The anti-war culture of Britain and America, strengthened by the horrors of World War II, had demanded that nations comply with the rule of law. One consequence of this impulse was the establishment of a War Crimes Tribunal at Nuremberg which tried the surviving leading Nazis on such charges as Conspiracy against the Peace and Crimes against Humanity, even though such crimes had not existed at the time they were committed. However imperfectly, the trials embodied the growing sense in the popular culture of the US and some other western states that international relations should be subject to law.

The same impulse had led to the foundation meeting of the United Nations (UN) in 1945 in San Francisco. The first session of its General Council met in London in 1946, and its HQ later settled in New York. The aim was to create an organisation founded on respect for human rights which would be more effective in securing peace than the old League of Nations. In fact, its direct influence has always been limited, but it became a key forum in which the superpowers fought out their struggle for hearts and minds. The United Nations became a kind of moral arbiter in the quarrels of member nations, and an environment in which contact could be maintained between competing forces so that disputes could be resolved by negotiation. In June 1950, when communist North Korea invaded the South, the UN passed Resolution 83 condemning the attack as an act of aggression and creating a United Nations Force which fought the war until its end in 1953. In a sense the Korean conflict became a 'just war' in a new era of conflicts. There was now a tribunal in which all countries needed to justify their actions, and Resolution 83 demonstrated an ability to impose sanctions on those who offended.

In fact this was an American war, for US forces dominated, suffering 36,516 dead, and this meant that the allied force reflected very closely the strengths and weaknesses of the United States military. After World War II America demobilised rapidly and its army was scattered across the face of the globe in forty-nine countries and six continents. Training suffered as a consequence and there was a startling rundown in equipment. This situation owed much to the outlook of the US public and its politicians; in short, to popular culture. Air power hypnotised US politicians, with its vision of war without the dreadful casualties of the landings at Okinawa or Omaha beach and the grim slog through Europe in 1944–5. The organisation of the US high command meant that the three services competed openly for resources, and members of Congress were highly conscious of the impact of lobbying on their electorates. For a nation in love with technology the air force offered impressive toys and great hopes. And above all, there was the Bomb, which until the late 1950s could only be delivered by the air force. As a result the army was neglected.

Against a well-prepared North Korean enemy the US Eighth Army barely survived. This was infantry warfare in a mountainous and seamed countryside where it was difficult to apply firepower, even when the air force's efforts were supplemented by the US navy's carriers. Soviet MiG fighters, mostly flown by Russian pilots, contested US air supremacy, but were defeated by the North American F-86 Sabre. Massive bombardment from the air destroyed the North's industrial base and damaged its army. US Marine forces landed in the rear at Incheon forcing a retreat. The US army then invaded North Korea, which collapsed; but this inspired China to intervene. Chinese regulars were well equipped and well trained for infantry warfare and drove back the Americans and their allies, primarily by infiltration tactics:

> The usual method was to infiltrate small units, from a platoon of fifty men to a company of 200, split into separate detachments. While one team cut off the escape route of the Americans, the others struck both the front and the flanks in concerted assaults. The attacks continued on all sides until the defenders were destroyed or forced to withdraw. The Chinese then crept forward to the open flank of the next platoon position, and repeated the tactics.[3]

At other times raw conscripts were thrown at US positions in human wave attacks redolent of eighteenth-century tactics, with appalling losses. In the end the war became a stalemate fixed along the 38th Parallel where it had begun and this was frozen by the July 1953 ceasefire which established a demilitarised zone.

The Korean War clearly showed the limitations of air power when use of nuclear weapons seemed impossible because it might precipitate a much wider conflict. Old-fashioned infantry tactics were essential, but the US army was hampered by its lack of resources and by the fear of casualties which had been so potent in western nations since World War I and was now increasing in strength. The Eisenhower administration (1953–61) in the US reacted to the experience of Korea with a 'New Look' policy which relied on massive nuclear retaliation delivered by the United States Air Force (USAF) which had become independent in 1947. This was despite its failure to produce a decisive result either in World War II or in Korea as its leaders had predicted. Fear of casualties was a powerful influence upon Eisenhower, who commented:

> Now our most valued, our most costly asset is our young men. Let's don't use them any more than we have to. For 40 years I was in the army, and I did one thing: study how you can get an infantry platoon out of battle. The most terrible job in warfare is to be a second lieutenant leading a platoon when you are on the battlefield.[4]

The result was what has been called 'Bilko's Army',[5] a large but ill-trained conscript force mainly stationed in the US, Japan and Germany, with no clear role and increasingly poor equipment. Eisenhower believed that the air force, and specifically Strategic Air Command (SAC), could deter the Soviet Union, while the navy could provide a flexible response to aggression across the globe. He was determined to fight only wars the US could win, avoiding conflict in states like Korea on the fringes of the communist bloc, which is why in 1954 he bluntly refused to help the French in their struggle against communist insurgency in Indochina. In Europe he was aware of US weakness and the feebleness of his allies, but there the balance of terror would keep the peace. Eisenhower was a highly experienced soldier, but he made no effort to create a unified command which would produce a single national strategy. Under him the rivalry between the services escalated, and their staffs barely consulted one another. America's enemies took note of its conventional weakness, but became fearful of its advanced nuclear weaponry.

War became an increasingly bitter bone of contention between the parties in US politics. Kennedy won the 1960 presidential election partly on the basis of a supposed 'missile gap', the notion that the USSR had a lead in missile technology, given credibility by the launching of Sputnik 1 in October 1957 and the early spectacular failures of the US Vanguard missile programme. It was against this background that in October 1962 Nikita Khrushchev tried to shift the nuclear balance of power in favour of the USSR by installing missiles in Cuba, precipitating a major crisis in that 'Autumn of the Missiles' which brought the world to the brink of nuclear destruction. For a moment the words of a satirical song had a terrible relevance:

And we will all go together when we go
What a comforting thought that is to know.
Universal bereavement, an inspiring achievement
Yes, we will all go together when we go.[6]

The depth of the crisis led to the establishment of a hotline between the US and Soviet leaders, and undoubtedly the proximity to apocalypse moderated behaviour on both sides.

But the commonest kind of war from the 1950s onwards was insurgency, usually directed by native peoples against colonial powers. Guerrilla warfare which mobilised a population against an enemy army was nothing new. The Jewish War of AD 66–70 cost Rome dear. In Revolutionary France, the uprising in the Vendée 1791–1801, essentially a protest against the anti-Catholic stance of the Republic and conscription, was a people's war, as suggested by its duration and the concessions to Catholicism which brought it to an end. In 1808 the Napoleonic conquest of Spain provoked a savage guerrilla war immortalised by the *Disasters of War* drawings of Goya. As the sheer firepower of western armies increased it was almost the only option for native peoples threatened by the colonial powers. Many of the resulting conflicts were of considerable duration. France began the conquest of Algeria in 1830, arousing deep hostility in the native population who could count on support and refuge in neighbouring Morocco. Based in Tlemcen, Abd al-Qadir launched a jihad, defeating the French in 1836 and establishing control over nearly two-thirds of the country, from which he was only ejected in 1847 when a third of the French army destroyed the crops on which his forces subsisted. In the enormous and wild Kabylia, Bou Baghla held out, defeating a French column at Tachekkirt in July 1854. After his death in 1855 a woman, Lalla Fatma, commanded the resistance. French settlers poured in, leading to another revolt in 1871. The Foreign Legion was born in Algeria in 1831, and it is hardly surprising that it became the world's first specialised counter-insurgency force. Tunisia was annexed in 1881, and in 1907 Morocco was partitioned, with Spain occupying much of the north. In the natural redoubt of the Rif mountains Abd-el-Krim rebelled against the Spanish, defeating their army and killing 8,000 troops. In 1925 he provoked the French by attacking their territory, and an army of 250,000 French troops eventually destroyed his Rif republic in 1926.

Russia faced a similar bitter resistance by Muslim mountain peoples in the long Caucasian War, 1817–64. Under Imam Shamil they fought off a major Russian offensive led by Prince Vorontsov in 1845. Between 1856 and 1859 a quarter of a million Russian troops finally brought the resistance to an end. Appalling hardships were inflicted upon the civilian population, and whole communities, like the Circassians, were resettled in other parts of Russia or expelled to the Ottoman lands, as a result of which hundreds of thousands died. The tribes of the steppe forest of northern Asia suffered in much the same way if they resisted. The US did not greatly desire to rule its various Indian tribes, but the growing population and its inexorable westward expansion destroyed or confined them to indifferent reservation lands. In 1898 the US invaded the Philippines, whose army capitulated after a brave resistance. However, a guerrilla war in the jungle continued until 1913. It is said that the Colt. 45 automatic pistol was commissioned by the US army which found that in the close-range jungle fighting they needed a weapon that could stop as well as kill an attacker. In the face of resistance the British displayed similar ruthlessness, massacring the Indian mutineers of 1857–9 and mowing down the Sudanese at Omdurman in 1898.

But after World War II suppressing insurgencies became more difficult for a number of reasons. The successful Irish revolt of 1919–22 set an encouraging example. Political organisation was becoming more sophisticated and Mao Tse-tung, the communist leader in China, formulated a blueprint of 'People's War' which was widely copied. Anti-colonial movements could generally attract some aid from the communist bloc. In a military sense the light high-powered weapons developed by the great powers leaked into the wider world, giving guerrillas formidable striking power. If guerrillas could never match the firepower of regular forces, they could now achieve a local superiority to deadly effect. Much, of course, depended upon the countryside and access to help. The jungle of Malaya provided shelter for the communist uprising there (1948–60), but the country was sufficiently distant from China to make assistance difficult. And the rebels were mostly Chinese, against whom the British mobilised the Malays. But crucial to its suppression, and that of the Mau Mau in Kenya, was the establishment of protected settlements, which isolated the population from the rebel elements as a step towards destroying the latter. The techniques of repression were well understood and well practised, but the problem was that they were now exposed to the gaze of American and European peoples whose cultural development caused them to regard such things as barbarism.

The crucial factor in any insurgency was that the guerrilla hid behind the civilian population. Mao argued that guerilla commanders must establish a close link between political ends by seeking a base of political support, and warfare. He stated bluntly that coercion was a vital element, though not the only one, in this process. And he argued forcefully that 'The guerrilla must move amongst the people as a fish swims in the sea.' This stratagem hazards the lives of innocents, but is justified by the end served. In practice, as the guerrilla movement escalates, it becomes increasingly able to force the civilian population to respond to its needs. In the Chinese civil war (1945–9) such tactics in enemy areas opened the way for the regular communist forces to advance from their well-established bases. The whole process was made possible by the growing disillusion with the nationalist regime. Guerrilla warfare depends upon a tight union between political and military preparation, and is the very epitome of Clausewitz's argument that war is the continuation of policy by other means. In military terms any insurgency which enjoys some real support poses very severe problems for regular forces. Their small units are exposed to hit and run attacks, but if they respond to an incident with massive fire-power they will alienate the population they need to conciliate.

The old imperial powers had been perfectly prepared to do this, but the growth of the media in the second half of the twentieth century thrust such nasty business right under the noses of the public in western countries. In Europe and the US the whole idea of the 'Laws of War' was based on the separation of soldiers and civilians and the immunity of the latter from the actions of the former. Moreover, in these states a civilian population, imagining itself immune from such horror, could not understand why and how they happened. Since the Amritsar massacre and the 'excesses' of the Black and Tans in southern Ireland, this cultural vulnerability has been a major military factor. Before then, and for a time after, authorities could get away with traditional methods which had always been hidden from sight, but this was no longer possible. Live TV reporting and the public reaction to it helped to bring about the US defeat in South Vietnam in the 1960s and '70s.

The French colony of Vietnam had been occupied by the Japanese, but on their defeat the Vietminh guerrilla movement which had fought very effectively against them claimed independence. The French reasserted their position as the colonial power, and initially enjoyed some success. However, after their victory in 1949 the Chinese communist government supplied much aid to the insurgents in the northern part of Vietnam. As a result the Vietminh defeated the French at Dien Bien Phu in 1954, leading to the Geneva Accords which gave independence to Cambodia and Laos and divided Vietnam at the 17th Parallel. The massive influx of anti-communist refugees into the south, especially Catholics, led to the formation of a South Vietnamese Republic, opposed to union with the North and backed by the US.

Eisenhower had refused to commit American forces to support the French in accordance with his military doctrine. But the growth of a Vietcong insurgency in the South supported by the North worried the US which was afraid that a collapse in South Vietnam would deliver Laos, Cambodia and perhaps even Thailand over to communism. President Kennedy, though hesitant about open intervention, was concerned that his domestic opponents would charge him with being soft on communism, and so permitted a drift into war in Vietnam by increasing volumes of material support and establishing a large-scale military advice effort for the South. As the Vietcong insurgency grew, US ground forces were committed by President L.B. Johnson to the Vietnam War in 1965.

This was emphatically not the kind of war Eisenhower had wanted to fight, and the US army was very badly prepared. US forces were trained to use massive firepower particularly in the form of air bombardment, but it was difficult to bring this to bear against an elusive enemy in the jungle. It took time to develop intelligence networks to rectify this situation. US army equipment was poor. The standard US light machine-gun remained the Browning Automatic Rifle, despite its many defects which had come to light during World War II, while well into the war US troops picked up the enemy's Russian-made AK-47 rifles which they regarded as far superior to their own. The Vietcong had excellent weapons, notably the Soviet Rocket Propelled Grenade launcher (RPG). Fighting at close range in the jungle was savage and casualties were heavy in combat units, although only a small part of the US army in Vietnam actually took part in combat.

The constraints of the Cold War age had a profound effect on the US. There was no question of using nuclear weapons. More surprisingly, it was judged politically inexpedient to bomb North Vietnam 'into the Stone Age' (in the popular phrase) because of world reaction, and even the port of Haiphong was not properly mined. Laos and Cambodia were safe havens where Vietcong and North Vietnamese units could rest and resupply, and though covert action was taken against these bases this was, until very late in the day, greatly circumscribed by the need to avoid breaking neutrality. The various arms of the US forces were very separate, so that army, navy and air force coordinated their efforts badly. In the north, along the demilitarised zone (DMZ), the US Marines fought a kind of private war, losing over 13,000 dead, roughly a quarter of the US total for the whole war.

In fact, given the extreme problems, US forces re-equipped and fought very well. The need for mobility produced air assault units equipped with helicopters like the Air Cavalry, which attacked the enemy directly on landing. Airborne units such as the 101st were converted to this role. They were supported by helicopter gunships which carried new weapons like the Minigun with its astonishing rate of fire of 3,000–4,000 rounds per minute. A new generation of mines like the Claymore, which could be used for offensive purposes, proved very effective. Above all, improved air cooperation could bring great power to bear even in small-unit encounters. Such firepower used indiscriminately took a grim toll of civilians as well as enemy fighters. The Americans and their South Vietnamese allies defeated the major communist Tet offensive of 1968 and virtually destroyed the Vietcong as a major force. After that the North Vietnamese Army (NVA) was obliged to carry the burden of the war.

But well before then, public support for the war was waning in the US. The years after World War II had seen a quite staggering rise in the standard of living in the US and many of its allies. People have rarely enjoyed membership of armies, and even in the era of nationalism in the later nineteenth century, there was resistance to compulsory military service. The two great wars of the twentieth century were fought with national conscript armies. But by the 1960s a new generation was growing up which perceived little gain and much personal loss in military service. The balance of nuclear terror appeared to make conventional armies out of date. At one and the same time the world seemed to live under the threat of nuclear annihilation and to enjoy effective immunity from war. With so much to live for young people focused protest increasingly on 'our boys', in that frightening slogan 'Hey, hey, LBJ, how many kids have you killed today!' Young Americans, largely middle-class college students, discovered that they could manipulate the media and especially television. In fact most of the fighting was done by regular volunteer units like the Marines and the Paratroops, but the media rarely considered such matters. The inequities of the US conscription system, with its numerous exemptions, came under severe criticism, as when people asked if more blacks were being drafted than WASPS. All this eroded the established connection between citizenship and military service.

Live coverage of the war by TV was riveting, but one-sided, and tended to convey the impression that the US and its allies were brutal. In fact all war is brutal and it cannot be fought in any other way, but this was not conveyed by TV coverage which all too often showed the effects of American firepower on civilians without being able to explain why this happened. Decisively, by 1968 the war seemed to be unsuccessful while the protest movement became ever more vociferous. Bereft of support,

President Johnson committed the US to a withdrawal, handing more of the war over to the Vietnamese with American support. His successor, Richard Nixon, placed great importance on bombing North Vietnam to maintain South Vietnam's independence, and this certainly worked well, but Congress felt he was committing the country to more war and placed a ban on aid, resulting in the collapse of South Vietnam in 1975. The victory of the North Vietnamese was an enormous blow to the US military, but hardly a triumph for communism. Vietnam feared China and allied with the Soviet Union against her, precipitating a war in 1979 which was not finally settled until 1989.

The Soviet Union suffered its own Vietnam when in 1979 it invaded Afghanistan in support of a Marxist government there whose anti-Islamic actions had aroused violent opposition. For ten years the Soviet army fought mujahideen, Islamic fighters who enjoyed the support of Britain and the US and many Islamic countries. The decisive Soviet weapon was the helicopter, which conferred mobility over the rugged terrain. It was, therefore, a severe blow when the US provided the mujahideen with the FIM-92 Stinger hand-held anti-aircraft missile system. Overall Soviet casualties were relatively modest, perhaps 30,000 dead in all, but the war cost the Soviets dearly in support from Islamic countries, and it increased financial pressure on their feeble economy, forcing a withdrawal in 1989. By this time, however, the Soviets had provided the Marxist government with an effective army which held power until 1992. By then the Soviet Union had ceased to exist and Russia, the main successor state, refused any more aid, causing it to collapse. There is a certain parallel between the defeats of the two superpowers in Vietnam and Afghanistan, but perhaps the real similarity is the recognition of how difficult it is to defeat an insurrection once it is well established.

But although 'people's war' commanded enormous attention in the 1960s and 1970s, the most dangerous and ultimately decisive events occurred in the field of conventional warfare. Prior to 1967 Israel had enjoyed limited US support, prompting the Soviet Union to buy Arab friendship by arming Syria, Egypt and Iraq who aimed to destroy her. But in the Six Day War (5–10 June 1967) Israeli forces overwhelmed those of Egypt, Syria and Jordan. The Israeli Defence Force (IDF) could muster less than 250,000 men against double that number, and had a motley collection of equipment, including Sherman tanks of World War II vintage. Its air force, with about 200 warplanes, spearheaded by 72 French Mirage IIIC and 36 Super Mystères, was numerically inferior to the 450 Egyptian planes, including many very modern Russian-supplied MiG-21s. Syria and Jordan also had substantial airforces.

But the IDF was well trained and flexible. It had adopted *Auftragstaktik* and practised the careful coordination of land and airforces in something closely resembling *Blitzkrieg*. A sudden strike by its planes destroyed the hostile airforces on the ground. Fast-moving ground assaults isolated Egyptian units whose doctrine, based on Soviet experience, called for defence in depth to repel the enemy who could then be crushed by massive counter-strokes. The Six Day War changed the map of the Middle East because Israel overran Sinai, the West Bank area of Jordan and the Golan Heights. It also sharpened the interest of the superpowers, with the US firmly supporting Israel as a surrogate and supplying equipment to match Soviet support for her enemies.

In 1973 a new Egyptian–Syrian alliance attacked Israel, and this time achieved complete surprise. One key element in the success of the Egyptian attack across the Suez Canal was the massive use by their infantry of anti-tank guided missile (ATGM) weapons to destroy Israeli tanks. But the Israelis adapted and with massive emergency US support beat off the enemy, after which Israel ceded Sinai to Egypt in return for diplomatic recognition. In the open territory of the Middle East, quite unlike the jungles of South America and South East Asia, conventional warfare worked. But it was in Europe that it was demonstrated to greatest effect.

The US army recovered from Vietnam and changed its very nature and much of its doctrine. In 1973 the US ended conscription, though men between 18 and 25 still have to register so that they can be conscripted in time of need; this was in fact considered during the bitter struggle after the Iraq War of 2003. Thus what emerged was an all-regular force which could be intensively trained. It strengthened its relationship with the airforce, developing the concept of 'AirLand Battle'. The problem this aimed to tackle was the overwhelming conventional strength of the Soviets and their allies, and their capacity to unleash massive tank armies against Western Europe which could raise only much smaller forces in response. US planners noted the events of the Arab–Israeli War of 1973 and decided that ATGMs could be deployed for aggression and not merely defence. This was possible because new missiles like TOW and Hellfire could be released with little exposure of the crews. They devised the notion of using highly mobile tank/infantry forces to strike into and disrupt the vast mass of an expected Soviet assault. Superior communications, increasingly by satellite, would enable their efforts to be coordinated and directed, and guaranteed support from the airforce.

The Vietnam War had forced the USAAF into the ground support role for which, at first, its aircraft and weapons were unsuited. Fast jets were not designed nor pilots trained to hit ground targets, and they proved to be very vulnerable to small-arms fire. As a result there was heavy reliance on the A1-Skyraider, a propeller-driven aircraft which was an obvious anachronism. But by 1977 the A-10 Warthog was coming into service specifically for ground attack. This was a heavily armoured plane designed around the GAU8-Avenger 30mm seven-barrelled cannon firing 4,200 rounds per minute, and capable of carrying a whole range of weapons. And by the end of the Vietnam War whole families of precision-guided munitions (PGMs) were coming into use. These 'smart bombs' could find their targets from a distance which protected the aircraft. On 13 May 1972 laser-guided Walleye missiles severely damaged the Thanh Hoa Bridge in North Vietnam which had previously been the target of 800 fruitless American attacks. Sophisticated pilotless aircraft (drones) were developed to find targets, and this combined with the new accuracy of weapons to make possible deep interdiction which would prevent the enemy from bringing up reserves to counter US thrusts.

The election of Ronald Reagan as US President (1981–89) brought a new spirit to the US forces. He was prepared to trust the professionalism of the generals and to give them the resources to bolster US strength; the invasion of Grenada in 1983 demonstrated a willingness to use this power. There was actually only limited opposition to this attack which revealed some very severe flaws in US operational abilities. As a result, the Goldwater Nichols Act of 1986 strengthened the power of the Chiefs of Staff, and though inter-service rivalries remained, cooperation increased radically. Suddenly US forces had real offensive capacity, and the Soviet ace in the hole, the European hostage, was trumped. This is not to say that a Soviet invasion of Europe could have been defeated by conventional means, but it now became much more problematic. This forced the Soviets to contemplate the modernisation of their conventional forces and those of their allies, demanding whole new weapons systems with complex communication networks, and imposing enormous costs on an increasingly moribund economic system.

But the killer blow came with Reagan's Strategic Defense Initiative (SDI), widely derided as 'Star Wars'. Reagan regarded MAD as a suicide pact, and he seized upon technological developments to force the creation of a system which would defend the US against any conceivable attack. Much of this was as fantastic as the name 'Star Wars' suggests. But powerful elements of the technology existed or were clearly foreseeable, and the Ballistic Missile Defense Organisation is now an established element in the US armed forces. Any response demanded technologies, especially information technologies, which the Soviet economic system simply had not developed. Their economy was in any case under serious pressure just to maintain standards of living. Energy exports were the great earner of foreign exchange for the Soviets, but the world price of oil fell sharply in the 1980s, a process hastened by US economic action. Overall attrition made a response to AirLand Battle and 'Star Wars' unthinkable, forcing the Soviet leadership to abandon the competition with the US, and this in turn led to the dissolution of the Soviet Empire in the years 1989–91. Military pressure was certainly not the only factor at work in the Soviet disintegration, but it was decisive; yet modern recollection of the collapse rarely dwells on it. This is because the fall of the Soviet Union ushered in an age of illusion, strengthening the anti-military elements in contemporary western culture.

It is hardly odd that the countries of Central and Eastern Europe which escaped from the Soviet embrace tended to emphasise their own efforts. It is perhaps more surprising that the Western European intelligentsia has never forgiven the US for the fall of the USSR which undermined its deepest convictions. Few European thinkers were communists (though some were), but after 1945 most shared a common conviction that the future was in some way 'collectivist'. The British Labour Politician R.H.S. Crossman, in his 1960 *Labour in the Affluent Society* was typical in his attitude:

Communism is still an inferior way of life compared to that of the Affluent Societies of the West. But this does not alter the fact that, in terms of military power, of industrial development, of technological advance, of mass literacy and eventually of mass consumption, the planned Socialist economy, as exemplified by the Communist States, is proving its capacity to outpace and overtake the wealthy and comfortable Western economies.[7]

This was conventional wisdom by the 1970s, and it somehow excused Europeans from challenging the Soviet Union. It justified the endless search for détente, enabling Europeans to demonstrate political sophistication, and to profit from the competition between the US and the USSR for their allegiance, by accepting the existence of the USSR and disdaining the US refusal to 'recognise facts'. When the USSR collapsed, they found their pretensions cruelly exposed, for those crude Americans were victorious and the collectivist future, a conveniently distant alternative to capitalism, vanished in a puff of smoke. It was unforgivable for the

US simultaneously to be right and to deprive Europe of its great bargaining position.

At the same time there was much talk of the 'peace dividend' and of beating swords into ploughshares. That this new world had been brought about by the black arts of war was, for Europeans, best forgotten, particularly as it reflected well on the US. And, perversely, the most serious military event of the period, Gulf War 2, contributed to that illusion. The US army was not at all enthusiastic about waging a war against Saddam Hussein's Iraq after his invasion of Kuwait in August 1990. They would be fighting the world's fifth largest army, over half a million strong, virtually in its own backyard. The Iraqi army was very experienced, having fought the long and bitter Gulf War against Iran in 1980–88. It was equipped with good Soviet armaments (including 500 T-72 tanks) and some advanced, mainly French, systems supplied during that war. It was feared that in the time taken to concentrate forces in the theatre Saddam's army would be able to harden its position and even to attack Saudi Arabia. Iraq was nothing like a first-class air power, but US forces lacked obvious bases in the area and might well find it difficult to bring their power to bear. Estimates of 20,000–30,000 casualties as the price of liberating Kuwait reflected the doubts in the US command. But in fact the US could hardly have chosen a better enemy.

Saddam's invasion of Kuwait alienated most of the Arab world and made possible United Nations sanction for a campaign against him; this ultimately attracted a strong coalition, though of its 940,000 troops over 700,000 were American. The AirLand Battle had been designed for use against the Russians in Central Europe. Saddam's army was Soviet-trained, and it lacked the capacity for fluid and coordinated movement which was the essence of AirLand doctrine. Moreover, Saddam distrusted his generals and created a creaky and slow centralised command system. This proved highly vulnerable to air interdiction which virtually destroyed the Iraqi communication network as well as essential bridges and other elements of infrastructure. After a sustained period of build-up, in which a large number of allies supplied a small number of troops, the air war was launched on 17 January 1991 and the ground war on 24 February: after 100 hours of fighting the Iraqis had been driven out of Kuwait and a ceasefire was in place.

In many ways the Gulf War flattered to deceive. Much attention was paid to the high-tech Stealth aircraft which could avoid radar, to smart bombs which could find their targets with precision, and to Cruise missiles which could be programmed to hit very specific targets. But most of the explosives dropped were dumb bombs. Air interdiction strikes did a magnificent job in paralysing the enemy without inflicting heavy civilian casualties which would have influenced UN opinion. But air strikes had relatively little effect on Iraqi tanks and infantry, which had to be destroyed by better trained and equipped US ground forces. They profited from their superior flexibility, which essentially derived from excellent communication and computer equipment. But it has to be said that the desert, while hardly comfortable, was an excellent operating environment for the highly mechanised US army. In Gulf War 2 the US fought the perfect enemy, and the staggering cheapness of the victory in human lives was deeply impressive. Only 148 US personnel died, 35 of them by friendly fire, and about the same number of allied troops, while the Iraqi military lost about 30,000.

Afterwards some military theorists suggested that the age of big armies was over. Digital communication had created a Revolution in Military Affairs (RMA) which meant that their units could be too easily detected by satellite and other means, and their key points were vulnerable to destruction by precision weapons. The notion of an RMA, however, made little allowance for the desert environment which made detection relatively easy. Weather was generally good, but its fluctuations often halted air bombardment, while even in optimum conditions front-line military targets were elusive. In a different theatre of war with a different geography and climate, finding and destroying targets might be much more difficult, and air interdiction might be as limited in its effects as it had been in Korea. Moreover, any degree of resistance in the air could further reduce effectiveness: AirLand War has never been tried against a strong hostile airforce. A more determined and more mobile enemy – Saddam's troops were peculiarly slow-moving – could make an enormous difference. So the argument against mass armies is moot. The belief that a large army would be so expensive that money could not be spent on modern weapons, thus rendering it vulnerable, is deeply entrenched, but must be regarded as non-proven. Many permutations of army size and weapons expenditure are possible. We cannot simply write off large conscript armies as ineffective.

But Gulf War 2 triggered much wider responses in western culture. A sense of invulnerability arose. The US appeared to be all-powerful (however much, in some circles, despised) and the feeling grew that nothing could happen to the people of the prosperous developed world. Europeans were nonplussed by the explosion of violence and genocide as Yugoslavia collapsed, leading to wars in Slovenia, in Croatia, in Bosnia and in Kosovo in 1991–9. Despite these horrors on its very doorstep it was not until 1994 that NATO tried to intervene under United Nations auspices. In 1995 a Dutch battalion of the international peacekeeping force guarding the 'safe haven' of Srebrenica stood by uselessly while Serbs massacred 8,000 unarmed Bosnian Muslims. The consequent outcry finally forced a more decisive NATO intervention, but the Kosovo War (1998–9) produced a similar paralysis ended by US aerial intervention, whose errors, inevitable though they were, provoked a western outcry but little enthusiasm for committing ground forces.

The break-up of Yugoslavia was a direct result of the Soviet collapse, but this was only one of the global repercussions of this momentous event. The Cold War was the continuation of broadly European and western control over the whole world. The US and the Soviet Union could not control all states all the time, but they could, at least up to a point, influence and restrain them. By the 1970s there were signs that this bipolar situation which had lasted since 1945 might be ending. The emergence of China from its long isolation created the potential for a third pole. In 1978 the Shah of Iran was overthrown and a new Islamic Republic, hostile to both the Soviet Union and the US, emerged. But when the Cold War ended, so did the restraining hand of the great powers, and the consequent numerous conflicts which erupted in the 1990s were deeply disconcerting, though for some time there was little sense of threat to disturb the sense of invulnerability of the western states.

Even the Islamic agitation against western interests and a series of attacks in the 1990s on US targets barely disturbed this complacency. On 26 February 1993 a car bomb was exploded in the World Trade Center in New York; bombings in Saudi Arabia in 1996 killed many Americans while US embassies in East Africa were targeted in 1998, and in 2000 the USS *Cole* was attacked by a suicide boat in Aden harbour. The culmination of these attacks came with the crashing of hijacked planes into the World Trade Center on 11 September 2001. Since the fundamentalist Taliban regime in Afghanistan had sheltered al-Qaeda and others, it was hardly surprising that the US invaded in October of that year. Their success was almost immediate because the Northern Alliance of leaders opposed to the Taliban lent their support and Kandahar, the Taliban's main base, was in US hands by the end of November. But the Taliban were by no means destroyed and the Byzantine passages of Afghan politics have proved as difficult for the US and its allies to navigate as for all previous invaders. Most decisively, the US attacked Iraq.

Amongst some of the US elite the illusion had grown, apparently confirmed by the easy initial success in Afghanistan, that the US was omnipotent. As a result, in 2003 the US reprised Gulf War 2 with the intention of overthrowing Saddam Hussein. On 20 March simultaneous air and land assaults were launched. Iraqi forces amounted to over half a million, roughly the same strength as in 1991, but their equipment had deteriorated, their training and morale were poor, and some of their commanders had been bribed. About 250,000 US troops attacked, supported by 45,000 UK personnel and a handful of others in Gulf War 3, which was deeply unpopular in the western world. Progress was rapid, with Baghdad falling on 9 April. US losses, at 139, were astonishingly close to those of 1991 despite the fact that the Iraqis were fighting in their own country. This victory was extremely impressive, but the fighting revealed weaknesses in the US forces which essentially sprang from their limited numbers. It was astonishing that US Marines, who are light infantry designed for short-term shock action, were sent far inland with very unsuitable equipment, such as lightly armed tractors designed for seaborne assault. They were held up at Nasiriyah by enemy irregulars, and suffered substantial losses. By contrast, no US tank troops were killed in the whole operation.

In the wake of the US victory large numbers of troops were withdrawn and, effectively, control over the Iraqi state was lost. The Saddam regime had favoured the Sunni to hold down the large Shi'ite population and the Kurdish minority of northern Iraq. The Sunni leaders lost their influence after the US conquest, and turned against the new rulers. The US enjoyed support from the Kurds of northern Iraq, but outside this zone they had no political base for their occupation and an anticipated handover to a native regime. In these circumstances civil war broke out, with numerous factions paying off old scores and all turning against the common enemy, the occupiers. Iran and Syria supported and armed some of these organisations, so that US casualties mounted. Radical Muslims, including al-Qaeda, sent volunteers and equipment to harass the occupiers. It was the kind of war the US army had lost in Vietnam and since sought to avoid – guerilla warfare, though this time in an urban setting. Armed insurrection in Iraq showed every likelihood of succeeding until the advent of a US troop surge in 2007. This vast increase in US troop numbers was allied to a deliberate conciliation of the Sunni in Iraq to create a political base for an Iraqi successor government. These are the classic divide and rule tactics of colonial powers, as adapted by Saddam Hussein. But the point is that Iraq swallowed more and more troops, and specifically more infantry, allowing a Taliban resurgence in Afghanistan.

Defeating insurgency is labour-intensive, and to succeed requires a fairly brutal mixture of carrot and stick. Insurgents cannot be put down by nice methods, and however subtle the rewards on offer the threat of violence, carefully graded, is essential because the guerrillas can apply murder and coercion in a much less inhibited way. The German treatment of subject peoples in World War II is highly illuminating. The Nazis were welcomed in much of Central and Eastern Europe as liberators from communism, but their brutal treatment of conquered peoples wasted this asset, and by 1942 significant guerrilla attacks threatened the area behind German lines. By contrast, in the West the Germans cultivated sympathisers in the occupied lands like Holland, and worked with well-disposed governments like those of Pétain in France and Quisling in Norway. It was only when German rule was threatened by the D-Day invasions that more violent methods were adopted, fanning resistance in the West. Until then the Germans played skilfully upon fear of communism and provided local elites with the carrot of a degree of autonomous rule, and the stick of threats of massive retaliation against uncooperative elements in the civilian population. Churchill's campaign to set Europe on fire was a spectacular failure. Even in Yugoslavia, where Tito's army has received much praise, the Germans were able to exploit divisions between Serbs, Croats and Muslims to minimise trouble until quite near the end.

Carrot and stick: these are the brutal and unavoidable realities of 'pacification'. The present struggle in Afghanistan is about establishing a broadly acceptable regime which will not permit guerrilla groups to operate. The US troop surge of 2007 achieved something like this in Iraq, allowing the emergence of an Iraqi government. But the process is ugly and results are bound to be slow. Western culture looks for instant and painless results, but that is not what they see on TV. 'Our guys' being violent is not a pretty sight, nor is the positive value of fear immediately clear. And our losses are not nice either. People look at these events through the tinted glasses of their own experience and their own values and find it difficult to understand what is happening. This is partly because Europeans and Americans think they have enjoyed peace, which they regard as the norm, since 1945.

This is a terrible illusion. The Chinese Civil War began long before World War II and ended only in 1949, and in 1950 the victorious communists invaded Tibet and subsequently joined the Korean conflict, which lasted until 1953. The Indochina War of 1946–54 drove the French from north Vietnam, but in 1954 they plunged into the Algerian war of independence which raged until 1962. Intermittent civil war has plagued most of the countries of South America. The division of British India in 1947 precipitated a series of massacres in which at least 500,000 died. India and

Pakistan subsequently indulged in bitter conflicts in 1965 and 1971, while after 1962 India became embroiled with China over their mutual border. More than four million died in the US war in Vietnam. Independence for the Congo in 1960 brought civil war which continues to this day. The Biafran war in Nigeria, 1967–70, cost over a million casualties. Turkey invaded Cyprus in 1974 and the island is still divided. From 1974 to 2002 Angola was ravaged by civil war. The complicated and bloody struggles in the Horn of Africa are still raging. From 1991 to 2002 Sierra Leone was torn apart by a civil war in which nearly 100,000 died. In 1979 China attacked Vietnam in a conflict which was not resolved for twenty years. Perhaps two million civilians died in the Soviet war in Afghanistan, 1979–89. The dead in the war between Iran and Iraq, 1980–8, seem to have numbered at least a million. In 1994 the world was appalled by the Rwanda genocide which cost perhaps 800,000 lives, while the Bosnian conflict after the break-up of Yugoslavia saw at least 100,000 dead. Europeans and Americans are privileged to have been mere spectators of these horrors, but should perhaps remember that many of these conflicts were waged in part on their behalf, and that they benefited even if they did not approve.

The insulation of western peoples from such realities means that they have little conception of what it is like to face real threat and criticise the reactions of those who do. A telling example is Israel. Since the Six Day War Israel has faced guerrilla action first by the Palestine Liberation Organization and latterly by Islamicist groups like Hamas in Gaza and Hezbollah in Lebanon. Their forces hide behind the civilian population which inevitably suffers in Israeli counter-insurgency operations. The result is heavy censure of Israel in the West. Hezbollah, to a degree, owes its very existence to these western inhibitions. Yet who is more to blame, those who deliberately put civilians in the firing line or those who kill them in consequence? And western complacency has little grasp of what is at stake in such conflicts. In 1967 the orders of a Jordanian brigade tasked to seize an Israeli settlement stated: 'The reserve brigade will commence a nighttime infiltration onto Motza, will destroy it to the foundation, and won't leave a remnant or refugee from among its 800 residents.'[8] The Palestinian National Charter made clear that their goal was the total destruction of Israel. In a raid on a block of flats at Kiryat Shmona in 1974 PLO gunmen deliberately threw small children out to their death. This sense of peril induces attitudes which are difficult to understand for people in the comfortable West, who perhaps should remember that in World War II the British and others were just as ruthless.

It is remarkable how insulated western societies are from war. In Europe and America relations between people are regulated by law and the notion of human rights has become very important. War is, in itself, an infringement of human rights and it cannot be sanitised. In the brutal business of killing, civilians will always suffer, and guerrilla war in its many manifestations deliberately creates the conditions in which this is bound to happen. Probably the best that can be achieved is to prevent attacks on civilian populations who are separate from any theatre of fighting, though even that is pretty difficult. This distance from war and its realities is made the greater because in the US and Europe soldiers are paid professionals, relatively detached from the rest of society. In 1973 the US effectively ended conscription. Germany retains conscription, but allows those called up to opt for civilian service and nearly two-thirds of draftees make this choice. In 1997 France ended conscription, a real landmark in view of the intimate connection with citizenship established at the time of the Revolution. In the West the citizen armies that fought the two great wars of the twentieth century have ceased to exist.

One of the most dangerous consequences of the open societies of western states is that they make it difficult to understand and face the new threat from radical Islam. The many distinct cultures in European and American societies see the Islamic communities in their midst as simply another cultural group which can be fitted in and regulated by political correctness. In one sense this is quite right, because most Muslims moved to western countries for the good life, a tribute to the attractive power of these societies. Their dilemma, essentially the same as that of any other immigrant group, is how to accommodate to a different world and yet retain something of their own identity. But this is more difficult for Muslims because Islam demands a unity of sacred and secular, the creation of an environment shaped by the demands of religion. Islam in power has historically been quite tolerant, but it has never tolerated living in a society it does not control. This is why secular states like Turkey have faced such grave difficulties.

The situation is complicated enormously by the fact that Islam is not a monolith. On the positive side this means that Islamic states are very diverse and within them there are people with interests as divergent as those who live in western countries. The idea of a clash of civilisations between the West and Islam is a dramatic and dangerous simplification. Threatening and hostile fundamentalism is confined to relatively few small groups which hate one another. Each conceives of itself as struggling for the soul of Islam, because that is their purpose, and attacking the West is merely a means. But of course these divisions also make the situation even worse.

Islam is an enormous world religion, but it lacks centres of authority comparable to the Papacy for Catholics or the various assemblies which govern the Protestant sects. The broad division is between the Sunni and the dissident Shi'ites, but each of these is subdivided, and even within such subdivisions there is often no clear spiritual leadership. In its absence radical groups can hope to create allegiances while secular powers often hold de facto religious authority. The bitter competition for mastery amongst all these forces generates extremism as each tries to outbid its rivals. The radical elements compete in anti-western agitation, setting up a violent syndrome which draws in others. The invasion and destruction of Taliban Afghanistan deprived al-Qaeda and other radical groups of a secure base. But giving the country a stable political regime which in the long run will deny its use to extremists is proving very difficult. Moreover, war in Afghanistan has made even worse divisions within Pakistan, which is taking on the aspect of a failed state that could fall into very dangerous hands. And Pakistan has nuclear weapons. The US reaction to 9/11, the invasion of Afghanistan, and even more the attack on Iraq with Gulf War 3, gave added credibility to al-Qaeda and its allies and rivals in the fundamentalist world. In effect a shouting match is now established, as radical groups of all shades within Islam compete with one another to rouse opinion against America and its allies.

Even more seriously, extremists like al-Qaeda see Islamic communities in western states as fifth columns by which they can infiltrate the West and attack its communities, all the while sheltering behind the western insistence on human rights. This gives them the option of denouncing countermeasures in the name of human rights in which they do not believe. They can recruit from young men who fear female emancipation deeply and are unhappy with their host societies for a whole gamut of reasons. In all societies many young men have many discontents, and extremism has always been adept at exploiting them. During the Cold War communists and other extreme left-wing political parties were skilful at playing upon their grievances, and even on the guilt feelings of the children of prosperous middle-class people. Islamic fundamentalism plays the same game, and the suicide bomber gives it enormous menace.

This is a new kind of war in which the guerrilla takes advantage of globalism to move from place to place, from Pakistan to Manchester, hiding amongst ordinary people and creating and profiting from networks of the dedicated and discontented. It is certainly not the case that émigré

Muslim societies in the West are naturally fundamentalist, let alone violent. But many in these communities support forced marriages and their concomitant, 'honour killings', which are sanctioned by fundamentalists. Older people dislike the fact that many of their young people have adopted western ways. Some young men hold menial jobs or are unemployed, and, as young men always have, they blame the society around them, the more bitterly in that many of their womenfolk have adapted better and landed more lucrative and secure positions. Thus militants can find a sea in which to swim even when they come from far away. And with this modest degree of sympathy, they can coerce others into silence. This abolishes the distinction between soldier and civilian every bit as effectively as full-scale conventional attack in World War II – we are now, as then, all in the front line.

There is a real potential for these guerrillas to gain access to deadly modern weapons. The World Trade Center was destroyed by extemporised weapons, civilian aircraft, but the collapse of the USSR left a great deal of nuclear material poorly guarded, while the security of Pakistan's fissile material is suspect. Even a quite ordinary bomb can be enhanced by the addition of low-grade nuclear material to make a so-called dirty bomb which could create a radioactive zone in the heart of a great city. And technology is not exclusive to the West. Its products are regularly used against us. Mobile phones commonly trigger bombs and guerrillas are adept at using the Internet to attack sensitive computer systems.

Even more dangerous is Iran, the only Shi'ite state in the world. Its rulers are religious leaders, the Mullahs, who have very obvious political goals. By mobilising radicals against the existing Sunni governments of the Middle East, they hope to revive the old dream of a Shi'ite empire. To strengthen their hand they support radical groups, especially Shi'ite Hezbollah in Lebanon, but also largely Sunni Hamas in Gaza. By supplying increasingly sophisticated missiles to these surrogates they hope to be seen as leading the war against Israel. This, of course, provokes Israeli reprisals and attacks, as in 2008, and they can then profit from western denunciations of Israel for its cruelty in launching such attacks. There is a readiness to sacrifice ordinary people, but of course the Iranian Mullahs are perfectly happy to do that in pursuit of their task, for this is a greedy and corrupt regime in which the Revolutionary Guard wages war on its own people and the rule of law counts for nothing. Iran is developing nuclear weapons. One evening in a small town in Iran which has one of these 'nuclear facilities', I heard it casually referred to as the 'bomb factory'. Iran might well conceive of giving fissile material to a radical group. Other states like Sudan harbour radical Islamic sympathies, and wealthy organisations in Saudi Arabia and elsewhere share some of their views.

Guerrilla war, therefore, enjoys considerable state support, and is now capable of reaching into the US and Europe whose peoples are no longer privileged spectators of distant conflicts. The real difficulty is that their extraordinary prosperity is a blinding force which hides the degree to which Europeans and Americans are hated, not just in the Islamic world but more widely, simply because they are rich and successful. Having relinquished their empires, Europeans seem to think they can now bathe in virtue and enjoy a peace-loving culture. They can shrug off the past airily, but for others it is well remembered as the cause of a present rather grim reality. In many places the struggle for independence has left a legacy of hatred, only increased by civil wars in which European powers have often had a hand, sometimes through devices like the British Commonwealth and the French Union (largely African). The French had a major role in the events which led to the Rwandan genocide in 1994, and although their activities were not as spectacular as the US intervention in Iraq, some 800,000 died in Rwanda, far and above the Iraqi total.

The small circle of wealthy and powerful states which constitutes the West has developed a culture of peace which is widely seen as entirely hypocritical, and not merely by Islamic peoples. Because it is at such odds with reality there is little chance that it will ever be very widely shared. The acceptance of United Nations authority is everywhere very limited, and while the belief in the value of abiding by western expectations of behaviour in conflict is widespread, this is only because the US and its allies are perceived as powerful. Europeans have tended to assume that spreading prosperity will also spread peace. However, some states, notably Iran, reject the benefits which participation in world trade and prosperity offers in favour of other values. And ruling elites do not always act rationally. As Foch remarked:

The Germany of 1914 would never have resorted to war if she had properly estimated her own interests. No appeal to arms was necessary. She had only to continue an economic development that was already penetrating every corner of the world.

Who would have dared oppose her? Her trade and commerce were moving forward with steady strides that left other nations behind. There was no need for Germany to resort to war in order to conquer the world.[9]

In any case, to suppose that any system of thought or behaviour will achieve universal allegiance is simply to repeat in different form the totalitarian error of thinking that uniform behaviour can be imposed on people. Conversion of the world to western values is simply not going to happen.

We should also beware of taking refuge in some of the silly clichés which have grown up. 'Nobody', it is often said, 'wants war': that is not true. War, even to the point of total destruction, was Hitler's preferred alternative to surrender and in 1945 he sacrificed millions to that end. The leaders of Japan were equally prepared to sacrifice their people, who were delivered from cataclysm only by the nuclear bombing of Hiroshima and Nagasaki which revealed to most (but not all) of their rulers the true hopelessness of their situation. There are plenty of regimes like that in the modern world. Ordinary people may not want war, but they do not get consulted much in North Korea or Iran, and they are despised by the leaders of organisations like ETA and the Real IRA. Religious zealots like those in al-Qaeda care little about the deaths of civilians and comfort themselves with the belief that divine reward awaits them on the other side.

But while Islamic fundamentalism currently attracts enormous attention, it is only one amongst many potential threats. Russia has shown an alarming belligerence in recent years, and in particular seems to want to dominate Central Europe and the states of Eurasia which once lay under the dominance of the Soviet Union. China, after a long eclipse, is emerging as a strong military power with a formidable nuclear capacity and a huge army. Her government has so far shown admirable restraint in military matters, save for some posturing on the subject of Taiwan. But her working alliance with Iran and Russia, aimed at keeping the US out of the affairs of Asia, brings her into association with two powers with enormous and dangerous ambitions and a readiness to use force. China is also the protector of the nightmare regime in North Korea whose nuclear arms threaten her neighbours. India and Pakistan have rockets and nuclear weapons and are bitter enemies capable of drawing others into their quarrels.

The conventional and nuclear forces of western states are probably sufficient to deter other nation states from directly attacking them. On any rational calculation even Iran and North Korea should recognise that. But what of indirect attack? Russia deliberately destabilises the weak states around it. She fomented racial tensions in Georgia to create the conditions to intervene in 2008. Her hand is very evident in Kyrgyzstan where disorders and persecution of Uzbeks can only lead to quarrels with Uzebekistan, creating conditions in which Russia can send in forces 'to keep the peace'. Russian attempts to dominate Poland, the Baltic States and Eastern Europe directly threaten European interests. At some point direct counter-threats may become necessary, and they demand armed force. How far the US will feel she needs to help European states who have shown little desire to help themselves is not at all clear. Another aspect of indirect attack is the increasing competition for resources, especially energy. China has shown itself ready to confront Brunei, Philippines, Malaysia, Taiwan and Vietnam over control of the Spratly Islands which, though covering less than 5 square kilometres, may sit on oil and gas reserves. Monopolisation of natural resources was an important element in the behaviour of the European empires of the nineteenth century and there is no reason to think that this cannot happen again, especially as resources are depleted.

The existence of dangerous regimes and numerous world flashpoints means accepting the need on a permanent basis to maintain, improve and develop a huge battery of weapons including nuclear ones. But technology in itself is no protection. Since the Military Revolution of the late nineteenth century, advanced technology has leaked from its inventors into the wider world. Now so developed is the global economy that US soldiers in Afghanistan use computers manufactured in China running software developed in India. And so many countries, some of them as dangerous as Iran, are capable of developing military technology apace and feeding it to other enemies, that western countries are locked into a race which they dare not lose, but cannot in any final sense win.

Military robots, particularly flying drones and miniature tanks, are remarkable weapons, and here the US has a considerable lead. 'Ember' is a robot the size of a paperback, now at an advanced level of development, designed to operate in swarms and to be so cheap that it can be thrown away once it has served its purpose. But the US has no monopoly, and others, including potential enemies, are already following this lead. Both Russia and China are in the field, while Hezbollah deployed four aircraft drones to fight the Israeli attack in 2006. Some of these weapons depend on satellite control, but already an astonishing number of states have established themselves in space. Nanotechnology promises new kinds of weapons, of the size of insects or even bacteria, and it is developing in all quarters of the globe.

More and more states can launch satellites which are the key to rapid communications and good intelligence, and computer technology is now widely diffused. China uses computer capacity to control its own citizens – it monitors Internet-café use consistently and is able to cripple the computer systems of other nations. GhostNet is a powerful force able to attack whole ranges of computers and is believed to have been devised by the Chinese People's Liberation Army signals division in Hainan. Even guerrillas and organised crime now use the Internet and have the potential to do great damage to economies dependent upon information technology.

M. Wynne, Secretary of the US Air Force remarked in September 2007, 'Tell the nation that the age of cyberwarfare is here.' Compromising the computer systems on which modern warfare depends, and even attacking the technological infrastructure of potential or actual hostile states, is perfectly possible, and has great advantages. In the spring of 2007 Estonia dismantled a Russian war memorial, and as a result suffered massive denial-of-service attacks – overwhelming requests for communication which simply saturated important computer installations in its economic infrastructure. The Russian war against Georgia in August 2008 was preceded by a series of cyber-attacks which damaged its state structures and cut its international communication links. In April 2009 there were reports of Chinese penetration of the US power grid and in May of that year the US Homeland Security admitted that its systems had been penetrated.

Such attacks have the great virtue of deniability. GhostNet appears to originate in China, but computers can be taken over and used by others. The shadowy Russian Business Network is often described as a criminal organisation specialising in cybercrime, but it has been used by governments anxious to hide their complicity in cyberwar. This crossover between state and illegal interests is deeply disturbing because war and criminality are closely connected.

South and Central America simmer with discontents and tensions, underlying which is the drugs trade. The worldwide appetite for narcotics, especially in western states, has created an enormous black economy whose corrupting force reaches out to undermine states far beyond South America. The government of Mexico is being destabilised by the drug organisations, the states of West Africa feel their influence, while parts of Spain and southern Italy are coming close to becoming independent enclaves where the state barely intervenes. In Naples middle-class people can now make modest but secure investments in drug deals in expectation of high returns, and so the tentacles of narco-crime extend ever further into wider sections of the community. And computer technology provides excellent communications for the drug networks. Even in tightly governed Northern Europe, drugs are increasingly available, their purity is improving and their price falling in a trade revolving around what are effectively 'no go' areas for police forces who are themselves becoming corrupted.

There is an intimate link between the drug trade and guerrilla warfare, most obviously in Afghanistan. The main export route from Afghanistan west via Turkey lies across Iran whose rulers are believed to take a cut of the business. The 'war on drugs' is not separate from other wars or even international diplomacy, but in itself is a real threat to western security for criminals find it convenient to take over state functions. In London councils lose control over housing units which, through a mixture of bribery and coercion, are controlled by criminals as safe houses. The front line against such activities is the police, but on 4 December 1997, Sir Paul Condon, former Metropolitan Police Commissioner, told parliament's Home Affairs Committee that there were an estimated 100–250 corrupt officers in the London force, and drug money is the primary source of corruption. Members of the British Crown Prosecution Service, responsible for bringing cases against those the police arrest, have been bribed. Large areas of great cities are highly dangerous and crime statistics visibly bear little relation to reality for they are simply a record of detected crime. Western nations face a series of interconnected struggles. Drug deals in London, Paris or New York fund attacks on coalition forces in Afghanistan, corrupt police, making detection and intelligence of movements less likely, help to fund Iranian ambitions to destabilise friendly regimes in the Middle East and weaken the uncertain authority of the Pakistan government.

The open society of western states has many enemies within. The fringe groups of the Left, who were particularly active in Germany and Italy, have been quiescent since their defeat in the 1970s and '80s. They have affiliations with the respectable Left and trade unions, which makes them very dangerous because through them they can tap into and manipulate the western culture of 'legalism'. The violent Right is gaining adherents in some European countries and in the US where a strong libertarian current of thought gives it connections with respectable circles. In the same way Islamic extremists have links with their 'moderate' communities. For all these groups, serving the drug networks offers money and access to clandestine communications. In Northern Ireland the various Irish Republican factions and their Loyalist counterparts compete for control of the drug trade in their communities. In Spain ETA, the Basque separatist guerrilla army, is a conduit for drugs from South America. In the US the various White Power groups are just as implicated in the trade. Western armies operate in Afghanistan, yet they do not prevent the massive export of drugs which finances their enemies.

The narcotics trade is a powerful threat because it offers the enemies of western states a source of income and a channel into the heart of their societies. The drug networks generate enormous wealth, and it is they who power the vast illegal trade in arms. Their leaders have no loyalties except to their own wealth, and they are perfectly happy to use guerrillas to protect their business. Legalising, regulating and taxing the drug trade is unknown territory, but it offers a serious prospect of breaking up the victorious internationalism of the drug gangs. And perhaps the dangers of legalisation are less than the risks of continuing to fight a lost 'war on drugs' which is demoralising the forces of law and order and killing western soldiers.

Since 1945 the apparent peace which western nations have enjoyed has given rise to the facile assumption that somehow their culture of plenty will spread effortlessly, but the reality is that the world of war has spread to them. Their immunity from war after 1945 rested on an enormous military preponderance which saw to it that while the blood of others was shed theirs, by and large, was not. This preponderance has been undermined by economic development, the advance of technology and the rise of new political and social forces. There can be no return to the situation of western supremacy, and common sense points to the need for sensible diplomacy, but in the end this must be based on military preparedness. Western people need to sharpen their perception of threats and steel themselves to the unpleasant task of doing something about them.

The chief obstacle to this is their cultural predisposition to pursue happy ideals, like free-range chickens or a carbon-free world, to contemplate illusions like the 'peace dividend' and to turn away from nasty realities like the face of war. This brings the reader to the central concerns of this book. It is patent that war will not go away. Since time immemorial it has offered, or at least appeared to offer, solutions to all kinds of problems. It can sometimes be prevented by persuasion or mediation, and the UN has played a notable part in this, but only when there is some predisposition amongst the parties to avoid conflict. In all too many conflicts since 1945 this has not been the case – the record rehearsed here shows that war has been continual since then despite the UN. War can be regulated, but only to the extent that there is a degree of perceived commonality between the combatants; witness the difference in German behaviour during World War II towards its western 'civilised' enemies and those in the East. But it can be held at bay, it can be deterred, by military strength. Weakness invites aggression. The breakdown of the steppe empires was the primary reason for the establishment of European world-empires which emerged in the eighteenth and nineteenth centuries, while the inaction of the 1990s permitted 9/11 and all that it brought in its train.

The absorption of war into popular culture is very recent. Until the Military Revolution of the late nineteenth century the conduct of war essentially stood outside the purview of human culture. War was shaped by the brute limitations of geography, topography and climate and by the possibilities offered by animal and human muscle-power. In that world of the close-order, close-quarter battle, success rested upon 'native skills', the abilities inherent in the ordinary life of the population. Because of their extraordinary lifestyle, steppe people were the supreme soldiers, and Europe stood outside their control only because of chance and circumstance. But equally by chance the steppe empires were in decline at the very moment when Europeans, through discipline, made the best possible use of firearms. This coincidence of events enabled western nations to replace the ascendancy of the steppe nomads. It should also give westerners cause to reflect on the transience and vulnerability of military power. Glory is always perilous because, while it evokes fear, it also creates hate, which is fertile in invention.

The long dominance of the steppe peoples has left a deep shadow on western culture. Phrases like 'Asiatic hordes' or 'the Yellow Peril' were deeply engraved upon the western consciousness and persisted even after the steppe empires had decayed and been superseded by western imperialism. Western scholars recast the wars of the fifth century BC between Greece and Persia as struggles between European freedom and Asiatic despotism, and some even argued that the western style of war was somehow related to democracy – an idea which Hitler and Stalin, amongst others, emphatically disproved. More dangerously, fear of the Asiatic is now projected upon Islam in the form of a clash of civilisations, as though Islam were simply a threatening monolith instead of a complex and fissiparous community whose diverse elements offer opportunity for alliance and friendship as well as conflict.

But every culture has its myths and illusions, and there is nothing inherently wrong with that of the West. It is self-indulgent, and self-deluding, but these are elements in all cultures. Its respect for the rights of individuals is praiseworthy. The problem is that many imagine that the norms founded on this respect can be applied to the chaotic world of war. Only a few, the naïve and the fantasists, think that war can be abolished, but many more think that it can be confined, restricted and controlled, and this is reinforced by a complacency founded on the apparent strength of western military power in relation to all others. But as the survey above has shown, the threats faced by western states are numerous, of enormous variety and deeply menacing. It is vital that western states change their culture in order to adapt. This is not a call for a cultural revolution of the kind achieved in Germany by Hitler in the 1930s. What is suggested is essentially that western states recognise that the values of legalism and respect for the individual which they prize cannot, except to their great disadvantage, be applied to the world of war.

The laws of war as we know them emerged in the eighteenth and nineteenth centuries at a time when it was unusually easy to distinguish between soldiers and civilians. But guerrilla war is based on the avoidance of this distinction and it is this kind of subversion which is presently the most obvious threat to western nations. The enemy within, the combination of native subversive forces, drug barons and hostile guerrillas, especially Islamic ones, is most immediately and obviously challenging and unwelcome to western culture. People chafe at airport restrictions but they are relatively minor inconveniences. The struggle against subversion is primarily an intelligence war, and that is a brutal and secret business. In the Cold War the intelligence services were free to act in a fairly untrammelled way, and they need to revert to that. No doubt in such a war the innocent and their human rights will suffer, but perhaps more innocents, and friendly ones at that, will suffer if the intelligence services are unduly restricted.

The appeal to international law to regulate conflict is a noble ideal, but it is not shared by many outside the sheltered world of western states, and it is dangerously unrealistic. In fact, the whole trend to regulate all aspects of human behaviour by law is a peculiarity of Europe and the US which has got out of control to the extent that it has become an employment scheme for lawyers who have lost any sense of reality. In 2009 it was reported that an eminent British lawyer was questioning the legality of killing by radio-controlled flying drones, on the grounds that it prevented the victims from defending themselves – as though the whole point of war is not to kill before you are killed. There is in fact a silly but growing tendency to regard even open enemies as though they are criminals who need to be tried by due process before we can proceed against them. But in the dark world of intelligence warfare, proof is an impossible luxury and Guantanamo Bay a necessity if we are not to liberate dangerous people into the world.

There is no means of enforcing international law on anything like an equable basis. US forces in Iraq and Afghanistan are accompanied by journalists, so that their every deed is reported, especially bad ones because they make good news. By contrast, Russia conceals repression in Chechnya so that international law cannot be applied. In Sri Lanka the state triumphed over separatists at the expense of their 'human rights', but the outcry was very limited indeed, because Sri Lanka was supported by China and enjoys the sympathy of many small states in the UN who have minorities they wish to suppress. Above all, the whole structure of international law favours the guerrillas against the conventional forces of states with open societies and thus shackles the responses to them. The UN condemns Israel and Hamas for the civilian casualties of the fighting in Gaza, but in practice all the blame falls on Israel because the UN can do absolutely nothing to restrain the guerillas who hide behind the unfortunate people of Gaza. Insurrectionary warfare demands that people choose, and uses force to influence their choices. In the present state of international law the guerrilla is effectively given a monopoly of the use of a vital kind of persuasion: coercion. And nation states are perfectly prepared to support guerrillas to put pressure upon their rivals. Pakistani support for guerrilla groups in its dispute with India over Kashmir is patent, but nothing has ever been done about it.

The muddled state of international law could in theory be modified by agreement, but in fact too many states have a vested interest in its distortions. So western states need to make it very clear that in any conflict the rules of engagement will take note of the confusion of civilian and soldier. If this is not done western soldiers will be inhibited in their conduct of operations and constantly looking over their shoulders lest they commit some infraction which in the circumstance of conflict cannot be avoided. And we need to be realistic about what happens when military force is applied, as it will often need to be. Armies are crude instruments and using them in any environment where there are lots of people will result in casualties to civilians. While every effort should be made to avoid this, it is going to happen and apologies afterwards will not make anything better and will undermine the morale of western forces.

In seeking alliance with states disposed to be friendly it should be recognised that insisting upon 'human rights' is foolish, the modern equivalent of the nineteenth-century habit of imposing 'white civilisation' upon others. The fact is that no single set of values can ever prevail worldwide, and western states should beware of thrusting theirs down the throats of potential friends. There are plenty of Islamic governments that loathe subversive fundamentalism because it is directed at them. They resent our arrogant imposition of our values upon them, and see in the restraints we impose on our troops evidence of a failure of will.

War challenges one of the most dearly held tenets of western culture: the sanctity of human life. This is bound to be the case in any society where great wealth offers boundless possibilities to young men and women so that loss seems all the more tragic. War demands its blood tax, and in one way or another it will be imposed. Counter-insurgency warfare is inevitably labour-intensive and, as we have noted, while technology can be useful it is also possessed by the insurgents, so the infantryman must go in to seek out his enemy. This means that forces must be structured around the small groups of brave fellows who actually do this, and that they will inevitably suffer losses. For most of human history, the long age of close-quarter close-order battle, this was simply accepted, as this book has shown. The glory and the prosperity of western nations were founded on military conquest, and because the military were removed from the mainstream of western societies casualties were simply a fact of life. The terrible human toll of the World Wars I and II the combined with rising standards of living since 1945 to change this, but only in a relatively few western nations. Elsewhere very different attitudes prevail – the suicide bomber is a powerful witness to that. There can be no return to the attitudes of the distant past, but we must accept that success and failure in war cannot and should not be judged by casualty numbers. The modern media in western countries has little expertise in military matters and little taste for acquiring any, and so measures success or failure in war in terms of the body count. Accepting this as the measure of success or failure is an invitation to more 9/11s. Moreover, media reporters rarely see the enemy and have no conception of what he is suffering.

The greatest challenge for western countries is to adjust a cultural outlook which, in a world of unprecedented economic well-being, has focused people's minds on individual satisfaction. Facing the present scale of threat could potentially undermine individual liberty and the rule of law, so safeguards are essential. War challenges long-established spending priorities. The idea that money should be spent not on perfecting society or self-indulgence (which are not very different), but on soldiers, military equipment and intelligence services whose workings are mysterious and threatening is deeply disconcerting. But such shifts are vital in view of the scale and range of threats that western nations face. And in any case, all culture must adjust to new realities, so it is perhaps best to make changes consciously and thoughtfully rather than under the pressure of events.

It is sometimes suggested that the risks are not really great, that small groups of hostile forces have nothing like the power that western nations enjoy. But this is merely an excuse for inaction. It is essential to have the will to fight, and if it is lacking and if there is no drive to develop skills in arms, and if soldiers are not loosed from the bonds of ideas which have nothing to do with war, then mere hardware will serve no purpose.

The Roman Empire in the fourth century had half a million men in arms, and none of its enemies could rival such glory; indeed, most could raise only the equivalent of a single legion, 6,000 men. But Rome's leaders did not focus on their enemies, and they preferred to fight one another. Now their empire is dust, their splendid cities are lost, and their glory is buried in earth.

NOTES

Chapter 1 The Many Faces of War

1. E.B. Sledge, *With the Old Breed at Peleliu and Okinawa* (Oxford: Oxford University Press, 1990), 260.
2. H. Nicholson, *Medieval Warfare. Theory and Practice of War in Europe, 300–1500* (Basingstoke: Palgrave, 2004), 21–2.
3. Lt-Col. John Blackader, *Life and Diary*, abridged by A. Crichton (Edinburgh: H.S. Baynes, 1824), 350.
4. Sun Tzu, *The Art of War*, tr. L. Giles (New York: Dover, 2002), 43.
5. C. von Clausewitz, *On War*, ed. M. Howard and P. Paret (Princeton, NJ: Princeton University Press, 1976), 110.
6. D. Ferry, *Gilgamesh. A New Rendering in English Verse* (Newcastle on Tyne: Bloodaxe Books, 1992), 3–4.
7. L. Miller, 'China. An Emerging Superpower?', *Stanford Journal of International Relations* (2006), 1.
8. V.D. Hanson, *Carnage and Culture. Landmark Battles in the Rise of Western Power* (New York: Anchor, 2002), 21.
9. *Matthaei Parisiensis, Monachi Sancti Albani, Chronica Majora*, ed. H.R. Luard, 7 vols (London: Longman, 1872), 3: 488.
10. Translation by P. Bookbinder, *Weimar Germany. The Republic of the Reasonable* (Manchester: Manchester University Press, 1996), 212.
11. Nicholson, *Medieval Warfare*, 22.
12. Patton, Speech of 5 June 1944 from www.pattonhq.com/speech.html.
13. Arrian, *The Campaigns of Alexander*, tr. A. de Selincourt and J.R. Hamilton (Harmondsworth: Penguin, 1971), 294.
14. Horace, *Odes*, ed. K. Quinn (Basingstoke: Macmillan, 1980), III.2.13; *The Poems of Wilfred Owen*, ed. J. Stallworthy (London: Chatto & Windus, 1994), 29.
15. Captain F. Majdalany quoted in J. Ellis, *The Sharp End: The Fighting Man in World War II* (London: Pimlico, 1993), 226, 107. In English public schools students live in separate houses which compete with one another in sport and, less obviously, in academic attainment.
16. *Mahabharata*, ed. R.V. Narayan (London: Heinemann, 1978), 156; *The Ramayana*, ed. R.V. Narayan (London: Chatto & Windus, 1973), 160.
17. Sledge, *With the Old Breed*, 315.
18. Captain Cochrane quoted in Ellis, *Sharp End*, 107.
19. Clausewitz, *On War*, 248.
20. Vegetius, *Epitome of Military Science*, tr. N.P. Milne (Liverpool: Liverpool University Press, 1993), 110.

21. *Selected Works of Mao Tse Tung*, 2 vols (London: Lawrence & Wishart, 1954), 2.129.
22. Clausewitz, *On War*, 4:11, 260.
23. Vegetius, *Epitome of Military Science*, 62.
24. In World War II a total of 185,000 aircrew served in the RAF. Approximately 70,000 were killed. I am presuming that World War II, aircrew were, broadly, the same kind of people who would have been army officers in World War I.
25. J. Boswell, *Life of Johnson vol.3 1776–80* (Edinburgh: Edinburgh University Press, 1994), 424.
26. L.P. Hartley, *The Go-Between* (London: Hamish Hamilton, 1954), 1.
27. The Revelation of St John the Divine, 6: 8.
28. Clausewitz, *On War*, 6:30, 515.
29. Ibid., 85.
30. Ibid., 4:11, 260.

Chapter 2 Many Worlds of War

1. The maker of the film *Dead Birds*, Robert Gardner, describes it on the website http://www.der.org/films/dead-birds.html. The film is of Grand Valley Dani, who are mountain Papuans in West New Guinea (Irian Barat, Indonesia), studied by the Harvard-Peabody Expedition (1961–3). The author wishes to thank the Concord Video and Film Council for giving him the opportunity to see again this film which he first saw on TV in the 1960s.
2. Quoted in J.N. Postgate, *Early Mesopotamia* (London: Routledge, 1992), 78, from J.S. Cooper, *The Curse of Agade* (Baltimore, MD: Johns Hopkins University Press, 1983), 50–1.
3. Quotations from W. Hamblin, *Warfare in the Ancient Near East to 1600BC* (London: Routledge, 2006), 222–3.
4. A. Kuhrt, *The Ancient Near East 3000–330BC*, 2 vols (London: Routledge, 1997), 1:71–2.
5. Quoted in Postgate, *Early Mesopotamia*, 252; Hamblin, *Warfare in the Ancient Near East*, 200, 199.
6. Hamblin, *Warfare in the Ancient Near East*, 226.
7. Ibid., 231.
8. *Ibid.*, 226, 230–4.
9. Quoted by Kuhrt, *Ancient Near East*, 515.
10. Quoted in A.M. Gnirs, 'Ancient Egypt', in K. Raaflaub and N. Rosenstein (eds), *War and Society in the Ancient and Medieval Worlds* (Harvard, Mass.: Harvard University Press, 1999), 77.
11. Quoted in Hamblin, *Warfare in the Ancient Near East*, 202.
12. Quoted ibid., 195.
13. Kuhrt, *Ancient Near East*, 211–12.
14. Quoted in B. and R. Allchin, *The Rise of Civilization in India and Pakistan* (Cambridge: Cambridge University Press, 1982), 307.
15. I would like to thank Keith Padgham, a PhD student in the Classics Department at Swansea University, for this information.

Chapter 3 Horses and Hoplites

1. Herodotus, *The Histories*, tr. R. Waterfield (Oxford: Oxford University Press, 1998), 7.9.2.
2. V.D. Hanson, *The Western Way of War, Infantry Battle in Classical Greece* (Berkeley: University of California Press, 1989), 157.
3. Xenophon, *Agesilaus*, 2.14 quoted in Sage, *Warfare in Ancient Greece* (London: Routeledge, 1996), 95–6.
4. J. Keegan in his Introduction to Hanson, *Western Way of War*, xii.
5. This is the essential case made by V.D. Hanson in *The Western Way of War*. For his other works in which the same ideas are propagated, see the 'Further Reading' at the end of the book.

6. Ulpian, *Digest*, 47.22.4 quoted by H. van Wees, *Greek Warfare. Myths and Realities* (London: Duckworth, 2004), 203.
7. Iran means the Land of the Aryans.
8. Ibid., 1.136.62.
9. Ibid., 6.112, 393.
10. Ibid., 7.228.484.
11. Ibid., 8.89.517.
12. Ibid., 9.49, 2–63 in Sage, *Warfare in Ancient Greece*, 92–3.
13. Plutarch, *Moralia*, 220A.
14. Xenophon, *Constitution of the Lacedaemonians*, 11.4–5 in Sage, *Warfare in Ancient Greece*, 29, 39.
15. Thucydides, *History of the Peloponnesian War*, quoted in Sage, *Warfare in Ancient Greece*, 44–6.
16. Xenophon, *Anabasis* 6.4.8 in Sage, *Warfare in Ancient Greece*, 153.

Chapter 4 The Glory of Empire, 336 BC–AD 651

1. The advice given by the Roman Emperor Septimius Severus (193–211) to his sons, according to Cassius Dio, *Roman History*, LXXVI.15.2, quoted by B. Campbell, 'The Roman Empire', in K. Raaflaub and N. Rosenstein (eds), *War and Society in the Ancient and Medieval Worlds. Asia, the Mediterranean and Mesoamerica* (Cambridge, Mass.: Harvard University Press, 1999), 231.
2. The cubit is a measure of length based on that of the forearm. It was, therefore, variable, but approximated to 18 in. or 45.7 cm.
3. Polybius, *Histories*, 18.29.1–30.4 quoted in Sage, *Warfare in Ancient Greece*, 169–70.
4. Arrian, *Anabasis of Alexander*, 1.15.4–8 in Sage, *Warfare in Ancient Greece*, 175.
5. Sage, *Warfare in Ancient Greece*, 195.
6. I Maccabees 1: 16–19.
7. Strabo, *Geographica* 15.2.1(9).
8. Pliny, *Natural History*, VI, 22.4.
9. Ashoka, Inscription, tr. in J. Keay, *India. A History* (New York: Grove, 2000), 91–2.
10. Quoted in D.A. Graff, *Medieval Chinese Warfare 300–900* (London: Routledge, 2002), 24.
11. B. Watson (ed.), *Records of the Grand Historian Jima Qian* (New York: Columbia University Press, 1993), 133.
12. *Shih chi*, 6,252 quoted in N. di Cosmo, *Ancient China and its Enemies. The Rise of Nomadic Power in East Asian History* (Cambridge: Cambridge University Press, 2002), 175, 203, 210.
13. Livy, *The Early History of Rome*, Books I–V, tr. A. de Selincourt (London: Penguin, 1987), 5.38.583–84.
14. Plutarch, *Lives: Aemilius Paulus*, 19.1–2, quoted by J.E. Lendon, *Soldiers and Ghosts. A History of Battle in Classical Antiquity* (New Haven, CT: Yale University Press, 2005), 203.
15. Second century AD, tr. in B. Campbell, *The Roman Army 31BC–AD337* (London: Routledge, 1994), 48.
16. Frontinus, *Stratagems*, 4.7.4 quoted in C.M. Gilliver, *The Roman Art of War* (Stroud: Tempus, 1999), 120 and for the Chinese see above, n. 10.
17. Caesar, *The Conquest of Gaul*, tr. S.A. Handford and J.F. Gardner (London: Penguin, 1982), 199.
18. Ibid., 181.
19. Ammianus Marcellinus, *Rerum Gestarum*, tr. J.C. Rolfe, 3 vols (London: Heinemann, 1950), 1.271, 285–7.
20. *Codex Theodosianus*, VII.22.1 quoted in Campbell, 'The Roman Empire', 234.
21. Ammianus Marcellinus, *Rerum Gestarum* 1.24,8.
22. Ibid., 2.73.
23. Ibid., 1.17, 17–21.

24. Ibid. 3.403.
25. E.A. Thompson, 'Zosimus and the Letters of Honorius', *Classical Quarterly*, 32 (1982), 445–62.
26. Vegetius, *Epitome of Military Science*, 18.
27. Eugippius, *Life of Saint Severin*, tr. L. Bieler and L. Krestan (Washington, DC: Fathers of the Church, 1965), Ch. 20.

Chapter 5 Ideology and Warfare, 500–*c*.1200

1. Koran, 8.15.
2. Koran, 2.210.
3. Constantinople was originally called Byzantium before Constantine shifted his capital there, and it later served as the capital of the Eastern Roman Empire which, after the fifth century, is generally called Byzantium.
4. Koran, 8.65.
5. Quoted in P. Brown, *The World of Late Antiquity. From Marcus Aurelius to Muhammad* (London: Thames & Hudson, 1971), 193.
6. Quoted in H. Kennedy, *The Armies of the Caliphs: Military and Society in the Early Islamic State* (London: Routledge, 2001), 23.
7. Al-Jahiz (*c*.781–Dec. 868 or Jan. 869) quoted in J.D. Latham and W. Paterson, *Saracen Archery: An English Version and Exposition of a Mameluke Work on Archery (ca. AD 1368)* (London: Holland, 1970), xxiii.
8. Gregory of Tours, *The History of the Franks*, tr. L. Thorpe (Harmondsworth: Penguin, 1985), Book 2, Ch. 37, 153–4.
9. Anon., *The Chronicle of 754*, in *Conquerors and Chroniclers of Early Medieval Spain*, tr. K.B. Wolf (Liverpool: Liverpool University Press, 1999), 145.
10. *Charlemagne to Abbot Fulrad, April 806*, in P.D. King (ed.), *Charlemagne. Translated Sources* (Lancaster: University of Lancaster Press, 1987), 260.
11. *Capitulary of Thionville, 806*, in King, *Charlemagne*, 248.
12. *Revised Frankish Annals for 774*, in King, *Charlemagne*, 110–11.
13. *Charlemagne to Fastrada September 791*, in King, *Charlemagne*, 309–10.
14. *Capitulary of Aachen of 811* in King, *Charlemagne*, 264.
15. J.L. Nelson (ed.), *The Annals of St-Bertin* (Manchester: Manchester University Press, 1991), 89.
16. *The Song of Roland*, tr. D.L. Sayers (Harmondsworth: Penguin, 1957), verse 98.
17. William of Poitiers, *Deeds of William, Duke of Normandy and King of the English*, ed. R.H.C. Davies and M. Chibnall (Oxford: Clarendon Press, 1998).
18. Widukind, *Rerum gestarum saxonicarum libri tres*, ed. G. Waitz (Hanover: MGH, 1882), 933.
19. Canon 2 of the Council of Clermont, 1095.
20. Fulcher of Chartres, *Historia Hierosolymitana*, tr. A.C. Krey in *The First Crusade* (Gloucester, Mass.: Smith, 1958), 117.
21. Abu Shama, quoted by H. Kennedy in *Crusader Castles* (Cambridge: Cambridge University Press, 1994), 59.
22. P. Contamine, *War in the Middle Ages*, tr. M. Jones (Oxford: Blackwell, 1984), 103.
23. Ouyang Xiu, quoted in P. Lorge, *War, Politics and Society in Early Modern China 900–1795* (London: Routledge, 2005), 39.
24. Quoted by W.H. McNeill, *The Pursuit of Power. Technology, Armed Force and Society since AD 1000* (Chicago: University of Chicago Press, 1982), 39.

Chapter 6 The Steppe Supremacy, *c*.1200–1683

1. A thirteenth-century Chinese annalist quoted in D. Sinor, 'Horse and Pasture in Inner Asian History', *Oriens Extremus*, 19 (1972), 171 (171–84) repr. as No. II in *Inner Asia and its Contacts with Medieval Europe* (Aldershot: Ashgate, 1977). Sinor himself

concluded (p. 171), that 'Until firearms came to dominate warfare, a well-disciplined, well-led Inner Asian cavalry force, provided that it was sufficiently large and disposed of an important reserve of mounts, was virtually invincible by armies of sedentary populations.'

2. Quoted in J. Keay, *India. A History* (New York: Grove Press, 2000), 248.

3. Quoted in P. Jackson, *The Mongols and the West, 1221–1410* (London: Pearson, 2005), 47.

4. The Persian Chronicler Juvaini quoted in J. Man, *Genghis Khan. Life, Death and Resurrection* (London: Bantam, 2004), 199.

5. From *sforzare*, to fight.

6. Ramon Muntaner, *Chronicle*, tr. Lady Goodenough, 2 vols (London: Hakluyt, 1920), 2, 457–8.

7. Quoted in J. Sumption, *Trial by Fire. The Hundred Years War II* (London: Faber, 1999), 379–80.

8. The phrase is used by J.A. Lynn, *Wars of Louis XIV 1667–1714* (London: Longman, 1999), 47–52.

9. Figures from M. Roberts, *Gustavus Adolphus and the Rise of Sweden* (London: English Universities Press, 1973), 126.

10. Mortimer, *Eyewitness Accounts of the Thirty Years War*, 55.

11. R. Barret, *The Theoretike and Practicke of Moderne Warres* (London: William Ponsonby, 1598), 2.

12. Quoted in C. Imber, *The Ottoman Empire* (Basingstoke: Palgrave, 2002), 259.

13. Paul Rycaut quoted in R. Murphey, *Ottoman Warfare 1500–1700* (London: UCL Press, 1999), 98.

14. Quoted in 'Timur', *Encyclopaedia of Islam*.

15. Nobunaga Chronicle quoted in D.M. Brown, 'The Impact of Firearms on Japanese Warfare 1543–98', *Far Eastern Quarterly*, 7 (1948), 242–3 (236–53).

16. Ibid., 240.

Chapter 7 Discipline, *c.*1683–*c.*1860

1. Lt-Gen. H. Bland, *Treatise of Military Discipline* (London: 1762), 24.

2. Translated and quoted in J.A. Lynn, *Wars of Louis XIV 1667–1714* (London: Longman, 1999), 27.

3. Quoted in R. Holmes, *Marlborough. England's Fragile Genius* (London: Harper, 2008), 205.

4. R. Muir, *Tactics and the Experience of Battle in the Age of Napoleon* (New Haven, CT: Yale University Press, 1998), 97.

5. Quoted in R. Holmes, 'Battle' in C. Townsend (ed.), *The Oxford History of Modern War* (Oxford: Oxford University Press, 2005), 226.

6. M. Glover (ed.), *A Gentleman Volunteer. The Letters of George Hennell from the Peninsular War 1812–13* (London: Heinemann, 1979), 15.

7. Quoted in C. Duffy, *Frederick the Great* (London: Routledge, 1985), 31.

8. Clausewitz, *On War*, 482.

9. Quoted in J. Keay, *India. A History* (New York: Grove, 2000), 392.

10. Claude Joseph Rouget de Lisle, verse 2 and chorus: tr. http://en.wikipedia.org/wiki/La_Marseillaise.

11. For Genghis Khan see above, 5, n.9. This quotation is taken from J.A. Lynn, 'Nations in Arms, 1763–1815', in G. Parker (ed.), *The Cambridge History of Warfare* (Cambridge: Cambridge University Press, 2005), 200. There is some doubt as to whether Napoleon ever made this speech in quite this form, which was designed to exaggerate the poor state of the army of Italy.

12. I have taken the phrase from J.R. Elting, *Swords around a Throne. Napoleon's Grande Armée* (London: Weidenfeld & Nicolson, 1989).

13. Ibid., 51.

14. Quoted by J.C. Herold, *The Mind of Napoleon* (New York: Columbia University Press, 1955), 217.
15. Glover, *A Gentleman Volunteer*, 90.
16. W.K. Thompson, *An Ensign in the Peninsular War. The Letters of John Aitchison* (London: Michael Joseph, 1981), 57–8.
17. Quoted in A. Forrest, *Conscripts and Deserters. The Army and French Society during the Revolution and Empire* (New York: Oxford University Press, 1989), 41.
18. Clausewitz, *On War*, VI: 30, 515.
19. If he ever did say this it suggests a familiarity with Adam Smith's *Wealth of Nations*, IV:7: 'To found a great empire for the sole purpose of raising up a people of customers may at first sight appear a project fit only for a nation of shopkeepers. It is, however, a project altogether unfit for a nation of shopkeepers; but extremely fit for a nation whose government is influenced by shopkeepers.'

Chapter 8 The Military Revolution

1. I.S. Bloch, *The Future of War in its Technical, Economic and Political Relations* (Boston: Ginn, 1902) abridged from the Russian original of 1898, xvi, lxi–lxii.
2. The phrase was coined by President Eisenhower in his farewell speech in January 1961: 'In the councils of government, we must guard against the acquisition of unwarranted influence, whether sought or unsought, by the military industrial complex. The potential for the disastrous rise of misplaced power exists and will persist. We must never let the weight of this combination endanger our liberties or democratic processes. We should take nothing for granted. Only an alert and knowledgeable citizenry can compel the proper meshing of the huge industrial and military machinery of defense with our peaceful methods and goals, so that security and liberty may prosper together.'
3. Quoted in J.M. McPherson, *Battle Cry of Freedom: The Civil War Era* (Oxford: Oxford University Press, 1988), 336.
4. Ibid., 327.
5. F. Trautmann (ed.), *A Prussian Observes the American Civil War: The Military Studies of Justus Scheibert* (Columbia: University of Missouri Press, 2001), 36.
6. Quoted in McPherson, *Battle Cry of Freedom*, 337, 334.
7. Quoted ibid., 809, 811.
8. Quoted ibid., 808–9, 778.
9. Quoted ibid., 786.
10. Union Colonel Theodore Lyman to his wife in 1864 quoted in R. O'Connell, *Of Arms and Men. A History of War, Weapons and Aggression* (Oxford: Oxford University Press, 1989), 198.
11. Quoted in McPherson, *Battle Cry of Freedom*, 730.
12. J.C. Hazlett, E. Olmstead and M.H. Parks, *Field Artillery Weapons of the American Civil War* (Champaign: Illinois University Press, 2004), 120.
13. Trautmann (ed.), *Prussian Observes the American Civil War*, 34.
14. John S. Mosby quoted in O'Connell, *Of Arms and Men*, 199.
15. Quoted in P. Wahl and D.R. Toppel, *The Gatling Gun* (New York: Arco, 1965), 12.
16. Quoted in G.C. Rhea, *The Battles for Spotsylvania Court House and the Road to Yellow Tavern* (Baton Rouge: Louisiana State University Press, 1997), 3.
17. Quoted in E.J. Milliken and P. Marks, *The 'Arry Ballads* (Jefferson, NC: McFarland, 2004), 107.
18. Quoted in G. Ryan, *Our Heroes of the Crimea* (London: Routledge, 1855), 50.
19. K. Marx and F. Engels, *The Communist Manifesto*, tr. S. Moore (1888; Harmondsworth: Penguin, 1967), 78.
20. Quoted in S.C. Neff, *War and the Law of Nations* (Cambridge: Cambridge University Press, 2007), 114.
21. Quoted in M. Ceadel, *Semi-detached Idealists: The British Peace Movement and International Relations, 1854–1945* (Oxford: Oxford University Press, 2000), 171.

22. Quoted in R. Chickering, *Imperial Germany and a World without War: the Peace Movement and German Society, 1892–1914* (Princeton, NJ: Princeton University Press, 1975), 322.
23. I.S. Bloch, *Is War Now Impossible?* tr. W.T. Stead, 6 vols (London: Grant Richards, 1899).
24. Quoted in C.E. Schorske, *German Social Democracy 1905–1917* (Cambridge, Mass.: Harvard University Press, 1983), 286.
25. K. Liebknecht, *Militarism and Anti-Militarism*, ed. G. Lock (Cambridge: Rivers Press, 1973), 9, Introduction, xi.
26. Quoted in M. Kitchen, *The German Officer Corps, 1890–1914*, (Oxford: Clarendon Press, 1968), 52.
27. Quoted ibid., 180.
28. Clausewitz, *On War*, II:5, 187.
29. Quoted in A. Horne, *The French Army and Politics 1870–1970* (London: Macmillan, 1984), 27.
30. Quoted in P.-M. de la Gorce, *The French Army: a Military-Political History*, tr. K. Douglas (London: Weidenfeld & Nicolson, 1963), 28.
31. Quoted in G. Wawro, *Warfare and Society in Europe 1792–1914* (London: Routledge, 2000), 206.
32. Ardant du Picq, *Battle Studies. Ancient and Modern Battle*, in *Roots of Strategy 2*, ed. S. Brooks (Mechanicsburg: Stackpole, 1987), 124,128, 196, 253.
33. Quoted by T. Wintringham, *The Story of Weapons and Tactics from Troy to Stalingrad* (Boston, Mass.: Houghton Mifflin, 1943), 155.
34. Quoted in R.R. Davis, 'Helmuth von Moltke and the Prussian-German Development of a Decentralised Style of Command: Metz and Sedan 1870', *Defence Studies*, 5 (2005), 84.
35. Quoted in G. Wawro, *The Franco-Prussian War. The German Conquest of France 1870–71* (Cambridge: Cambridge University Press, 2003), 47.
36. See Appendix 1, Table 2 .
37. Hilaire Belloc, *The Modern Traveller* (London: Edward Arnold, 1898), 42.
38. Quoted in W.S. Hamer, *The British Army. Civil–Military Relations 1885–1905* (Oxford: Clarendon Press, 1970), 28.
39. G.F.R. Henderson, *The Science of War* (London, 1905), 148.
40. W. Churchill, *The Boer War* (London: Leo Cooper, 1989), 110.
41. W. Balck, *Tactics*, tr. L.R.M. Maxwell (London: Sands, 1899), quoted in M. Howard, 'Men Against the Fire. The Doctrine of the Offensive in 1914', in P. Paret (ed.), *Makers of Modern Strategy: from Machiavelli to the Nuclear Age* (Princeton, NJ: Princeton University Press, 1986) 519.
42. Quoted in D. Porch, *The March to the Marne. The French Army 1871–1914* (Cambridge: Cambridge University Press, 1981), 163.
43. 'Recessional', published in the London *Times* in July 1897.
44. See Appendix, Table 2.
45. Quoted in H. Strachan, *European Armies and the Conduct of War* (London: Routledge, 1983), 1008.

Chapter 9 Industrial Killing

1. F. Scott Fitzgerald, *Tender is the Night* (1934; Harmondsworth: Penguin, 1963), Book 3, Ch. 1, 125.
2. H. Strachan, *The First World War I: To Arms* (Oxford: Oxford University Press, 2001–), 290.
3. Terraine, *White Heat*, 101.
4. Maj.–Gen. Sir Edward Spears, *Liaison 1914* (London: Eyre & Spottiwoode, 1968), 36.
5. Quoted by M.S. Neiberg, *Fighting the Great War. A Global History* (Cambridge, Mass.: Harvard University Press, 2005), 11.

6. Quoted by Terraine, *White Heat*, 108, 94.
7. Rommel in his *Infanterie greift an* [Infantry Attacks] (1937); tr. D. Fraser, *Knight's Cross. A Life of Field-Marshal Erwin Rommel* (London: Harper, 1993), 29.
8. Quoted in Terraine, *White Heat*, 108.
9. Quoted ibid., 89.
10. E. Marsh (ed.), *Collected Poems of Rupert Brooke* (London: Sidgwick & Jackson, 1929), 144.
11. Strachan, *First World War I*, 437.
12. General Ludendorff, *The Coming War* (London: Faber & Faber, 1931), 71; see also 141.
13. J.C. Powys, *War and Culture* (New York: Shaw, 1914; Village Press, 1975), 24, 39.
14. M. Brown, *Tommy Goes to War* (London: Dent, 1978), 21, 245.
15. 'Oh where are my officers?' Quoted in Terraine, *White Heat*, 89–90, 93.
16. Major Stanley Washburn, British Military Observer with the Russian forces quoted in Charles F. Horne and Walter F. Austin (eds), *Source Records of the Great War, Volume III, 1915* (Indianapolis: The American Legion, 1931), 186.
17. D. Lloyd George, *War Memoirs*, 6 vols (London: Nicholson, 1933–6), 1.602.
18. Corporal Gale of 14th Division quoted in L. Macdonald, *To the Last Man: Spring 1918* (London: Viking, 1998), 92.
19. R.H. Lutz (ed.), *The Causes of the German Collapse in 1918*, tr. W.L. Campbell (Stanford, CA: Stanford University Press, 1934), 71–2.
20. Quoted in B.I. Gudmundsson, *Stormtroop Tactics. Innovation in the German Army, 1914–18* (Westport: Praeger, 1989), 144.
21. Captain R. Binding quoted in Terraine, *White Heat*, 288.
22. General Ludendorff, *My War Memoirs 1914–18*, 2 vols (London: Hutchinson, 1919), 2: 542.
23. Quoted in M.S. Neiberg, *The Second Battle of the Marne* (Bloomington: Indiana University Press, 2008), 198 n. 29.4
24. T. Travers, *How the War Was Won: Command and Technology in the British Army on the Western Front, 1917–1918* (Barnsley: Pen and Sword, 2005), 87.
25. Lutz, *Causes of the German Collapse*, 82–3.
26. Quoted in Travers, *How the War Was Won*, 153–4.
27. British Official History quoted in Terraine, *White Heat*, 312.
28. Quoted in Neiberg, *Fighting the Great War*, 352.
29. Clausewitz, *On War*, 1:3, 101.

Chapter 10 Culture and Warfare in the Age of Total War, 1919–1945

1. Vegetius, *Epitome of Military Science,* tr. N.P. Milner (Liverpool: Liverpool University Press, 1993), 62.
2. R.H. Lutz (ed.), *The Causes of the German Collapse in 1918*, tr. W.L. Campbell (Stanford, CA: Stanford University Press, 1934), 88.
3. P.A. Thompson, *Lions Led by Donkeys: Showing how Victory in the Great War Was Achieved by Those Who Made the Fewest Mistakes* (London: Werner Laurie, 1927). The phrase was given even wider currency by K. Clark in his *The Donkeys* (London: Hutchinson, 1961) which attributes this phrase to the Germans:

Ludendorff: The English soldiers fight like lions.
Hoffmann: True. But don't we know that they are lions led by donkeys.

But this same phrase had earlier been used of the French army in 1870–1.
4. Quoted in B. Bond, *British Military Policy between the Two World Wars* (Oxford: Clarendon Press, 1980), 58.
5. Quoted by E. Bobo, 'Scientists at War. The Development of Radar and Jet Propulsion in Britain', in G. Jensen and A. Wiest (eds), *War in the Age of Technology. Myriad Faces of Modern Armed Conflict* (New York: New York University Press, 2001), 242.

6. P. Fussell, *Wartime. Understanding and Behaviour in the Second World War* (Oxford: Oxford University Press, 1990), 3.

7. Quoted in J. Ellis, *The Sharp End. The Fighting Man in World War II* (London: Pimlico, 1990), 366.

8. Quoted by S.J. Lee, *The European Dictatorships 1918–1945* (London: Methuen, 1987), 78.

9. Quoted in S.G. Fritz, *Frontsoldaten. The German Soldier in World War II* (Lexington: University of Kentucky Press, 1995), 199.

10. General Rokossovsky quoted in R. Overy, *Russia's War* (London: Penguin, 1997), 87.

11. J.W. Dower, *War without Mercy. Race and Power in the Pacific War* (New York: Pantheon, 1986), 203, 247.

12. Ibid., 7.

13. Captain W. Knowlton quoted in M. Hastings, *Armageddon. The Battle for Germany 1944–45* (London: Macmillan, 2004), 87.

14. Quoted in A. Beevor, *D-Day. The Battle for Normandy* (London: Viking, 2009), 249.

15. Ibid., 248.

16. Fritz, *Frontsoldaten*, 61; Fussell, *Wartime*, 9.

17. Quoted in Hastings, *Armageddon*, 160.

18. Generalleutnant Schimpf, 3rd Paratroop Division quoted in Beevor, *D-Day*, 283.

19. Quoted in J. Latimer, *Alamein* (London: Murray, 2002), 28.

20. J.C. Lebra-Chapman, *Japan's Greater East Asia Co-Prosperity Sphere in World War II: Selected Readings and Documents* (Kuala Lumpur: Oxford University Press, 1975), 157.

Chapter 11 A New Age of War

1. G. Santayana, *Soliloquies in England: and Later Soliloquies*, No. 25 *Tipperary* (London: Constable, 1922), 102. This quotation is often attributed to Plato, notably on the walls of the Imperial War Museum in London built in 1936, but there appears to be no basis for this.

2. London *Times*, 17 December 1966.

3. B. Alexander, *How Wars Are Won: The 13 Rules of War from Ancient Greece to the War on Terror* (New York: Crown, 2002), 22.

4. D.D. Eisenhower, 'President's New Conference on March 17 1954', in S.C. Sarkesian and R.A. Vitas (eds), *US National Security Policy and Strategy: Documents and Policy Proposals* (New York: Greenwood, 1988), 57.

5. The reference is to Sergeant Bilko, the leading figure in a long-running TV comedy show of the 1950s set on an army base whose denizens have no interest in military matters or war and run their affairs as a kind of comic and mildly criminal mafia.

6. Tom Lehrer, 'We Will All Go Together When We Go', from the 1959 live album *An Evening Wasted with Tom Lehrer*.

7. R.H.S. Crossman, *Labour in the Affluent Society*, Fabian Tract 325 (London: Fabian Society, 1960), 9.

8. T. Segev, *1967: Israel, the war, and the year that transformed the Middle East,* tr. J. Cohen (New York: Metropolitan Books, 2007), 191.

9. Quoted in R. Neillands, *Attrition. The Great War on the Western Front – 1916* (London: Robson, 2001), 116–17.

FURTHER READING

Chapter 1 The Many Faces of War

J. Black, *Why Wars Happen* (London: Reaktion, 1998).
A. Gat, *War in Human Civilization* (Oxford: Oxford University Press, 2006).
D. Kagan, *On the Origins of War* (London: Hutchinson, 1995).
J. Keegan, *The Face of Battle: A Study of Agincourt, Waterloo and the Somme* (London: Jonathan Cape, 1976).
W.H. McNeill, *The Pursuit of Power* (Chicago: University of Chicago Press, 1982).
R.L. O'Connor, *Of Arms and Men. A History of War, Weapons, and Aggression* (Oxford: Oxford University Press, 1989).
M. van Creveld, *Technology and War from 2000 BC to the Present* (London: Brassey's, 1991).

Chapter 2 Many Worlds of War

B. and R. Allchin, *The Rise of Civilization in India and Pakistan* (Cambridge: Cambridge University Press, 1982).
N. di Cosmo, *Ancient China and its Enemies. The Rise of Nomadic Power in East Asian History* (Cambridge: Cambridge University Press, 2002).
W. Hamblin, *Warfare in the Ancient Near East to 1600 BC* (London: Routledge, 2006).
A. Hyland, *The Horse in the Ancient World* (Stroud: Sutton, 2003).
L. H. Keeley, *War before Civilization* (Oxford: Oxford University Press, 1995).
P.B. Kern, *Ancient Siege Warfare* (Indianapolis: Indiana University Press, 1999).

Chapter 3 Horses and Hoplites

G. Davies, *A History of Money from Ancient Times to the Present Day* (Cardiff: University of Wales Press, 2002).
V.D. Hanson, *The Western Way of War. Infantry Battle in Classical Greece* (Berkeley: University of California Press, 1989).
T. Holland, *Persian Fire. The First World Empire and the Battle for the West* (London: Little, Brown, 2006).
K. Raaflaub and N. Rosenstein (eds), *War and Society in the Ancient and Medieval Worlds. Asia, the Mediterranean, Europe and Mesoamerica* (Cambridge, Mass.: Harvard University Press, 1999).
M.M. Sage, *Warfare in Ancient Greece. A Sourcebook* (London: Routledge, 1996).
H. van Wees, *Greek Warfare. Myths and Realities* (London: Duckworth, 2004).

Chapter 4 The Glory of Empire, 336 BC–AD 651

P. Cartledge, *Alexander the Great. The Hunt for a New Past* (London: Macmillan, 2004).
A. Goldsworthy, *The Complete Roman Army* (London: Thames & Hudson, 2003).
D.A. Graff, *Medieval Chinese Warfare 300–900* (London: Routledge, 2002).
P. Heather, *The Fall of the Roman Empire. A New History* (London: Macmillan, 2005).
R. Thapar, 'From State to Empire in Early India: The Mauryan Period', *Historical Research*, 79 (2006), 287–305.
B. Ward-Perkins, *The Fall of Rome and the End of Civilization* (Oxford: Oxford University Press, 2005).

Chapter 5 Ideology and Warfare, 500–c.1200

J. France, *Western Warfare in the Age of the Crusades 1000–1300* (London: UCL Press, 1999).
G. Halsall, *Warfare and Society in the Barbarian West, 450–900* (London: Routledge, 2003).
H. Kennedy, *The Armies of the Caliphs. Military and Society in the Early Islamic State* (London: Routledge, 2001).
A.R. Lewis, *Nomads and Crusaders A.D. 1000–1368* (Bloomington: Indiana University Press, 1988).
J. Pryor, *Geography, Technology and War. Studies in the Maritime History of the Mediterranean 649–1571* (Cambridge: Cambridge University Press, 1988).
G.S. Sandhu, *A Military History of Medieval India* (New Delhi: Vision, 2003).
R.C. Smail, *Crusading Warfare, 1097–1193* (2nd edn, Cambridge: Cambridge University Press, 1995).

Chapter 6 The Steppe Supremacy, c.1200–1683

K. Chase, *Firearms. A Global History to 1700* (Cambridge: Cambridge University Press, 2003).
D. Goffman, *The Ottoman Empire and Early Modern Europe* (Cambridge: Cambridge University Press, 2002).
J. Gommans, *Mughal Warfare. Indian Frontiers and High Roads to Empire 1500–1700* (London: Routledge, 2002).
B.S. Hall, *Weapons and Warfare in Renaissance Europe* (Baltimore, MD: Johns Hopkins University Press, 1997).
H. Inalcik, *The Ottoman Empire. The Classical Age 1300–1600* (London: Weidenfeld & Nicolson, 1973).
P. Lorge, *War, Politics and Society in Early Modern China 900–1795* (London: Routledge, 2005).

Chapter 7 Discipline, c.1683–c.1860

J. Black, *European Warfare, 1453–1815* (Basingstoke: Macmillan, 1999).
J.A. Lynn (ed.), *Feeding Mars* (Boulder, Col.: Westview, 1993).
R. Muir, *Tactics and the Experience of Battle in the Age of Napoleon* (New Haven, CT: Yale University Press, 1998).
K. Pomeranz, *The Great Divergence. China, Europe and the Making of the Modern World* (Princeton, NJ: Princeton University Press, 2000).
N.A.M. Rodger, *The Command of the Ocean. A Naval History of Britain, 1649–1815* (London: Lane, 2004).
D. Showalter, *The Wars of Frederick the Great* (London: Longman, 1995).

Chapter 8 The Military Revolution

M. Ceadel, *Semi-detached Idealists. The British Peace Movement and International Relations, 1854–1945* (Oxford: Oxford University Press, 2000).

A.R. Lewis, *Nomadas and Crusader A.D. 1000–1368* (Bloomington: Indiana University Press; 1988).

M. Kitchen, *The German Officer Corps 1890–1914* (Oxford: Clarendon Press, 1968).

J.M. McPherson, *Battle Cry of Freedom. The Civil War Era* (Oxford: Oxford University Press, 1988).

H. Strachan, *European Armies and the Conduct of War* (London: Routledge, 1983).

B.D. Taylor, *Politics and the Russian Army. Civil–military Relations, 1689–2000* (Cambridge: Cambridge University Press, 2003).

G. Wawro, *Warfare and Society in Europe 1792–1914* (London: Routledge, 2000).

Chapter 9 Industrial Killing

A. Clayton, *Paths of Glory. The French Army 1914–18* (London: Cassell, 2003).

E.J. Erickson, *Ordered to Die. A History of the Ottoman Army in the First World War* (Westport: Greenwood, 2000).

B.I. Gudmundsson, *Stormtroop Tactics. Innovation in the German Army, 1914–18* (Westport: Praeger, 1989).

J. Morrow, *The Great War in the Air. Military Innovation 1909–21* (Shrewsbury: Airlife, 1993).

M.S. Neiberg, *Fighting the Great War. A Global History* (Cambridge, Mass.: Harvard University Press, 2005).

J. Terraine, *The White Heat. The New Warfare 1914–18* (London: Sidgwick & Jackson, 1982).

Chapter 10 Culture and Warfare in the Age of Total War, 1919–1945

C. Bellamy, *Absolute War: Soviet Russia in the Second World War: a Modern History* (London: Pan, 2009).

J. Black, *World War Two. A Military History* (London: Routledge, 2003).

B. Bond, *British Military Policy between the Two World Wars* (Oxford: Clarendon Press, 1980).

J. Buckley, *Air Power in the Age of Total War* (London: UCL Press, 1999).

J. Ellis, *The Sharp End. The Fighting Man in World War II* (London: Pimlico, 1990).

J.C. Hsiung and S.I. Levine (eds), *China's Bitter Victory. The War with Japan, 1937–1945* (New York: Sharpe, 1992).

M.S. Sherry, *The Rise of American Air Power. The Creation of Armageddon* (New Haven, CT: Yale University Press, 1987).

Chapter 11 A New Age of War

F.A. Gerges, *The Far Enemy. Why Jihad went Global* (Cambridge: Cambridge University Press, 2005; 2nd edn 2009).

M. Hastings, *The Korean War* (London: Michael Joseph, 1987).

A.R. Lewis, *The American Culture of War. The History of US Forces from World War II to Operation Iraqi Freedom* (London: Routledge, 2007).

B. Palmer, *The 25-Year War: America's Military Role in Vietnam* (New York: Simon & Schuster, 1985).

K.M. Pollack, *Arabs at War: Military Effectiveness, 1948–91* (Lincoln: University of Nebraska Press, 2002).

R.F. Weigley, *The American Way of War* (Bloomington: Indiana University Press, 1973).

APPENDIX I: TABLES

1. The Battles of the Franco-Prussian War, 1870–71

Battle	Date	German Nos + guns	German Casualties	French Nos + guns	French Casualties
Wissembourg	4.8.70	60,000+144	1,500	8,000+12	2,000
Froeschwiller	6.8.70	75,000+300	10,000	37,000+101	20,000
Mars-la-Tour	16.8.70	80,000+130	16,000	127,000	16,000
Gravelotte	18.8.70	188,332+732	20,163	112,800+520	12,000
Sedan	1.9.70	200,000+774	9,000	120,000+564	annihilation

2. Dates of the Commanders of 1914–18

Name	Nation	Dates
J.D.P. French	Britain	1852–1925
D. Haig	Britain	1861 (19 June)–1928
J. Joffre	France	1852–1931
H.P.B.O. Pétain	France	1856–1951
F. Foch	France	1852–1925
Conrad von Hotzendorf	Austro-Hungary	1852–1925
H.J.L. von Moltke	Germany	1848–1916
E. von Falkenhayn	German	1861(11 Sept.)–1922
Grand Duke Nikolai	Russia	1856–1929

INDEX